BERLIN REPLAYED

BERLIN REPLAYED

Cinema and Urban Nostalgia in the Postwall Era

Brigitta B. Wagner

UNIVERSITY OF MINNESOTA PRESS
MINNEAPOLIS • LONDON

A portion of chapter 4 previously appeared in "10 August 1994: One Month after X-Filme Founding, Filmboard Berlin–Brandenburg Paves Way for New Productions in the German Capital," in *A New History of German Cinema,* ed. Jennifer M. Kapczynski and Michael D. Richardson, 530–36 (Rochester, N.Y.: Camden House, 2012).

The author gratefully acknowledges the DEFA Foundation for generously providing selected images for this book. http://www.defa.stiftung.de/

DEFA STIFTUNG

Published by the University of Minnesota Press
111 Third Avenue South, Suite 290
Minneapolis, MN 55401-2520
http://www.upress.umn.edu

Library of Congress Cataloging-in-Publication Data
Wagner, Brigitta B.
Berlin replayed: cinema and urban nostalgia in the postwall era / Brigitta B. Wagner.
Includes bibliographical references and index.
ISBN 978-0-8166-9171-5 (hc)
ISBN 978-0-8166-9174-6 (pb)
1. Berlin (Germany)—In motion pictures. 2. Berlin (Germany)—Civilization—20th century. 3. Cities and towns in motion pictures. I. Title.
PN1995.9.B47W34 2015
791.430943′155—dc23 2014043040

Printed in the United States of America on acid-free paper

The University of Minnesota is an equal-opportunity educator and employer.

21 20 19 18 17 16 15 10 9 8 7 6 5 4 3 2 1

To

GERTRUD, HEINZ, *and* BERNHARD WAGNER,

drei Berliner Kinder

CONTENTS

ABBREVIATIONS AND TERMS

BArch	Bundesarchiv-Filmarchiv (Federal Film Archives)
BFF	Berliner Filmförderung (Berlin Film Funding)
BPB	Bundeszentrale für politische Bildung (Federal Agency for Civic Education)
Bundestag	German Parliament
CDU	Christlich Demokratische Union (Christian Democratic Union)
CGI	computer-generated imagery
DEFA	Deutsche Filmaktiengesellschaft (German Film Company)
DFFB	Deutsche Film- und Fernsehakademie Berlin (German Film and Television Academy Berlin)
DFFF	Deutsche Filmförderfonds (German Federal Film Fund)
DK	Deutsche Kinemathek (German Cinemathèque)
FBBB	Filmboard Berlin–Brandenburg (regional film funding body for Berlin and Brandenburg from 1994 to 2004)
FDJ	Freie Deutsche Jugend (Free German Youth)
FFA	Filmförderungsanstalt (German Federal Film Board)
FRG (BRD)	Federal Republic of Germany, the official name of West Germany and Germany today (Bundesrepublik Deutschland); "Germany" used with films designates German productions released before the end of the Second World War in 1945
GDR (DDR)	German Democratic Republic, the official name of East Germany (Deutsche Demokratische Republik), 1949–89
GmbH	Gesellschaft mit beschränkter Haftung (limited liability company)

HFF — Hochschule für Film und Fernsehen "Konrad Wolf" (Academy for Film and Television "Konrad Wolf")
HICOG — Allied High Commission for Occupied Germany
MBBB — Medienboard Berlin–Brandenburg (Media Board Berlin–Brandenburg, regional film and media board, since 2004)
SED — Sozialistische Einheitspartei (Socialist Unity Party)
SOZ — Soviet Occupation Zone (Sowjetische Besatzungszone); used here to designate films made in the East from 1945 to 1949
SPIO — Spitzenorganisation der Filmwirtschaft (the [West] German film industry's umbrella organization)
Trabi, Trabant — East German car manufacturer
VBF — Verband Berliner Filmtheater (Association of Berlin Film Theaters)
Wende — "turning point," referring to events leading up to and following the fall of the Berlin Wall in 1989 and German unification in 1990

INTRODUCTION

AUF *WIEDER*SEHEN, BERLIN!

RETROSPECTION AND PRODUCTION

Saying good-bye to Berlin—a pastime of twentieth-century German regime change—meant reencountering and repurposing the city's previous filmic images and asserting its new ones. Established as computer culture was transforming methods of storing and circulating digitized film files, the unified New Berlin has had an exceptional relationship to cinema. No other city in the 1990s and early 2000s so publicly and consistently relied on films to narrate and picture its contested pasts, nor was another city so dependent on new and archival moving images to legitimate its present and imagine its future. Though Berlin's filmography is as old as cinema's first public screenings in 1895, and though Kaiser Wilhelm II was known to be a savvy early adopter of cinema's ability to record and project monarchical and urban spectacle before his abdication in 1918, two events or conditions of the century were predominantly responsible for the city's unique dependence on film.[1]

The first of these was the violent destruction of the built city, particularly in the final two years of the Second World War; the second resulted from its postwar division into four Allied sectors and eventually into Eastern and Western halves, separated from 1961 to 1989 by the Berlin Wall. After all, the consolidation of the German Empire in 1871, following victory in the Franco-Prussian War, had extended the Prussian capital's administrative and symbolic function to the entire German nation and justified large-scale construction and urban development initiatives. In the decades before the First World War, but also significantly in the interwar period, Berlin enjoyed rapid population growth and evolved into a modern industrial powerhouse and an important, internationally recognized political and cultural center. New architecture and infrastructural expansion lent the city a sudden visual splendor in keeping with modern urban and national aspirations, first of the Wilhelmine era, and then of the Weimar Republic and the Third Reich. The Second World War did not simply destroy Berlin; it erased the achievements of a built city that was still nascent.

To understand the intertwined nostalgic allure and danger of Berlin's pre–air raid archival views in postwall Germany, one has to revisit the bombed residential and industrial buildings, rubble-filled streets, cramped quarters, and interrupted infrastructure of the immediate postwar years. This backdrop of jagged ruins and mounds of brick and stone quickly generated a cycle of didactic "rubble films" *(Trümmerfilme),* including Wolfgang Staudte's exploration of German guilt and trauma in *Die Mörder sind unter uns* (*The Murderers Are among Us,* SOZ 1946) and Roberto Rossellini's plea on behalf of Berlin's suffering civilian population in *Germania anno zero* (*Germany Year Zero,* Italy/SOZ/France 1948). Walking through the streets also reminded Berlin's inhabitants of what had been lost in 363 aerial attacks: 39 percent of the city's apartments and 50 percent of its residential space.[2] Much damage befell Berlin's six central districts, where the city's cultural capital, representative Prussian architecture, and government buildings were concentrated; artillery shells and street fighting in the Battle of Berlin in spring 1945 caused additional destruction to Berlin's museums. Only twenty of four hundred cinemas were functional. A quarter of the city streets and most bridges, trains, trams, and automobiles were completely or partially destroyed. Statistics estimate wartime population loss at 26.6 percent.[3] The city has never recovered its prewar population of nearly four and a half million.

Berlin's physical transformation altered the value of the city's surviving visual archive. Indeed, the loss of personal possessions through emigration, bombardment and artillery, forced migration to concentration camps and POW prisons, and expulsion from the Eastern provinces left many Germans and Berliners without their prewar photographic heritage. At the same time, the Third Reich's careful documentation of the war and the Holocaust produced film footage and photographs of National Socialist atrocities that were difficult to displace, especially under Allied Occupation and in the American-led process of de-Nazification. In its final years as the sovereign German capital, Berlin had been the seat of a government that had instigated another world war, invaded numerous countries, justified genocide, and subjected its civilians to the violence of total war. Looking back at the city through the technologies of photochemical resemblance could be personal and local or collective and national, not to mention deeply traumatic and highly politicized, for both civilians and Germany's victims.

Two postwar artifacts—a film sequence and a book of photographs—help to illustrate the complications of urban retrospection after 1945. In July, just months after German capitulation, an American warplane carried unusual cargo in its bomb bays: 16mm cameras loaded with Kodak color film stock. Later edited into Jost von Morr and John Lionel Bandmann's compilation film *Ein Tag im Juli, Berlin 1945* (One day in July, Berlin 1945, FRG 1975), this aerial footage drifts over the eerily empty city center in three long takes. For two and a half minutes, the mobile camera reveals the contiguity of this vast cemetery of vacant streets; hollow, roofless buildings; and thinned-out patches of trees. The camera's privileged height, the airplane's motion, and the shots' duration suggest that there is no intact city just beyond the frame. Famous buildings and symbols of power, such as the Reichstag and the Hohenzollern monarchy's City Palace (Stadtschloss), were not spared the damage of more anonymous residential houses; their size merely left a larger footprint of battered and sundered facades on the cartographic specter below. Cinema, unlike photography, could survey the extent of the destruction in real time, over vast stretches of terrain. Whether walking through the city in 1945, watching von Morr and Bandmann's film in West Germany in 1975, or attending a repertory screening of a rubble film just after the political turn *(Wende)* of 1989–90, inhabitants and more geographically dispersed spectators encountered a marred cityscape that changed their relationship to Berlin's prewar and present built form. The city's prewar filmic past could only arrive in the present by way of (or in a detour around) death and ruins, while the city's new architecture and films, whether intentionally or not, remained in perpetual dialogue with their preferred and rejected precursors.

Photographer Otto Hagemann and art historian and National Gallery director Paul Ortwin Rave's book *Berlin: Vor der Zerstörung aufgenommen* (Berlin captured before the destruction) was in its second print run by 1949. It consists of Rave's introduction, Hagemann's prewar architectural photographs of Berlin's prominent historical and notable modernist buildings, and Rave's short descriptions of the structures, including their dates of construction and their fate in 1945. Embossed on the cover is simply the word BERLIN above the city's coat of arms, an upright bear with flaring tongue and outstretched paws. Though 1949 saw the formal establishment of the West's Federal Republic of Germany (FRG) in May and the East's German Democratic Republic (GDR) in October, Berlin before its destruction was the cultural heritage of both East and West Berliners and all Germans. The book is a curiosity of the early postwar years and, though simple enough in its premise, betrays the conundrum of backward glances: an urban nostalgia that both re-presents the lost, organic, or whole city to readers and observers who wish to retrieve it and makes this mediated retrieval contingent on the knowledge of its impossibility. What's more, the war's devastation of urban space could not be blamed solely on the Allies; some degree of responsibility, indeed, guilt, for Berlin's disfigurement lay with the very population that had suffered in its ashes.

The joy of accessing vanished sights was at best ambiguous, as many ruins and voids attested to a vanquished political and cultural grandeur that Berlin and Germany had worked so hard to construct in the late nineteenth and early twentieth centuries. A case in point are Hagemann's photographs of the Potsdamer and Anhalter Bahnhöfe, large train stations, expanded and rebuilt in the 1870s, that brought long-distance rail traffic from the south to the busy environs of Berlin's Potsdamer Platz and Askanischer Platz. While the photographs herald the dignity of arrivals to and departures from the capital of the unified German Reich on facing pages, Rave's brief accounts of their charred interiors, structural damage, and destroyed platform halls both enhance and undercut the pleasures of trumping history. In his conclusion, he offers a solution for those too pained or discouraged by the discrepancies between past and present. Much like the wave of popular, rural *Heimat* (homeland) films of the 1950s, he urges readers to look beyond the city, to its "outskirts," which, in their unaltered nature, could offer more "hope for a new life than the immeasurable hills of rubble located in its interior."[4]

If both kinds of photochemical retrospection—the filmic and the photographic—could trap observers in a nexus of knowledge and longing, new film production was instrumental in reconstructing Berlin both during the Cold War and after the fall of the Berlin Wall. In both periods, cinema offered not only a means of political and geographical reorientation in the filmic and built Berlin but also new geographies of distribution, exhibition, reception, and retrospection that situated the city within the two Germanys, the unified FRG, Europe, or the greater world. While the GDR's state-run DEFA (Deutsche Film Aktiengesellschaft) Studios manufactured an image of the capital, East Berlin, that was consistent with the preoccupations of the ruling (and censoring) Socialist Unity Party (Sozialistische Einheitspartei, SED), the West Berlin film industry reflected the half-city's stature as a capitalist outpost of Western democratic freedom. Whether nonfiction or narrative, films set in the postwall city had to contend with competing urban visions and spatial legacies left behind, for instance, by Weimar Germany's cinematic modernity and frenzied angst, fascism's self-aggrandizing and sanitized urban postures, and divided Germany's demarcated political loyalties and sociocultural territories. Framing and choreographing profilmic urban space for the camera, arranging the logic of its cinematic spatial relations through editing, and organizing the filmic city's geographies of exhibition link the production and dissemination of cinematic space to knowledge, memory, and use of the built city.

The present study is neither a seamless history of cinema in Berlin nor a lexicon of Berlin films, of which there are thousands. Rather, I take as my point of departure three necessities of the postwall city: (1) the urgent need to validate the 1991 decision of the Bundestag (the German parliament) to return the unified federal government (then housed in Bonn) to a capital so strongly associated with the Nazi and SED dictatorships; (2) millennial Berlin's need to maintain the performance of its political, architectural, and cultural ideals after the government's arrival; and (3) a unified film and media culture's need to circulate images of the city that could aid the integration of Berliners and Germans socialized on opposite sides of the border through common filmographies and frames of visual reference. The urban planner and sociologist Claire Colomb has approached the New Berlin through the built city's public displays of reinvention, noting, "No other historical capital city has had to 'market' its capital function with slogans and image campaigns in order to underpin its present-day legitimacy."[5] Though postwall Berlin's thoroughly planned and marketed negotiations with historical events and with new and old architecture have perplexed and fascinated scholars and practitioners across several disciplines, there is very little sustained analysis of the role of moving images in this process.[6]

Because built cities are already multifaceted entities, they are difficult to grasp through the tools of one discipline. The study of cinematic cities requires, furthermore, attention to culturally and historically specific geographies and locations and an awareness of how moving image media construct and circulate representations of place and urban space; relying exclusively on one or the other disciplinary perspective neglects much of what films and archival footage convey.[7] The kind of urban analysis that I am undertaking in *Berlin Replayed* therefore interrogates the German capital's moving image legacy at the intersection, rather than at the respective centers, of German cultural studies and film and media studies. Moreover, it seeks productive exchange between often distinct areas of film research: theories of medium specificity, histories of production and reception, and close audiovisual analysis.

Cinematic space is not constructed in a vacuum of fictional worlds and artistic innovation but reflects on and can even change the built city. Investigating Berlin's urban-cinematic feedback loop reveals how and why particular films and city images continue to shape the city's history, spatial relations, and collective urban nostalgia. Since the early 2000s, film scholarship has increasingly recognized cinematic space's cartographic and archival potential. Whereas Giuliana Bruno has argued that "film is modern cartography" in its mobile, haptic mapping of culture, place, and emotion, Tom Conley has maintained that "film *is* a map" whose "symbolic and political effectiveness is a function of its identity as a cartographic diagram."[8] The *Wende* necessitated new ways of thinking about European space generally, but Germany's unification, and particularly the visible, physical integration of Berlin's two halves, foregrounded the geographical and cartographic information contained in the city's new and old moving images. In their anthology *Taking Place,* Elena Gorfinkel and John David Rhodes ask "how" films "can act as archives of specific places."[9] In his film essay *Los Angeles Plays Itself* (United States 2003), filmmaker Thom Andersen not only isolates the function of location, backdrop, and studio sets in the construction of Los Angeles's city image but, importantly, demonstrates his observations across several thematically grouped fragments of film. This acknowledgment of films' often subtle yet interlinked assumptions about place and geography exposes the effects of an accumulation of cinematic urban views and spatial relations through time.

In questioning cinema's role in urban nostalgia and reinvention, *Berlin Replayed* looks not to discrete films that signify in isolation but rather to clusters of historically related films that, together, portray complicated and sometimes contradictory versions of urban space. Organized as case studies, the individual chapters blend concerns with medium-specific properties of mobile resemblance and culturally specific forms of didactic geography. Because postwall retrospection and revival frame contemporary reception of the older films, I explore their Berlin geographies in tension between the historical exigencies of their production and the cultural and geographical politics of their more recent screening contexts. As postwall film funding policy in the capital region initiated a resurgence of commercial film production in and around unified Berlin, I also analyze the recharted terrain of successful Berlin films made during the tenure of Filmboard Berlin–Brandenburg (FBBB) from 1994 to 2004. As films that had to demonstrate the dual competence of Berlin and its film industry, these newer works can hardly be separated from past guises of the built city and from the earlier films that captured these.

The book's four themes—remake, generation, virtuality, and orientation—reflect the selective pasts and recurrent titles of the New Berlin's repertory film programming as well as the spatial and indexical preoccupations of its successful millennial productions. As politicians, planners, architects, and marketers strove to persuade inhabitants and visitors of Berlin's positive, shared pasts and all-German *(gesamtdeutsch),* European, and global future, the 1920s, the prewall 1950s, the *Wende,* and the transformative present all became audiovisual commonplaces. To make sense of these revived Berlins and their ongoing influence on the city's evolving layout and image at home and abroad, this study places their internal, narrative geographies in dialogue with their changing geographies of reception and with the intersecting demands and desires of the city's decision makers and film professionals. The past and present must be considered together.

FILM IN TIMES AND PLACES

Approached as cultural objects of shifting meaning and value, the films in this book invite complex intertemporal and geographical negotiations with longing. A number of questions arose in the choice of films to examine. Why have some titles screened more frequently in postwall Berlin than others? Which periods, such as the Third Reich, were generally excluded from film retrospectives, and which ones were consistently revived?[10] Which spatial histories did these preferred films recirculate, and in which institutional contexts, in which parts of the city? How did this new reception relate to the geopolitical discourses that surrounded the films' initial production and release? Had the films been known in both the East and West, and did their reception and circulation patterns change significantly during and after the Cold War? Because individual acts of film retrospection are dependent on opportunities *to retrospect,* access to repertory films and archival fragments is largely dictated by the institutions and businesses responsible for restoring prints, planning film series, programming film festivals and television schedules, mounting museum exhibitions, and licensing and distributing films for theatrical rerelease and home entertainment. In particular, organized theatrical retrospectives *concentrate looking* around contemporary interest in the past (in themes, periods, and formal characteristics), often in conjunction with other urban cultural events.

The versatility of individual Berlin films for updated cultural frameworks of remembrance and renewal places their reactivated cinematic space in perpetual dialectical relation to the present. Much like the philosopher Hans-Georg Gadamer's insistence on the history of effect *(Wirkungsgeschichte),* my emphasis on films' dual or ongoing reception acknowledges "*the fusion of these* [present and historical] *horizons supposedly existing by themselves.*" This effected understanding is a logical consequence of historical consciousness, and the confrontation of the two horizons—of tradition and hermeneutic retrospection—generates a productive "tension between the text and the present." As Gadamer proceeds to argue, "the hermeneutic task consists in not covering up this tension by attempting a naïve assimilation of the two but in consciously bringing it out."[11] Making sense of films' recontextualization and recirculation in the present requires a return to their successive horizons of meaning, particularly to the original conditions that gave rise to their conceptualization and framing of urban space. One might think of these films as kicking up historical dust and triggering multilayered familiar and altered responses each time they are screened. Because the meaning of cinematic space becomes fluid over time, revived images of Berlin are subject to ideological slippage and inversion, depending on how they are being used and who is viewing them.

To screen or see cinematic space again in the first fifteen years following the fall of the Wall was to select or accept specific confrontations with the urban past. Control over archival images countered the uncertainties of postwall urban planning and development. While television and, increasingly, the Internet revived Berlin images across great distances, theatrical retrospectives and repertory screenings affirmed collective and personal memories of place in the city's physical and mediated public sphere. New and old audiences learned to discern historical cityscapes in Berlin's transitional form, gained exposure to previously unknown East or West German filmmaking traditions, or developed a cult appreciation for a small canon of films, notably Walter Ruttmann's *Berlin. Die Sinfonie der Großstadt* (*Berlin: Symphony of a Great City,* Germany 1927), Gerhard Klein's *Berlin—Ecke Schönhauser* (*Berlin—Schönhauser Corner,* GDR 1957), and Wim Wenders's *Der Himmel über Berlin* (*Wings of Desire,* FRG/France 1987)—pillars of the book's first three chapters.

In the early 2000s, material traces of Berlin films and Berlin-themed series were visible for several days and weeks throughout the city in posters, postcards, magazine advertisements, and subway monitors. These retrospectives and revivals also mapped an exhibition terrain from Wilmersdorf, Schöneberg, and Kreuzberg in the West to Potsdamer Platz along the former East–West border to Mitte and Prenzlauer Berg in the East. Some films and screenings had such great cultural political value that they justified temporary alterations in urban infrastructure. An apex of this public appreciation for Berlin's film history was the eightieth anniversary of Ruttmann's city symphony.

More than any other title in the city's filmography, *Berlin. Die Sinfonie der Großstadt* has reappeared at every turn in postwall retrospection and thus serves as a common thread throughout this book. After the Second World War, and, even more so, after the Cold War, this document of the lively Weimar metropolis became the standard against which all subsequent built and filmic iterations of the city were measured.

On September 24, 2007, I flew to Berlin for the premiere of a new restoration featuring Bernd Thewes's reconstruction of Edmund Meisel's original score, to be performed by Frank Strobel and the Rundfunk Sinfonieorchester Berlin. The gala event took place, not in a cinema, but at the Friedrichstadtpalast, a large and glitzy venue usually reserved for musical revues. Located in the heart of Mitte, the core of Old Berlin, the theater is just a few blocks north of Bahnhof Friedrichstraße, an important junction of long-distance, regional, city train (S-Bahn) and subway (U-Bahn) lines that used to mark a key point of arrival and departure to East Berlin. The street Friedrichstraße, once bisected by Checkpoint Charlie, had also become a principal site of postwall renovation and construction aimed at restoring some of its prewar commercial flair and bustle. That the film was introduced by politicians and leading cultural figures in the presence of Ruttmann's daughter and rights holder, and at such a significant location, is testament enough to its accumulated cultural prestige. The mise-en-scène of the evening did not, however, end there. The S-Bahn, a cosponsor of the screening, ran a historical "special train" to Friedrichstraße.[12] Recalling the film's age as well as its montaged promise of the coordinated tempo of a modern, world-class city *(Weltstadt),* the S-Bahn's participation in the spectacle helped to stage an urban narrative of continuity and renewal that far exceeded the film itself.

Few individual films have repeatedly commanded the city's resources like Ruttmann's, but, when embedded in new retrospective geographies, they can change the way that inhabitants use urban space. Like the reactivated narrative

A trailer for *Berlin. Die Sinfonie der Großstadt* (Germany 1927) advertises an upcoming screening at Kino Central in 2010. Courtesy of the author.

geographies in revived films, film exhibition topographies reactivate spatial relations and spatial memory. In August 2011, on the eve of the fiftieth anniversary of the erection of the Berlin Wall, an exhibit titled *Flimmern auf dem Eisernen Vorhang* (Flickering on the Iron Curtain) opened at the Galerie Zero in northeastern Kreuzberg. The event commemorated the eleven-year history of West Berlin's border cinemas *(Grenzkinos),* U.S.-sponsored movie theaters that catered ideological transgressions to East German spectators in the 1950s and that mostly went out of business when the Wall cut off their source of revenue and political purpose.

In a clever orchestration of repurposed and reactivated locations, the organizers made forgotten Cold War topographies around Schlesisches Tor (an area now known for its clubs, cafés, and Easyjetsetters) both visible and functional. While audiences in the nearby music venue Lido, whose facade still evokes a movie theater, could watch *Der Teufel spielte Balalaika* (*Until Hell Is Frozen,* FRG 1961), the last film shown there before the border was sealed, Galerie Zero's visitors stepped onto a floor map charting the divided city's film political border.[13] Amid documents, archival footage, and interviews, Bernd Feuerhelm, who had been a *Halbstarke* (a German brand of rebellious postwar youth), was on hand

Visitors step onto a map on the floor of the exhibit *Flimmern auf dem Eisernen Vorhang* in 2011. Photograph courtesy of the author.

to provide authentic memories of East–West border culture and its particular expression among 1950s Berlin teenagers.[14]

The exhibit and retrospective, which also extended to newer venues such as the Deutsche Kinemathek's Arsenal cinema at Potsdamer Platz, revised urban space in ways that are important to my use of the term *spatial memory.* First, the retrospective included films, such as Gerhard Klein's *Eine Berliner Romanze* (*A Berlin Romance,* GDR 1956) and Georg Tressler's *Die Halbstarken* (*Teenage Wolfpack,* FRG 1956), that depict the Berlin space of prewall East and West German teenagers.[15] The revival of these cinematic spaces could provide knowledge of earlier topographies to younger spectators and elicit affective responses from both groups that remembered the films and the sector boundaries and those that did not. Second, the exhibit brought opposing generational claims to the neighborhood into dialogue. The mobilization of the postwar generation's memories took place in a part of town that was undergoing rapid gentrification. The gallery's location could thus unite memories of the Cold War past, transitory functions of the hipster party street, and contemporary frustrations with postwall urban development, such as the corporatization of the River Spree, Kreuzberg's internationalization and rocketing real estate prices, the imminent arrival of the nearby and formerly Eastern district of Treptow, and neighborhood *(Kiez)* rivalries between Kreuzberg in the West and Friedrichshain in the East. In the triangular relation between historical profilmic space, preserved cinematic space, and the changing built city, spatial memory of a given place remains a negotiation between virtual and physical geographies.

REPETITION AND DISSEMINATION

Retrospective structures position Berlin's moving images within larger spatial arguments, but cinema also produces city images and urban nostalgia through film's propensity for repetition. Whether in their original medium or in the proliferation of their subsequent forms of dissemination, films are designed for reuse and replay. From the sequential frames of a strip of film to the photochemical striking of countless positive prints to the rewind functions of projectors, VCRs, and DVD players to more recent means of bookmarking, ripping, burning, uploading, downloading, streaming, and embedding digital film files on the computer, the creation and screening of a film rely on various mechanisms of repetition. If the first city films depicted street views in long takes from one camera position, early filmmakers quickly realized that they could manipulate urban space through trick photography and editing. The Lumière brothers' *Démolition d'un mur* (*Demolition of a Wall,* France 1896) and Frederick S. Armitage's *Demolishing and Building Up the Star Theatre* (United States 1901) demonstrate cinema's capacity to revise urban space through temporal reversal. The same impulse to resurrect a demolished wall or building helps to explain both the appeal and the effect of repeated exposure to cinematic cities. Cinematographic technology records profilmic space, but it also enables this space to return, to puncture the physical and immediate authority of the present built city with portals to the past.

Today there are many ways to encounter photochemical and video traces of past cityscapes and their geographies. Not only can Web users search for specific film sequences and locations on video platforms such as YouTube and Vimeo but they may also post their own audiovisual content according to keywords as well as the date and place of recording. Film retrospection has ceased to be the domain of local, public film retrospectives and theatrical revival alone; nor is it any longer constrained by the fixed times and unifying public sphere of network and cable television schedules, as one technology after the other has provided means of recording films and television programs for later, individualized consumption. While this diverse media landscape has greatly fractured the collectivity of retrospection, it has also increased individual agency in accessing and sharing archival images of place. Successively new formats of film storage and acquisition (DVD, Blu-ray, DVR, digital film files, and online streaming) have expanded opportunities for private, small-group, piecemeal, and binge retrospection.

At the turn of the millennium, however, the retrospective culture of home entertainment still centered on ownership of physical media, video store rentals, and repetitions in television programming. Allowing consumers an unprecedented intimacy with older films, these forms of access brought images of past places into private homes for personal and semicollective consumption. In her study of home viewing, *Beyond the Multiplex,* Barbara Klinger investigates, among other topics, the ways in which American college students of that era derived pleasure from "multiple viewings" of films. As she finds, the "replay value" of a given feature might lie in its familiarity, its aesthetic complexity, its therapeutic qualities, the memorization of its dialogue, or, most significantly for the repetition of place, its provocation of nostalgia. "Nostalgic impulses for re-viewing," she concludes, "signal how individuals within a generation comprehend not only themselves and their peer group but also broader histories that define their social experience."[16] While constructing generational, often gendered cohesion, home re-viewing also encourages emotional engagement with revisited places.

Just as the proliferation of available films and means of consumption both empowered individual choice and reinforced group identities in the German media landscape, network and cable television at the time must be understood as a collective backdrop to personal expression with a remote control. A feature, a historical documentary, or a news report might be viewed in its entirety, repeatedly, with interruption, or not at all. Similarly, not all Berliners attended local, Berlin-themed film retrospectives. Participation in collective urban-cinematic nostalgia for Berlin and in the anticipation of the city's future must thus be conceived as neither obligatory nor uniform nor necessarily active. Nonetheless, all of these options and means of exposure were curated. Together, they formed an audio-visual architecture of the urban past whose contours could be encountered at home, in cinemas and museums, and on public, outdoor monitors. Anyone moving through this network of Berlin images in and beyond the city would come into contact with portions of this constantly flowing archive. Footage seen on television or in the cinema might reappear a week later in a public space and could be juxtaposed immediately with its surroundings.

Thus, though generational affiliations gave important impetus to Berlin's film retrospection and new productions, the ubiquity of these images also ensured that Berlin nostalgia would transcend the barriers of age and personal experience. Alison Landsberg's concept of cinematic prosthetic memory can be helpful here. As "advanced capitalism and an emergent commodified culture" invent new forms of dissemination and push content beyond national reception, she has argued that nonorganic, mediated memories "become part of one's personal archive of experience."[17] In this way, exposure to archival footage and repertory films furnishes

A public monitor informs crowds at Potsdamer Platz's Sony Center about the square's history, 2010. Photograph courtesy of the author.

spectators across space and time with a collective nostalgia for urban pasts through which they themselves may never have lived. These affective relations to the historical places, people, and events depicted in films become a global, empathetic tool kit, which Landsberg likens to a prosthetic limb. The availability of contradictory Berlin images—of destruction and construction, of ruptures and continuities, of East and West—educated the masses to perceive and mourn the city's losses. It is not hard to understand how the postwall generation, confronted with the archival evidence of National Socialism and 1945, also came to desire a return to the dynamic 1920s metropolis.

LOCATION POLITICS

Remembering and *reimagining* the city went hand in hand with *re-imaging* it. Representations of the New Berlin in films must thus be understood in dialogue with the politics of the production location. As a skyline of construction cranes heralded the architecture of a new order, federal and regional politicians, film professionals, and international corporate investors were eager to rebuild Berlin's lapsed reputation for commercial film artistry, a valuable cultural cachet of the Weimar era.[18] A good past was a good *film* past, and during Berlin's vibrant interwar period, the Ufa Studios in Potsdam–Babelsberg had cultivated a number of stars, directors, and cinematographers, whose features not only drew domestic acclaim but also played on the international market, for example, Friedrich Wilhelm Murnau's *Der letzte Mann* (*The Last Laugh,* Germany 1924), Fritz Lang's *Metropolis* (Germany 1927), and Josef von Sternberg's *Der blaue Engel* (*The Blue Angel,* Germany 1930). After passing through Nazi hands and becoming the East's state-of-the-art, yet SED-controlled, DEFA Studios, the new Studio Babelsberg was just one element in an ensemble of film institutions forming Germany's restored capital of production and symbolic capital of film history and continuity.[19] After decades of migration westward, the FRG's film industry had established strongholds elsewhere, and the FBBB was tasked with integrating the East and West Berlin industries and with establishing a strong brand name within existing production geographies (e.g., Bavaria and North Rhine–Westphalia). Diverting federal and regional coffers toward development, production, and postproduction financing, the FBBB had to ensure that films made in the capital region would reflect well on the service location.[20]

When, in 2004, the film-centric FBBB was superseded by the more comprehensive regional media organization Medienboard Berlin–Brandenburg (MBBB), the incoming management was careful to fête the Filmboard's statistical achievements, which it was eager to uphold, surpass, and extend across multiple platforms. The FBBB's investment of 171 million euros into 1,430 film projects had paid off when these productions, in turn, spent 477 million euros in the region.[21] Beyond regional profit, however, the more than four hundred features supported by the FBBB had generated new images of an exciting city in flux. By 2007, Berlin–Brandenburg had become a popular location for international coproductions, and the Federal Government Commissioner for Culture and the Media initiated the German Federal Film Fund (Deutscher Filmförderfonds, DFFF) as a means of strengthening the domestic film industry, while also attracting the larger production budgets often furnished by foreign partners. The image of Berlin and Germany in these films, which typically gain distribution beyond Europe, can hardly be neutral.

As the films that most visibly construct Berlin's spatial relations for the global market and most persuasively advocate the service location through production values, these costly coproductions (one of the film industrial futures of this book's concerns) demonstrate the importance of location political analysis for any discussion of film geography. Rather than situating this discussion exclusively within or outside the films themselves, I understand location politics to be a negotiation between (1) urban discourse contemporary to the film's moment of production or revival; (2) the shifting cultural political agendas underlying a film's development, funding, and production; (3) formal choices of how to frame, edit, and otherwise present urban space; and (4) degrees of resemblance and conspicuousness.

Tom Tykwer's global action thriller *The International* (United States/FRG/United Kingdom 2009) provides a case in point. Opening the fifty-ninth Berlin International Film Festival, the film premiered just steps away from Potsdamer Platz, where a red observation platform invited festivalgoers and passersby to survey all that had changed in the twenty years since the fall of the Wall. Once the marginalized border between East and West, the now built-up square was draped with an enormous placard welcoming jury president Tilda Swinton, Tykwer (German cinema's own "international"), and festival director Dieter Kosslick to the "Platz to be." *The International* merely begins in Berlin before proceeding to showcase other metropolises, such as New York, Milan, and Istanbul. Nonetheless, its opening scene could not be more conspicuously set in the German capital. What's more, it evokes the high stakes of Cold War espionage by reserving Berlin a place in the politics of flashy, more contemporary global intrigue.

Shot in fall 2007, the film introduces one of the New Berlin's celebrated architectural and infrastructural feats, the Central Train Station, which had finally been completed in spring 2006. A gleaming glass structure just north of the new government district, the station symbolically unified the city's long-distance rail traffic while offering a view of its new architecture of power. An Interpol agent meets with an informant in a car in the station's parking lot as his partner (played by Clive Owen) scans the location from a distance. A wide shot displays the station's facade, its sign, "Berlin Hauptbahnhof," clearly legible. At the bottom of the frame, a legend further explicates, in English, "Central Station Berlin, Germany." Over the next three minutes, portions of the sign appear in seven shots, should there be any doubt as to where this conversation about the international arms trade is taking place. Before the film's title even appears on-screen, the station serves as a geographically specific calling card. Though Berlin does not figure in the remainder of the film, it supplies the narrative point of departure, the place that instigates the subsequent whirlwind of stunning international backdrops. Through conspicuous narrative placement and framing, this cinematic intervention secures the New Berlin's membership in the club of world-class cities, at least cinematically.

Receiving its German investment from the inaugural reserves of the DFFF, *The International* stood alongside a spate of English-language features that combined international stars with extensive location shooting in Berlin–Brandenburg: *Speed Racer* (United States/Australia/FRG 2008), *The Reader* (United States/FRG 2008), *Valkyrie* (United States/FRG 2008), *Inglourious Basterds* (United States/FRG 2009), *Unknown* (United Kingdom / France/FRG / Canada / Japan / United States 2011), and *Hanna* (United States/United Kingdom/FRG 2011). If regional funding boards have capitalized on cinema's potential as an economic and cultural investment (akin to tourism) in a given part of the country, the DFFF's broader, national approach asserts the German pedigree, albeit partial, of each funded project. As transnational film financing and global story lines proliferate, the visibility and narrative use of place stake an audiovisual claim in real and virtual worlds already saturated with images of other cities. As with films funded by one or more regional

The International (2009) clarifies its location. Frame still.

boards, the screen time and presentation of German cinematic space in DFFF features must not be taken for granted.

Berlin's appearance in films after the *Wende* was tied to a new politics of picturing place, and the DFFF's complicated evaluation system reveals the extent to which postwall filmmaking in Germany has become entangled in discourses of location, resemblance, and recognition. In a numeric "Test of Characteristics for Feature Films," the evaluation committee quantifies the German and European qualities of each application, assigning, in the section on "cultural content," the highest value of 3 points to the use of "German landmarks" or "German locations" and to the preparation of a final version "in the German language."[22]

The International's conspicuous framing and naming of the Central Station is merely an exaggerated example of the cultural and geopolitical work that filmic representations of place can accomplish. As the DFFF's distinction between "landmark" and "location" makes clear, big-budget production funds and capital region resources are the implicit, but also explicit, province of producers and filmmakers who render Berlin identifiable. While landmarks display "clearly German subjects, no matter where they are shot," locations provide "the place where imagination is transposed into a film work." Official examples of landmarks, such as Berlin's Reichstag, Hamburg's Reeperbahn, or even prototypical landscapes and architecture ("Black Forest cottage"), are thus contrasted with a more general German space of narrative action.[23] A filmmaker who avoids landmarks would likely miss a few points on the tally sheet, whereas one who combines obviously German locations with indisputable landmarks stands a better chance of getting the film made.

CASES OF URBAN NOSTALGIA AND FILM GEOGRAPHY

Berlin Replayed's progression of chapters forms a loose chronology of temporal and spatial concerns that make sense of cinema's postwall privilege in visualizing Berlin's past, present, and future. Chapters 1 and 2 lay a historical foundation for Berlin's filmic representation in the 1920s and 1950s, two eras of acceptable all-German memory that, in postwall retrospection, could elide the perceived missteps of the Third Reich and the GDR. Chapter 3 looks more closely at the decade surrounding the *Wende*, whereas chapter 4 examines the FBBB's prolific years in the late 1990s and early 2000s. Though all four chapters negotiate some degree of nostalgia for the past built city, chapters 1 and 3 revisit the medium specificity of this longing. Chapters 2 and 4 emerge from the respective geopolitics of early Cold War and postunification Berlin, both places in which films were instrumental in conciliatory reconstructions of all-Berlin space.

Each chapter's cluster of films or audiovisual objects generates new questions about spatial memory and urban space. Chapter 1's emphasis on the remake asks how Ruttmann's city symphony came to be Berlin's mediated "origin" and how the newer images of documentarian Thomas Schadt's *Berlin: Sinfonie einer Großstadt* (Berlin symphony, FRG 2002) relate to the earlier film's legacy. Chapter 2 examines the narrative geographies of Gerhard Klein's Eastern *Eine Berliner Romanze* and *Berlin—Ecke Schönhauser* and Georg Tressler's Western *Die Halbstarken* and *Endstation Liebe* (*Last Stop Love,* FRG 1958) alongside the intersector mobility of 1950s Berlin film culture to probe the generational nuances of belonging in the divided city. Chapter 3 explores Potsdamer Platz, Berlin's most complicated and symbolic place of layered, contradictory histories, through cinematic and new media representations of what I call *urban virtuality* in Wenders's late–Cold War *Der Himmel über Berlin* and media artist Joachim Sauter and computer programmer Dirk Lüsebrink's interactive map and film archive *The Invisible Shape of Things Past* (1995 to present). Proposing *cartographic indexicality* as a post-*Wende,* new media shift away from the *cinematographic indexicality* of resemblance in chapter 1, I suggest the increasing appeal of mapping moving images not to their lost, profilmic referents but to their permanent, geographical coordinates. Finally, chapter 4 approaches the successful partnership of the FBBB and the production company X-Filme Creative Pool through the location politics surrounding the production and distribution of Tom Tykwer's *Lola rennt* (*Run Lola Run,* FRG 1998) and Wolfgang Becker's *Good Bye, Lenin!* (FRG 2003). Together, these case studies present Berlin's unique relationship to moving images as an ongoing process of emotional, ideological, spatial, and historical reorientation—an affective hermeneutics that takes place between Berlin's moving image archive and its evolving built form.

Berlin's future and future images are beyond the purview of the present study. New technology continues, however, to change the ways that the past may be called up, positioned, and circulated. On one hand, the current age of computer-generated imagery (CGI) offers greater possibilities for manipulating cinematic space. Destroyed buildings rise again in period pieces while more recent architecture is eliminated from the skyline. The Brandenburg Gate may be enhanced and doubled for the car-racing protagonist's intercontinental triumph in *Speed Racer,* a film in which all global roads lead to Berlin. The pasts of Berlin cinema's future may thus be beholden neither to the built city's voids and ruins nor to its archival views. How the German and international film industries wield this technology, and to which ideological purposes, remains to be seen.[24]

On the other hand, the rise of social media, the prevalence of affordable video-recording and mobile devices, and widespread access to editing software have renewed interest in moving images' relation to profilmic space. The documentation of *being here/there* has become a daily practice on Facebook walls and in Twitter newsfeeds. Web users search and cite places at historical moments while relying on GPS technology to tag personal images with geographical coordinates. Place is turning into its images, into an archival aggregate grouped by keywords and location. Moving images of place may be carried in the pocket of a mobile user and played anywhere, against any physical backdrop.

Cartographic indexicality is rehabilitating the belief in what one sees, even as CGI calls the old (photochemical) cinematographic indexicality into question. It is in part *because* they are moored to geography that new digital images and digitized old ones can serve so many simultaneous cultural purposes. As new media theorist Lev Manovich puts it, "remixability has become a built-in feature of the digital networked media universe," and "users themselves have been gradually 'modularizing' culture."[25] The shifting contexts of repurposed material have become a crucial feature of critical analysis. In the study of urban nostalgia and film geography, one might ask how cultural remixers embed or invert the moving images they use.

Film sequences and fragments have become tools (like rulers or calculators) for measuring and exploring profilmic space virtually. As the federal and regional film industries were devising new ways to assure German and Berlin spaces' place in cinema, a number of multimedia projects advanced new geographical approaches to Berlin. In summer 2011, the Hong Kong–based artists and architects Laurent Guitierrez and Valérie Portefaix convened a brainstorming session at Berlin's Kunstquartier Bethanien. After the successful exhibition of *Runscape* (2010), which included a film of their son running parkour through Hong Kong spaces known from cinema, the duo announced their new project, *Runscape Berlin.* I joined a group of architects, artists, and art historians to discuss Berlin's representational challenges, complex geography, and long filmography. Video-mapping Berlin through film historical spatial memories and contemporary affective geographies would require, we decided, new strategies. The camera would have to behave differently in a different city.

One week later, the gallery Program|Initiative for Art and Architecture Collaborations held its interdisciplinary workshop, *rePLACE BERLIN,* to "artistically research and investigate" personal, routine urban pathways, submitted anonymously to the organizers. From these, the group would develop innovative ways to represent current inhabitants' interactions with their surroundings.[26] Once again, new strategies for mapping Berlin's spatial relations and detecting urban change called for a combination of artistic and theoretical modes of inquiry. Once again, the questions asked of Berlin were posed in relation to other metropolises, in this case Beirut and Beijing. To see past the city's clichés, we armed ourselves with analog and digital devices—from sketchpads and bicycles to digital cameras and audio recorders. After all, re-*placing* Berlin meant confronting its physical discrepancies and communicating the results visually, textually, and aurally to others. My own video experiment, *Bunker/weg (Pathway to the Bunker),* traced a mundane route from a residential building to a former air-raid bunker recently transformed into luxury condominiums. The camera's record of the space between the two points was aligned, not with my eyes, but with the movements of my body. The images thus revealed many invisible aspects of a spatial memory poised between two moments in time.

I returned to Program a few months later to present a remixed video exhibition, *Bau/Rückbau (Build/Unbuild),* on the relationship of cinema to construction and demolition, particularly in the history of the GDR's Palace of the Republic (Palast der Republik). Asking the audience to watch, not film sequences, but the building itself, and to treat the image fragments not as an installation but as a coherent cinematic projection, I wanted to demonstrate the migration of spatial meaning across modes of filmmaking, across time, and even across cities. The point was to let space tell its own story, inscribed in the many ideological approaches that have attempted to make it visible. While studying Berlin's images, I have come to make my own, to participate critically in and observe their dissemination.

Bau/Rückbau (2011) at Program. Photograph courtesy of Lena Kilkka Mann and Kino Satellite.

I began researching *Berlin Replayed* before digital remediation and remixing were quotidian practices, let alone critical ones, and I have finished the book at a time when scholarship is finally embracing the methodologies and expanded digital tool kit of critical media practice. Berlin's period of physical transformation after the Wall was also one of technological transition in which collective desires for past and future spaces intersected with new means to service those desires. In the epilogue, I explore briefly three innovative versions of cartographic indexicality, in which moving images are reunited with their profilmic locations. Postwall Berlin's culture of cinematic retrospection occurred at a unique moment, a time poised between an indeterminate physical form, virtual promises of the city to come, and the archival boom of digitization. It was a time when the city was an urban laboratory, not only for Germany, but for the world at large.

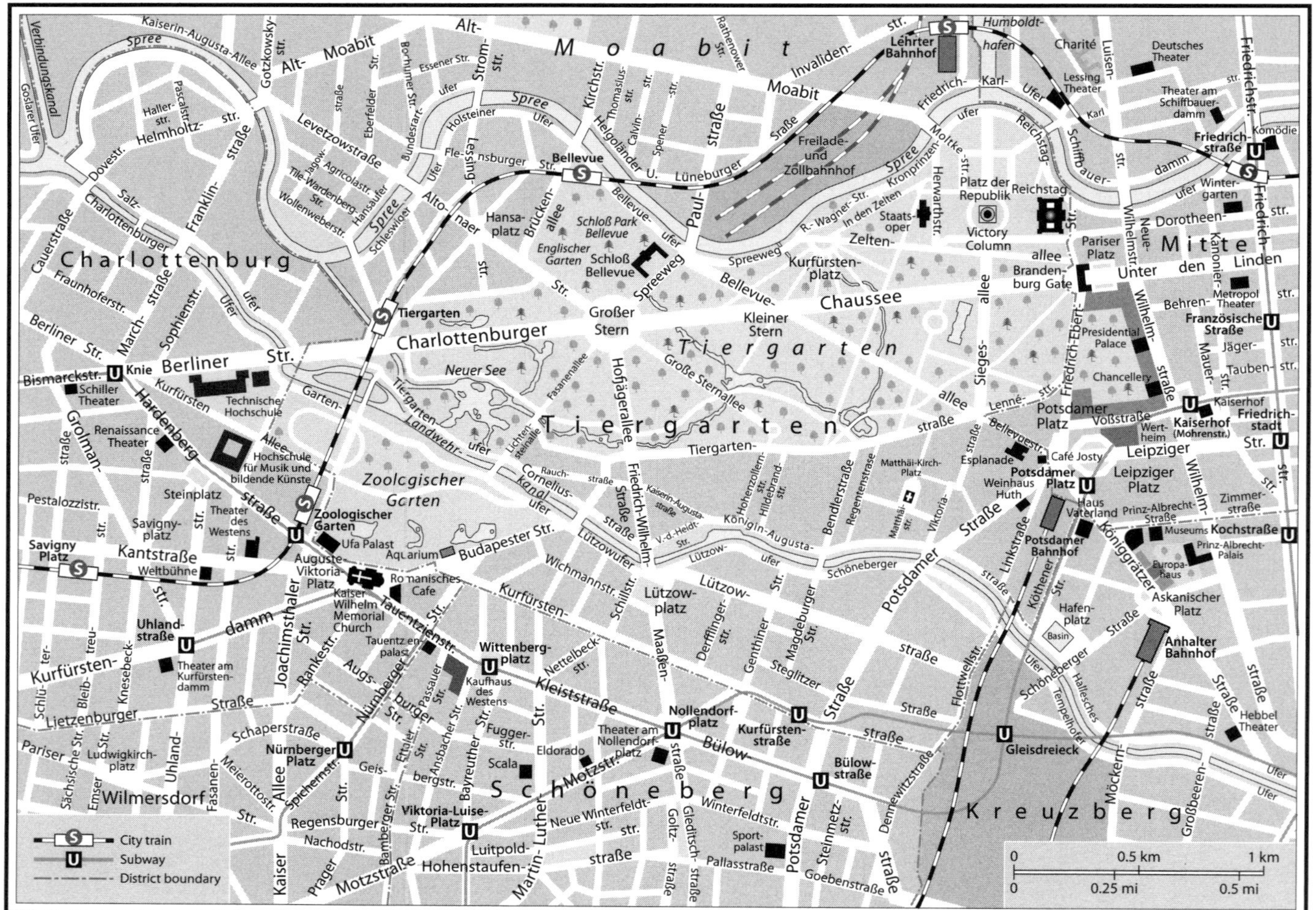
Moabit
Charlottenburg
Tiergarten
Mitte
Schöneberg
Kreuzberg
Wilmersdorf
Zoologischer Garten
Lehrter Bahnhof
Freilade- und Zollbahnhof
Reichstag
Platz der Republik
Victory Column
Staatsoper
Brandenburg Gate
Pariser Platz
Unter den Linden
Presidential Palace
Chancellery
Potsdamer Platz
Leipziger Platz
Potsdamer Bahnhof
Anhalter Bahnhof
Askanischer Platz
Haus Vaterland
Café Josty
Weinhaus Huth
Wertheim
Europahaus
Prinz-Albrecht-Palais
Museums
Deutsches Theater
Lessing Theater
Theater am Schiffbauerdamm
Komödie
Wintergarten
Metropol Theater
Schloß Bellevue
Schloß Park Bellevue
Englischer Garten
Großer Stern
Kleiner Stern
Neuer See
Technische Hochschule
Hochschule für Musik und bildende Künste
Schiller Theater
Renaissance Theater
Theater des Westens
Ufa Palast
Aquarium
Romanisches Cafe
Kaiser Wilhelm Memorial Church
Tauentzienpalast
Kaufhaus des Westens
Theater am Kurfürstendamm
Theater am Nollendorfplatz
Eldorado
Scala
Sportpalast
Hebbel Theater
Gleisdreieck
Kurfürstendamm
Charlottenburger Chaussee
City train
Subway
District boundary
0 0.5 km 1 km
0 0.25 mi 0.5 mi

Berlin, 1927

1

REMAKE

Berlin Symphonies and the Myth of the *Weltstadt*

A CITY REMADE

In her installation *Berlin Remake* (United States 2005), American filmmaker and video artist Amie Siegel confronts the representational problem that the twenty-first-century German capital had become. Through a dual-channel video projection, she places two Berlin scenes—one from a series of East German DEFA films and one from a series of contemporary shot reconstructions—side by side on a white wall. Although Siegel does not identify the films, their historical periods are revealed foremost in their location shots of East Berlin.[1]

Whether bearing witness to postwar rubble, vast stretches of the Berlin Wall, or socialist architecture in its prime, the DEFA shots contrast greatly with Siegel's meticulous postwall reconstructions: views of renovated squares and houses, unwalled streets, and brightly repainted satellite-city highrises. With each juxtaposition, the viewer must literally do a double take to process the temporal disjunction yet spatial correspondence between the two images. In the artist's own words, this intersection of historical moments and both "physical" and "cinematic" landscapes provokes "an uncanny dialogue between past and present, suggesting how architecture (film locations) reveals, embeds and sometimes denies history."[2] *Berlin Remake* is not a film but a critical apparatus for representing urban change. As such, it offers a strategy both for encountering Berlin and for understanding its legacy of contradictory film images. The only way to account for altered appearances in this city, the installation seems to suggest, is to film a geographical location twice, to place competing temporalities in simultaneous relation to each other, to poise the act of seeing, dialectically, between Berlin's present and past.

The doubling inherent in *Berlin Remake*'s design attempts to envision the "feeling of unease" that has pervaded postwall discourse on the city.[3] With numerous

Berlin Remake (2005), here a view of Berlin's Gendarmenmarkt, at KW Institute for Contemporary Art. Courtesy of Amie Siegel.

sites suspended, after the political turn *(Wende)* of 1989–90, between historical associations and future architectural projections, Berlin has become the paradigmatic city for theorizing the virtual presence of the past. In language recalling archeological layers and supernatural phenomena, scholars and artists have repeatedly cited the postwall city's "haunted" quality. In 1997, the historian Brian Ladd attributed this prevalent urban characteristic to the tendency of memories to "cleave to the physical settings of events" there. For the geographer Karen Till, it was the "practices and politics of place-making" in the New Berlin that continually rehearsed and re-presented the city's pasts. Urban planner Claire Colomb has more recently approached Berlin's reinvention as an act of staging and marketing the city image.[4] Certainly the city's twentieth-century history of radical regime change supplied the same location with a range of preferred and shunned connotations.

This ambivalence lingered particularly around Berlin places that were most symbolic of National Socialist ideology, Holocaust atrocities, wartime damage, and the injustices of East Germany's ruling SED and state security apparatus (Stasi). Understandably, Berlin's municipal and federal governments, cultural politicians, urban planners, city marketers, tourism companies, business leaders, news media, and artists struggled to identify appropriate all-German *(gesamtdeutsch)* traditions for the unified city, while also acknowledging its troubled history. Prussian, Weimar, Nazi, and Cold War pasts were present in Berlin's built and absent architecture, its prewar structures *(Altbauten)* and postwar and postwall voids, and physical incongruities in the cityscape challenged overly optimistic claims to newness.

In the 1990s and early 2000s, quotidian confrontations with Berlin's disputed legacies required little more than going for a walk, opening a newspaper, or turning on a television. While *Stolpersteine* embedded in sidewalks tripped pedestrians into an awareness of names and addresses of deported Jews, debates over contested spaces, such as those surrounding the future of (East) Berlin's Palace of the Republic (built on the former grounds of the Hohenzollerns' City Palace), occupied the public sphere. Photographs, films, and television programs played a pivotal role in this renewed attention to the city that would once again serve as the German capital and seat of government; they reminded local, national, and international readers and viewers how the city had once looked.

Moving images, in particular, not only circulated invisible urban views in those years but also reanimated them. Far more ghostly than the ruin, monument, and void, cinema fostered both a public consciousness of what Berlin used to be and strong notions of what it should become (again). Whether rescreened in retrospectives, revived in new prints, programmed on television, or sampled as archival excerpts, films could disseminate city images from various eras of Berlin's political legitimation or, if shown often enough, align the city with a favored past. As *Berlin Remake* demonstrates, historical views of the city call into question their more recent counterparts. Containing just enough spatial and architectural information to confirm their shared geographic origins, the dual frames demand to be related, to have their differences narrated. Siegel's juxtaposition therefore gives form to the risk of temporal irreconcilability and, in this way, theorizes access to simultaneous visions as a proof of transience, much like literary scholar and media artist Svetlana Boym's fragile cinematic metaphor for nostalgia. Writing about Europe's complex, emotional, and ironic relationship to the past in the 1990s, Boym describes this longing for lost places and times as "a double exposure, or a superimposition of two images—of home and abroad, past and present, dream and everyday life." The tension of this permanent state of duality remains unresolvable, because the "moment we try to force" the superimposition "into a single image, it breaks the frame or burns the surface."[5] This self-destruction of the material of preservation punishes cinema's hubris, mediated revivification's claim to "have it all."

Siegel's title and format underscore the correspondence between remaking a film and remaking a city, but original films and their remakes appear on a screen together as rarely as past and present skylines share the physical horizon. Remakes offer discrete, aesthetic experiences, and their initial exhibition and reception can be separated by decades from those of their sources. They also appear at different times in the lives of their spectators. While younger viewers may not know that a new film has revisited old material, older ones encounter remakes in reference to their own biographies and in a dynamic relation to the reception of the earlier film. The advent of a remake often becomes an opportunity to take a second look at the original. Remakes attune audiences who have seen both films to differences in social attitudes, fashion, technology, star culture, geopolitics, and place; they also attest to the cultural conditions and values that warrant their (re)production at all. Because these films are generally the province of fiction, Siegel's installation signals all the more that a remake of Berlin film scenes is a documentary matter. Whether as a nondistinctive backdrop or a location of known landmarks, the Berlin of these new and old fictional fragments bears witness to the historicity of place.

No single title in Berlin's vast filmography has resurfaced more often and widely than Walter Ruttmann's *Berlin. Die Sinfonie der Großstadt* (*Berlin: Symphony of a Great City,* Germany 1927), nor has another Berlin film warranted a remake as prominent as documentarian and photographer Thomas Schadt's *Berlin: Sinfonie einer Großstadt* (*Berlin Symphony,* FRG 2002). Ruttmann's nonnarrative urban cross-section film, which approaches the city with the observational sobriety of the New Objectivity *(Neue Sachlichkeit)* and the occasional graphical frenzy of Expressionism, has become the primary cinematic document of Weimar Berlin's golden interwar years. Perpetually revived, cited, and programmed, the film's portrayal of a modern, populous, and lively city haunted postwall Berlin's cosmopolitan aspirations. Famed for its experimental montage of a day in urban life and its prewar views, this audiovisual symphony of place depicts a modern city through rapid cuts, traffic, machinery, and rushing pedestrians. Offering precisely the kind of usable past that the New Berlin required, the film supplied a metropolitan model, a place to look forward/back to amid the constructions and reconstructions of the capital. The immediate postwall era, like the 1920s, was "a period of very self-conscious, not to mention self-interested, questioning of what Berlin represented, how it embodied the broader spirit of the age, what made it unique and how it should be presented to the world."[6] *Berlin. Die Sinfonie der Großstadt* could attest to the city's former stature as a world-class metropolis *(Weltstadt)* over 4 million and circulate a positive history that predated Nazism and the national shame and worldwide trauma of its aftermath.

If the multitude of Berlin-themed film retrospectives revived selective histories and contributed to public urban reeducation about past Berlins, the regional and federal politics of film production assured that new features would disseminate fresh interpretations of the city. The appearance of Schadt's remake coincided conspicuously with the early years of the Berlin Republic. Its production both staged the film as an homage to Ruttmann and reflected a self-congratulatory sense of accomplishment in the city and in the film industry. Through the boldness of this cinematic enterprise, the refurbished city would seem to have regained its past attributes were it not for Schadt's aesthetic choices. His deliberately slower rhythm and effort to meditate on the past as well as document the present introduced a note of critique into this new city symphony and the New Berlin. *Berlin: Sinfonie einer Großstadt* responded to and intervened in the unquestioned circulation, recycling, and cultural authority of historical images, particularly those of Ruttmann's Berlin.

Ruttmann's iconography of the city became so ubiquitous and malleable after 1945, and even more so after the *Wende,* that sequences from his film had come to dominate representations of Berlin before the Second World War.[7] Postwall urban marketing similarly upheld the primacy of interwar Berlin's renowned tempo and entertainment culture by promoting "a cosmopolitan, open, youthful city using images and terms that allude to Weimar Berlin of the 1920s." At the same time, urban planners continued to preserve the integrity of Berlin's neighborhoods *(Kieze)* via building codes of the nineteenth century.[8] While the New Berlin looked back to its future, *Berlin. Die Sinfonie der Großstadt* became something of a foil to Leni Riefenstahl's *Triumph des Willens* (*Triumph of the Will,* Germany 1935), the Nazi propaganda film typically called on to demonstrate the aesthetics of German fascist order and obedience in other documentaries. Anton Kaes has argued of fiction films set in the Third Reich that the "past cannot be recovered and re-experienced, since it is not out there to be visited and photographed like a foreign country: the past always has to be reconstructed, reconstituted, represented based on representations that already exist."[9] Nonfiction views of place wield tremendous authority in this process because their existence presupposes the camera's immediate access to profilmic space at a specific point in history. The privileged authenticity of historical moving images becomes dangerous when it begins to preclude nuance, explanation, and contradictory evidence.

Though it does not include a single frame from Ruttmann's film, Schadt's remake engages with the legacy of the 1927 city symphony by answering its images with new ones. Thus adding his own vision of the city to the relativizing "language of images,"[10] Schadt's Berlin of 2002 enables the interfilmic equivalent of Siegel's juxtaposition. This interplay of urban versions requires both medium-specific and cultural-historical scrutiny if the evolving mythology of real and filmic Berlins is to be understood and invoked responsibly. Schadt's cinematic remaking of Berlin demands a reassessment of Ruttmann's original hand in its making. The relational quality of the cinematic urban remake invites dialogue between the two films but also between the films and the built city. The complex receptive afterlife and changing cultural value of *Berlin. Die Sinfonie der Großstadt* can be separated neither from capital politics nor from the film medium's claims to indexicality, spatial memory, and urban nostalgia. After all, the film's persuasive modernity continues to challenge Berlin's contemporary image campaigns.

ORIGINAL CITY

The extraordinary cultural prestige and public presence of *Berlin. Die Sinfonie der Großstadt* in and beyond the unified capital enact a longing for and mediated return to an elective home. Because cinematographic technology relies on the camera's direct access to profilmic space, on the generation of countless copies from the same negative, and on a comparable viewing experience across a wide geographic area, it can unite local spaces of recording with remote spaces of consumption. Though cinema's promise of overcoming physical distance with mediated proximity usually refers to space, it can also refer to time. Films repeat the presence of past profilmic space with each new screening.

The historian and cultural critic Walter Benjamin recognized the invention of "technological reproducibility" as a paradigm shift away from an original artwork's authority and unique aura. His arguments on the relation of originals to copies offer a provocative point of departure (and inversion) for theorizing *Berlin. Die Sinfonie der Großstadt*'s acquired cultural function as Berlin's origin. By destabilizing the unique here and now of an original artwork, the mass distribution of photographic and cinematographic reproductions allows the copy to travel and places it "in situations which the original itself cannot attain." While a painting might hang in a museum, its photograph appears in books and magazines (and, today, on websites, which users can access with a smartphone while crossing the street). Reproducibility, argues Benjamin, can similarly devalue (by making widely available) "a landscape moving past the spectator in a film." The implication is that profilmic space, too, is original, a historical intersection of place and time that the camera reproduces on film and that the photochemical printing process further replicates.

Curiously, Benjamin then abandons the comparison between artworks and landscapes. Reproducibility "touches on" a work of art's "authenticity," which, he claims, is "more vulnerable than that of any natural object." What the reproduction and its mobility obscure is the original artwork's relation to "physical duration" and "historical testimony." The authentic work bears the marks of time, a gradual corruption halted by the late nineteenth and early twentieth centuries' new promise of cinematographic eternity. Film wrests the object from the process of aging and "actualizes" this reproduction in any number of locations and receptive surroundings even as the original artwork continues to acquire the patina and inevitable damage of its long physical existence.[11]

It would be a mistake, however, to dismiss the lesser vulnerability of profilmic space. As early travel films demonstrate, cinema brought views of the world to spectators who could not always, for socioeconomic and logistical reasons, visit these sights themselves. Whereas filmed natural landscapes—seasides, mountains, and fields—might have suggested permanence, urban views presented street scenes and cities-in-progress (e.g., the construction of Manhattan's skyscrapers).[12] These actualized cities that cinematographic technology recorded and brought to distant spectators nonetheless originated from a field of view before the camera. Devaluation of a unique place this way yielded access to its cinematographic image—the knowledge that a given filmic representation signified a profilmic Berlin. Like original artworks, this original city, then, existed in relation to its reproductions. Recording technology preserved a version of the original, a state in its history, but *not* the original in flux, throughout time.

Accelerated urban change can quickly produce discrepancies between the original city and its reproduction. Berlin's specific history and evolving physical form have especially dramatized this disparity. When, in the late 1930s, Benjamin described the loss of aura and observed fascism's "*aetheticizing of politics,*" which would culminate in war, he could hardly have anticipated the extent to which the world and his own Berlin would be transfigured by military aggression.[13] "Origin" took on a second meaning in the capital of the Third Reich, transformed, by 1945, through National Socialist urban planning, Allied air strikes, and violent street combat into a cityscape of rubble and ruin.

Writing in 1972, and expanding many of Benjamin's observations, John Berger frames the relation between image (here an original painting) and subject as a question of survival. While images came into existence "to conjure up the appearance of something that was absent," societies gradually appreciated "that an image could outlast what it represented." Increasing cultural reflection on these remainders could remind later beholders of "how something or somebody once looked—and thus by implication how the subject had once been seen by other people." Additional historical distance from an image allowed "the specific vision of the image-maker" to be "recognized as part of the record."[14] Art history thus recovers contexts, details, and narratives contained in the painting, in the fact of its creation, and in its cultural and physical endurance.

Though made with 1927's technology par excellence of visual reproducibility, *Berlin. Die Sinfonie der Großstadt* is not simply a cinematographic facsimile of Weimar Berlin. Much like a unique painting or sculpture, rather, Ruttmann's film has outlasted its built referent and gained authority as a discrete artwork and historical document both of urban space and of authorial intention in the form of montage. Paradoxically, a film is an original artwork already designed for mass reproduction, but its inherent mobility and repetition can enhance rather than cheapen the physical bond between the artwork and the profilmic cityscape. Cinematographic technology, far from depriving the original city of its aura, could provide Weimar Berlin's nearest indexical relative, the moving image, for permanent retrospection. With time, *Berlin. Die Sinfonie der Großstadt* has taken on its own aura—not of uniqueness but of temporal and spatial discrepancy and repeated consumption.

Throughout the 1990s, enthusiasm for the Weimar era accompanied preparations for the arrival of the federal government in its piecemeal relocation from Bonn to Berlin. The city's temporal indeterminacy, including a strategic bracketing of the Third Reich's blight on German democratic idealism, had become a hallmark of capital marketing strategy. In 1999, for example, weekly news magazine *Der Spiegel* heralded the New Berlin with a cover story whose art depicted a unified (and already successfully integrated) cityscape as an oversized, ascendant air balloon carrying the weight of a much smaller globe. Proclaiming Berlin's "journey to becoming a world-class city," the cover advertised forty pages on "Germany's New Old Metropolis."[15] While such invocations of Weimar ambitions helped the news media reassure a skeptical public of the city's readiness to function as the capital of a unified Germany,[16] cultural and architectural developments in the built city reinforced the naturalness of these prewar associations. The rebuilding of Potsdamer Platz included both a replica of the square's original traffic light, erected in 1924, and a touristic Café Josty, an allusion to the prewar café of the same name. False historical facades gave built form to scaffolding all around the nearby octagonal Leipziger Platz. Across from Alexanderplatz, the facade of the Haus der Elektroindustrie displayed (now long-faded) passages from Alfred Döblin's 1929 novel *Berlin, Alexanderplatz*. From 2003 to 2005, Anhalter Bahnhof's portico, all that remains of the once massive train station, underwent renovation. Cabarets and sex clubs emulated the perceived greater political wit, social experimentation, and gender fluidity of the Weimar metropolis, while architect Daniel Libeskind's Jewish Museum celebrated the loss and reinstatement of the city's German-Jewish culture. At almost any tourist site, black-and-white postcards of Berlin's prewar architecture displayed nostalgic Wilhelmine and Weimar photographs of buildings that had since been destroyed or greatly altered.

A June 1999 *Der Spiegel* cover advertising the new-old world-class city. Courtesy of *Der Spiegel.*

Reviving Weimar diversity and cultural production—the "good" Germany cultivated abroad—provided a politically secure means of transit between the city's present transformation and its future opportunities.

The Nazi *Reichshauptstadt* had been the place in and from which Adolf Hitler's government had justified a gradual erosion of civil liberties; state racism; a meticulously planned genocide targeting Jews, homosexuals, political dissidents, the mentally ill, and various smaller religious and ethnic groups; and a war that had left millions dead around the globe. These policies and actions in turn served as the legitimation of postwar Allied occupation and the division of Berlin into French, British, American, and Soviet sectors, the country into four corresponding zones and, by 1949, into two states later separated by a wall. By embracing the Weimar city image, the Federal Republic and its new and old citizens could, as Till has argued, counteract their "strong dissatisfaction with, and anger toward, the pasts embodied through National Socialist and Cold War Berlins that continued to define Germany's place in the contemporary world even after unification."[17] Regardless of their socialization in the East or the West, Germans could rediscover in Weimar Berlin shared democratic origins and a prewar, pre-Holocaust national understanding that could alleviate Nazism's lasting, negative stereotypes of the brutal German perpetrator, willing population, and aggressive, warmongering nation.

Weimar imagery's positive spin on Berlin's past helps to explain its utility at the turn of the millennium, but it does not account for the more melancholic pleasure of selective revisiting. In Boym's formulation, nostalgia is both "a longing for a home that no longer exists or has never existed," with its attendant "sentiment of loss and displacement," and "a romance with one's own fantasy."[18] Berlin's mediated abundance of filmic, photographic, and literary imagery from the 1920s constructed a collective narrative of loss that paralleled the fragmented and architecturally incongruous cityscape.[19] By positing Weimar Berlin as the city's physical and psychical origin, city marketers, urban planners, government representatives, and news outlets helped legitimize the desire for a return (e.g., through mediated time travel) as an all-German matter of "going home."

ACCESSING PLACE

Berlin. Die Sinfonie der Großstadt holds a repository of urban information, an archive of movement and surface detail that can continually be reactivated and reentered. In her exploration of cinematic time, Mary Ann Doane asks, "What exactly is being archived in the preservation of an early film"? Observing that film as a "historical artifact" and the moment as a "historical event" are "inextricably welded together," she concludes that the "task" of "film as an archival process" becomes "that of preserving time, of preserving an experience of temporality, one that was never necessarily 'lived' but emerges as the counterdream of rationalization, its agonistic underside—full presence."[20] Much like the early single takes (1895–96) of France's and Germany's respective pioneering film families, the Lumières and Skladanowskys, Ruttmann's film exhibits a fascination with the objects, people, street views, and phantom rides of urban quotidian experience. The streets, squares, buildings, and machines of *Berlin. Die Sinfonie der Großstadt* offer glimpses of the spatial distribution of buildings, the flow of traffic, and the mass production of goods. The film archives actions and activities requiring the full presence of spatial duration—a knowledge that photography alone cannot provide.

As an archived film, a film cited as archival footage in other films, and a film that archives unique urban information in its own shots and frames, *Berlin. Die Sinfonie der Großstadt* beats the odds of silent film obscurity in a country whose Weimar film holdings, due to the Second World War and the material fragility of nitrate prints, can too often be "presumed lost" *(gelten als verschollen).* Doane describes the film archive as "always a wager about the future: a future screening, a future interpretation,"[21] and the survival of Ruttmann's film in its many copies and successive modes of preservation has had much to do with projections of the continued importance of Berlin and of the film's ongoing privilege in documenting the Weimar city. With the exception of *Menschen am Sonntag* (*People on Sunday,* Germany 1930), a semifictional realist collaboration between future Hollywood émigrés Billy Wilder, Edgar G. Ulmer, and Robert and Kurt Siodmak, few of the city's nonfiction films of the period are widely screened today.[22]

Despite the triumphal ubiquity of Ruttmann's images, their perpetual emergence from the archive also accentuates the physical inaccessibility of their time and place of origin. Positioned as exiles to their elective home, the film's postwall spectators may only return to the Weimar city virtually. The film, whose cinematic mechanism awakens and fulfills desire through repetition, is all that is left of the original city, the mythical place in which today's ruins and fragments were once whole, today's voids once occupied. Quite the opposite of the displaced protagonist in Vladimir Nabokov's 1925 short story "A Guide to Berlin," the spectator of today seeks to regain the past through the accidental details preserved by the film medium. Conversely, Nabokov's expat, a white Russian from St. Petersburg, must preemptively chronicle his present ride in a streetcar. He encounters even this banal, everyday occurrence with a prescience of human and urban transitoriness:

> The horse-drawn tram has vanished, and so will the trolley, and some eccentric Berlin writer in the twenties of the twenty-first century, wishing to portray

> our time, will go to a museum of technological history and locate a hundred-year-old streetcar, yellow, uncouth, with old-fashioned curved seats, and in a museum of old costumes dig up a black, shiny-buttoned conductor's uniform. Then he will go home and compile a description of Berlin streets in bygone days. Everything, every trifle, will be valuable and meaningful: the conductor's purse, the advertisement over the window, that peculiar jolting motion which our great-grandchildren will perhaps imagine—everything will be ennobled and justified by its age.[23]

In this act of what Boym terms "anticipatory nostalgia," Nabokov's protagonist inverts the work of today's film archivists, who preserve, restore, reconstruct, and decode past images.[24] Having access to the profilmic or, in this case, pro-literary event, he teases the historian of the future who will only be able to guess that which the inhabitant of 1925 takes for granted. Although the protagonist's own migration is the result of previously unforeseen historical events, he cannot foretell exactly which catastrophe will befall the cityscape of Berlin. On this point, the reader–historian of today wields an ironic clairvoyance over Nabokov's mnemonic tricks. The victory is bittersweet, however, because the knowledge and residues of wartime destruction render even the protagonist's imagined museal recovery of the past all the more difficult.

In the age of CGI, the ability to manipulate *cinematographic indexicality* and spectators' assumptions of visible truth paradoxically grants all the more authority to the implied physicality of past profilmic objects and the archival footage that contains their representations. The digitization of visual culture and the increasingly widespread use of the Internet since the 1990s have hardly cured us of our fascination with resemblance, reproduction, and the historical accuracy of imitations. Even blockbusters' manipulation of bodies and environments in the computer animation of actual or once existing objects still requires the mathematical approximation of architectural and cartographic accuracy or, in the case of human movement, careful monitoring of the motion of real bodies. With the aid of social-networking and video-sharing platforms, individual computer and mobile device users have also become amateur producers of public images. With ever-new means of posting information from their own daily lives, they populate cyberspace with photographs and videos that, through place tagging or geographical keywords, correspond to specific locales.

When one considers the investment of postwar film theorists such as André Bazin and Siegfried Kracauer in reality, in cinema's predilection for reproducing the world, it is no surprise that *Berlin. Die Sinfonie der Großstadt* has also become film history's *ur*-representation of Berlin. In 1945, Bazin's essay "The Ontology of the Photographic Image" celebrated cinema as "objectivity in time," a mechanical, objective reproduction of the duration of things or "change mummified."[25] Cinema becomes, accordingly, the temporal extension of a photograph's claim to the objects before the camera. This is a physical claim by which the photograph and object "share a common being," which Bazin likens to a fingerprint's trace of a unique finger or a photochemical "impression" much like the molding of a death mask.[26] Comparing the photographic image to the affective immediacy of a "phenomenon in nature," he suggests that "reality" is transferrable to its reproductions. Bazin's emphasis on photographic and cinematographic "credibility"[27] is related to Kracauer's later insistence, in his 1960 *Theory of Film,* on cinema's affinity for representing physical reality. Beyond simply recording that which is before the camera, cinema also shares with photography the capacity for revealing this reality.[28] Welding the ability to capture duration and change to the spatial, causal, temporal, and hermeneutic endlessness of physical existence, Kracauer singles out the street as the privileged location of cinema's "inherent affinity" for "the flow of life."[29]

Though both Bazin and Kracauer argue in ways that reduce cinema's formal potential to realism, their preference for film's recording function is instructive for approaching shots or short sequences that reproduce specific locations. At the beginning of *Berlin. Die Sinfonie der Großstadt,* a train cuts across the countryside, its wheels intercut with the oncoming tracks, electric wires, and phantom rides through an increasingly industrial landscape. This bravura locomotive entrance to the city culminates with the engine's arrival at Anhalter Bahnhof, the end station of trains from Munich, Dresden, Leipzig, Vienna, and Basel, among others. From the camera's position at the front of the train, the spectator shares, in these final fifteen seconds, the point of view of the machine itself, gliding through oncoming space. This temporal extension of space conveys countless details, much like those observed by Nabokov's protagonist. One may note the speed of the engine or of the camera's advance; the stationary trains on tracks to the left and right of the frame; the arches and decorative details of the station's brick entryway; the bright light coming through the windows of its dark interior; the moisture on the tracks ahead; the curious hut perched just overhead; a signal pole; a boy, briefly visible, strolling along the platform; a sign, barely legible, revealing the name of the station.

Duration, coupled with the motion of the camera, allows the spectator, then and now, an experiential knowledge of Anhalter Bahnhof circa 1926–27. Though Roland Barthes, in *Camera Lucida,* distinguishes film from photographs through cinema's implication of an off-screen space where the actors go on living, and through its temporal continuousness, his observations on photography articulate

The train's arrival at Anhalter Bahnhof in *Berlin. Die Sinfonie der Großstadt.* Frame still.

an emotional response to photochemical processes that film also elicits. Just as he identifies the essence of photography as "that-has-been" (the fact that a photographic image presupposes a referent), this cinematic snapshot, a single take from Ruttmann's film, indicates the veracity of both a place and an action.[30] A train arrives at Anhalter Bahnhof. For Barthes, photographic technology enables a form of physical and emotional contact between the body or object in the image and a temporally distant observer. As he puts it, quite like Bazin, "the photograph is literally an emanation of the referent. From a real body which was there, proceed radiations which ultimately touch me, who am here."[31] It is not the image's objective representation that, in Barthes's view, defines photography but rather visual recording technology's relation to loss. The film frame may suggest an intact world and the real, mobile life beyond its edges, but film shares with photography its growing historical distance from a once existing profilmic subject. If Berlin's cinematographic original city bears witness to past architecture's having been, Schadt's millennial city symphony provides the physical confirmation of this architecture's later durability, transformation, fragmentation, or absence.

The cinematographic index, like Charles Sanders Peirce's sign for which it is named, "physically, causally, or symptomatically" structures the relation between the signifier and signified, the filmic image and its referent.[32] By aligning a scientific indication of the once-real past with the shot's capacity to archive the "manifold contingencies that seem to specify modernity,"[33] cinematographic indexicality substitutes the knowledge of loss (distance) with the apparatus's potential for resemblance, reanimation, and repetition (proximity). Ruttmann's self-mythologizing description of his production process emphasizes the immediacy of the camera's recordings, which the rescreened archive promises to restore:

> I had to work without a studio, without built sets, under difficult circumstances, constantly underway with my small detective-camera lurking at the ready. I had to enter the life of the big city, to film without being noticed, for none of the subjects were to be aware of the filming and thus, with the knowledge of being "filmed," begin to "act."[34]

Despite his exaggeration of the extent to which his camera remained hidden and his scenes unstaged, he did capture the movements and spatial and social patterns of the city. The spectator of today thus retrieves the accidents, coincidences, and routines of Berlin's past and, indeed, may perceive in these images, far more than the eternal youth of the city's copy, a direct physical and affective relation to the Weimar city itself.

Barthes's concepts of "studium" and "punctum" seek to validate precisely this more emotional regard toward a photograph and its referent. Whereas the studium accounts for the general, cultural interest in the photograph, a quality that can be named and objectively discerned, the punctum is visceral and personal enough to challenge a conceptualization via language; it "rises from the scene, shoots out of it like an arrow, and pierces me."[35] It is the addition of subjective interest, "what I add to the photograph and *what is nonetheless already there.*"[36] Whereas one form of punctum manifests itself in detail, another is rooted in time. For Barthes, the pain of this second element lies in a photograph's betrayal of "death in the future."[37] Its human subjects will die or have already died, and its scenery has surely changed. The New Berlin's persistent revival of Ruttmann's metropolis has been double-edged, for it is not only the urban population that the film commemorates. The enjoyment of *Berlin. Die Sinfonie der Großstadt*'s replayed city conceals a nagging awareness that the industrial processes, articles of Weimar fashion, uninterrupted blocks of buildings, and modes of transportation that enter its frame are merely the intangible remnants of what they portray.

Just as film's referents remain photochemically visible (but just out of physical reach), the unique spatial properties of the medium suspend haptic intimacy with place between a three-dimensional participation in the on-screen world and the rational disavowal of its flat surface. German applied psychologist and Harvard professor Hugo Münsterberg, who wrote an early theory of film before his death in 1916, and Weimar aesthetic theorist and later émigré Rudolf Arnheim independently conceptualized the cinematic depth effect through a conspiratorial spectator, who is able, at once, to perceive and deny a film's three-dimensionality. Calling this effect "something in between" 2-D and 3-D or both "plane and solid," Arnheim illustrates the point with a shot from *Berlin. Die Sinfonie der Großstadt.* As two trains cross the frame at Gleisdreieck's two-level U-Bahn station, their opposing screen directions (one approaching, the other receding from the plane of the screen) indicate 3-D movement.[38]

Like the generative relationship between an original place and its film reproduction, the spectator's real exploration of space in duration and illusory depth renders filmic forays into Weimar Berlin all the more personal. In her investigation of cinema's emotional geographies, Giuliana Bruno recognizes film's overlap between spatial and affective encounters as a function of its "habitability." The haptic interior of spectators' mobile cinematic surroundings "provided the modern subject with a new *tactics* for orienting herself in space and for making 'sense' of this motion, which includes the motion of emotions."[39] Postwall cinematic time travelers have been able to "reenter" Weimar Berlin on-screen; what they have gleaned from and felt in that "plane and solid" place has contributed to their knowledge of the city and their emotional ties to its memory.

In its relationship to profilmic space and its potential for wide dissemination, film enables historical places both to become part of individual, personal memory and to be perceived and shared by large collectivities. Writing of old family photographs and experiences of the Holocaust, Marianne Hirsch describes a particular form of intimate recollection for a past that is not one's own. Calling this phenomenon "postmemory," she distinguishes it from memory "by generational distance and from history by deep personal connection."[40] The possibility of experiencing genuine, if mediated, pastness through photography and film's emotional, visceral bridges across time also allows groups separated by geography, age, gender, class, and religion to share filmic places, even when they have not visited these in the same moment, under the same conditions of reception.

Such bridges also unite nations. In his formulation of "nation" as an "imagined political community," Benedict Anderson attributes much of the modern sense of belonging to a larger, "limited and sovereign" group-space to the technologies of "reproducibility and dissemination."[41] *Berlin. Die Sinfonie der Großstadt*'s hegemonic portrayal of the Weimar capital in the decade and a half after unification had much to do with the film's unusual accessibility to traditional cinema audiences and frequent citation in Berlin's public space and museums; but this predominance of Ruttmann's cityscape also succeeded through its availability on familial television sets, in schools and universities, and in perpetually updated video and DVD releases. Effectively providing what the sociologist Maurice Halbwachs termed a "collective framework" for the postwall nation of troubled master narratives, Ruttmann's Berlin was just the kind of "instrument" employed by "the collective memory to reconstruct an image of the past" that was "in accord, in each epoch, with the predominant thoughts of the society."[42] Collective memories of and urban nostalgia for the future's Weimar lineage could rally the population, whose organic, divided memories and asymmetrical experiences of the *Wende* offered little cohesion, around a spatiotemporal point of pride and "authentic" Germanness.

But Berlin's marketing was not only directed inward. *Berlin. Die Sinfonie der Großstadt* continued to sell Germany abroad and to a new generation of young, cosmopolitan urbanites drawn to the city's spirit of renewal and creativity. Calling for adjustments to the notion of "collective memory" in the age of mass culture and globalization, Alison Landsberg acknowledges memories that eschew organic experience, traditional group identities, and purely national belonging. Instead, she makes a compelling case for "prosthetic memory," which accounts for (1) nonorganic memory gained through mediated representation; (2) memory worn like an artificial limb and resulting from the experience of a given representation; (3) the commodification and circulation of these mediated memories; and (4) the political usefulness of mediated memories in producing empathy and alliances beyond one's limited, subjective experience.[43] By addressing more global structures of moving image circulation, this concept suggests a means by which filmed places encourage identification with and understanding of historical events, distant locations, and foreign cultures.

Just as the film's influence exceeds one historical moment of reception, its representation of Berlin transgresses German borders. Ruttmann's images of the Weimar city are as persuasive as they are pervasive at home and abroad. Together with the *Wende* as a Berlin media event and the postwall city as a perpetual construction site, they contributed to the millennial perception that the city's past and present were exhaustively documented. When Thomas Schadt took up the challenge of an updated film symphony for the New Berlin, he was conscious of having to create a catalog of images in opposition to the existing ones. "At every street corner," he observed, "lurks the all-annihilating cliché, the conventional image."[44] *Berlin. Die Sinfonie der Großstadt*'s acquired representative function in and for the New Berlin makes it all the more necessary to interrogate the ideological frameworks that gave rise to Ruttmann's images in the first place. Their postwall shroud of nostalgic retrospection obscures both the experimental ethos of their production and their controversial relationship to Weimar Berlin's ambivalent international modernity.

BERLIN 1927

In 1920, the city consolidated a number of outlying smaller cities, towns, and districts into the coherent urban entity of Greater Berlin (Groß-Berlin). No longer the seat of the Hohenzollern monarchy, the new-old capital of the Weimar Republic was a place of sudden expansion and population growth, of postwar democratic and diplomatic ambition, and of industrial prowess and modernization. Politically young, architecturally imaginative, culturally vibrant, and forward thinking, 1920s Berlin drew frequent, if wishful, comparisons both to established European cosmopolitan centers like London and Paris and to Chicago and New York, whose growing outline of skyscrapers epitomized American modernity, industrial might, and capital.[45] As in the postwall era, Berlin was caught between self-congratulatory articulations of what it was or had just become and equally grandiose projections of its urban aspirations. Efforts of politics, industry, and culture to assert the city's unique place in the world after Germany's defeat in the First World War were accompanied by the desire to keep pace with other world-class cities. Whereas the first of these impulses emphasized the singularity of place, the second favored proofs of cosmopolitan belonging.

The internationally celebrated yet debt-ridden postwar German film industry that could bolster these city images was located largely in and just outside the capital. Like Berlin, however, it was poised between demonstrations of financial and cultural autonomy and concessions to Americanization through Hollywood's encroachment on the German exhibition landscape. Production firms struggled to generate films that were at once culturally German enough for domestic audiences and had enough general appeal to make a profit on the American market.[46] As reflections of national space, cultural production, and economic potency, films could help disseminate empowering visions of place and demonstrate one form of Germany's successful transatlantic and international commerce.

The built city and feuilletons reflected Berlin's actual progress but also contributed to the city's exaggerated performance of modernity. Already by the beginning of the twentieth century, signs, advertisements, and newspapers had converted the cityscape into a legible space that inhabitants could apprehend and absorb while in motion.[47] The city existed in perpetual dialogue with its own displayed claims. Emblematic of the age were Berlin's new West End (around the

Kaiser Wilhelm Memorial Church and Kurfürstendamm) and Potsdamer Platz, a junction of six streets, the Potsdamer Bahnhof (and nearby Anhalter Bahnhof), the U-Bahn, and several tram and bus lines. While literary journalists portrayed Kurfürstendamm as "the site of speed and simultaneity, entertainment and irresponsibility; of variety, exchange, appearance, steady innovation," Potsdamer Platz's commotion of vehicles, pedestrians, travelers, cultural venues, and commerce similarly made it an ideal showcase for the Weimar Republic's "marked celebration of surface culture in everyday urban life."[48] Still, not all of Potsdamer Platz's potential for modernization was realized. Though architect Erich Mendelsohn's sleek, decoratively unencumbered, white Columbushaus was erected there between 1930 and 1932, minister of urban planning Martin Wagner and minister of transportation Ernst Reuter never managed to carry out their plans for a renovated, futuristic Platz that could function both as a prominent, world-class node *(Weltstadtplatz)* and a more organized infrastructure for traffic regulation *(Verkehrsplatz).*[49]

In the years leading up to *Berlin. Die Sinfonie der Großstadt,* the city's administration began, with hopes of improving the local economy, to collaborate with industrial and tourism interests in promoting Berlin as a business and travel destination. In 1927, the newly consolidated Exhibition, Trade Fair, and Tourist Office of the City of Berlin (Ausstellungs-, Messe-, und Fremdenverkehrsamt der Stadt Berlin) launched a marketing campaign called "Everyone Once in Berlin" *(Jeder einmal in Berlin),* which relied as much on modern attractions as on established Berlin architecture to entice visitors.[50] The conceit of the campaign suggested that German citizens (and international visitors) had to *see* the city with their own eyes and to experience it with all their senses to believe in their postwar nation.

Throughout the decade, the increasing electrification of the city, which rose dramatically in 1927 owing to widespread electric signage, could both attest to Berlin's achievement of modern luxury and international, world-class standards and convince German *Provinzler* of the capital's shining urban example. In October 1928, the Union of Berlin Traders and Industrialists (Berliner Kaufleute, Unternehmer, und Großindustrie) presented *Berlin im Licht* (Berlin in Light), a four-day program of events celebrating the effect of lights in the city. Including spot-lit buildings, parades of car lights and electric signs, and live radio reporting impressions from a Lufthansa plane flying overhead, the initiative mobilized public space around the idea of Berlin's technological advancement.[51] While architecture began to substantiate these claims through the smooth facades and horizontal lines ideal for electric advertisement, cinema could reinforce Berlin's electric industry both through its dissemination of brightly lit nocturnal streets

Otto Umbehr's publicity collages for *Berlin. Die Sinfonie der Großstadt* highlighted Berlin's Americanized modernity. Courtesy of Filmmuseum Berlin–Stiftung Deutsche Kinemathek.

and through German cinematography's mastery of artificial light.[52] *Die Sonne der Stadt* (The sun of the city, Germany 1925), an industrial short sponsored by the electric company Elektrowerke AG, even implies that populations suffering in the gloom of provincial towns might attain some of the glamour of the capital through electrification. In his tongue-in-cheek 1929 poem "Besuch vom Land" (Visit from the countryside), Erich Kästner pokes fun at rural tourists' reactions to the sensory overload at Potsdamer Platz: "They stand, confused, at Potsdamer Platz / And cannot take the din. / The night lights up in kilowatts / A young miss says hoarsely, 'Come here my Schatz.' / And shows far too much skin."[53] In the end, distracted by the light and noise, the disoriented rubes are run over by the square's merciless, surging traffic.

The big city of Weimar fiction films was often explicitly or implicitly identified with Berlin, even when not diegetically set there. A place of organized crime, brazen sexuality, class struggle, and surveillance, these studio cities rehearsed the politics, technologies, temptations, and economic hardships of an interwar metropolis caught between poverty and materialism. Street films *(Straßenfilme)* such as Karl Grune's *Die Straße* (*The Street,* Germany 1923) and Joe May's *Asphalt* (Germany 1929) opposed the sexual, feminine lure of the street to the secure home life and modest aspirations of the petty bourgeoisie. While Fritz Lang and Thea von Harbou's *Dr. Mabuse, der Spieler* (*Dr. Mabuse, the Gambler,* Germany 1922) and *Metropolis* (Germany 1927) display the dangers of unfettered capitalism, their late Weimar collaboration, *M* (Germany 1931), presents the city as a cartographic, surveillant network, as well run by police as by criminals. Friedrich Wilhelm Murnau's *Der letzte Mann* (*The Last Laugh,* Germany 1924), Georg Wilhelm Pabst's Viennese *Die freudlose Gasse* (*The Joyless Street,* Germany 1925), Phil Jutzi's *Mutter Krausens Fahrt ins Glück* (*Mother Krause's Journey to Happiness,* Germany 1929), and Slatan Dudow's *Kuhle Wampe oder Wem gehört die Welt?* (*Kuhle Wampe, or Who Owns the World?,* Germany 1932) thematize the compromised morality and financial struggles of individuals and families adversely affected by the loss of work and means due to old age, war, inflation, and, later, the Depression. Late Weimar films such as Jutzi's *Berlin, Alexanderplatz* (Germany 1931) and Gerhard Lamprecht's *Emil und die Detektive* (*Emil and the Detectives,* Germany 1931), perhaps in partial response to financial constraints on the studios and changing aesthetic interests, began to include more scenes shot on location.[54]

The high production values of numerous Weimar city films can mask the financial and transnational underpinnings of these exemplars of German cinematic space, atmospherics, and set design. In 1924, the U.S. Dawes Plan relaxed the scale of Germany's reparation payments, ended postwar inflation, and enabled the country to accept Allied loans. While this American support helped to stabilize the economy, it also allowed vertically integrated Hollywood studios to proffer needed production funds in exchange for German distribution of American films. In 1925, the most famous of these arrangements, the Parufamet Agreement, provided Germany's powerful Ufa studio (Universum-Film Aktiengesellschaft) with a credit of four million dollars and established a Paramount-Ufa-Metro-Goldwyn distribution company. The U.S. and German interests each controlled 50 percent of the joint company, but Ufa, which went on to make *Metropolis* and *Asphalt,* was also required to exhibit twenty Paramount and twenty MGM films per year in its chain of theaters. Though the American partners pledged to fund German productions and to ensure exhibition of a portion of Ufa's production output in the United States, they reserved the right to alter German films for the U.S. market.[55]

The German government's response to cinematic Americanization through strict quota laws further polarized German film culture around questions of national identity in the years leading up to and following the production of *Berlin. Die Sinfonie der Großstadt.* After 1925, German companies wishing to distribute American films could only obtain one import license per German feature film produced. With German producers dependent on American capital, German distributors eager to reach the promised number of American imports, and German exhibitors forced to show often second-rate American features, the motivations of all three sectors of the industry were at cross purposes.[56] German studios and their U.S. partners soon found that they could satisfy contingency laws with "quota quickies" *(Kontingentfilme)*—rushed, cheaply made productions that could expedite access to coveted import licenses.

The trade press followed these developments with keen, critical interest. By 1929, after another adjustment to the law, the *Lichtbildbühne* asked, "What is a German film?" Frustrated at the updated decree's failure to provide "a clear, appropriate definition of the term," the article proceeded to outline the ironies of the new system, which seemed to hamper as much as foster a homegrown German cinema. A film that counted toward quota fulfillment had to have (1) at least its studio sequences filmed in Germany, (2) a minimum length of fifteen hundred meters, (3) a minimum of fourteen days of studio time, and (4) public screenings arranged by the responsible distributor. Because these regulations excluded accepted practices of transnational filmmaking (multiple-language versions shot in Germany but released in several countries, foreign adaptations of German work with a German filmmaker and actor, or productions shot in multiple countries with too few days in Germany), many German films could not be legally recognized as "German features."[57] In turn, this risked the goodwill of German studios' American investors and U.S. distribution partners.

Despite these challenges to the quality and dissemination of German cinema, the Weimar film industry continued to cultivate a self-image of elite artistry, technological innovation, and international importance. In October 1927, Ernst Jäger, editor in chief of the daily *Der Film-Kurier*, welcomed producer Erich Pommer's prodigal return to Ufa (after a stint at Paramount and MGM) in an enthusiastic article titled "The German Special-Film Will Always Succeed in America." The piece's subtitle, "The Meaning of the Ufa Brand Name in America," betrays a naive belief in the motives of U.S. studios, which were, after all, the competition on Germany's domestic market. Rather than addressing Ufa's budgetary crisis or the ills of the quota system, Jäger reinstates Pommer (and German cinema) as an internationally recognized mark of quality: Pommer "not only has a local reputation, he is equally important for all film countries and all film people."

In rhetoric reminiscent of Berlin's unique urban choreographies that doubled as cosmopolitan displays, Jäger praises Pommer's professional accomplishments as both triumphs for "German prestige" and "German art" and a measure of "world-class quality." Paraphrasing Pommer, Jäger outlines a niche for German "special-films" at the U.S. box office and predicts a future of eager U.S. exhibition of German films.[58] When seen against the film industry's climate of foreign cultural threats and nationalistic pride, neither *Berlin. Die Sinfonie der Großstadt*'s production nor its portrayal of the modern, interwar capital was neutral.

Beyond controlled studio lots and purely commercial calculations, filmmaker–artists around the world began, in the 1920s and early 1930s, to venture into the urban streets and to seek new hybrid, experimental modes of representing real cities and their inhabitants. Whether attempting lyrical evocations of place, as in Charles Sheeler and Paul Strand's poetic rendering of New York in *Manhatta* (United States 1921), or advocating cinematography's role in the revolutionary principles of urban space, as in Dziga Vertov's *Chelovek s Kino-apparatom* (*Man with a Movie Camera*, USSR 1929), these films reinvigorated film art's relation to place and also kept international cities in view. Challenging filmmakers to comprehend the totality of a place or to translate multisensory impressions into visual imagery and a musical score, city films may be considered in part a conflation of geographic, cultural specificity (place) and aesthetic competition (the technological and artistic ability to represent place). In just a few years, these cinematic cities came to include René Clair and Alberto Cavalcanti's respective versions of Paris in *Paris qui dort* (*The Crazy Ray*, France 1923) and *Rien que les heures* (*Nothing but Time*, France 1926); Mikhail Kaufman and Ilya Kopalin's *Moskva* (*Moscow*, USSR 1927); Joris Ivens's Rotterdam and Amsterdam in *De Brug* (*The Bridge*, The Netherlands 1928) and *Regen* (*Rain*, The Netherlands 1929); Jean Vigo's Côte d'Azur in *À propos de Nice* (Regarding Nice, France 1930); and László Moholy-Nagy's *Impressionen vom alten Marseiller Hafen (vieux port)* (*Impressions of the Old Marseille Harbor,* Germany 1929) and *Berliner Stilleben* (*Berlin Still Life,* Germany 1931).[59]

Berlin. Die Sinfonie der Großstadt, a pioneering film of this aesthetic trend, ironically owes its production to Americanization and contingency law's unexpected by-product: modest funding for independent, experimental projects.[60] Deutsche Vereinsfilm AG produced Ruttmann's film for Fox-Europa, the German affiliate of Hollywood major Fox, over a one-year period. Formed in 1926 expressly to manufacture quota films, Fox-Europa was nonetheless in the hands of personnel who understood film as art: general director and Austrian producer Julius Außenberg and supervisor Karl Freund, a cinematographer who regularly collaborated with reputed directors of high (commercial) film art such as Lang, Murnau, and Carl Theodor Dreyer.

From the beginning, all involved parties envisioned *Berlin. Die Sinfonie der Großstadt* as an artistic venture, a revolution in filmmaking by some of the Weimar film industry's top minds. Credited with the initial idea for the film was Austrian screenwriter Carl Mayer, who had written numerous city films, such as *Die Straße, Der letzte Mann,* and Fox's Murnau feature *Sunrise* (United States 1927), and who spoke of *Berlin. Die Sinfonie der Großstadt*'s potential to re-create the sensual experience of the city. For Ruttmann, a painter turned filmmaker, the city symphony could continue the exploration of abstract form, movement, and classical music begun in his animated *Opus* (Germany 1921–25) series of "absolute films" while also signaling a departure into the realm of "living," indexical film material. Freund, who had shot *Der letzte Mann* and *Metropolis,* extolled his innovative use of a hidden camera and specially treated film stock and fueled the production myth of a Berlin captured unawares. The composer Edmund Meisel, who had recently compelled Soviet spectators with his music for Sergei M. Eisenstein's *Bronenosets Potyomkin* (*Battleship Potemkin,* USSR 1925), hoped that his listeners would recognize the music of their daily lives in *Berlin. Die Sinfonie der Großstadt*'s score.[61] By eschewing a conventional plot, Ruttmann planned to demonstrate that "life, everyday life, is exciting and incredibly dramatic, even without literature and theater." Fox-Europa's support for the film's unusual position between avant-garde experiment and popular cinema allowed Ruttmann to create art for the masses "without all the compromises."[62]

Ruttmann's justification for his nonnarrative urban subject as well as his approach to editing recall the promotional efforts of Berlin's tourism industry and the descriptive enthusiasm of its feuilletons:

> *Berlin,* the most interesting of all cities, because it is the youngest of all metropolises of the world, because it is *the* city that is still in the process of

> becoming and not already suffocating behind façades, weighted down by its own monumentality, *Berlin,* a city of ubiquitous aspiration, is the center, theme, and lone actor of my symphonic work.[63]

Difficult to pinpoint through its resistance to the "restlessness" of his "lens," the Berlin that Ruttmann sought to record through careful observation was also governed by his postproduction process of montage and the film's structural elements of five acts or symphonic movements throughout a typical Berlin day. Building this whole from small, thematically and formally grouped shots, he hoped to create "a complex machine, that can only function if even the tiniest of its parts fits into the others with the most exact precision."[64] While some of the film's framings in factories evoke the matter-of-factness of photographer Albert Renger-Patzsch's new objective fascination with architecture and machinery, *Berlin. Die Sinfonie der Großstadt* itself becomes a machine—one constructed for the transference, translation, and dissemination of visceral information about the urban environment.

If shooting and editing the film required the patience of a "hunter" and a meticulous technician, viewing it provided a sensory, lived-through experience *(Erlebnis),* "an intoxication of movement." His film, declared Ruttmann, was no mild "picture book." Rather, its novelty derived from the onslaught of vicarious urban sensations, which spectators could learn to experience *(erleben)* cinematically.[65] Through its innovative form, *Berlin. Die Sinfonie der Großstadt* encouraged viewers to become as bodily engaged in the prosthetic urban *Erlebnis* as visitors to an amusement park.

The grandiosity of the film's premiere both attested to the scale of expectations for *Berlin. Die Sinfonie der Großstadt* in Germany's political and film capital and, in retrospect, underscored what the industry felt was an absurd and self-crippling decision by the quota board to deny such a groundbreaking film the status of a "German feature." Opened on September 23, 1927, at the Tauentzienpalast, a large movie palace in Berlin's West End, Ruttmann's city symphony was staged not only as a musical extravaganza with Edmund Meisel's seventy-five-piece orchestra but also as a film-historical event.[66] In this way, the director and his team deliberately encouraged their audience to align German cinema's artistic and technological advancement with Berlin's progress as a city.[67] Advertisements and opening night accounts indicate that both the premiere and subsequent screenings were preceded by a series of early shorts under the title *Kintopp vor 20 Jahren* (Cinema 20 years ago). After laughing at the apparent primitiveness of these older films, the audience may well have been overwhelmed by the technical virtuosity of *Berlin. Die Sinfonie der Großstadt*'s cinematography, editing, and experimental score.[68]

Destined for wide distribution, the film could also convey images of Berlin's industrial strength and world-class postures to curious filmgoers in the provinces and non-Germans abroad in a mediated inversion of "Everyone Once in Berlin." Instead of everyone traveling to Berlin, Berlin could travel to everyone. As one trade article argued, this rural and foreign interest in the film would be "a significant indication of its potential economic success."[69] As substantiated through repeated screenings, long exhibition runs, and distribution geographies, *Berlin. Die Sinfonie der Großstadt* enjoyed an unusual degree of attention for what the quota board had designated a *Kulturfilm* (a genre of information and educational films often limited to the domestic market). In addition to screening three times a day at the Tauentzienpalast for several weeks, the film opened in Hamburg, Leipzig, Frankfurt, Munich, and Breslau in fall 1927. Just two weeks after the film's Berlin premiere, *Der Film-Kurier* ran a front-page notice announcing a scheduled screening and appearance by Meisel at the Roxy Theater in New York. In 1928, *Berlin. Die Sinfonie der Großstadt* had a second run in Berlin, and by the end of that year, it had opened in Salzburg, London, Prague, Paris, and Tokyo.[70] The film garnered domestic and international acclaim, in all of these instances, as an aesthetic experience of great cultural value.

Despite these accolades, Fox-Europa could not release a *Kulturfilm* in exchange for an import license. Ruttmann and his team's model of creative resistance to German film culture's impoverishment through quota films seemed jeopardized in the very act of proving its concept. As *Lichtbildbühne*'s Rudolf Kurtz complained, the quota board's decision to "write off" this "consummate film masterpiece" as "commercially second rate" would complicate the future of German film experimentation, which was already beholden to American capital. He reasoned that, should this mistake not be corrected, "it might never again occur to an American company to use their funds to produce first-rate, culturally valuable films for the Germans." Similarly outraged, Hans Feld condemned the German authorities for not supporting the film that *Der Film-Kurier* deemed "the greatest, fundamentally important film event in years."[71] Through this controversy, *Berlin. Die Sinfonie der Großstadt*'s images of the city gained even greater prestige within the Weimar film community.

BERLIN IS AND ISN'T BERLIN

While the film industry could adopt *Berlin. Die Sinfonie der Großstadt*'s audiovisual dynamism as a symbol for the city's viability as a location of German cultural production, critical responses to the film centered on how its radical form related to the built city and what it meant to represent a city cinematically at all. Many critics, though baffled by Ruttmann's nonnarrative montage, were nonetheless eager to associate the fast-paced filmic city with the actual place. The *Reichsfilmblatt* declared the film "too interesting" to be "boring," while Kurtz thought it successfully evoked the feeling of a "world-class city," *Der Kinematograph* that of "an American literary tempo." At home, the *Berliner Tagesspiegel* credited the film with holding up a mirror to "our everyday life," while further afield in Hamburg, one critic described its task as "comprehending optically the totality of the theme 'Berlin.'"[72] It would seem that the film universally brought to mind not only the place it purported to depict but also a slew of Berlin's modern attributes.

The film itself demonstrates a surprising tension between its degree of conspicuousness (the clarity of its performance of a specific place) and its competing aesthetics of geographical indeterminacy. Already in *Berlin. Die Sinfonie der Großstadt*'s title, "Berlin" is qualified as *the* symphony of *the* major city. In German, *Großstadt* refers to any large city and lacks the uniqueness of the *Hauptstadt,* a country's capital. Nor does Ruttmann's title take up the ambitious term *Weltstadt,* which appears in Leo de Laforgue's Third Reich endeavor *Symphonie einer Weltstadt* (Symphony of a world-class city, Germany 1943), a sanitized (re)makeover of the wild Weimar metropolis that was released more modestly after the war as *Berlin, wie es war* (Berlin the way it was, FRG 1950). While Berlin was *the* largest *German* "big city," it was only one big city among others.

Berlin. Die Sinfonie der Großstadt begins with a manifesto-like aesthetic transformation and a sense of clear, cartographic direction as animation becomes live action and as the countryside gives way to urban surroundings. The film opens with a shot of water, whose undulations suggest nature's fluidity and a kind of rhythmic *ur*-motion. The play of light and dark on the water's surface is superseded by animated horizontal, black-and-white bars that are eventually joined by a rectangular and semicircular form. As in Ruttmann's *Opus* series, these forms exhibit a relation to each other, one seeming to propel the other in alternating counterclockwise rotation. All of the graphic elements (lines, semicircle, and rectangle) begin to move at an increasingly frenzied pace until the two forms are replaced by two diagonal white lines that fall repeatedly across the frame. A dissolve to a graphical match of two railway crossing barriers performs Ruttmann's transition from abstract animation to cinematographic indexicality.

Reprising early cinema's fascination with the arrival of trains, the next shot features a locomotive rushing diagonally across the frame.[73] With the direction of motion thus set, the film establishes a visual lexicon of movement, speed, and geography in which the graphic elements of the animated sequence are reconstituted as the experience of train travel. Rapid transitions ensue between four shots: (1) a high-angle view of the oncoming tracks; (2) a tracking shot of horizontal electrical wires; (3) a close-up of the engine's wheels; and (4) a phantom

From water to abstract forms to cinematographic indexicality in *Berlin. Die Sinfonie der Großstadt.* Frame stills.

A locomotive racing toward the city in *Berlin. Die Sinfonie der Großstadt*. Frame stills.

ride through the approaching landscape, alongside the infinite stretch of wires. The montage of this sequence not only identifies spectators with the vantage point of the engine; it constructs their perceptual journey as a blend of visual rhythm and spatial progression.

After several repetitions and variations of this core imagery, longer phantom rides (a variation of shot 4) document the transition from countryside to urban outskirts. Trees, fields, and distant villages give way to bridges. A sign announces, "BERLIN 15 KLM," its arrow upholding the train's direction of travel. The camera-train passes a gasworks, several construction sites, and a massive railroad yard. The city now lines the tracks, its buildings displaying the painted advertisements of urban goods and services. In a variation of shot 1, several tracks converge in a further confirmation of the engine's approaching destination. The train slows as it glides into Anhalter Bahnhof, a distinct Berlin location, and, insisting on this specific place of arrival, Ruttmann slowly dissolves between the engine's forward motion into darkness and a dolly shot into the bright sign, "BERLIN." The letters emerge from the background and expand beyond the limits of the frame. There is no question, at least lexically, where the spectator is. Only in Berlin does the engine stop, dripping with condensation.

Upon entering Berlin in the usual early-twentieth-century way, the spectator does not immediately encounter busy streets as would a train traveler leaving the station.[74] Instead, the initial elevated views of the city defamiliarize touristic knowledge. These privileged shots of Old Berlin are static and not quite high enough to evoke the aerial technologies of airplane or Zeppelin travel. While they function as establishing shots from above, they are at odds with the film's greater project of exploring urban life at street level. *Berlin. Die Sinfonie der Großstadt*'s earlier insistence on direction, location, and signage gives way to disorientation, as landmarks and touristic sights (e.g., the City Palace, the Berliner Dom, and the Nikolaiviertel) are rendered unrecognizable. Even the average Berliner, though perhaps able to identify the buildings, would not be familiar with the camera's position. What's more, the first shots at ground level fail to deliver the cosmopolitan bustle promised by literary accounts of the city; rather, they feature ghostly views of empty, early-morning streets. Already at this preliminary stage, the film's more anonymous Berlin deviates from that of guidebooks and tourism boards.

This initial contrast between the indisputable geography and energy of the train's journey and the stillness of the sleeping, unremarkable city exposes, if inadvertently, the gap between rhetorical celebrations of Berlin's worldly allure and parallel, more critical assessments of its enduring provincialism. Just as some writers bolstered Berlin's marketing campaigns, numerous Weimar intellectuals resisted these narratives. In an essay bemoaning Berlin's "chronic traffic ailments,"

Signs for Berlin, en route to and in Anhalter Bahnhof. *Berlin. Die Sinfonie der Großstadt.* Frame stills.

The city from above and its empty morning streets. *Berlin. Die Sinfonie der Großstadt*. Frame stills.

Austrian expat journalist and cultural critic Joseph Roth playfully deflated the pomp of Potsdamer Platz's (and Europe's) first traffic light in 1924: "It is now two weeks since the traffic control tower was put up. One had an expectation, perhaps, of something soaring and magnificent. But one day there stood a little gray metal stump of a tower, with large, and at that stage, still-closed round eyes on its top edge." Though the lights were intended to regulate traffic without human intervention, "the traffic regulator," Ross reported, "remains the blond, chunky policeman on his wooden platform."[75]

These critiques of the city could also be humorous and satirical. In his 1928 lampoon "Herr B. W. Smith besichtigt die Leipziger Straße" (Mr. B. W. Smith takes a look at Leipziger Straße), Lion Feuchtwanger imagines an English tourist's nonplussed reaction to Leipziger Straße, the major Berlin thoroughfare linking Friedrichstraße to Potsdamer Platz: "All in all it was nothing special for Mr. B.W. Smith / this Leipziger Straße of the capital of the German Reich—Berlin. / He came to the following conclusion: / I won't say 'first-rate.' I'll say in goodwill, 'not bad.'"[76] Unlike *Berlin. Die Sinfonie der Großstadt*'s exalted traffic montage (which includes but also does not conspicuously identify Potsdamer Platz) or the film's display of shop windows and electric signs, such alternative viewpoints make the extent of Berlin's constructed modernity comprehensible today.

Because the attributes of Ruttmann's filmic city could so cursorily be taken for those of the real Berlin, the film's negative reviews pondered the distinction between the two. In his first response to the film, Siegfried Kracauer, then a prolific cultural critic for the *Frankfurter Zeitung,* articulated concerns about the relationship of form to place that would continue throughout his later oeuvre as a film theorist. He dismissed the film as a "great disappointment" because Ruttmann failed to capture the Berlin of a "chronicler." His primary grievance, however, was structural and thus targeted the very foundation of the film's aesthetic innovation. As Kracauer put it, Ruttmann's choice of form—the film symphony—predetermined the film's content or, rather, lack thereof. That is, even before Ruttmann and his team "saw anything, they already had ideas—easily reeled off literary ideas." Rather than observing the city as it was, they could seek out images that confirmed impressions already disseminated by the print medium. Kracauer's logic suggests that cinematographic indexicality could, through montage, be misused as proof of the written word. "Is this Berlin?" he asked in 1927. "No," he concluded, "it's a dreadful impression, produced by a certain way of thinking that is more than embarrassing."[77]

Kracauer's early admonishment of Ruttmann makes only a mildly political argument, but his partiality toward chronicled nonfiction films and his warning against superficial observations and juxtapositions came at a time when a different, more dangerous strain of antimetropolitanism was spreading among National Socialists. In 1928, a young Joseph Goebbels, Nazi *Gauleiter* of Berlin, published an anti-Semitic attack on the multicultural and leftist intellectual flair of the West End, around Kaiser Wilhelm Memorial Church: "One would so gladly believe that it is the national elite stealing day and night from the dear Lord on Tauentzien Avenue. It is only the Israelites." Implying that Jews and foreigners were corrupting national culture, he proceeded to disavow the very cosmopolitanism that city officials and *Berlin. Die Sinfonie der Großstadt* had worked so hard to display: "The German people is alien and superfluous here. To speak in the national language is to be nearly conspicuous. Pan-Europe, the *Internationale,* jazz, France and Piscator—those are the watchwords."[78] The big city, for Goebbels, was not an appropriate source of national renewal.

That same year, Kracauer refined and more overtly politicized his critique of Ruttmann's film. He argued that the filmmaker had failed to understand Berlin's "social, economic, and political structure." Lacking "human concern" and "a particular vantage point" that would allow for analysis, the cross-section film, he insisted, left "the thousands of details unconnected, one next to the other, inserting at most some arbitrarily conceived transitions that are meaningless."[79] Kracauer's antiformalist condemnation of *Berlin. Die Sinfonie der Großstadt,* an argument he continued to develop from his own later vantage point as an émigré in New York, is interesting in its evolving dogmatism, particularly for Kracauer's own conflations of film and place. In 1928, he was unable to grant Ruttmann the legitimacy of artistic experimentation, to contextualize the film as an extension of the filmmaker's prior work with paint on filmstrips. Nor did he recognize the film's affinity with Bauhaus artist László Moholy-Nagy's 1923 screenplay draft of an unrealized project titled *Dynamik der Großstadt,* which approached "the city as an experience, a process, rather than as an object."[80]

Weimar Berlin was a place of political and socioeconomic upheaval. Kracauer expected Ruttmann's film not simply to reflect these contradictions but to embed them as well as formalism itself in the rhetoric of a larger argument, as would his favorite counterexample, Dziga Vertov, in *Chelovek s Kino-apparatom.* By 1947, he would devote an entire chapter of *From Caligari to Hitler,* in which he explores a fascist teleology in Weimar cinema, to montage. Kracauer's anger toward *Berlin. Die Sinfonie der Großstadt* would hardly be veiled as a postwar disappointment in the film's referent; the Weimar society in Ruttmann's film had, according to the critic, "managed to evade revolution and now, under the stabilized Republic, is nothing but an unsubstantial conglomeration of parties and ideals. It is a shapeless reality, one that seems to be abandoned by all vital energies."[81] By the time he wrote *Theory of Film,* Kracauer would use *Berlin. Die Sinfonie der Großstadt* to model montage's antirealist abuse of film's recording function, its direct relation to profilmic space. If the endlessness of physical existence was one of cinema's five inherent affinities, the cinematic simultaneity of Ruttmann's cross section served as a poor example of a contiguous geography.[82] Together, Kracauer's history of German cinema and general theory of film posit *Berlin. Die Sinfonie der Großstadt*'s dual betrayal of the Weimar city: first, by recording the wrong city and giving it the wrong shape, and second, by becoming the (wrong and already fractured) archival record of the lost place.

In 1928, however, spectators could still pose the question of the film's resemblance to the city as a matter of cinematic, not political, merit. In a good-humored review, the poet and critic Ernst Blass approached the city symphony from the perspective of a native Berliner, wondering, "But which of the images have symbolic power, visualize Berlin?" While Blass struggled with the film's form and, like Kracauer, could not reconcile the filmic city to its profilmic space, he remarked of its varying degrees of conspicuousness, "Where the film presents images of Berlin, it rarely conveys Berlin, and where it conveys Berlin, it especially doesn't present Berlin." The most obviously referential images of the city, Blass implied, did not capture the spirit of the place, while those that truly evoked Berlin's atmosphere occurred in indeterminate spaces and framings. Blass concluded with an inversion of the film's recording function: "The film credits the city with its own essence. It is what it claims Berlin to be."[83] If *Berlin* was not Berlin, which place was it?

Following its prelude, *Berlin. Die Sinfonie der Großstadt* begins to feature images of activities common to all big cities: traffic, work, crowds, food production and consumption, shopping, flirtation, and entertainment. The body of the film avoids the direct naming of the city; it also effaces the ground-level panoramas, touristic compositions, and maps that would locate Berlin's various neighborhoods. The film's division into temporally distinct acts further underscores the universality of the day's activities and emphasizes this thematic action over cartographically accurate spatial relations and distinct places.[84] Cars, horses, buses, streetcars, and bicycles obey traffic regulations and compete for space as they move in alternating screen directions. Human forms rush across the streets, dodging the steady flow of vehicles, or wander past shop windows advertising modern luxuries. Even class difference is neutralized as the arrival of white-collar commuters is intercut with workers streaming into factories. The machines of mass production organize the goods of mass consumption: lightbulbs, milk, bread, and newspapers. Ruttmann's editing, which groups images according to the type of activity and the time of day, offers the impression that the city moves in a coordinated tempo that cuts across spatial separation and class distinction.[85] Berlin is not coded as Berlin; it is simply a city.

Markers of a city. *Berlin. Die Sinfonie der Großstadt.* Frame stills.

HERMANN TIETZ
GROSSE
BEKLEIDUNGS-W CHE
Hildebrand
SCHOKOLADE
Moslem
PROBLEM

In 1925, Kracauer, anticipating Benjamin's later thoughts on reproducibility and dissemination, astutely observed the way that new levels of cultural mobility were affecting modern travel. "As the world shrinks thanks to automobiles, films, and airplanes," he wrote, "the concept of the exotic in turn also becomes relativized." Despite the film's promotional resonance with the German film industry and Berlin tourism, *Berlin. Die Sinfonie der Großstadt* did not merely exoticize the German capital for national and international consumption; rather, it demonstrated the monotony of modern travel. In an era in which "one hotel is like the next, and the nature in the background is familiar to readers of illustrated magazines," travel served as an affirmation of sameness, of belonging on an international scale.[86] In cinematic terms, *Berlin. Die Sinfonie der Großstadt* displayed the familiar—urban activities and indeterminate spaces that could exist anywhere, given that the city was "big" enough. A *Berlin* that was and was not Berlin could circulate this locational slippage and deliver cinematographic proof of a German urban modernity that was at home as much in Berlin as elsewhere.

AFTERLIFE AND REVIVAL

The Second World War altered the relevance of *Berlin. Die Sinfonie der Großstadt*'s faithful or fanciful correspondence to the profilmic city. Unlike the majority of critics, who responded to the film as a reflection of Berlin at the time, Kurt Pinthus evaluated it according to its future screening contexts. He argued that the "early antics of cinema" in the four shorts that typically preceded the film's first run preserved "nothing of the countenance and essence of their time and their humanity." By contrast, he maintained, "even after thirty—after three thousand years—Ruttmann's film will at least reveal the countenance of the city of Berlin as far as the film technology and cinema of 1927 are capable of this. If not, as well, the countenance and essence of today's humanity."[87] Like Nabokov's protagonist, Pinthus was aware of the present as the future's past and of contemporary cinema as the future's archive. Although he did not predict a radical change in the built city, he projected *Berlin. Die Sinfonie der Großstadt*'s film historical significance into successive eras of retrospection. The observations of Nabokov and Pinthus, made at the height of Weimar Germany's stabilized period, take on a prophetic air in light of the destruction caused by preemptive urban planning for Hitler's world capital Germania, American and British air warfare, and combat in Berlin's streets in the final stages of the Battle of Berlin. Such alterations in the cityscape changed the meaning of prewar moving images of the city. The authority and enormous cultural capital of Ruttmann's *Berlin* seemed to grow in proportion to the built city's physical damage.

During the Third Reich, *Berlin. Die Sinfonie der Großstadt* was systematically disavowed by Nazi efforts to control the representation of the capital, but this enforced denial, inversion, and invisibility also attested to the strength of the film's Weimar city image. Though the film was no longer shown, Ruttmann continued to make industrial and propagandistic documentaries until his death in 1941.[88] He directed several short city films on Düsseldorf, Stuttgart, and Hamburg and even shot a discarded frame narrative for Leni Riefenstahl's *Triumph des Willens*.[89] Nonetheless, footage from *Berlin. Die Sinfonie der Großstadt* came to connote all that the Nazis abhorred in urban modernity. Rolf von Sonjevski-Jamrowski's *Blut und Boden: Grundlagen zum Neuen Reich* (Blood and soil: Foundations of the New Empire, Germany 1933), about the misfortunes of a farmer's family forced to relocate to the big city, even used shots and sequences from Ruttmann's film to signal a corrupt and declining urban culture.[90] Claiming to be influenced by Ruttmann (as well as Riefenstahl), Leo de Laforgue began *Symphonie einer Weltstadt* in the Olympiade year 1936 but revised the idea of the cross-section urban symphony to include more classical touristic sights and less viscerality. Ironically, de Laforgue's National Socialist remake was banned by censors in 1943, purportedly for fear that intact, prewar views of Berlin could demoralize German civilians confronted with the transfigured cityscape of aerial bombardment. Instead, de Laforgue's material became the misleading stock footage for several Nazi entertainment films, including Volker von Collande's *Zwei in einer großen Stadt* (*Two in a Big City*, Germany 1942) and Wolfgang Liebeneiner's *Großstadtmelodie* (*Melody of a Great City*, Germany 1943).[91] Ruttmann's images, though out of circulation, remained invisibly present in their Nazi counterparts of ordered urban space.

After the war, *Berlin. Die Sinfonie der Großstadt*'s reception changed once again as the film took on a strategic cultural political function in both German states—one that would intensify after unification. By October 1950, de Laforgue's renamed *Berlin, wie es war*, offset by Friedrich Luft's didactic voice-over, was offering last looks at the prewar, albeit Nazi, capital, using the Brandenburg Gate logo of the old "Everyone Once in Berlin" campaign to advertise a perverse cinematic trek to "Berlin the Way It Was." While Laforgue's film could only be seen too late and never gained the popularity of the Weimar film, Ruttmann's city symphony could finally be seen again.[92] *Berlin. Die Sinfonie der Großstadt* was, from the 1950s onward, shown repeatedly in the Federal Republic of Germany as a masterpiece of German film history. In 1962, the West's Film Evaluation Commission for Youth and School unanimously approved the film for use in schools and film clubs with the rationale that it "conveys the no longer reproducible atmosphere of the 1920s to today's spectators." The commission explained further, "The film doesn't necessarily show the typical Berlin of this period, but rather, more generally, the typical features of a large German city."[93] Not only did commission members find new value in the film's potential to document an irretrievable historical moment;

Publicity for *Berlin, wie es war* (1950) using the familiar logo of "Everyone Once in Berlin." Courtesy of Deutsche Kinemathek.

it extended the film's documentary function to all German cities (e.g., Frankfurt am Main and Dresden). Thus, copies of the "original city," Germany's original *lost* city, came to stand in not only for Berlin's profilmic space but also for other, nonidentical urban locations rendered similar through destruction.

Berlin. Die Sinfonie der Großstadt was broadcast repeatedly on West German television after 1969.[94] The film's more modest, rather academic presence in the film culture of the German Democratic Republic, however, likely arose from a need to justify appropriate German cinematic traditions before 1946, the year of DEFA's founding.[95] In 1964, the State Film Archive of the GDR made the film available to film clubs throughout East Germany in one of the distribution season's fifteen circulating series. Under the banner of "International Documentary Production," Ruttmann's *Berlin. Die Sinfonie der Großstadt* stood alongside films from socially conscious filmmakers like Vertov, Joris Ivens, and John Grierson. In 1970, the year of the Lenin centennial, *Berlin. Die Sinfonie der Großstadt* was shown in the retrospective *Dokumentarfilm im Zeitalter Lenins* (Documentary film in the age of Lenin) at the International Leipzig Documentary and Short Film Week for Film and Television.[96] If Ruttmann's early penchant for formalism and his subsequent National Socialist career threatened the film's utility for socialist society, GDR film historians also found ways to rehabilitate *Berlin. Die Sinfonie der Großstadt* as a forerunner to DEFA's documentary and realist aesthetics. Its high degree of "authenticity" and creative contribution to the "art of montage" could offset some of its political weaknesses, and the analysis of these diverging qualities could lead to "realizations about the principles and problems of the documentary film genre" more generally.[97] At the same time, the film's importance for Berlin's history was not lost on Eastern critics, who, like their West German counterparts, recognized, in 1962, that the film could "today impart to us an image of the Berlin of that time which, through the destruction of the Second World War, is especially valuable."[98]

In 1982, a decisive shift in the film's screening contexts occurred. Although Edmund Meisel's original score had been lost, piano directions for smaller theaters were rediscovered and provided the basis for a reconstructed live accompaniment. Presented that year as a special event in the Berlin International Film Festival's retrospective, *Berlin. Die Sinfonie der Großstadt* enjoyed a second world premiere. Suddenly the exemplar of film history became a high cultural event. The film, along with conductor Mark Andreas [Schlingensiepen] and his orchestra, traveled to Düsseldorf, Amsterdam, Rotterdam, the Hague, Frankfurt, and Brussels, and the performance aired on television.[99]

Beyond merely witnessing the Weimar built city for postwar audiences, *Berlin. Die Sinfonie der Großstadt* became the locus of a collective, prosthetic nostalgia for the physically inaccessible cityscape that was at once Berlin and all the other lost cities in both Germanys. One Berlinale journalist mourned, "We left the Zoo-Palast, looked at the store colonnades, hotels, and high-rises and at fakes and neon, and realized that we will go on having to pay for the insanity of a war. The symphony is over, and Berlin has not remained Berlin." A gap had emerged between the presumed "optimism" of Ruttmann's Berlin of tempo and activity and the "melancholy" of postwar spectators, who brought an awareness of "transitoriness" to the film.[100]

The more the film, in its perpetual revival, came to connote urban loss, the more cultural, political, and archival forces emphasized the reconstruction of the original *Gesamtkunstwerk* of the film's 1927 premiere. Not only was it possible to safeguard and restore the film for new cultural contexts; the re-creation of the multisensory aesthetic experience of *Berlin* also betrayed a need to reconstruct, reanimate, and revisit, at one remove, the multisensory city.

During Berlin's concurrent East–West 750th anniversary celebrations in 1987, Ruttmann's film enjoyed its highest level of cultural esteem. The West's Bundesarchiv discovered, in its holdings, a Library of Congress print of *Berlin. Die Sinfonie der Großstadt* containing an extra thirty-one meters of footage, and Mark Andreas prepared an embellished Meisel score with a seventy-five-person RIAS Youth Orchestra.[101] In a year of cultural political focus on all aspects of Berlin's history, the city symphony's third act (the one most concerned with "tempo") played at West Berlin's official opening gala on April 30, 1987, in the massive International Congress Center. In July, the entire film was screened with live accompaniment at Berlin's largest outdoor concert venue, the Waldbühne. In December, the Freunde der Deutschen Kinemathek held a retrospective in honor of Ruttmann's one-hundredth birthday, and the Deutsches Filmmuseum sponsored a screening of *Berlin. Die Sinfonie der Großstadt* with live orchestral accompaniment in Frankfurt am Main's Mozart-Saal der Alten Oper.[102] Each of these venues blurred the boundary between the movie theater and the locations of high cultural performance.

Not to be outdone, East Berlin's festivities included an impressive series of film retrospectives with themes such as *Filme über Berlin* (Films about Berlin), *Berliner Filmemacher* (Berlin filmmakers), and *Berliner Geschichten* (Berlin stories). Although the official festival guidebook named only those Weimar films that overtly addressed class struggle, *Berlin. Die Sinfonie der Großstadt* was indeed presented in a retrospective of *Welterfolge aus Berlin* (World-class hits from Berlin) in the Camera art house program at East Berlin's Babylon Cinema.[103] As in the West, the Weimar city and its film heritage received public and intellectual attention as the GDR's premiere film journal, *Film und Fernsehen*, ran a special issue highlighting the era and as the Academy of the Arts (Akademie der Künste) sponsored a December symposium on "The Berlin of the Weimar Republic—a Center

Tempo at Potsdamer Platz in Weimar Berlin. *Berlin. Die Sinfonie der Großstadt.* Frame still.

of Film Theoretical Thought."[104] East Berlin, too, commemorated Ruttmann's birthday with an additional December screening at the Babylon. Hailed in the East as "the only classical German documentary film" and in the West as "the fascinating document of a Berlin that no longer exists today,"[105] Ruttmann's film provided, even before the *Wende,* a common ground for all-German cultural memory.

After unification, *Berlin. Die Sinfonie der Großstadt* became a mainstay of the city's smaller art house and revival houses *(Programmkinos),* many subsidized by federal funds. The film's attractiveness as a live event figured both in a pan-European initiative and in Berlin's new youth culture. In 1995, the film once again garnered public attention when Mark Andreas developed a new score with sixty young musicians from Paris, Berlin, and Moscow. Initiated by the Paris Goethe-Institut and financed by all three cities, the project was seen as a means of preparing the youths of Europe "to live together in an international world" and of "reconnect[ing] Russia to European contexts."[106] In the widened geopolitical framework of postcommunist Europe, Berlin and *Berlin. Die Sinfonie der Großstadt* occupied a central position: as a geographical location linking Eastern and Western

Europe and as a "European" cultural product. Echoing earlier sentiments about the film's restorative function for all German cities, one article reinscribed the Berlin of Ruttmann's urban symphony as "a metropolis in the heart of Europe."[107]

European integration and the return of the capital to Berlin preoccupied debates about the city throughout the 1990s. As Franz Schoser, an industry leader, put it, Berlin now had to convey a city image on par with those of other European capitals: "If in Frankfurt a new bank tower goes up, Berlin does not need to get nervous. But when Jacques Chirac in Paris has the Champs-Élysées spruced up, then Ku'damm, Alex[ander Platz], and Potsdamer Platz need to radiate international flair again." He extended this urban presentation, as well, to development and renewal projects: "If in Budapest and London new residential and business quarters go up, Neukölln and Wedding must also get a 'face lift,' and the reserves in the long isolated surrounding areas must be reactivated."[108] In this context of intra-European competition and cooperation, *Berlin* became representative of the shared cultural heritage of countries undergoing an abrupt shift in their political relations. The new live performance of *Berlin. Die Sinfonie der Großstadt* opened on August 29, 1995, at the Haus der Kulturen der Welt in Berlin before traveling to the Dom Kino in Moscow on September 2 and to the Théâtre National de Chaillot in Paris on September 15.[109] The near-simultaneity of these events united the three cities around a series of Berlin images that were being universalized as a lost European time and space.

The postwall use of *Berlin. Die Sinfonie der Großstadt* was not, however, limited solely to the projects of high culture. As the New Berlin became attractive to a young, German and international generation of artists and students, Ruttmann's film found a new following in Berlin's neighborhood theaters and began to appear in experimental contexts.[110] From 1995 onward, the electronic music duo Tronthaim performed a live accompaniment to *Berlin. Die Sinfonie der Großstadt* in Berlin and other European cities. The performance, in which a DJ and a keyboardist mediated Weimar Berlin for an audience familiar with montage, music videos, and video scratching, blurred the atmospheres of cinema and club. The musicians themselves made explicit their intention to link Weimar Berlin to the postwall Berlin of youth culture: "The result [of this musical approach] is a performance that transfers the ecstatic pictures of 1927 into the reawakened Berlin of the 21st century."[111] In one performance at the Kino Blow Up in Prenzlauer Berg, the film was followed by a party with DJ Hertzfeldt.[112] The youthful audience could experience Ruttmann's tempo and disputed formalism as just that—historical wallpaper in a city of multiple historical surfaces. When the film, whose pace appeared faster as a result of the music, ended, the party of twenty-first-century Berlin continued; it was a seamless transition.

A postcard advertising Tronthaim's performance of *Berlin. Die Sinfonie der Großstadt* in 2001. Courtesy of Tronthaim.

Whether appropriated by cultural politicians or by youth culture, *Berlin. Die Sinfonie der Großstadt* assumed a level of recognition and a degree of public access that city marketers and cultural agents could continually draw on. After 1989, Berlin's attractiveness as a location of personal and artistic experimentation, entrepreneurialism, low-cost living, large-scale building projects, and international tourism generated the city's new millennial "hype." Nonfiction films such as Hubertus Siegert's *Berlin Babylon* (FRG 2001) explored the mystique of the city's construction sites; fiction films such as Tom Tykwer's *Lola rennt* (*Run Lola Run*, FRG 1998) and Leander Haußmann's *Sonnenallee* (*Sun Alley*, FRG 1999) catered respectively to the techno and retro energies of a youth culture fascinated by both Berlin's club scene and GDR fashion and design. An optimistic city government dared to bid for the 2000 Summer Olympics in 1991–93, so soon after the *Wende*, and later boasted of the emerging government district (Regierungsviertel) and the new-old capital's multicultural openness. The new city image generated a climate of urban pride, historical awareness, and high expectations for the future; it also justified a bold cinematic venture: the commissioning of a new Berlin symphony. Ruttmann's *Berlin* seemed ripe for a remake.

BERLIN 2002

From the earliest press coverage of the production of Thomas Schadt's *Berlin: Sinfonie einer Großstadt* in 2001, it was clear that the project's investors anticipated not just a film but also a film-historical and grand cultural event. By then, Schadt, who had studied at the Deutsche Film- und Fernsehakademie Berlin in

Berlin. Die Sinfonie der Großstadt (1927): Licensing before and after the *Wende**

Type of Use	*1970s–1990*	*1990–2011*
Use in German Television Productions	108	282
Use in Communal Cinemas and Festivals	61	272
Use in International Television Productions	82	264
Use in Film Productions	26	90
Use with New Live Music	—	39
Use in Museum Exhibits	3	33
Use in Theater Productions	3	15

* These figures are approximations provided by Ruttmann's rights' holder, Eva Riehl, in an e-mail to the author, September 22, 2011. They are based on her records since acquiring the film rights in the 1970s. The numbers reflect only those uses of the film that required Riehl's consent. For instance, these numbers include neither screenings of the film in the GDR nor illegal or amateur uses of Ruttmann's material.

the 1980s, was a professor of direction and documentary cinema at the Filmakademie Baden-Württemberg in Ludwigsburg, where he later became the artistic and then executive director. A regular contributor to numerous German television stations, he had also recently won a special Adolf Grimme Prize as well as a German Television Prize for *Der Kandidat* (The candidate, FRG 1998), his documentation of the election campaign of Gerhard Schröder, whose tenure as chancellor coincided with the relocation of the government to Berlin.

Funded with an unusual amount of capital for a television-produced documentary (two million DM) and shot, luxuriously, over more than one hundred days, *Berlin: Sinfonie einer Großstadt* was already scheduled a year in advance of its release to open at Berlin's Staatsoper Unter den Linden.[113] In a process of exchange much like that of Meisel and Ruttmann, the composers Helmut Oehring and Iris ter Schiphorst worked closely with Schadt to develop a score for the Südwestrundfunk-Orchester.[114] In addition to the premiere and several live performances, the film was set to open in cinemas and to screen both on the public ARD (channel 1) and the highbrow French–German cable channel Arte.

Production choices and film publicity encouraged the association of the two city symphonies. Schadt, like Ruttmann, used a 35mm camera, black-and-white film stock, and available light. Throughout the shoot, he made explicit references to Ruttmann's filming process and even produced several thematically similar shots of urban life. A bilingual lobby card particularly emphasized the desired continuities between the two historical moments:

> Berlin finds itself during the second decade after the fall of the Wall in a vivid and exciting period of transformation. Tracks of history meet a new emerging city. Different faces, different cultures—capture the spirit of the New Berlin that echoes the Roaring Twenties! 75 years after Walter Ruttmann's spectacular work, "Berlin Symphony" invites you to explore this metropolis. Thomas Schadt, one of Germany's most renowned documentary directors, guides you from morning to evening through a day in Berlin.[115]

While the rhetoric of this advertisement merges Berlin's newness with the city's Weimar legacy, it strategically elides less popular pasts. At least in theory, Schadt's film was meant to bridge the eras, to prove, after the Wall, the New Berlin's self-identity with the mythical democratic, culturally vibrant, and liberal city before the war.

In practice, however, Schadt's stance toward the earlier film was fraught as Ruttmann's *Berlin. Die Sinfonie der Großstadt* challenged his understanding of the postwall city. Careful to draw a distinction between a remake of shot correspondences and a new interpretation or new production, he insisted on the difference

Thomas Schadt shooting *Berlin: Sinfonie einer Großstadt* at Potsdamer Platz. Courtesy of Filmmuseum Berlin/Deutsche Kinemathek. Photograph by Peter Schnitzler.

between the two films.[116] When Eva Riehl, Ruttmann's daughter and rights holder, forbid him to use footage from *Berlin. Die Sinfonie der Großstadt,* Schadt decided to avoid archival materials altogether and instead sought ways to depict history "in the form of traces." Eschewing the rapid cutting of modernist montage, he developed historically conscious atmospherics of longer takes and slower movements that showcased locations of urban change, development, improvisation, and neglect. Haunted by the omnipresence of Ruttmann's images, Schadt vowed to "shoot past all existing images" of Berlin.[117] Though he often invoked Ruttmann as an inspirational force, he also remained skeptical of the earlier filmmaker's depiction of the Weimar city. His exclamation "Look here [Ruttmann], at what's become of your city of the future"[118] harbored much resentment toward the ongoing authority and circulation of Ruttmann's Berlin and also betrayed a note of *Schadenfreude. Berlin: Sinfonie einer Großstadt* never quite emerged from the nostalgic discourse surrounding its film-symphonic predecessor. Instead, Schadt's emphasis on the projects' divergent cityscapes only further accentuated the irreparable loss of the 1920s metropolis.

Part filmic reconstruction and part meditation, the film recalls Boym's distinction between a restorative nostalgia that seeks to return to, recover, and rebuild the national past and its myths and a more reflective nostalgia that "lingers on ruins, the patina of time and history" in more individual and collective iterations that savor the ruptures between past and present.[119] *Berlin: Sinfonie einer Großstadt* takes up both of these. Indeed, the same film that was to establish and safeguard the continuity of the Weimar and postwall city also had to account for the New Berlin's changed surface. On one hand, Schadt upholds Ruttmann's temporal structure of a day in Berlin (though with many annual events included) and revisits certain visual motifs from the earlier film. On the other hand, he inverts the *Erlebnis* of Ruttmann's *Berlin. Die Sinfonie der Großstadt* by exchanging tempo for evocations of absence: times, events, structures, and functions unseen.

The very first shots of *Berlin: Sinfonie einer Großstadt* seem to proceed directly from the end of Ruttmann's *Berlin,* in which swirling fireworks (the last of the day's entertainments) and the rotating searchlight of the 1926 Radio Tower puncture the night sky. The opening low-angle shot frames the ledge of a building against the darkness as several searchlights dance across the gloom. Fireworks enter the frame, briefly lighting the statue perched there. Subsequent shots reveal the Gendarmenmarkt's classical ensemble of churches and a concert hall, an area meticulously restored by the East German government for the city's 750th anniversary. Crowds press together before the Brandenburg Gate. It is New Year's Eve in Berlin-Mitte, one of the districts most aligned with Old Berlin and most changed by postunification building projects. The camera, in turns, drifts past or halts on the faces of revelers. A child's sparklers give way to a young man dancing in a club, his spiked hair illuminated by a strobe light. A cigarette, drinks, and the limbs of dancers come into view and disappear again in the alternation of light and dark. The score swells and dies down as eerie, extended notes elicit expectations of sudden exposure. Of what? Ruttmann's evening of electric urban delights has become the early morning of Berlin's postwall clubland.

All too abruptly a man turns a wheel in a brightly lit factory, and familiar, sober views of mechanized production follow. Conveyor belts advance and sort pills, beer bottles, cigarettes, and passports. Schadt then cuts between elevated cityscapes attesting to the wee hours, the thinning numbers on the club dance floor, and the *Berliner Morgenpost* and loaves of bread in various stages of their mass production. Shots of empty streets and buildings, many identifiable, establish the stillness of the slumbering population. Schadt's symphony of *a* big city hardly masquerades as *any Weltstadt* when a lone car creeps toward the Victory Column or when the Eastern Television Tower dominates the skyline. Despite his wish, like Ruttmann, to foreground Berlin's general urban qualities rather than its specific iconic identity,[120] *Berlin: Sinfonie einer Großstadt* does much to align both the New Berlin's achievements and its shortcomings with the city's unique history.

Mass production in Ruttmann (*above*) and Schadt (*right*). Frame stills.

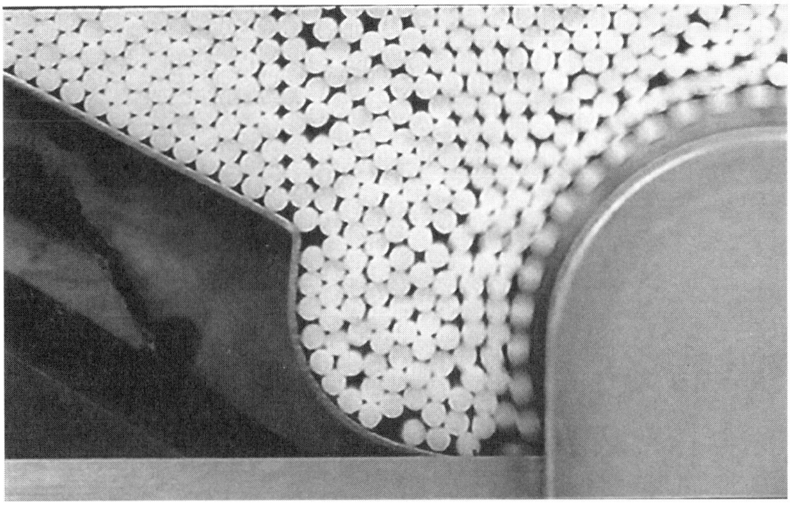

Schadt's citations of *Berlin. Die Sinfonie der Großstadt*'s imagery often reproduce form at the expense of function and content at the expense of form. In this way, elements of formal and thematic continuity comingle comparisons of the 1920s and early 2000s with the repeated exposure of their superficiality. While shots of the quiet city at dawn function in both films to portray the quotidian awakening of Berlin, once experimental modernist compositions of machines at work seem outdated in Schadt's otherwise contemporary photographic and observational approach to his subjects.[121] Elsewhere Schadt takes up Ruttmann's thematic cues but avoids integrating these images into the montage's larger formal structure. His lions fed at lunchtime no longer contribute to a patterned use of animals to comment on human actions and the violence of urban modernity; rather, Schadt's lions are little more than visual vestiges of Ruttmann's *Berlin. Die Sinfonie der Großstadt.* Reconstruction thus rests on diurnal markers and purloined motifs that ensure the inherent relation between the two films.

Poised between acts of homage and iconoclasm, Schadt infuses *Berlin: Sinfonie einer Großstadt* with a didactic antimetropolitanism. As one critic remarked cynically, "this 'Berlin Symphony' would function best as an ad for the marketing organization 'Partners for Berlin.' In addition, all remaining Goethe-Instituts in this world can also anticipate a wonderful, image-boosting educational film."[122] While Schadt does indeed engage with a number of positive preoccupations (youth culture, ethnic diversity, prestigious international events, Prussian heritage, and post-unification architecture) of Berlin's millennial marketers, his heavy-handedness crystallizes around the city's controversial past.

Choosing the newly restored and modernized Reichstag as a site of literal and figurative historical reflection, Schadt suggests that no celebration of the New Berlin should exclude an acknowledgment of the city's role in military aggression and crimes against humanity. The touted democratic transparency of the building's new glass-and-mirror cupola provides a reflective surface from which he repeatedly transitions between present and past. From a shot of human forms moving along the cupola's double-helixed pathways, the film cuts to a reflection of legs fragmented in its vortex-shaped mirror. Racked focus reveals an image of the Reichstag in its Wilhelmine glory. The camera tilts down a stand of nostalgic postcards of prewar Berlin; these are followed by Prussian statuary, the likes of Moltke, Roon, and Bismarck, underscored with dramatic military drumbeats. Schadt returns to this device to present an image of the Reichstag fire of 1933, followed by the columns of the 1936 Olympic Stadium, an enduring Nazi edifice, framed ominously against the sky. At other moments, the Reichstag is associated with the graffiti and occupation of the Soviet Army in 1945, with the Berlin Wall and Cold War division, and with the architectural remnants of wartime destruction. Replacing Ruttmann's act intertitles, which heralded transitions in the day's rhythm, Schadt's postcards assign historical gravity to present-day activities.

Typical of Schadt's pedagogical tendency, which he attributes to the needs of a general or international audience,[123] is the proximity of a sequence filmed in the Jewish Cemetary in Schönhauser Allee and a Neo-Nazi rally in one of Berlin's Eastern districts. Close-ups display the Hebrew inscriptions on the headstones of generations of German Jews. In long shot, patches of sunlight shimmer across the graves, which are protected by trees and ivy. The camera then tilts downward to a sign commemorating German pacifists who were hanged by the SS for hiding in the cemetery. Shots of construction sites, including Potsdamer Platz, link the two locations. Smiling skinheads wave banners and glance at the camera. Far from delivering a Berlin that has outgrown German guilt and successfully regained cosmopolitan legitimacy, Schadt undercuts such aspirations with manipulative edits and sequencing.

The film's emphasis on fragments similarly disrupts the continuity and nostalgia evoked by the conceit of a remake. Ruins, voids, and construction sites provide evidence of lost structures and functions and expose spaces forgotten and transformed through war and division. In a phantom ride reminiscent of a sequence in Ruttmann's film, a boat passes under a bridge in Berlin's canal system. Instead of signaling the midday doldrums that followed lunchtime in 1927, however, Schadt's

Reflecting German history at the Reichstag in *Berlin: Sinfonie einer Großstadt*. Frame stills.

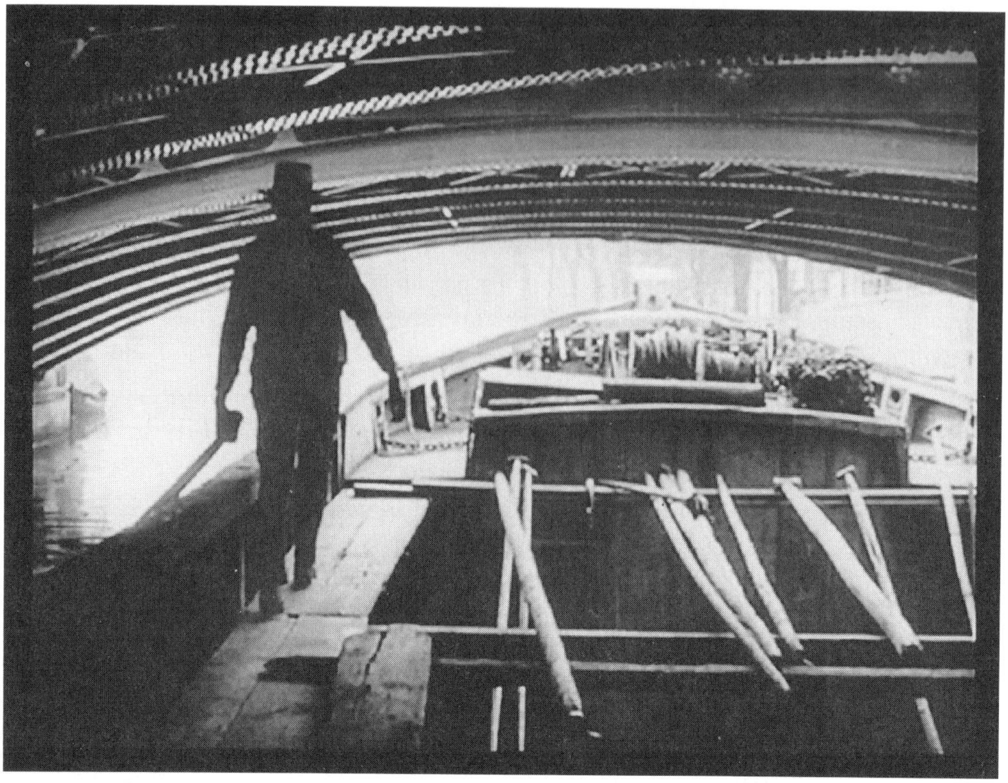

Berlin's canal system in Ruttmann (*above*) and Schadt (*below*). Frame stills.

boat drifts along the Landwehrkanal and the Spree to reveal a few isolated, architecturally incongruous apartment buildings, the Museum Island of Old and East Berlin cultural capital and the still standing Palace of the Republic, which once housed the GDR parliament and a popular leisure center. Where Berlin's waterways once served industry, they now guide tourists and spectators alike through the narrative of urban loss, postwar reconstruction, and unification.

One postwar image of the damaged Reichstag yields to a series of carefully composed tableaux emphasizing architectural juxtaposition: lone apartment houses, their exposed firewalls bearing witness to construction sites, to a monument to workers' failed 1919 Sparticist Uprising, or to grassy vistas; the graffiti-covered Kino Sojus against the Eastern concrete-block satellite city of Marzahn; the Anhalter Bahnhof ruin in front of a modern office building; the broken spire of the Memorial Church rising from the tangle of a postwar sculpture; an angular modern sculpture in the foreground of the West's Radio Tower; and, finally, the Potsdamer Platz construction site. Once the destination of Ruttmann's Berlin-bound train, Anhalter Bahnhof is, in Schadt's film, only one ruin among many. Potsdamer Platz, once a lively center of traffic and entertainment, is revealed as a myth under reconstruction. New corporate buildings rise up around a former watchtower of the East German border guards; there is no time to wait for the dust of the *Wende* to settle. The structures and spaces of Weimar's aspiring world-class city have been removed, reassigned, or replaced, and, as Schadt's choice of images suggests, a return based on facades is not possible.

Schadt's reflective assault on the New Berlin's marketing hubris does, however, allow the city one legitimate identity: that of innovative appropriation of historical artifacts and transitional spaces. A void between buildings doubles as a grazing ground for circus animals. The Ernst Thälmann Memorial, covered with graffiti, provides a varied terrain for skateboarders while an empty lot is repurposed as an urban driving range. At the Love Parade, two young men transform gas masks into a fashion statement. This Berlin of improvisation does not mourn the passage of time, but rather indulges in the pleasures of an ephemeral cityscape, in sudden appearances and just as sudden erasures.

There is, however, something inconclusive about Schadt's use of fragments to distinguish between the two urban eras. Berlin's ruins and voids signal historical rupture and engender creativity, but they also attest to a missing whole, a mythical *ur*-city. Like films, they contain an archive of knowledge about the past and invite speculation as to the materials, dimensions, and uses of the complete structures they represent. The ruin and the void extend meaning backward in time as they interrupt the built city of the present. Existing neither fully in their current contexts nor wholly in their past functions, they not only memorialize loss but also encourage projections of a virtual totality.

Anhalter Bahnhof, one of Schadt's sites of reflection in *Berlin: Sinfonie einer Großstadt*. Frame still.

One of many improvised spaces in *Berlin: Sinfonie einer Großstadt*. Frame still.

Schadt's historically conscious aesthetics hardly forecloses correspondences between Weimar and postwall Berlin; rather, it introduces a means of safe conduit between the two. Just as *Berlin: Sinfonie einer Großstadt* begins with fireworks reminiscent of *Berlin. Die Sinfonie der Großstadt*'s ending, its last shot of water recalls Ruttmann's opening image. This temporal figure eight links the films and their historical moments in eternal repetition. Though Schadt insists that "it is no longer necessary to be familiar with both films" and that "there are many people who don't know the old Ruttmann film but have seen mine," he admits that his film functions "on two levels—for those who know the Ruttmann film and for those who do not." In what he terms "the half-distance" between Berlin's 1927 and 2002 filmic versions,[124] the spectator occupies an ambiguous position between two sets of images. To know both is to seek one in the other, as in Siegel's split-screen *Berlin Remake.*

Whereas some Weimar critics responded hostilely to Ruttmann's portrayal of Berlin, their postwall counterparts evaluated *Berlin: Sinfonie einer Großstadt* alongside its predecessor. They either emphasized the New Berlin's search for legitimacy through an updated city symphony or decried the film's failure to promote the new metropolis as Ruttmann had the old.[125] One reviewer complained that the film "barely conveys the feeling of a metropolis."[126] For Schadt, however, the New Berlin could not be a metropolis in Ruttmann's sense:

> Back then [in 1927], Berlin was clearly a metropolis. There was London, there was Paris, there was Berlin, and beyond that there were Rome and maybe five American cities. But today, Berlin is not a metropolis. Maybe it will become one—the city is certainly moving in that direction. But compared to London, Paris, Mumbai, and Saõ Paulo—and thank God I've also been to these cities—Berlin is provincial. In its tempo, in its people.[127]

Though hardly evoking a global megacity, Schadt's twenty-first-century interpretation of Berlin works to adjust regional, national, and international perceptions of Germany's revived capital. Offering new images for dissemination at home and abroad, *Berlin: Sinfonie einer Großstadt* responds to *Berlin. Die Sinfonie der Großstadt* through imitation, inversion, and irreverence. With it, Ruttmann's film is contextualized, its authority contained. A cinematic return to Weimar Berlin is possible, but only when mediated by new images. Between the dramatic arrival of a train at Anhalter Bahnhof and the jagged contours of the station's ruin lies a punctum of spatiotemporal indeterminacy, the promise of a return that is at once exposed as an illusion—a persistent double vision.

WEDDING

1. Scala Filmtheater
2. Conny/ABL Lichtspiele
3. Schiller-Lichtspieltheater
4. Mercedes-Palast
5. **Tivoli**
6. Pamela-Lichtspiele
7. Rialto-Palast-Lichtspiele
8. **Theater des Weddings**
9. **Prinzen-Palast**
10. Marienbad-Lichtspiele
11. Kristall-Palast
12. **Corso**
13. Neue Alhambra
14. **Rio-Lichtspiele**
15. **Record-Lichtspiele**
16. **Atlantic**

TIERGARTEN

17. **Aladin-Lichtspiele**
18. **Camera**
19. Primus-Palast
20. BTL-Lichtspiele

KREUZBERG

21. **Centrum Tageslichtspiele**
22. **City-Lichtspiele**
23. Oranientheater
24. **Texas-Lichtspiele**
25. **Filmbühne Naunynstraße**
26. Kino am Heinrichplatz
27. Colosseum
28. **Oppelner Lichtspiele**
29. **Stella Palast**
30. Casino-Lichtspiele
31. WTB-Lichtspiele
32. **Lido-Lichtspiele**
33. **Wiener Lichtspiele**

NEUKÖLLN

34. Luna
35. Kamera Filmtheater
36. Lux Filmtheater
37. Orion Lichtspiele
38. Filmeck Britz
39. Echo Tonfilmtheater
40. **Olympia Filmbühne**

West Berlin cinemas along the border with the Soviet sector before 1961.

2

GENERATION

A 1950s Place for *Us*

A COMMON GROUND

In fall 2005, Germany's public ARD television station broadcast a popular six-part documentary titled *Unsere 50er Jahre (Our 1950s).*[1] Combining interviews with archival footage, the series strategically interwove oral histories from the GDR with those from the FRG. The carefully chosen subjects illustrated a range of postwar youths and young adult types: the expellee from the former Eastern provinces; the returning POW; the Americanized young rowdy; the idealistic socialist; and the entrepreneur of the West's Economic Miracle *(Wirtschaftswunder).* A companion book, bearing the subtitle *How We Became What We Are,* claimed to offer for the first time "a lively, comprehensive, all-German portrait of a decade at the end of which Germany and its people would never be the same."[2] The Germany evoked here was an inclusive one of elided difference and mutual understanding, one in which the prewall East German experience could be reframed as belonging to *us all.*

Just a few months later, *Der Spiegel*'s special issue "The 1950s: From Land of Rubble to Economic Miracle" proved less conciliatory, presenting the decade as a decidedly West German phenomenon. While Klaus Wiegrefe extolled the founding years of the Federal Republic and explained the renewed fascination with the 1950s as nostalgia for the West's postwar economic prowess, an article in the comparatively slim section on the early GDR dismissed any legitimate antifascist and reconstructive enthusiasm in the East with phrases such as "From the Supposedly Better Germany to the Next Dictatorship."[3] With the 2006 World Cup on the horizon; a generation of wartime and postwar rubble kids recently in office;[4] and Angela Merkel, the new chancellor, former Easterner, and Germany's first female head of state, representing the Christian Democratic Union

(Christlich Demokratische Union, CDU), the party initiated by Konrad Adenauer, a retrospective glance to the 1950s could function as an affirmation of the FRG's current pathway. In aligning the decade of the FRG's birth with the early years of the Berlin Republic, *Der Spiegel* demonstrated an alternative to *Unsere 50er Jahre*'s juxtaposition of East and West German anecdotal history; namely, it cast the forty years of German division as a deviation from the FRG's master narrative of postwar democratic and economic success. Lest the 1968 generation's critique of the conservativism and National Socialist continuities of the Adenauer era (1949–63) dampen the spirit of self-congratulation, Wiegrefe suggested that this conflict, too, had been "overcome" like the Cold War and the trauma of a divided nation.[5]

By the late 1990s and early 2000s, a cycle of generously budgeted star vehicles, both features and miniseries, had rallied the competing East and West German memory cultures (and their attendant ticket sales and television ratings) around historical events and German suffering in which both sides could participate: the good old Weimar days of German–Jewish musical camaraderie in *Comedian Harmonists* (*The Harmonists,* FRG/Austria 1997); an unlikely lesbian affair between a German and a Jew in wartime in *Aimée & Jaguar* (FRG 1999); German Jews surviving the Second World War in picturesque Africa in *Nirgendwo in Afrika* (*Nowhere in Africa,* FRG 2001); multigenerational and inclusive *Ostalgie* (nostalgia for the East) in *Good Bye, Lenin!* (FRG 2003); feminist resistance and German–Jewish solidarity in the Third Reich in *Rosenstrasse* (FRG/The Netherlands 2003); coming of age during the triumph of the FRG's 1954 World Cup win in *Das Wunder von Bern* (*The Miracle of Bern,* FRG 2003); Hitler's humanity and the fall of Berlin in *Der Untergang* (*Downfall,* FRG/Austria/Italy 2004); romance amid firebombing in *Dresden* (FRG 2006); and the good Stasi officer in *Das Leben der Anderen* (*The Lives of Others,* FRG 2006). *History, the German Blockbuster,* or, more often, the blockbuster-melodrama, offered enjoyable ways to mourn adjacent losses and to cultivate a pride in real and fictional exceptions to the dictatorships of the Third Reich and the GDR's ruling SED.[6]

In Berlin, Cold War topographies remained important attractions for urban tourism even as their traces began to vanish. Just as the public recourse to the bustling Weimar metropolis had (re)generated the all-German *(gesamtdeutsch)* myth of the New Berlin, the revival of the 1950s generally and of prewall Berlin specifically emphasized postwar commonalities, indeed even spaces and modes of cultural, political, and social exchange, that complicated the easy separation of East and West German experience. Already conditioned from 1946 to 1949 to participate in the black market, "an interstitial space, a place of ambiguity and messiness, of movement and constant change," postwar Berliners of all sectors

Der Spiegel displays Western memories of the German 1950s in 2006. Courtesy of *Der Spiegel*.

maintained, as Paul Steege has argued, the "everyday power to shape their world in spite of occupiers,' municipal authorities,' and party political leaders' various claims to power."[7]

When one considers the extension of this local negotiation of all-Berlin culture into the period between the founding of the two German states in 1949 and the sealing of the German–German border in 1961, the city emerges as something of a heroic last holdout to the unnatural division of the nation. A space that thwarted control from above through daily contact between sector populations, 1950s Berlin could, in the postwall era, model what Ernest Renan once called a "spiritual principle" of nation: "the desire to live together, the will to perpetuate the value of the heritage that one has received in an undivided form."[8] As a subversive site of real, potential, and retrospective postwar German–German consensus, a place where the rhetoric of one superpower might be unmasked at the next street crossing, 1950s Berlin satisfied a need to isolate a uniquely German, populist resistance to Allied Occupation and the division of Germany—one that could counteract the social and economic disparities felt by Easterners and (West) Berliners in the wake of postunification East–West integration.

Film production and exhibition proved a crucial means by which the Western Allies, particularly the U.S. occupying forces, but also East German cultural politicians and Soviet occupation authorities, competed for the minds of Berliners, especially the mobile, youthful demographic born between the late 1930s and the immediate postwar era.[9] The cinema was no exception to the built city's constant relay of surplus ideologies, and the same young people whose earliest memories were of war, death, deprivation, and destruction could now enjoy East and West German variants of urban reconstruction, economic recovery, leisure, and dreams for the future. At the same time, postwar teenagers' indulgence in the pleasures of peacetime, however tenuous along the front lines of the Cold War, was overshadowed by the detrimental effects of the Second World War on family life. As sociologist Helmut Schelsky observed in an influential 1957 study of "skeptical," rebellious German youths,

> the tearing apart of families through the military service of the husbands and sons, and, at times, even the wives and daughters; the loss of many close relatives, especially fathers, through war, expulsion, and transport from the homeland; the loss of economic, often professional stature of many social classes; the long and straining captivity of many husbands and fathers as POWs; and of course the loss of property and household effects through the bombing as well as the housing shortages and cramped quarters of the postwar period all greatly shook up the usual foundations of family life.[10]

While film politics sought to distinguish between East and West Berliners' access to films, their filmgoing experiences, and, indeed, the ideological content of new productions, Schelsky's catalog of ordinary grievances suggests a strong basis for more complex cinematic affinities between young East and West Berliners in the damaged city.

More than any other features shot in Berlin in the 1950s, the teen films of director Gerhard Klein and his young screenwriter Wolfgang Kohlhaase, both East Berliners, and of Viennese filmmaker Georg Tressler and his youthful West German collaborator, journalist Will Tremper, demonstrate the East and West's differentiated yet overlapping discourses on Berlin's Cold War geography, postwar youth culture, film exhibition, and reunification. Released within a two-year period in which both East and West German authorities and their respective media grappled with the phenomenon of rowdy, delinquent (mostly working-class) teens and young men known as *Halbstarken* (the "half-strong"), Klein and Kohlhaase's DEFA features *Eine Berliner Romanze* (*A Berlin Romance,* GDR 1956) and *Berlin—Ecke Schönhauser* (*Berlin—Schönhauser Corner,* GDR 1957) and Tressler and Tremper's *Die Halbstarken* (*Teenage Wolfpack,* FRG 1956) and *Endstation Liebe* (*Last Stop Love,* FRG 1958), bankrolled by Wenzel Lüdecke's Inter West Films, mapped this wider social problem onto the specific politicized terrain of Berlin.[11]

Following the popularity of American rebel, rock 'n' roll, and social problem films such as *The Wild One* (United States 1953), *On the Waterfront* (United States 1954), *East of Eden* (United States 1955), *Blackboard Jungle* (United States 1955), *Rebel without a Cause* (United States 1955), and *Rock Around the Clock* (United States 1956) in West German and West Berlin cinemas, both DEFA's and the West's recovering film industries lagged behind in producing homegrown entertainments for this age group. While the FRG was turning out countless colorful *Heimat-* and *Revuefilme,* mass entertainment that precisely rejected the ambivalence of postwar urban views, DEFA sought to master the elusive, unequivocal socialist realist narrative, one of positive heroes and ideological clarity, of socialist *Aufbau* (construction of a new society) and politically correct resolutions.[12]

The Klein–Kohlhaase and Tressler–Tremper productions, particularly the more overtly intertextual and conspicuously compared *Die Halbstarken* and *Berlin—Ecke Schönhauser,* adapted the American films' themes of youth alienation, juvenile crime, generational conflict, and teen romance to a more nuanced East or West German idiom.[13] Learning from Weimar street and milieu films, postwar rubble films like Gerhard Lamprecht's *Irgendwo in Berlin* (*Somewhere in Berlin,* SOZ 1946) or Roberto Rossellini's *Germania anno zero* (*Germany Year Zero,* Italy/SOZ/France 1948), a wave of later Italian neorealist films released in both the East and West, and international thrillers set in the city, such as George Seaton's *The*

Big Lift (United States 1950) and Carol Reed's *The Man Between* (United Kingdom 1953), the highly competitive East and West German film industries began to reinvent location Berlin as an exciting, dangerous backdrop to Cold War espionage, illicit cross-border romance, intersector crime, and everyday ideological clashes. These productions included *Krimis* like Erich Freund's *Zugverkehr unregelmäßig* (Irregular train service, GDR 1951) and Franz Cáp's *Die Spur führt nach Berlin* (*International Counterfeiters,* FRG 1952/1958) and love stories between East and West Berliners such as Kurt Maetzig's *Roman einer jungen Ehe* (*The Story of a Young Couple,* GDR 1952) and Victor Vicas's *Zwei unter Millionen* (Two among millions, FRG 1961). Several Berlin films of the time depicted uncompromising geopolitical boundaries: Slatan Dudow's plea for socialist feminism, *Frauenschicksale* (*Destinies of Women,* GDR 1952); Arthur Maria Rabenalt's tourist romp *Frühling in Berlin* (Springtime in Berlin, FRG 1957); the heavy-handed children's films *Alarm im Zirkus* (*Alarm at the Circus,* GDR 1954), from Klein and Kohlhaase, and *Sheriff Teddy* (GDR 1957), from Heiner Carow; and Gerd Oswald's teen crime film *Am Tag als der Regen kam* (*The Day It Rained,* FRG 1959). Prewall Berlin films from both Germanys not only represented the city's existing division; they circulated images of this morally ambiguous site of German separation and contact to their broader populations.

Owing to their common subject matter, shared stylistic imperatives, and interlinked production and reception histories, the four Klein–Kohlhaase and Tressler–Tremper films offer together a far more complicated picture of how spaces of exhibition, the built city, narrative space, and the imagined city related to each other within and beyond the divided Berlin of open borders. Shot on the streets in realist black and white, cast with newly established male leads and attractive ingénues, and released in East–West turns, *Eine Berliner Romanze, Die Halbstarken, Berlin—Ecke Schönhauser,* and *Endstation Liebe* not only created a dialogical framework for understanding the frustrations of young people in a city that was still clearing the rubble of a failed political regime; they legitimized the ways in which East and West Berlin youths *used* the city. The teenagers who occupied the spaces within, between, and around these films engaged with Berlin on their own terms; their memories of the city's political interstices would be instrumentalized once the fall of the Wall and unification restored reciprocal mobility across Cold War borders.

PREWALL MOBILITY AND THE CINEMA

In the immediate aftermath of the Second World War, even as Berlin was quartered into French, British, American, and Soviet occupation sectors much like the country's occupation zones, this centralized site of national heritage remained a unique location for all-German encounters, exposure, and exchange. Even after the Soviet Blockade and Allied Airlift of 1948–49, currency reform, and the founding of the two German states, daily life in the city was "weakly 'defined' both politically and structurally."[14] Despite the new Allied boundaries, East and West Berlin still functioned, in many respects, as a single city. U-Bahn and S-Bahn lines continued to connect Berlin's two halves, and residents in traditionally bordering neighborhoods such as Friedrichshain and Kreuzberg, Treptow and Neukölln, and Prenzlauer Berg and Wedding continued their daily commerce. Both populations thought nothing of crossing the border for employment. By 1961, West Berlin industry was relying on more than fifty-six thousand of these *Grenzgänger* from the Soviet Sector; in turn, roughly thirteen thousand West Berliners were still commuting to work in East Berlin when the border was closed that August.[15] Discrepancies in the exchange rate (usually four East marks to one West mark) and asymmetrical access to consumer goods and produce drove much of this traffic. Indeed, West Berliners lacking basic goods and services could find these in the East, while East Berliners and GDR citizens at large relied on West Berlin for certain necessities and luxury items.

A popular street for East–West exchange: Badstraße in Wedding, January 1954. Courtesy of Landesarchiv Berlin.

Despite this ongoing interdependence of the two populations, Erika Hoerning warns that the quotidian persistence of a "self-evident feeling of belonging together" quickly gave way to an awareness that one was standing "at the fork of two political systems."[16] The United States and the Soviet Union were increasingly invested in Berlin's symbolic potential. While both the FRG and the GDR laid claim to Berlin and called for reunification *(Wiedervereinigung)* throughout the 1950s, architectural building races between the West's Ernst-Reuter-Platz and Kurfürstendamm and the East's Alexanderplatz and Stalinallee were visibly transforming the divided city.[17] Unity remained an elusive, idealistic goal as political events repeatedly exposed the fragility of Berlin's intersector mobility. When, on June 17, 1953, East German workers protested the SED's demand for a 10 percent increase in productivity norms to cover the GDR's financial losses, the U.S. occupation authorities prevented West Berliners from entering East Berlin to support the demonstrators.[18] In a bitter foreshadowing of life without freedom of movement, the border between East and West Berlin remained sealed for a week after the incident.

Intersector mobility had its advantages and risks as Berliners negotiated currencies, location of employment, and place of residence. A salary exchange policy *(Lohnumtausch)* assured that the border-crossing workforce would not be shortchanged. While East Berliners working in the West benefited from the percentage of their salary that was paid one to one in East marks, West Berliners employed in the East lost roughly 50 percent of their salary via currency exchange and required additional compensation. Those West Berliners who worked for political and cultural organizations in the East, however, effectively forfeited their right to the West's exchange benefits, though the GDR tried to amend this loss with an allowance *(Einkaufsberechtigung)* for certain groceries.[19] Gradually, the U.S. Marshall Plan and the FRG's subsequent economic boom diminished the appeal of jobs in the East and fostered an increasingly unidirectional flow of labor from East to West Berlin.

Despite these economic inequities (but also because of them), the Cold War's capital of ideological warfare could also function as a site of communication and comparison, of immediate rather than projected alternatives. In 1950s Berlin, the proliferation of propaganda in a variety of media (newspapers, radio, newsreels, feature films, and the ever more prevalent television) both provided continual access to competing political viewpoints and enabled transgressions into what Katie Trumpener has termed "an interior, extraterritorial world not defined or circumscribed by Cold War borders and polarities."[20] Whereas currency reform introduced economic disparity between East and West Berliners, cultural affinity prolonged a sense of shared space and common references. Venturing forth into this murky, slippery ideological terrain would hardly have necessitated a serious act of espionage; one could transgress in the turn of a dial, in the flip of a switch, in a conversation with family members from "over there," in the casual glance at a newsstand or a political poster, or in a simple jaunt to the nearest cinema, just over the border.

Paradoxically, the cinema in prewall Berlin served both to differentiate East and West German positions and to maintain the all-German cultural and social proximity of Berliners as well as visitors from the greater GDR. Initially lacking the number of new features that postwar audiences demanded, theater owners and distributors in both Germanys turned to past hits, precisely those films that might recall German popular culture before the defeat of the Third Reich. Between 1946 and 1959, East German cinemas screened more than two hundred revivals, mostly Nazi entertainment films and the occasional Weimar silent. Evidencing more a war of distribution and access than merely one of new production, the comparative German film industrial landscapes of the 1950s mapped competing desires both to participate in all-German cultural production and to demonstrate allegiance to the superpowers. Although the West restricted the importation of DEFA films and released only a handful of East German titles throughout the decade, DEFA's Progress-Film-Vertrieb distributed more than seventy West German features, many of them new comedies and *Heimatfilme* by popular directors from the Nazi Era.[21] While GDR theaters screened more than 140 Soviet films and only three American titles from 1950 to 1957, cinemas in the West hosted an average of 225 American features annually until 1959.[22]

Neither DEFA's modest annual production plan and required ideological bent nor the West's largely relocated film industry could compete with Hollywood's intact studios, production values, and spectacle. While the old Ufa studios lay, rather fortuitously for DEFA, in the Soviet Zone, just outside West Berlin, much of West German production now centered on Munich and Hamburg. The German cinematic tradition, which had flourished in Berlin before and during the war, became fragmented as numerous directors, stars, and production personnel gradually fled to the FRG. If studios in Berlin's Western occupation sectors supplied only 17 percent of film production in the Western zones between 1945 and 1951, the city's open borders nonetheless facilitated extended structures of all-Berlin cinematic collaboration.[23] While the 1952 GDR Filmmakers' Conference explicitly called for new screenwriters with literary talent who could infuse films with correct Marxist–Leninist ideals, Stalin's death, the workers' uprising, and the SED's subsequent declaration of a New Course in 1953 brought about a relaxation of German–German film relations.[24] Not only did DEFA take the opportunity to plan several coproductions with companies in the FRG and other Western

European countries; it also engaged well-known West German actors and continued to draw up to 70 percent of its studio employees from West Berlin.[25]

Just as opportunities to work for DEFA enticed West Berlin film professionals to lend their craft to state socialism, the Western sectors' varied exhibition terrain encouraged primarily East Berliners to cross the border for new cinematic thrills. A case in point was the Kurbel's long run of *Gone with the Wind* (United States 1939) from 1953 to 1956. This epic color melodrama on the resilience and reconstruction of the fallen post–Civil War South may have had particular resonance in Germany at the time; the film attracted thousands of visitors, not only from East and West Berlin but also from other regions in the GDR.[26]

By the early 1950s, the U.S. military and West Berlin governments had grasped the potential for cinema to motivate ideological restlessness among Easterners eager to see new American and West German features. While Oscar Martay, film officer in the Information Services Branch of the Allied High Commission for Occupied Germany (HICOG), contributed momentum to the establishment of the West's Berlin International Film Festival in 1951, his idea to initiate a program of specialized screenings for East Berliners in theaters along the East–West sector boundaries institutionalized a year-round culture of cinematic border crossing. With only four cinemas in the American sector in 1945, West Berlin could, by summer 1957, boast 264 theaters and 128,437 seats (roughly 1 seat per 17 inhabitants) in contrast to East Berlin's 96 venues.[27] At officially designated "border cinemas" *(Grenzkinos),* the number of which fluctuated around twenty-three throughout the decade, East Berliners with proper identification could pay a mere twenty-five West pfennigs to attend daytime (and later also evening) screenings of films banned in the East. Participating theater owners, in turn, received a generous tax break and were reimbursed at a rate of one to one for tickets sold in East marks.[28]

In cinemas that might blare Dixieland jazz over the loudspeakers, young East Berliners in particular could satisfy their curiosity about the sensationalist western, crime, gangster, and war genres that, according to GDR authorities, "offend[ed] against moral principles," "incit[ed] to murder and crime," and "propagat[ed] racial hatred, militarism and war as unavoidable."[29] In 1956 and 1957, internal GDR reports estimated that twenty-six thousand East Berliners attended the border cinemas each day, while the West German trade press reported four and a half million tickets sold at border cinemas and an additional six million sold at half price in West Berlin's regular theaters during the same period.[30] Carefully tracking this exhibition trend, *Filmblätter,* the news organ of the West German film industrial alliance Spitzenorganisation der Filmwirtschaft (SPIO), printed a postcard from a thankful Leipzig resident who had seen two West German films at the

Autograph seekers outside the Filmbühne Wien on Kurfürstendamm during the 1955 Berlin International Film Festival. Photographed by Horst Siegmann. Courtesy of Landesarchiv Berlin.

Camera Cinema at Potsdamer Platz. While Progress maintained that U.S. distributors were blocking the release of American films in socialist countries, visitors to the GDR capital could defy such political limitations to socialist entertainment in a visit to a border cinema.[31] As Kohlhaase later remarked on the duality of state versus individual determination in cinematic border crossing, young East Berliners and East Germans could "attain the unattainable" American culture "in one evening in the cinema."[32]

In the warmer months, the Berlinale and the Waldbühne in the West and various venues in the East staged mass outdoor screenings. While the festival reintroduced some of the cinematic glitz and international attention of Berlin's Weimar years, it also appealed to the memories of a slightly older generation socialized in the 1930s and 1940s. Fêting German stars of that era, the festival organizers hoped "to cash in on nostalgia by appealing to a common cultural experience of the Nazi period to unite a divided population."[33] Locations like Potsdamer Platz, once a center of traffic and urban entertainments, could be reactivated for all-German use at the convergence of the British, American, and Soviet sectors.

Trips to the Waldbühne's Film-Bühne Wien, deep in Berlin's West End, required a more deliberate geographical transgression. One 1950 Waldbühne screening of Carol Reed's *The Third Man* (United Kingdom/United States 1949) pulled out all the stops to foster a tongue-in-cheek awareness of Berlin's absurd political position. Drawing twenty-five thousand Easterners, the evening featured comical repartee about East German politicians, musical performances, an appearance by popular Austrian actor Paul Hörbiger, and back-to-back projection of East and West German newsreels.[34] The East, for its part, turned its 1951 international World Youth Festival into an occasion to expose West Berlin young people to progressive films that they might not see elsewhere. While many participants streamed over to the West's border cinemas, GDR media reports indicate that East Berlin could, for once, preempt a West Berlin release: Vittorio De Sica's much anticipated *Ladri di biciclette* (*Bicycle Thieves,* Italy 1948), one of the exemplars of the neorealist aesthetic that inspired Klein, Kohlhaase, Tressler, and Tremper to turn to Berlin's streets.[35]

Though the East's cinematic didacticism could hardly compete with the West's emphasis on entertainment, it is important to acknowledge the multiple and shifting compositions of cinematic border crossers in the 1950s. In a 2011 initiative to raise awareness of this geographical history on the fiftieth anniversary of the construction of the Berlin Wall, the exhibition *Flimmern auf dem Eisernen Vorhang* (Flickering on the Iron Curtain) collected oral histories of East and West Berliners who engaged in this activity. A self-identified *Halbstarke* from northern Kreuzberg, actor and dancer Bernd Feuerhelm remembers both pretending to be an East Berliner to get into cheap screenings at the border cinemas (a common practice for young West Berliners in border neighborhoods) and watching DEFA fairy-tale films in nearby Taunus Lichtspiele in East Berlin.[36] At odds with the (socialist) workday, the *Grenzkino* program's initial privileging of late morning and afternoon screenings may have appealed to social groups that had disposable time during the day. Certainly these cinemas were widely understood to be the domain of lower-class, undiscerning youths rather than of border-crossing cinephiles.[37] Depending on the films shown, however, audiences might vary according to age, gender, class, and residence. In addition, most official border cinemas were clustered along popular streets for intersector commerce *(Grenzhandel)* that often featured several regular cinemas as well (see the map at the beginning of this chapter). Thus, even if the ostensibly "Eastern" audiences in border cinemas sat among fellow *Grenzgänger,* some may have ventured into the more expensive regular cinemas or visited nearby businesses. In all of these variations, not only the border cinema but also the cinema at large was very much a space of real and potential social contact between East and West Berliners.

Presumably "East" Berlin women in front of an advertisement for special screenings for GDR spectators at Kreuzberg's Stella Filmtheater, 1955. Photograph by Kurt Schymatzek. Courtesy of Landesarchiv Berlin.

As relations between the GDR and the FRG grew strained in the late 1950s, SPIO and the West's Association of Berlin Film Theaters (Verband Berliner Filmtheater, VBF) increasingly politicized the geography of film spectatorship. SPIO's careful monitoring of the slightest alterations in DEFA's output, of the East German taste for imports, and of East and West Berlin's exhibition landscape betrayed conflicting concerns: the cultural and ideological competition between the two Germanys and the economics of film industrial reunification, however unlikely this was becoming. In a regular column in *Filmblätter,* the VBF followed the development of the All-Berlin Cultural Program (Berliner Kulturprogramm) from 1957 to 1958. Designed to sustain East Berliners' interest in shared cultural experiences, the Cultural Program allowed them to attend theater and musical performances, museums, libraries, the Berlin Zoo, and various sports events and festivals in West Berlin at a discounted one to one exchange rate. Subsidized with two and a half million marks from the Federal Republic, the program initially excluded Berlin's cinemas.[38]

Feeling slighted, the VBF argued that films and the cinemas that screened them were the principal attraction for East Berlin border crossers and that West Berlin film theaters had, after all, first instituted discounts for Easterners. The association proceeded to condemn the high cultural bias of the All-Berlin Cultural Program as an ineffective propaganda strategy:

> It's not a visit to the Botanical Garden, the Zoo, an ice-skating rink, a roller rink, an operetta performance, a concert, etc. that will endanger the East German government, but rather the film screenings with weekly newsreels and films from the West that will transmit the western way of life. Even the theater can by no means as clearly promote western tendencies as film, with very few exceptions, is wont to do. An unheard of political mistake has been perpetrated.[39]

Three months later, the VBF recast its role in promoting German–German cultural relations as a heroic form of reunification "from below." In place of DEFA's East–West coproductions, which failed to prepare East and West Germans for actual unity, the VBF imagined an idyllic week of free intersector film access in which Berliners from all sectors could interact. Exceeding the general concern of the West German film industry, the VBF saw itself as "the bridge between East and West in terms of visits to the cinema."[40]

When, in August 1958, all West Berlin cinemas were invited to join the Cultural Program, it was under the condition that the discount apply only to films of high merit, those deemed culturally worthwhile (*wertvoll* and *besonders wertvoll*) by the Film Evaluation Commission. An attempt to appease East and West German criticism of typically sensationalist border cinema fare, the film policy of the Cultural Program effectively ended the *Grenzkino*'s special economic and geographical status. Lamenting the lost profits of diverse, nonedifying programming, the VBF was quick to articulate the border cinema's legacy as a pioneering social force that had advanced the "merger of both halves of the city."[41] In this tone of self-congratulation, the VBF maintained the visibility of Berlin's unique politics of exhibition and spectatorship within the greater West German film industry.

For young people, but also for journalists and film professionals, the divided city offered a rich and varied program of films primarily from the United States, Western Europe, and Soviet bloc countries. With New Waves emerging in France, Italy, Great Britain, and Poland as well as ample access to the latest Hollywood productions, Berlin's filmmakers and critics (whether from the East or the West) belonged to a filmgoing culture that was at once officially determined and seemingly limitless. In this way, viewing habits of local filmmakers, screenwriters, cinematographers, and actors must be considered as potentially promiscuous and ideologically ambiguous as those of the teenagers who crossed the inner-Berlin borders for cinematic and other cultural entertainments. This is not to say that all members of this unique film culture participated equally in its formation, circulation of references, and intersector influences; far more, the multiplicity of this cultural environment demands a nuanced recognition of the various kinds and degrees of contact and proximity within and between the films made there.

Despite the East's official ban on violent American genres, both the Klein–Kohlhaase and Tressler–Tremper films are replete with references to American cinema, particularly the films of rebel icons Marlon Brando and James Dean. While method actors Dean and Brando created antiauthoritarian characters who were at once tough and deeply vulnerable in *Rebel without a Cause, The Wild One,* and *On the Waterfront,* Richard Brooks took a sociological approach to juvenile delinquency in *Blackboard Jungle*'s inner-city public school, his black-and-white cinematography heightening the film's effect of documentary realism.[42]

For Klein and Tressler, both trained as documentary filmmakers, and Kohlhaase and Tremper, who got their start at newspapers, cinematic realism was paramount, particularly for the portrayal of youths in urban space. Both Klein's cinematographer Wolf Göthe and Heinz Pehlke, the cameraman of *Die Halbstarken,* made use of special high-speed film stock and available light to produce a grainy black-and-white image evocative of newsreels.[43] Beyond the American example, both production teams admired the subtle storytelling and quotidian simplicity of neorealist narratives. For Kohlhaase, it was the Italians' "particular view of reality," their choice of "the everyday" as "a subject," that seemed so new; for Tressler, who had made the Vienna social problem film *Unter 18* (*Under 18,* Austria 1957) between his two Berlin features, films like Federico Fellini's *I Vitelloni* (The idlers, Italy/France 1953), "about normal young people, who want to get out and experience things," provided the inspiration for *Endstation Liebe.*[44] Tremper, a self-described visual writer, had specific Berlin locations in mind as he prepared *Die Halbstarken,* and though he and Tressler disagreed on these, they shared a strong sensibility for milieu.[45]

This turn to the streets, to the public and semipublic spaces where the city's postwar youths congregated and, occasionally, grew unruly, constructed interfilmic and intersector affinities of a generation that behaved differently within their respective capitalist and communist political structures. As the GDR location in which the cultural influence of the U.S. occupation forces was most palpable, East Berlin was both the East German point of entry into this Americanized space and a platform from which the SED could vehemently denounce U.S. popular culture. The four films' choice of location and rather unusual foregrounding of German youths' rebellious streak (in comparison to the FRG's sanitized Peter Kraus rock 'n' roll cycle and DEFA's "do the right socialist thing" approach to children's entertainment) assured the films' rhetorical contact between sectors at the time of their production and release.[46]

The political exigencies of the divided but permeable Cold War mediascape, its offensive and defensive strategies, placed the films and their makers in dialogical structures that can only be understood in the Greater Berlin context and in the wider spheres of GDR and FRG spectatorship and reception. Though the two teams approached 1950s Berlin with varying degrees of referential fidelity and deviated in their solutions to the *Halbstarken* problem, they provided points of communication that muddied these very attempts at ideological clarity. Thus Tremper could recall a 1956 interview at East Berlin's Deutschlandsender (a radio station directed at West Berlin listeners) in which he and Kohlhaase discussed the crisis of German youth in *Die Halbstarken* and in the upcoming *Berlin—Ecke Schönhauser.* Klein, after a 1956 screening of *Eine Berliner Romanze* in Karl-Marx-Stadt (Chemnitz), could ask his young audience to suggest the title of his next film and hear a resounding "*Halbstarke*" in response. Hans Modrow, then the leader of the East's youth organization Free German Youth (Freie Deutsche Jugend, FDJ), could proclaim the rough cut of *Berlin—Ecke Schönhauser* the "exact foil" to *Die Halbstarken.* Ekkehard Schall, the male lead in *Berlin—Ecke Schönhauser* (already an actor at the Deutsches Theater in the early 1950s and Bertolt Brecht's son-in-law by 1961), could remember having seen *Die Halbstarken* and numerous American youth films in West Berlin. When GDR authorities complained that the DEFA film was mistaken in depicting youth unrest in the land of *Aufbau,* West Berlin's RIAS (Radio in the American Sector) could even choose to broadcast an unedited scene from *Berlin—Ecke Schönhauser* in all-German solidarity.[47]

Against this contradictory backdrop of purported political independence and actual cultural exchange, the four teen films built bridges not only between Berlin's sectors and Germany's zones but also to a future in which the authenticity of youth experience in the divided city became a matter of film retrospection and memory.

IDEOLOGICAL LANDSCAPES

From 1956 to 1958, the East and West German public spheres expressed heightened concern for the behavior of postwar youths. Though gangs had emerged in both German states and had committed petty crimes, vandalism, and public disturbances in several cities and towns, Berlin became the principal target of critique. It was, after all, the place where 41 of the 128 larger incidents (those involving more than fifty participants) occurred between 1955 and 1958.[48] GDR authorities conveniently attributed this decidedly unsocialist, destructive streak to Western influences and claimed that in the "few cases" in which "groups of young rowdies" had surfaced in the East, they had been reading "such literature smuggled in from West Germany or West Berlin" or "visiting West Berlin cinemas and doubtful dance halls."[49] East German reviews of *Eine Berliner Romanze* and *Berlin—Ecke Schönhauser* generally applied this sentiment to the predicaments of the films' young East Berliners, but West German critics of *Die Halbstarken,* too, blamed Berlin's higher rate of juvenile delinquency on "the unique circumstances of the divided, torn apart Berlin."[50] At the site where German political and cultural autonomy most visibly broke down, the new "skeptical" teen generation could seek out stronger, more sovereign alternatives to the GDR and FRG or reject these altogether. How the DEFA and Inter West films presented Berlin's contested terrain reveals much about the limitations of film propaganda in realist approaches to urban space.

Shot in summer 1955, *Eine Berliner Romanze* premiered in May 1956, just in time for DEFA's tenth anniversary celebrations. The one-hundredth feature by the first German film company to be licensed after the war and the latest contribution from national prize recipients Klein and Kohlhaase, this cross-border love story also arrived in the midst of a Cold War thaw following Nikita Khrushchev's denunciation of Stalin that winter.[51] Its urban reunification fantasy posited a cinematic solution for aching all-German hearts too big for sector boundaries.

When Uschi (Annekathrin Bürger), a sixteen-year-old East Berlin salesgirl, meets West Berliner "Lord" (Uwe-Jens Pape), she is charmed by his portable radio and suave manner. Initially Lord's worldliness trumps the simple, more earnest affections of his friend and romantic rival Hans (Ulrich Thein), who struggles to find work in West Berlin. While Uschi dreams of becoming a model in the West, Hans tries to impress her with material goods. He buys Lord's radio on installment, pays the tuition for her modeling school, and passes off a friend's place as his own. Hans's mother, with whom he lives in a miserable basement apartment, scolds him for his wastefulness; Uschi's good socialist parents criticize her enchantment with the West and remind her of where she belongs. After discovering that Hans is not an affluent, independent exemplar of the Economic Miracle, Uschi reassesses their relationship and realizes that her love transcends not only German division but also material wealth. With her mother's blessing, she invites Hans to visit her family, and the film ends with the implication that the young couple will find happiness in East Berlin.

DEFA press and promotional materials explicitly articulated both the shortcomings of Western representations of Berlin and GDR cinema's role in fostering spectators' desire for reunification. Whereas West German images of the city "were too vague, too done up, just not true" and failed to depict "serious efforts

Uschi and Hans in *Eine Berliner Romanze*. Photographs by Waltraut Pathenhaimer. Courtesy of the DEFA-Stiftung.

to become one again," the responsible artist should fulfill "only one task" in this "unhealthy situation of life in a divided city," that is, help Berliners "find their way to each other again so that the body of the city once again becomes whole." Taking quite literally the sexual implications of this merger of bodies and urban space, one handbill, depending on how one unfolds it, even combines cartoons of a boy and a girl on a park bench; East and West Berlin location names; a subway map of East Berlin, including several cinemas in which the film is presumably playing and the West's more proletarian neighborhoods; and an abstract illustration of the boy's blue silhouette and the girl's red one overlapping in an all-German purple. Above them a swath of yellow bears the phrase "love that knows no boundary posts" as arrows point in four directions. A bit of the yellow taints the boy's head, but not the girl's; is it perhaps the green of U.S. occupation?[52]

Similarly, Klein and Kohlhaase hardly shy away from representing the border. *Eine Berliner Romanze* immediately locates the spectator in the divided cityscape with a fade-in to a busy street corner across from an HO-Laden, one of the GDR's state-owned department stores, which made roughly 75 percent of its profits from West Berlin consumers in the early 1950s.[53] Pedestrians move in and out of frame, and as the camera pans right, a paternalistic narrator declares, "Today we want to tell you a little story from the big city Berlin." The motion reveals a map of the city, and the narrator resumes, "It is the story of two young people." The words "West Sector" and the thick black line of the inner-Berlin border are now visible. As the pan continues from West to East, the voice-over explains, "The boy lives in that part of the city that one calls the 'West Sector' . . . and the girl lives in East Berlin." Over a shot of a sidewalk and street, this unidentified male further specifies the film's topography, placing Uschi, a sales trainee, at the large HO store on Alexanderplatz. "It is a special day for Uschi," he intimates as the camera now pans left along the side of the HO building. This objective statement of facts and series of nonfiction images give way to the fictional world of the narrative as Uschi's face appears in close-up, an iris-out from the facade. Her story literally emerges from the surface of the city.

Having already left no doubt as to Berlin's cartographic parameters, the film persists in this didactic marking of territory. Border crossing, particularly from East to West, becomes a highly stylized act of transgression. Seeking refuge in the street after an argument with her family, Uschi meets her friend Gisela, who invites her to see the aptly titled *Lockende Sünde* (Tempting sins) in the West Sector. Although Uschi refuses to watch such a "stupid" film, she agrees to accompany her friend along the way.

A shot of the girls walking screen left dissolves to the sign "END OF THE DEMOCRATIC SECTOR OF GREATER BERLIN." A dramatic drum roll marks

A handbill for *Eine Berliner Romanze* opens into a map of East and West Berlin's border zone. Courtesy of Bundesarchiv-Filmarchiv.

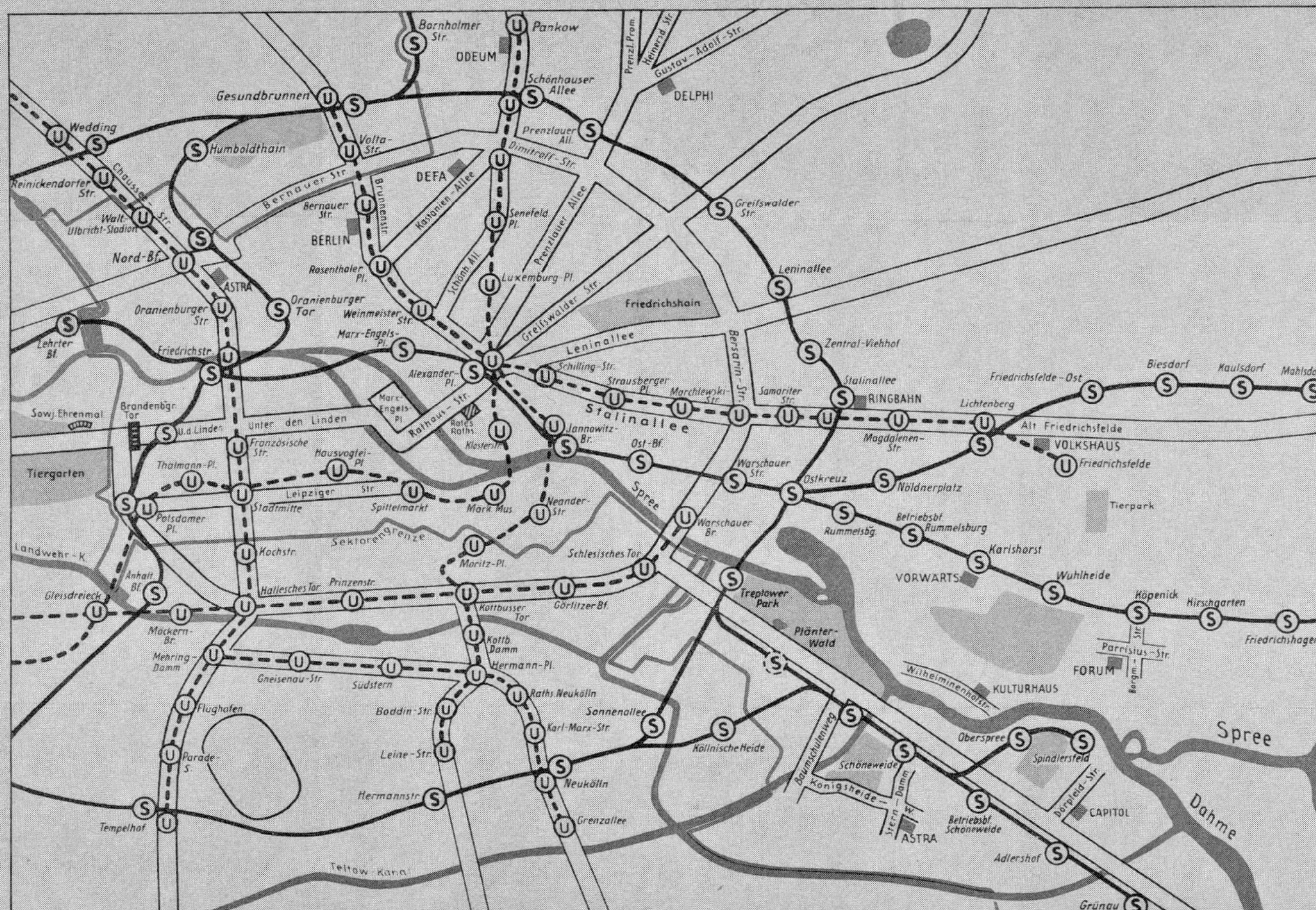

(204) Ag 214/56 DDR Nr. 66/56

the spatial transition as the narrator returns, "There's been a border as long as Uschi can remember." The camera tracks left around the first sign to reveal the quadrilingual warning "YOU ARE ENTERING THE AMERICAN SECTOR," while the voice-over proceeds, "and one goes over there and comes over here. And one calls oneself 'East Berliner' or 'West Berliner.'" A West Berlin department store then stands in an empty evening street as the narrator concludes, "Just the way one used to call oneself 'Berliner.'" In the next shot, damp streets and sidewalks reflect the neon lights of a busy Western shopping district. Günter Klück's jazzy melody underscores the glittering surface of a moving streetcar, a parked Volkswagen, and a series of building facades, whose bright signs "Radio," "Nescafé," and "Woolworth" promise Western abundance and luxury. Finally, Uschi and Gisela stand in front of the marquee and display cases of the Astoria cinema, and the spectacle of border crossing is complete.[54]

Though subsequent transitions between sectors are far more understated, these early sequences effectively establish Cold War boundaries as both interruptions in geopolitical contiguity and ceremonial observances of spatial unity. Neither characters nor spectators may "enter" West Berlin without first reading the signs. Just as the language of demarcation includes and excludes, informs and directs, these phrases pause the narrative over real distances that would be quickly traversed on foot. An admonishment to walk, not run, over the border, to take the time to acknowledge what these signs are separating, Klein's insistence on visualizing the site of German division also suggests a narrative that would itself be impossible without a mobile, border-crossing camera.

The voice-over disappears for much of the film, though East–West boundaries and cultural markers remain. One sector sign pointedly opposes Hans's modest Western means to his love in the East; the neon-lit "Hotel am Zoo" and a poster for *East of Eden,* which had opened in the West in summer 1955, locate Uschi and Hans's visit to a boxing match in downtown West Berlin. When Uschi, after another disagreement with her parents, catches the U-Bahn from Warschauer Straße in Friedrichshain, her older brother (Hartmut Reck) urges the conductor to stop the train. Helpless, the conductor replies, "But the train's moving. The next stop's the West Sector." In each of these instances, Klein conveys the shift between ideologically distinct geographies through signs, screen direction, and audiovisual codes of the glossy or impoverished West. To know Cold War Berlin, even as a cinematic city, is to know at all times where one is within it.

The film's ending, however, destabilizes the very geographical clarity that its beginning so carefully constructs. Uschi collects Hans from the West Berlin demolition site where he has been working and invites him to meet her parents. In the final shot, the two walk toward an elevated U-Bahn station that recedes

Uschi crosses the border in *Eine Berliner Romanze*. Courtesy of the DEFA-Stiftung.

into the distance. Framed by several converging diagonals, they move toward the city's vanishing point as the narrator, absent since the first border crossing, observes, "Yes. Now they are a real couple. One of thousands in Berlin. Or, as we say here, they're 'going together.' And together they'll also find their place, Uschi and Hans. In the midst of our life, where there's work, something to fight for, and love."

Although the narrator associates "our life" and even the "we" of local idiom with the socialist ideal of collective struggle and the rewards of love, the last image preserves a degree of geographic uncertainty for the uninitiated spectator. Though the film generally follows a consistent logic of cartographic direction (screen left for the West, screen right for the East), it is not clear that Uschi and Hans are in the East or even heading that way. The station displays no signs, and rather than walking toward it, the couple continues along the sidewalk, parallel to the tracks. It takes a sharp eye to spot slightly blurred posters for New York and the British Lux soap on a nearby advertising column, and there are few pedestrians and cars on the street. Indeed, it is possible that Uschi and Hans are walking into their socialist future in Kreuzberg, along the U1, which runs on elevated tracks through

Uschi and Hans walk into the city and into their future in *Eine Berliner Romanze*. Courtesy of the DEFA-Stiftung.

much of West Berlin and has its end station at Warschauer Straße, an established locale in Uschi's border-crossing repertoire.

Conversely, only those familiar with the view from Prenzlauer Berg's Dimitroffstraße station (today the Eberswalder Straße stop) would be able to locate the pair definitively along the U2 in the East, with the distinctive spire of Segenskirche vaguely discernable in the distance. Did a socialist advertising column really advocate trips to New York and cosmopolitan beauty products? Did Klein, for logistical reasons, dress up the East as the West or else intentionally scramble the Cold War visual codes the film had begun by upholding? The answer, in this case, is less important than the complexity of the image that survives. One of film theorist and cultural critic Siegfried Kracauer's five "inherent affinities" of the cinema (all of which advocate cinematic realism's indexical relationship to objects before the camera) is particularly suggestive here: "the indeterminate," that quality of photography and film by which "natural objects" are "surrounded with a fringe of meanings liable to touch off various moods, emotions, runs of inarticulate thoughts." Referring to "psychophysical correspondences" relaying information between the mind and the physical world, he claims that "a film shot does not come into its own unless it incorporates raw material with its multiple meanings."[55] Much like the street views of early cinema, the framing of this final shot betrays a carefully chosen vantage point, one that maximizes the visible elements of urban life in a stretch of intact cityscape and, in this case, also masks determinate geographical clues.

Klein and Kohlhaase's 1956 novellization of *Eine Berliner Romanze* similarly preserves this ideal Berlin. Here the director and screenwriter make no grand statements about Uschi and Hans's socialist future; they simply conclude, "And Berlin, the city, takes them in."[56] The city that incorporates Uschi and Hans, absorbs them into adult society, is "Berlin," a much broader concept than the film's narration implies. If the narrator initially laments Berlin's division, the final shot recuperates a single urban space, a lost unity regained through geographical indeterminacy.

Eine Berliner Romanze depicted the city's internal political boundaries only to collapse them through love; *Berlin—Ecke Schönhauser* raised the stakes of Cold War border crossing by more overtly vilifying the West. Responding to critiques of both *Eine Berliner Romanze*'s overly conciliatory portrayal of West Berlin and *Die Halbstarken*'s perceived failure to probe the sociological roots of unrest among postwar youths, Klein and Kohlhaase now attempted to correct their ideological course with a less ambiguous narrative geography and closer examination of East Berlin teenagers' home lives and consequent vulnerability to the dangers of the West.[57]

Written in 1956, toward the end of the thaw, and released in fall 1957, *Berlin—Ecke Schönhauser* refers, in its title, to the corner of Schönhauser Allee and Dimitroffstraße, where five streets, the U2, and several tram lines converge. At this busy Prenzlauer Berg intersection, the young construction worker Dieter (Ekkehard Schall) regularly meets the seamstress Angela (Ilse Pagé), the film fanatic "Kohle" (Ernst-Georg Schwill), and the high school dropout Karl-Heinz (Harry Engel), whose affluent parents are secretly planning to move to the West. After Karl-Heinz, who supplements his allowance with petty criminal activity in West Berlin, dares Kohle to smash a street lamp for one West mark, the friends and their extended group of rowdies are interrogated by a friendly, well-intentioned *Volkspolizist* (Raimund Schelcher). At a dance, Karl-Heinz steals a girl's East German identity card to pawn in the West; Dieter, who has fallen in love with Angela, comes under suspicion. Eager to confront the thief, he and Kohle discover Karl-Heinz on the run from a manslaughter he committed in West Berlin. When Karl-Heinz threatens Dieter with a pistol, Kohle throws a brick at his head, knocking him cold. Fearing that they have inadvertently killed their friend, Dieter

Karl-Heinz, Angela, Dieter, and Kohle on the streets in *Berlin—Ecke Schönhauser*. Photograph by Holstein, Schneider. Courtesy of the DEFA-Stiftung.

and Kohle flee to a youth refugee camp in West Berlin, where Kohle dies accidentally. Disillusioned, Dieter returns to East Berlin, where the pregnant Angela awaits him.

Like *Eine Berliner Romanze*, *Berlin—Ecke Schönhauser* establishes its location in the first shot. A long, almost 360 degree pan explores a richly textured street scene. Pedestrians and a hand-drawn cart pass before the camera; in the background, a streetcar runs beneath the elevated U-Bahn tracks, along which a banner advertises *Neues Deutschland,* the SED party newspaper. The camera comes to rest as the word "BERLIN" emerges in a matter-of-fact sans serif font from the center of the frame's several converging diagonals before moving to the upper left to accommodate the italic, more personalized "*Schönhauser Corner.*" In only a few seconds, the graphic arrangement of the film's title has produced at least three variations in meaning: (1) (All-) "Berlin" (a)rises from the New (East) Germany; (2) (All-)Berlin overwrites the New (East) Germany and thus *is* the New Germany; and (3) the (East) Berlin location "Schönhauser Corner" overwrites, dominates, and dismisses both grand propagandistic notions of (East) Germany's

The graphic arrangement of the title sequence. Courtesy of the DEFA-Stiftung.

newness and the controlling rhetoric of official state news. Though *Neues Deutschland* evokes the GDR of socialist *Aufbau,* the term preserves a polysemic quality in which the differentiation of East and West Germany is at once acknowledged and disavowed.

Once again, Klein and Kohlhaase's efforts to avoid geopolitical ambiguity along the inner-Berlin border evince a rather contradictory use of urban space. Though this opening sequence clearly positions the camera at the corner of Dimitroffstraße (known before and after the Cold War as Danziger Straße), the film's title is aligned with Schönhauser Allee, a street name that did not change under socialist rule. While the team's working title, *Wo wir nicht sind* (Where we aren't), alluded to the film's final sentiment, the police officer's plea for collective socialist vigilance against the Western enemy, the words "Berlin—Schönhauser Corner" harbor a variety of connotations that predate the East German state. Joshua Feinstein has noted, in particular, the ironic contrast between the film's setting in a working-class and petty bourgeois neighborhood of prewar buildings *(Altbauten)* and the "stately bombast of some socialist urban renewal scheme." While he interprets the title sequence as a reconciliation of the "ordinary" and the "actual" with the promise of a "new society,"[58] this initial play of words also resonates significantly in discussions of reunification and all-German cultural tradition. As one critic for *Die Zeit,* a West German weekly, put it, "What's meant is Schönhauser Allee, that traffic artery in Northeastern Berlin, whose heavily stuccoed Wilhelmine façades, along with the more petty bourgeois than revolutionary demeanor of its residents, still exude much of the Old Berlin flair." The review then goes on to compare the milieu of Klein and Kohlhaase's Berlin to that of Alfred Döblin's 1929 novel *Berlin, Alexanderplatz,* which took place among the lower classes of Old Berlin's Alexanderplatz and Scheunenviertel.[59] DEFA publicity materials, too, encouraged an association of timelessness, not with Schönhauser Corner, but with the behavior of Berlin youths generally; a turn-of-the-century Heinrich Zille sketch of young people dancing could relativize the exploits of East Berlin's border-crossing teenagers and young adults as perennial antics rather than cause for socialist alarm. The film's location could thus be understood, within and across East and West German reception, as both geographically specific and temporally layered.

Berlin—Ecke Schönhauser's first shot betrays the unstable relationship between word and image; its second one reinforces, in contrast, a spatial and lexical barrier between East and West. As in *Eine Berliner Romanze,* Klein employs sector signs and a mobile camera to convey narrative geography and political division. A young man (Dieter) runs beneath the quadrilingual sign "YOU ARE ENTERING THE AMERICAN SECTOR" at Checkpoint Charlie. The camera pans 180 degrees to follow his motion before coming to rest on the equally clear phrase "BEGINNING OF THE DEMOCRATIC SECTOR OF GREATER BERLIN." Even before Dieter starts to recount his story to the police officer in flashback, his action propels the spectator from the space between the two German states to a firm ideological ground. Indeed, it is only when Dieter has narrated his way to this point that the plot reconnects with the present. Having returned from the West to the refuge of Schönhauser Corner, he stands at the entrance of Angela's building, ready to face his socialist future.

Berlin—Ecke Schönhauser, in contrast to its predecessor, enlists the West sector as a cautionary tale rather than as an attractive, viable alternative to life in the GDR. Careful audiovisual signposting via landmarks, objects, and aural cues aligns West Berlin with Cold War criminality, militarism, and the sensationalism of the tabloid press. The first shot of the West presents the busy commercial district surrounding the Bahnhof Zoo. In the background, the ruin of the Kaiser-Wilhelm Memorial Church stands as a reminder of wartime destruction. A swish pan cuts to the interior of the train station, where an old newspaper seller advances

Dieter runs from West to East in *Berlin—Ecke Schönhauser.* Courtesy of the DEFA-Stiftung.

toward the camera, proclaiming the headline, "Atom bombs for the Federal Armed Forces! *Der Telegraf*! 55 Billion for Rearmament!" He moves off-frame to reveal Karl-Heinz in an illegal currency transaction with a West Berlin black marketeer; it is clear that the "crimes" of the West German state have corrupted at least one East Berlin border crosser.

In a later scene, it is Kohle who ventures westward after an altercation with his brutal stepfather. A familiar pan between sector signs establishes his cinephilic escape route into the French sector, most likely Wedding. As he makes his way past the cinema's sidewalk display cases, a newspaper seller once again reinforces acoustically the West's dubious politics and superficial concerns: "Soraya Expecting after All . . . *Die Bild-Zeitung* . . . 10 Pfennig." Referring to the difficulties of Soraya Esfandiari, the half-German wife of the Iranian Shah, to conceive an heir, this announcement signals Karl-Heinz's arrival, awkward dismissal of Kohle, and disappearance into a Volkswagen with two West Berlin criminals. If mention of "Soraya" had served in *Eine Berliner Romanze* as Lord's capitalist compliment to Uschi, his implication that she, too, could achieve fame and fortune, Kohlhaase's revised allusion to star culture now casts the pregnant Soraya as a harbinger of the moral decline of Eastern youths. From a seemingly innocent visit to the cinema to the violence and sexual promiscuity of Kohle's film noir *The Flanagan Boy* (United States 1953) to real acts of murder, the West's worship of wealth is, in *Berlin—Ecke Schönhauser,* hardly worth the perils of border crossing.

After Kohle and Dieter flee to the West *(Republikflucht),* they sit, forlorn, beneath a "relief organization" poster as loudspeakers intermittently underscore their location, "Last train station in the West sector." This escalation of quotidian border crossing to defection receives its due punishment; the boys' refugee camp is populated with unfeeling psychologists, disaffected youths, and a sadistic guard, whose club-wielding violence prompted at least one West German critic to compare the compound to a concentration camp.[60] Put off by the Cold War bias of the camp's administrators, Dieter, who remains stubbornly independent of both Western and Eastern propaganda, gradually realizes the price of West German freedom and asks one of his interrogators, "If I came here of my own free will, I can also leave if I feel like it, can't I?" After Kohle's death from a botched poisoning trick seen in a forbidden film, Dieter manages to escape and, like the more than twenty-three thousand returnees *(Rückkehrer)* in the fifteen- to twenty-five-year-old age group in 1956, find his way back to the East.[61]

Despite such overt concessions to GDR cultural politics, Klein and Kohlhaase came under attack at the 1958 Film Conference for relying too heavily on realism's socially critical, rather than socialist, strain and for appealing to bourgeois entertainment values.[62] Nonetheless, *Berlin—Ecke Schönhauser* was immensely popular. Like *Eine Berliner Romanze,* it was a rare, lucrative DEFA film, one that appealed to a broad public far more than the studio's typical antifascist and political fare and, as a result, sold nearly two million tickets in four months.[63] Both films were celebrated for their realistic portrayals of life in the divided city and of the tribulations of German youths as well as for their relative freedom from DEFA's usual didacticism. Imperfect cinematic socialism validated the lives of those who "don't or don't yet live in such comfortable buildings as those in Stalinallee."[64]

Within and beyond Berlin, Klein and Kohlhaase's "Berlin films" engaged with Cold War Germany's complex spectatorship and intermingled film cultures. *Junge Welt,* the news organ of the FDJ, reported long lines for *Berlin—Ecke Schönhauser* at East Berlin's Babylon and Colosseum cinemas, the latter of which was renovated in the months prior to the film's premiere.[65] Located on Schönhauser Allee, the Colosseum addressed precisely those local teenagers who might otherwise be prone to border crossing. For once, DEFA had a few films that could pique the curiosity of the West, and *Junge Welt* made much of West German actor and director Dieter Borsche's appearance at a screening of the film in the Babylon.[66]

The West German press responded enthusiastically to Klein and Kohlhaase's teen films. While *Film-Echo* touted *Eine Berliner Romanze* as the East German answer to Helmut Käutner's interzonal romance *Himmel ohne Sterne* (*Sky without Stars,* FRG 1955), Anna Teut of *Die Welt* looked beyond the necessary socialist elements of *Berlin—Ecke Schönhauser* to the film's elicitation of unity within the postwar generation: "In the perspective of the young people, two worlds come together that, in the divided city, can't be as strictly separated as proponents of the Cold War would have it anyway." She then went on to call for the film's release in the West, a request that went unfulfilled.[67]

The Klein and Kohlhaase films may not have reached the greater FRG population through traditional theatrical distribution, but they did take part in new televisual strategies to attract and unite East and West German audiences. Accelerating production of television sets between 1956 and 1957 and eventually surpassing the FRG's manufacturing of the units, the GDR embraced the propagandistic potential of this new medium to maintain all-German cultural ties across Allied zones.[68] In addition to their cinematic release in the East, *Eine Berliner Romanze* and *Berlin—Ecke Schönhauser* were broadcast on television a few months later in an effort to avoid competition between the two media. Indeed, the East German channel Deutscher Fernsehfunk was instrumental in advertising *Berlin—Ecke Schönhauser*; one broadcast on the eve of the premiere introduced the film's young stars.[69] Since much early television spectatorship in the East involved collective viewing rooms, the West German trade press feared that GDR television could become a major source of anti-West propaganda.[70]

Though it is impossible to estimate just how many Westerners partook in the broadcasts of Klein and Kohlhaase's Berlin films, this Western window into DEFA's blocked exports must not be discounted. As for the East, television programming of the two features provided viewers well beyond Berlin with simultaneous access to representations of the city's Western sectors. Even after the thaw, *Eine Berliner Romanze* enjoyed an extensive run on television, airing eight times between July 1956 and October 1959. *Berlin—Ecke Schönhauser* was broadcast twice in fall 1957 and again just a few weeks before the Berlin Wall was constructed. Once the border was closed, both films effectively disappeared from GDR television until the *Wende* era.[71] In the period of prewall division, however, a mediated and collective experience of Berlin's open borders and youth culture circulated freely. The West that these films cited was still a place to be visited—in West Berlin and in its cinemas.

THE POLITICS OF AUTHENTICITY

Unlike their Eastern counterparts, Tressler and Tremper avoided Cold War Berlin's notorious landmarks; indeed, they steered clear of narrative geopolitics altogether. Effectively denying the existence of the inner-Berlin border, *Die Halbstarken* and *Endstation Liebe* nonetheless engaged in city-wide discourses on the postwar generation. Both during their production and after their release, the press attributed the films' referential fidelity to West Berlin to their authentic portrayal of young Berliners and neorealist renderings of milieu. If *Eine Berliner Romanze* and *Berlin—Ecke Schönhauser* embedded the frustrations of youths within the specific confrontation of two political systems, the Inter West features imagined a Berlin that may never have been divided in the first place.

Die Halbstarken, like *Blackboard Jungle* and *The Wild One,* opens with a disclaimer that at once condemns the actions of the film's characters yet morally justifies the act of spectatorship. Jan Borchert (Christian Doermer) runs into his estranged older brother Freddy (Horst Buchholz) at a public swimming hall. Having left the family after a disagreement with their authoritarian father, Freddy, the charismatic leader of a gang of rowdies, seems to be doing well for himself with a job at a gas station and a pretty, but conniving, young girlfriend named Sissy (Karin Baal). While Freddy and his friends plan the elaborate robbery of a postal truck, Jan mistakes his brother's apparent wealth for legitimate financial success and asks him for three thousand marks to settle an ongoing feud between their parents. Freddy, who pledges to give up his criminal exploits after this final heist, encourages Jan to participate. When the robbery fails to yield the anticipated cash, Sissy and some of the others turn on Freddy. His leadership at stake, Freddy and his remaining followers decide to rob the villa of an Italian café owner. In the process, Sissy shoots Freddy, who, with Jan's help, stumbles into police custody.

The film's sensationalist plot and the real incidents from which it derived prompted several debates in the public sphere before and during shooting. Journalists worried that *Die Halbstarken*'s depiction of youth violence might instigate new outbreaks of riotous behavior, as had *Blackboard Jungle*.[72] To counteract charges of exploitation, the Inter West team invited more than a thousand young people to join the mayor of Kreuzberg and Buchholz, a native Berlin son, in a discussion at the Palladium Theater.[73] Despite such publicity stunts, engineered primarily by Tremper, West Berlin's senator for youth and sports Ella Kay condemned the film for defaming the city's teenagers and refused to support its production: "Such a film is only useful if it shows a way out and can help change things."[74]

More positive coverage of the production phase celebrated location shooting and the local pedigrees of the young cast (often heard in their speech) as *Die Halbstarken*'s chief merits. Though the film includes several exterior shots on streets and sidewalks, Tressler hardly identifies these with Berlin. Instead,

Freddy and Sissy stand at the center of the gang. Jan is off to the right. *Die Halbstarken*. Courtesy of Deutsche Kinemathek.

the apartment blocks in the distance, the busy street in the background of an ice cream parlor, the dingy courtyard of Sissy's building, and the S-Bahn arches and highway overpass at the scene of the robbery might be anywhere in (West) Germany. The press, however, eagerly reported the distinctly West Berlin neighborhoods in which the crew had filmed: Wedding, Charlottenburg, Lankwitz, Spandau, and Wannsee. While Buchholz was living in Kreuzberg at the time, Karin Baal, chosen from among seven hundred for the role of Sissy, was hailed as a working-class "film-addicted, little girl" and "a 'basement-dwelling kid'"[75] from Wedding (both neighborhoods bordering those of their Eastern counterparts and fans). Hans-Joachim Ketzlin, who played one of Freddy's more loyal disciples, similarly drew accolades for his convincing demeanor: "With his flattened boxer's nose, friendly-yet-cynical Marlon Brando gaze, and gum-chewing lower jaw, he appears to be 'the' rowdy, bar none."[76]

Just as André Bazin theorized, in 1948, the benefits of "an amalgam" of professional and nonprofessional "players" for "that extraordinary feeling of truth that one gets from the current Italian films," the West German print media's frequent recourse to the "truth" of *Die Halbstarken*'s "faces that were, in part, actually brought into the studio from Berlin's streets," promised to extend the real city into the anonymous Berlin of the diegetic world.[77] The implied contiguity of street to stardom, of juvenile crime to successful genre picture, of *Halbstarke* to filmgoer, certainly contributed to the film's association with production location West Berlin, even where Tressler's images failed to evoke distinctive Berlin and Cold War topographies.

A few perceptive critics looked past the film's rather clumsy narrative and mediocre acting to praise *Die Halbstarken*'s refreshing, low-key approach to Berlin. The *Frankfurter Allgemeine Zeitung* expressed surprise that the film took place in a "New Berlin" without the very visual accoutrements that usually distinguished the city, "advertising surfaces, cultural posturing, and heroic poses." In his review of the West German film industry's 1956 output, Oskar Kalbus panned *Die Halbstarken* for its confusion of generic elements but lauded its cinematography for elevating the film "beyond the usual German framework." Pehlke's camera, he went on to rhapsodize, had "captured the streets of Berlin so well that even the famous Italian neorealist flicks couldn't have done it better."[78] On one hand, such enthusiasm for a "new" unadorned, quotidian cinematic city welcomed the film's formal rupture with the elaborate studio sets of Weimar, National Socialist, and existing West German film traditions. Tressler and Tremper's attempt to dramatize juvenile delinquency by insisting on the natural correspondence between actors, characters, and setting could dispel with overt markers both of place and boundary. On the other hand, *Die Halbstarken*'s territorial vagueness could better uphold West German cinema's "Inter West" aspirations by allowing the film to resonate interculturally West of the Iron Curtain.

Beyond neorealist comparisons, reviews were quick to bring the film into dialogue with its American predecessors, with Western European cinema, and with a more widespread phenomenon of youth rebelliousness. Typical was *Filmblätter*'s defense of the film as "a well-made crime film" with "nearly American spunk,"[79] something that could benefit the domestic box office. Authenticity took a turn here, away from claims of realist milieu, to the West German film industry's legitimate attainment of qualities found in more prominent national cinemas, particularly those of some NATO countries. Buchholz, who had played a sympathetic Soviet soldier in *Himmel ohne Sterne* and would see his star rise rapidly and internationally after *Die Halbstarken,* seemed now to be both "on the trail of Marlon Brando in 'The Wild One'" and in the process of "being molded into a German

Karin Baal, an authentic Berliner. *Die Halbstarken.* Courtesy of Deutsche Kinemathek.

James Dean, the tough guy with a soul, even an overly sensitive soul, if need be."[80] Newcomer Karin Baal, for her part, came across as "a slightly raw, backstairs version of the difficult, sweeter Marina Vlady,"[81] the young French actress, who had appeared not only in Rolf Thiele's *Sie* (She, France/FRG 1954) but also in numerous French and Italian productions released in both the FRG and the GDR. Through narrative and stylistic imitation as well as the conscious construction of fresh postwar star personae, West German cinema could assert its variant of a cultural and geopolitical comeback.

Just as the film's realist approach to Berlin helped to articulate Germany's participation in this new, transnational strain of postwar film art, a rejuvenated film industry could work to promote, if indirectly, the politics of the Adenauer government. Publicity materials proclaimed *Die Halbstarken* "a German contribution to an international problem," and Viktoria von Ballasko, who played Freddy and Jan's mother, maintained that it was "not a postwar or mere milieu problem" because young people were acting up "in Sweden as well as in Germany and elsewhere."[82] The historian Uta Poiger has argued compellingly that such efforts to align West German youth culture with that of the Western Allies signaled an emerging Cold War liberal consensus, in which the FRG could "[participate] in the West's fight against totalitarianism" by depoliticizing cultural consumption. While the GDR gradually withdrew from a "stance that promised an accommodation of *Halbstarken* styles and increasingly reverted to earlier attacks that labeled both young German rebels and American popular culture fascist," the FRG could more easily and strategically come to terms with Americanization.[83] Seen from this perspective, one not far removed from DEFA critiques of Tressler and Tremper, *Die Halbstarken* lets West Germany off the hook for the effects of the Third Reich, the war, and their immediate aftermath on teenagers of the Economic Miracle.

The film's audiovisual repression of Berlin's obvious Cold War cultural and political topographies cuts, however, two ways, particularly as turning one's back on the border is still a form of acknowledging its presence. Released in September 1956, just four months after *Eine Berliner Romanze* mapped a city of all-German love, *Die Halbstarken*'s intermingled local (urban), (trans)national (cinematic), and international (political) receptive discourses placed its geographical omissions nonetheless in structures of interfilmic communication and meaning. Just as *Berlin—Ecke Schönhauser* amended the representation of urban space in *Eine Berliner Romanze, Endstation Liebe* revised and further elaborated *Die Halbstarken*'s anonymous portrayal of West Berlin.

A Berlin romance without borders, Tressler and Tremper's new collaboration could undermine the Cold War ideological function of specific West Berlin locations and thus, indirectly, respond to DEFA's more polarizing view of the divided city. Rejoining the production team, Horst Buchholz provided visible continuity between the delinquent Freddy and the slightly more mature Mecky, a brash lady's man, who bets his fellow factory workers five marks that he can seduce the new employee, Christa (Barbara Frey), by the end of the weekend. When she initially rejects his advances, Mecky visits her family's apartment and invites her to a wrestling match. Suspicious of Mecky's intentions, Christa's younger brother Uli (Peter-Uwe Witt) tags along. The wrestlers' performance prompts a youthful riot, from which Mecky and Christa escape to Kurfürstendamm. As they sit in an abandoned truck musing about the future, Mecky realizes that Christa will not be the usual conquest. Like West Berliner Hans in *Eine Berliner Romanze,* he invites his date to a friend's apartment, which he pretends is his own.[84] After a misunderstanding, Christa leaves. The next day Mecky attempts to stamp out his growing affection for Christa but in the end must admit that he has fallen for her. After a soccer game, an awkward meeting with Christa, a bar brawl with a friend, and a visit to an ex-girlfriend, Mecky goes in search of his new love and ultimately

Mecky and Christa on the streets of Berlin in *Endstation Liebe.* The film poster at the left comments reflexively on the pathway from street to stardom. Courtesy of Deutsche Kinemathek.

finds her in their truck. By Monday morning, they are back at the factory, an established couple.

Klein and Kohlhaase's evocations of downtown West Berlin range from a center of capitalist consumption to the origin of cross-border crime. By portraying "Kudamm," Bahnhof Zoo, and environs as a modest backdrop for young love, *Endstation Liebe* inverts these negative attributes of place. Department store display cases like the ones that frame Uschi's longing for consumer goods in *Eine Berliner Romanze* serve, in Tressler and Tremper's film, to furnish Mecky and Christa with a protected intimacy. Helmuth Ashley's camera refuses dramatic framings of the products on view; instead, the mannequins and objects in the cases provide a tranquil space for communication in contrast to the chaotic motion and noise of the riot.

Christa and Mecky's movements around the glass facades parallel their growing attachment as well as the breakdown of Mecky's bravado. When Christa, still unaware of his designs, compliments him on his bravery and protective instinct during the commotion, Mecky glides around the edge of the display case and glances back at her. In this play of emotional and visual transparency, character psychology takes precedence over props. Martin Böttcher's melancholic harmonica-led score emphasizes romance and vulnerability where Günter Klück's brassy border-crossing number in *Eine Berliner Romanze* had insisted on the false promise of Western surfaces. The provincial West Berlin of *Endstation Liebe* is one of empty sidewalks and frosty air. When this evening scene continues in front of Bahnhof Zoo, the train station appears in the background as a mere rectangle of diffused light. The neon signs of postwar buildings remain small and blurred in the distance; they, too, are secondary to the romantic progression in the foreground.

Though the film opens in the Osram lightbulb factory, the Inter West team carefully avoids signage and establishing shots that would confirm the location. Mecky, like his Eastern counterparts Hans and Dieter, is a blue-collar worker, and the spaces he traverses (the prewar buildings, the sidewalks, the soccer field) are not particular to the West. Originally titled *Zeit bis Montagfrüh* (Time until Monday morning), the film explores the temporal and atmospheric elements of daily life.[85]

With *Endstation Liebe,* Tressler and Tremper managed to curb their penchant for exaggeration, and, ironically, West German critics' approval of this improvement recalled East German reviewers' initial endorsement of *Eine Berliner Romanze* and *Berlin—Ecke Schönhauser.* While *Hamburger Abendblatt* proclaimed *Endstation Liebe* "a foil" to *Die Halbstarken, Deutsche Woche* marveled at this "poetic realist rowdy film, a film on the trail of *Menschen am Sonntag,*" a 1930 realist experiment in which four young people enjoy a Sunday around Berlin's Wannsee

Tressler's approach to downtown West Berlin: protective intimacy and a modest Bahnhof Zoo in *Endstation Liebe.* Courtesy of Deutsche Kinemathek.

and Nikolassee.[86] Claiming the Weimar city as an aesthetic, all-German forerunner to 1950s West or East Berlin was by no means a neutral act in an era of pointed calls for reunification and careful construction of competing memory cultures. A film like *Menschen am Sonntag (People on Sunday),* which the Western press had previously invoked in discussions of *Eine Berliner Romanze,*[87] still resonated in both film cultures as a reminder of a common, prefascist filmographic past.

Though the West German press ignored any possible exchange with the DEFA films, Tressler and Tremper's new approach to West Berlin migrated much of *Die Halbstarken*'s external Berlin discourse into *Endstation Liebe*'s cinematography. GDR critics had praised Klein and Wolf Göthe for creating "an unmistakable Berlin atmosphere" in *Berlin—Ecke Schönhauser,* and Tressler and Ashley could now boast a similar accomplishment: "It is after all a joke that two Viennese guys, Georg Tressler and cameraman Helmuth Ashley, had to come to the Spree, in order to make one of the most Berlin-like films we've ever seen."[88] As the *Süddeutsche Zeitung* put it, Ashley's camera, interested in "the streets of the big city and the life of the little people," offers "no accusation, no bragging, just statement. Critique of the times is indirect and impartial. And everything is visual."[89]

Tressler and Tremper's competitive urban authenticity depoliticizes Berlin, but to what end in the history of the films' reception? By excluding Berlin's unique visual characteristics or else inverting their presentation, *Die Halbstarken* and *Endstation Liebe* convert the profilmic spaces of 1950s Berlin into anonymous cityscapes, postwar Western European backdrops to the conflicts of youth. Urban space becomes a generic element, a context for criminal and romantic encounters, a cinematic necessity without a place-name. West Berlin, like the Berlin of Weimar and National Socialist productions as well as the postunification city, could masquerade as many places in the service of mass entertainment.

On another level, the films' absence of Cold War borders approximates West Berlin's status as both an outpost of Western freedom and a prison, surrounded on all sides by the GDR. Incorporating the city's noncontiguity with the FRG into their spatial understanding, the films imagine West Berlin as both any city in the FRG and as a self-sufficient, limitless city. Indeed, why should young West Germans and West Berliners seek adventures in socialism when their own Berlin offered the full spectrum of youth entertainments and experiences? A cinematic city without borders could provide a fantasy of real freedom, of Western ideology extended infinitely.

The ambiguity of contextual knowledge versus spatial experience in the Inter West films also suggests, however, a third possibility. The films' target audience of West German, West Berlin, and Eastern border-crossing teenagers would have known that *Die Halbstarken* and *Endstation Liebe* were shot in Berlin. While young West Germans had already encountered West Berlin as a distant, mediated, and fictionalized space, Berliners would have been better equipped to recognize the absence of the East and to enjoy the films' fictional and authentic postures. An imagined (West) Berlin that was at once borderless and ideologically unassuming would have catered precisely to East and West German fantasies of reunification. Those young people who sat in West Berlin cinemas watching Tressler and Tremper's films could experience an ideal projection of their city in an idealized space for all-German encounters. As the VBF boasted in October 1958, "in our cinemas, nations and, even more so, zones are forgotten."[90] Within the unique exhibition culture of West Berlin, *Die Halbstarken, Endstation Liebe,* and the dreams they contained were available to both Germanys.

DEFIANCE AND DESIRE

Though beholden to processes of political and cultural differentiation, the DEFA and Inter West teen films also encouraged an all-German generational stance in the divided city and in the greater GDR and FRG. Retrospectively, the films' common source material and pop cultural references, the filmmakers' self-conscious imitation of American and Italian styles and genres, and the porous prewall public sphere did much to confirm young Berliners' similarities across sector boundaries. Rejecting the authority of the postwar societies that seek to contain their disruptive energy and mold them into ideal citizens of East and West Germany, the characters in all four films might also be understood to recuperate their right to belong together, a right forfeited by the parental generation's mishandling of history.

In each of the films, the home, a cramped space of ruptured kinship and oppressive and contradictory moral standards, motivates the teenagers' exodus to the streets. In *Eine Berliner Romanze,* Uschi's family crowds a kitchen dominated by her sturdy mother (Erika Dunkelmann). Not only is this space the locus of imposed gender norms as Uschi peels potatoes; it is the site of the family's ideological conflict as her parents and brothers work to curb her errant individualism. When Uschi declares her intention to become a model in the West, her mother slaps her. In the next shot she wastes no time crossing Warschauer Brücke with a suitcase. For the fatherless Hans, home is a small kitchen with a bed. After a date with Uschi, he returns to find his mother still awake. She confronts him with his radio installment plan and complains that they do not even have enough money to pay for his sister's shoe repairs. With little privacy to change his clothes, he replies bitterly, "What do you want from me? For a few measly marks I wash cars, at night when other people are sleeping. That's why I gave up boxing even though Kora said I had the best right hook of all time. You think I shouldn't have anything else on my mind but my sister's shoe soles?" As a train whistles in the background, he leaves, slamming the door. For both Hans and Uschi, family life presents an obstacle to personal ambition.

In *Die Halbstarken,* the Borchert household is ruled by a domineering father, who blames his wife for a failed investment in her brother's business. When he discovers that Jan has seen Freddy, Herr Borchert declares, "You will no longer meet Alfred, not even 'by chance'! If he can't conform to the social order, he can go ahead and lead his life however he wants. It's not my concern anymore." Disowning his older son, he soon commands the younger one to leave home as well. Herr Borchert is not, however, the only adult male to fail the postwar generation. The house porter Prillinger (Egon Vogel, who also plays a druggist in *Eine Berliner Romanze*) is only too willing to sell Freddy an old gun, the very prop that precipitates his downfall. As for the fatherless Sissy, her young though weary mother hangs laundry in the courtyard. When Sissy arrives, she scolds her, "Can't you ever stay at home when I have a big load of laundry? It's really terrible with you!"

The premature independence, even arrogance, of *Die Halbstarken*'s teenagers bespeaks a disdain for a society of hypocritical role models. As Freddy reassures Jan about a stolen car, "Other people do worse things! You have to read the newspaper. You're old enough! Chiefs of police . . . mayors. . . . Just recently they even caught a district court judge!" Though not explicit, these more general indictments of authority resonate with continuities of National Socialism in postwar public life. At the Palladium event in spring 1956, Buchholz reflected a cynicism similar to that of his character when he reminded the audience of *Halbstarken* that they had lived through the last days of the war and spent the early postwar years providing for their families.[91]

In their efforts to examine the causes of *Halbstarken* attitudes, Klein and Kohlhaase similarly condemned the moral ambiguity of adult characters in *Berlin—Ecke Schönhauser.* While Angela's mother, a war widow who "doesn't want anything that hurts anymore," sends her daughter out of their one-room apartment twice a week to spend time alone with her married boss, Kohle's alcoholic stepfather beats the boy regularly. Echoing an outdated rhetoric of order and obedience, he effectively drives Kohle onto the streets and into West Berlin cinemas. Hedging their bets on the future of the FRG, Karl-Heinz's bourgeois parents maintain bank accounts in the West and hardly qualify as exemplars of "the workers' and farmers' state." Dieter's parents died in the war; his older brother and guardian, a *Volkspolizist,* has trouble communicating with him. Stubbornly individualistic, Dieter feels constrained by the collective strictures of GDR society and asks, "Why do you guys have so many rules and regulations? If I stand on the corner, I'm a rowdy. If I dance the boogie, I'm American. And if don't tuck my shirt in my pants, it's politically incorrect." Whether in the East or the West, these young skeptics expose the faulty foundation of their new societies, a German past embedded (like the undetonated bomb at Dieter's construction site) in the soil of the city.

In *Endstation Liebe*, the motherless Mecky shares an apartment with his father. Their caregiving roles reversed, Mecky comes and goes as he pleases. Publicity materials for prospective exhibitors provided an extensive sociological explanation for his wise-cracking veneer:

> But why is he like this? Born in 1936. An A+ in school for recycling old paper, an ugly scar on his leg from fire bomb ashes, at fourteen a crack black marketeer of American cigarettes; today he has experienced everything for which his father needed twice as many years. Mecky knows everything, can do everything. Mecky is always on the ball.[92]

Though this background surfaces nowhere in the film, it reveals a common perception of the bitter life events of young people, particularly of men in their early twenties, who had already experienced National Socialism, de-Nazification, occupation, division, and the transition from postwar scarcity to the promises of East or West German reconstruction. The slight age difference between the male and female actors and protagonists in these films brings the contours of this evolving intergenerational tension into relief. Even the fatherless but financially better off Christa is stifled by her family's petty bourgeois ambitions. Though the antithesis to Sissy's teen femme fatale, she, too, seeks autonomy outside the home.

In all four films, the streets offer love, adventure, and freedom. Converting public spaces into private ones, the couples Uschi and Hans, Angela and Dieter, and Christa and Mecky map romantic itineraries onto Berlin's busiest and most marginal terrain. A stroll through the city, the *Spaziergang*, functions as the prelude to a binding relationship or, in the case of Angela and Dieter, to sexual consummation.

Whereas home life demanded order and restraint, German young people could express themselves differently beyond the confines of "family, school, church congregation, and youth organization." Urban life abounded in opportunities for spectacle and embodied thrills, and in the protective atmosphere of "commercially mediated public spaces like cinemas, bars, ice cream parlors, soda shops, etc.," 1950s youths could gather "with little regulation."[93] While Uschi visits the cinema, a carnival, and a boxing match in the West, Freddy and his gang transform a café into a dance hall during an extended rock 'n' roll sequence. In this truly indulgent interruption of the narrative, the camera captures the actors' swinging hips, clapping hands, and intricate footwork for a full two minutes. At

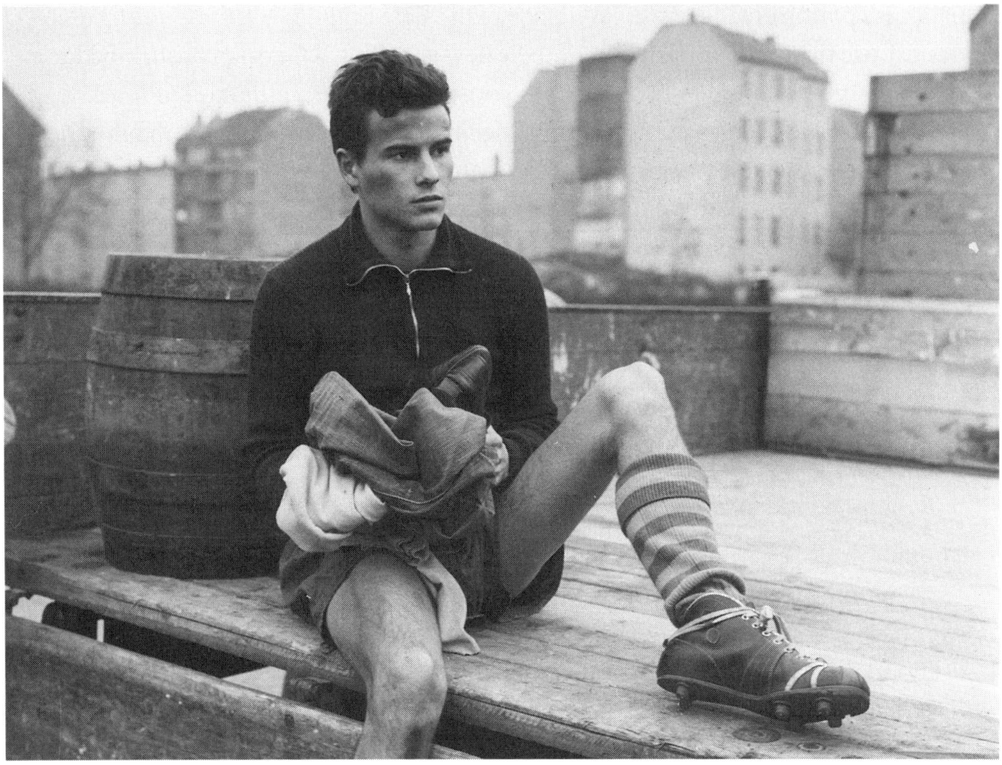

Mecky, brash and vulnerable, against a backdrop of prewar buildings in *Endstation Liebe*. Courtesy of Deutsche Kinemathek.

one point Freddy, clad in shiny, black leather pants reminiscent of Elvis Presley, grins conspiratorially and winks at the camera. Though loosely aligned with Sissy's perspective, surely this privileged repartee with Buchholz was meant for an audience that could appreciate the music, the motion, the gesture, and the star. A similar musical transformation of space occurs at the staged wrestling *(Catcher)* match in *Endstation Liebe*. To calm an unruly, disappointed crowd, the venue proprietors play a rock 'n' roll record that, instead, incites the younger spectators to leap onto their chairs and into the wrestling ring. Anticipating the Bill Haley concert riots later in 1958, this long interlude depicts a pleasure-seeking German youth of unbridled physicality.

Even *Berlin—Ecke Schönhauser* features a dance sequence. Though shot in East Berlin's Prater on Kastanienallee, one of the many streets merging into Schönhauser corner, it presents precisely the type of modern dancing and Western dress disavowed by the East's Committee for German Unity: "The young workers of the German Democratic Republic show, however, little understanding for Americanised 'jam sessions,' 'spivvy' [*sic*] clothing and so on, and they themselves take

Dancing in *Berlin—Ecke Schönhauser* (*above*; photograph by Holstein, Schneider, courtesy of the DEFA-Stiftung) and *Endstation Liebe* (*below*; courtesy of Deutsche Kinemathek).

steps to prevent any such activities in public places."[94] Although several critics complained of the scene's length, its inclusion in the film both strengthens the interfilmic alliance between the DEFA and Inter West productions and reclaims Americanized dancing as an acceptable activity for East German youths.

The films' teenagers find in the city streets the space and privacy lacking in postwar housing conditions. Turning their backs on home, they seek alternatives to their work lives and limited means in urban entertainments and in their cliques. The presence of groups of young people in public, the very corner loiterers *(Eckensteher)* to whom Dieter referred, provokes scenes of collective adult censure in both *Die Halbstarken* and *Berlin—Ecke Schönhauser.* Tressler and Tremper, clearly attempting to mollify their detractors, made comical use of the gang's mascot and aspiring *Halbstarke,* little Wölfi (Wolfgang Heyer), to convey divergent generational values. Hoping to participate in the evening's criminal activities, Wölfi approaches Freddy, Jan, and Günther (Jo Herbst) in a brand-new striped blazer. When Freddy mocks his "carnival jacket," Wölfi insists, "But Freddy, it's my best piece. I put it on especially for tonight!" In a display of his absolute power, Freddy then challenges the boy to throw the jacket away. Wölfi obliges instantly, tossing it into the street and even kicking it.

As he glances proudly back at Freddy, a middle-aged woman enters the frame and grabs Wölfi's arm. "Hey! Now you pick that . . . get the jacket, you little louse, you!" The older boys laugh as a small, indignant crowd forms. One man asks, "What's going on here?" to which a woman replies, "Didn't you see it? He just threw away a perfectly good jacket!" The older boys leave Wölfi at the mercy of the gathering and proceed to steal a car. The episode's punch line comes when the car runs over the jacket. As the angry adults look on, Wölfi picks it up and walks off crying.

This scene served as a sociological centerpiece for Tressler and Tremper's ploy to temper the thrill of juvenile delinquency with an appropriate measure of adult disapproval. An excerpt of dialogue from the scene even appeared in *Süddeutsche Zeitung* prior to the film's release as evidence of *Die Halbstarken*'s serious, nonexploitative agenda.[95] In their screenplay, Tressler and Tremper elaborated this dialogue into a chorus of baffled voices across gender and class boundaries:

ENERGETIC WOMAN: A little guy like that should be brought directly to the police. Couldn't his mother take better care of him?

WORKING WOMAN: What, when she's stuck at work like me?

MAN IN SPECTACLES: Come on, there are millions of good kids—it's always the minority that stands out.

WOMAN SELLING FRUIT: You know, if a boy like that had a proper upbringing, this kind of thing wouldn't happen.

Wölfi's action provokes disapproval from the older generation in *Die Halbstarken*. Frame still.

> MAN IN SPECTACLES: Sometimes there aren't any parents, and sometimes they simply just don't bother enough! Then the children seek out their own diversion. You can imagine where that leads.[96]

Though this more extensive set of conjectures does not survive in the film's final version, the critique of the parental, wartime generations persists in the figure of Herr Borchert. Having dismissed all social responsibility for his sons, he acknowledges them only when it is already too late: "My sons—Freddy and Jan."

Berlin—Ecke Schönhauser's answer to Wölfi's jacket pointedly replaced the destruction of private goods with the vandalism of public property. As young East Berliners sing and dance beneath the U2 tracks, an older worker comments, "They don't know what to do with their energy!" Karl-Heinz dares Kohle to smash a street lamp, to which Kohle replies, "What's it worth to you?" When Karl-Heinz offers him one East German mark, he counters that it would not even cover the price of a film ticket, presumably in the West. With the wager raised to "one West mark," Kohle finally agrees. He shatters the bulb with a stone, and glass falls on the head of a passerby. Immediately, pedestrians rush at the boys, "You guys are crazy!" A woman runs into the group and tries to hit Kohle. "Man, you, louse, you! Somebody should slap you right away, you!" The *Volkspolizei,* among them Dieter's brother, arrive almost instantly, and a growing crowd looks on as the teenagers are led to the police station.

Despite variations in the destroyed object and the degree of public response, both scenes reflected the all-German postwar sentiment that willful damage to property ran counter to the logic of reconstruction. The widespread loss of one or both parents in the war invested those adults who had survived with a more collective, public disciplinary role. Whereas these representatives of German values and social order resisted the changed styles and mannerisms of the postwar youths, the younger generation, hardened by a childhood of rubble and ruins, sought quick routes to economic success in peacetime.

Berlin—Ecke Schönhauser's young people posing in character under the U-Bahn after Kohle breaks the lamp. Publicity still. Photograph by Holstein, Schneider. Courtesy of the DEFA-Stiftung.

West Berlin and its open door to American popular culture prove fertile ground for teen dreams in the DEFA and Inter West films. Geographical and moral transgressions are mere means to an end. In *Eine Berliner Romanze,* Uschi seeks the kind of fame that only the West can provide; the struggling Hans, who regrets his lapsed boxing career, recalls the thwarted ambitions of Marlon Brando's character in *On the Waterfront.* In *Die Halbstarken,* Freddy's fantasies of a bourgeois lifestyle include the purchase of a Buick. He assures the greedy Sissy, "Once I'm on top, you can have whatever you want from me: a villa, fur coats, diamonds." For her part, Sissy is quick to identify with the wealth and glamour of movie stardom. In response to Jan's confusion about the spelling of her name with an *i* or a *y,* she asserts, "With *y*—like Romy." Aligning herself with the popular young actress Romy Schneider (who would appear in two films with Buchholz in 1957), Sissy also alludes, in her name, to Schneider's role in Ernst Marischka's successful *Sissi* costume trilogy (1955–57) about a princess who becomes the empress of Austria.[97]

In *Berlin—Ecke Schönhauser,* Dieter dreams of owning a motorcycle. He asks Angela what kind of men she likes, to which she responds, "Doctors and boxers." When he presses her further, "I mean how they look," she replies, "Like Marlon Brando." Although he is no Brando, Dieter maintains his independence at work, prompting the company FDJ leader to compare him to Tarzan. Proud of the one hundred or more films he has seen in the West, Kohle imagines life as a cinematic adventure and proposes that he and Dieter travel abroad. In *Endstation Liebe,* Mecky and Christa sit in their truck in a West Berlin junkyard fantasizing about international travel and famous friends: "To Italy, to Spain, or to the Riviera to visit Grace Kelly. . . . Then maybe Africa, Morocco . . . and then a little bit of the South Seas." Immobile in their broken vehicle and gazing through the windshield, a makeshift screen, Mecky invites Christa to America to visit Louis Armstrong. These projected geographies, known from the cinema and illustrated magazines, offer to transport the films' characters and their spectators beyond Berlin's circumscribed political borders.

While the young people in all four films fall short of their goals and must instead settle for the law and love, their Berlin audiences could leave the theater with dreams intact. Travel to exotic locales was as real as the next film, and sudden stardom, both 1950s German film industries would have teen girls believe, was waiting in the next newspaper advertisement. Like Karin Baal, the lead actresses Annekathrin Bürger, Ilse Pagé, and Barbara Frey were all chosen from the Berlin masses.[98]

Eine Berliner Romanze, Die Halbstarken, Berlin—Ecke Schönhauser, and *Endstation Liebe* mirrored the social reality of Berlin's postwar generation but also

Dreams that money can buy in *Eine Berliner Romanze* (*above*; photograph by Waltraut Pathenhaimer, courtesy of the DEFA-Stiftung) and *Die Halbstarken* (*below*; frame still).

preserved their fantasies—imagined futures cut short by political events. Paradoxically, the efforts of Klein and Kohlhaase to distinguish DEFA teen films from West German and U.S. features ensured that *Eine Berliner Romanze* and *Berlin—Ecke Schönhauser* would remain in dialogue with these over time. With their notable presences and absences, the 1950s Berlin films of Klein, Kohlhaase, Tressler, and Tremper archive information about the city's unique prewall culture. A rediscovery of the films is the rediscovery of shared urban experience. Film revival, then, becomes a means of tracing historical development, of making sense of the New Berlin through the city's earlier contiguity.

A GENERATION RECLAIMS ITS CITYSCAPE

Since their initial release, the films have reappeared at significant moments in Berlin's history; *Berlin—Ecke Schönhauser* and *Die Halbstarken,* often remembered together, have become popular revivals within and beyond the postwall city. Retrospection of DEFA films has, however, remained contentious in the unified Federal Republic as the polarities of Cold War film historiography and cultural memory gradually give way to more inclusive formulations of the German past.

At the turn of the millennium, historian Irmgard Wilharm warned against the direct comparisons between the GDR dictatorship and the FRG democracy that Germany's dual film histories might promote. Instead, she advocated an approach of "asymmetrical integration" that would acknowledge the divergent developments of the two German states and the imperfect parallelism between compared elements.[99] The long reception of the 1950s Berlin films merits similar caution. When, for example, both populations celebrated a first wave of nostalgia for the 1950s in the late 1970s and 1980s, the occurrence signaled a shared need to assess their states' respective postwar accomplishments but also drew important distinctions between the East and West German experience of the intervening years.

In 1978, *Berlin—Ecke Schönhauser* toured East German cinemas as one of thirty films commemorating more than thirty years of DEFA production. The postwar generation greeted the film fondly, and numerous critics infused their reviews with personal memories of the prewall city. Jutta Voigt recalled her own border-crossing youth and praised the film for retaining "so much Berlin-feeling, realism, fidelity to details, and precision of conflict through the years."[100] In 1985, Hannes Schmidt reminisced that the film had been one of the most meaningful of his youth and claimed that one could still find the East Berlin of the 1950s in the contemporary city.[101] Written decades after the construction of the Berlin Wall, such comments were bittersweet, identifying youth and young adulthood with lost mobility.

Peter Kahane, a filmmaker of DEFA's last generation who is best known for his critical East Berlin drama *Die Architekten* (*The Architects,* GDR 1990), responded cinematically to this retrospective melancholy surrounding Klein and Kohlhaase's film. In his own youth film, *Vorspiel* (*Ready for Life,* GDR 1987), set in the provincial town of Schönebeck, a young *Halbstarke* stands in front of a sign for the communal cinema Aktivist and asks, "What's a 'retro-spec-tive'?" The cinema is where the local teenagers, including Tom (Hendrik Duryn) and his crush, Corinna (Susanne Hoss), flee for some autonomy from the adult world and its proscriptions. As the two rehearse backstage for their upcoming drama school auditions in East Berlin, a scene from *Berlin—Ecke Schönhauser* plays in the background. Later in the film, Corinna's father (Hermann Beyer), a former rowdy, lies in bed with an old girlfriend, who has just asked him to play a 1950s record "again." As the doo wop ballad trills the English "night after night," he reminds her of the "jeans and Elvis pompadour" that had scandalized socialist authorities when they were in school. Though he has found his place in East German society, and though Schönebeck's new teenagers have the mopeds and motorcycles that Dieter could only imagine, there is something wistful in Kahane's comparison. After all, the young people ride only to the edge of town, and the GDR of the 1980s seems to have youth rebellion on repeat and under control.

Though the 1950s influenced West German retro youth fashions of the 1980s, the decade's films had generally been dismissed by the reigning directors of the Young and New German Cinema and consistently undervalued by film historians.[102] Western responses to the revival of *Die Halbstarken* combined affirmative memories of West German reconstruction *(Wiederaufbau)* with an awareness of youth culture's leftist social critique of the late 1960s and 1970s. In 1981, Manuela Reichart of *Die Zeit* could relish a feminist rediscovery of Karin Baal's ruthless young vixen as well as the material objects of the Adenauer era, "black-and-white striped club chairs and the handheld hole puncher at the lotto counter."[103] In the 1990s, the West German film industry's principal contribution to the rebel film genre and to the myth of a larger West German youth movement could provide, as Jürgen Felix would argue, a historical orientation for young people lacking authentic ties to the origins of protest culture.[104]

In 1987, during the all-German 750th anniversary of Berlin, all four DEFA and Inter West youth films were once again explicitly aligned with the city. While both *Eine Berliner Romanze* and *Berlin—Ecke Schönhauser* screened in the State Film Archive's series *Berlin im Film—Film in Berlin* (Berlin in Film—Film in Berlin), one of several East Berlin retrospectives that would tour the entire GDR, *Die Halbstarken* and *Endstation Liebe* appeared in West Berlin's *Berlin und das Kino* (Berlin and the Cinema).[105] As public reminders of a Wall-less Berlin, the films could both prompt the reflection of those who had crossed its 1950s sector boundaries and instruct new generations in the spatial limitations of their more concretely and irrevocably divided city. As institutions in both halves of Berlin competitively recounted the city's history, albeit from biased perspectives, their asymmetric cultural capital revealed complementary forms of incompleteness. Though very few filmgoers, and only those from the West, would have been in the position to gain an overview of both retrospective programs, the Berlin youth films might be seen as place-markers of their absent counterparts. A longing for lost geographies required a figurative and perhaps furtive glance across the Wall.

After the *Wende,* DEFA films became artifacts of an endangered, illegitimate cultural heritage subsumed by the Federal Republic. In 1992, DEFA was dissolved as an independent entity, its Babelsberg studios sold off to the French conglomerate Compagnie Générale des Eaux (CGE), their directorship in the hands of Western New German cineaste Volker Schlöndorff.[106] At first, political unification seemed to promise new opportunities for DEFA's film catalog within broader German culture. In 1990, the Berlinale shone its international, A-list spotlight on the famous forbidden films *(Kaninchenfilme)* of the 1965–66 production year; among them was Klein and Kohlhaase's fourth Berlin collaboration, *Berlin um die Ecke* (*Berlin, Around the Corner,* GDR 1965/1990), which extended the rebel generation's social criticism to the workplace. The films' delayed reception in the Western festival's acclaimed category International Forum of New Cinema (known for its discovery of fresh, young talent and challenging aesthetics) catalyzed "a feeling of bitterness, bitterness about the loss that the creative potential of [the GDR] had suffered, about the loss of imagination, of critical edge."[107] As East German filmmakers and filmgoers came to terms with these features' suppressed efforts at social reform, West German film culture had to confront the sudden expansion of the FRG's filmography. The films of the Cold War opponent had become, overnight, the unexpected archival and cultural political responsibility of the Federal Republic.

The rise of the Berlin Republic and its attendant construction boom and changing capital image required the careful management and validation of multiple urban pasts. As its central neighborhoods and former border zones grew more integrated and attracted a new, post–Cold War expat community fascinated by communist culture, Eastern and Western archival views of Berlin became staples of the city's unified exhibition landscape. This interest in DEFA's film heritage was rather exceptional in the greater FRG, where so few East German features were known.

In the late 1990s, the DEFA-Stiftung (DEFA Foundation) and its distribution partner Progress-Film-Verleih as well as video and DVD distributor ICESTORM

Entertainment began working to safeguard and publicize the hundreds of features, documentaries, animated films, and shorts that the studios had produced over nearly five decades. As products of a dictatorship that had meddled in all levels of media and artistic creation, these films appeared tainted both to Western audiences and to many former Eastern critics of GDR society. In a 2001 issue of the East-inflected *Beiträge zur Film- und Fernsehwissenschaft,* scholars pondered, "DEFA Film as National Cultural Heritage?" Giving voice to a widespread wariness of East German cinema, political scientist Klaus Finke questioned the extent to which positive memories of the GDR should be encouraged through its film legacy. Instead, he advocated screenings that connected the films to public debates about the SED regime and demanded that a contextualization of the films' politicized aesthetics should override their purely formal or nostalgic celebration.[108]

For the institutions charged with their protection and future all-German cultural value, such a critique could only be useful if the films were to have opportunities to become known in the first place. Appealing for widespread support of DEFA heritage, Jürgen Haase of Progress asked, in the same year,

> What does the repertory film need?
>
> Brave distributors, theater owners, and institutions, unusual concepts for ensuring that film classics aren't forgotten. Political and financial support (for the sake of cultural identity) that, after all, represents a country and, in the European context, a shared responsibility like, for example, a European distribution and cinema initiative dedicated to the repertory film.[109]

Without new audiences and new screening contexts, even DEFA's revival hits, often poised between socialist kitsch and criticism of the system, could foster no future nostalgia.

Klein and Kohlhaase's 1950s Berlin films counted among a rare number of DEFA titles that film programmers could consistently schedule. In Berlin in particular, postmillennial revival venues and small, independent cinemas *(Programmkinos)* such as the Arsenal (now arsenal institut für film und videokunst e.V.), Filmkunsthaus Babylon (now Babylon Mitte), Lichtblick, Blow Up, Nickelodeon, Central, BrotfabrikKino, Börse, and, later, the Deutsches Historisches Museum's Zeughauskino, mostly in the former East or close to the border, regularly presented DEFA films and Berlin-themed retrospectives. While *Berlin—Ecke Schönhauser* was screened in the 2001 series, *Brennpunkt—Mauer im Film* (Focal Hotspot: The Berlin Wall in Film) and the 2003 series *Berlin—Prenzlauer Berg,* the Berlinale showed *Eine Berliner Romanze* in 1991 and 2006. Addressing a dual clientele of ostalgic Easterners and younger, new arrivals from the West and abroad, Berlin's cinemas (re)introduced postwall spectators to the emotional topography of East–West border crossing.

As the DEFA Berlin films, particularly *Berlin—Ecke Schönhauser,* became mainstays of the city's revival houses, *Die Halbstarken* and *Endstation Liebe* were broadcast regularly on the Federal Republic's expanded cable television system. With extensive runs on both Filmpalast and Premiere Nostalgia from 2000 to 2005, Tressler and Tremper's youth films circulated as hallmarks of Horst Buchholz's early career, of Adenauer era cinema, and of 1950s Berlin.[110] When Bernd Eichinger, a proponent of (West) German cinema's more commercial camp, produced a series of "German Classics" for television in the mid-1990s, a remake of *Die Halbstarken* (The hooligans, FRG 1996) was among them. Offered the role of Herr Borchert to Til Schweiger's Freddy, Buchholz refused, claiming that he would have betrayed his generation and its investment in his *Halbstarken* persona.[111] Through this gesture, the actor not only acknowledged a collective identification with the film; he also articulated the fragility, indeed preciousness, of a generation's mediated, heroic vision of itself.

Despite the New Berlin's vibrant revival culture, contact between East and West German filmographies remained limited in the early 2000s. Like the Deutsches Historisches Museum's exhibit on the nation's division, the physical layout of which required visitors to pass through East and West German versions of history separately to gain an overview of both, film historians and programmers within and beyond Germany were initially reluctant to explore the aesthetic, social, political, and historical conversations that integrated retrospectives might provoke. The Museum of Modern Art's successful traveling film series, the West German *After the War, before the Wall* (2003), and the East German *Rebels with a Cause* (2005) were a case in point. With few exceptions, scholars and film institutions at the time upheld cinema's Cold War borders or, at best, encouraged reenactments of filmographic and ideological standoffs. As the city that had belonged to both Germanys and that was evolving daily before the eyes of its postwall inhabitants, Berlin and its wider mediated image posed a challenge to film retrospective politics. In the refurbished capital, but also in the greater FRG, it was advantageous to present evidence of harmonious urban wholeness and East–West contact, mutual desire, and camaraderie. Seen together, the DEFA and Inter West Berlin youth films of the 1950s reveal a larger geographical story, one that resides within and between the built city, its filmic representations, and its film cultures. As the Klein–Kohlhaase and Tressler–Tremper films returned to the city's cinemas, Berlin, the common ground of prewall all-German culture, could once again—through images—become *ours.*

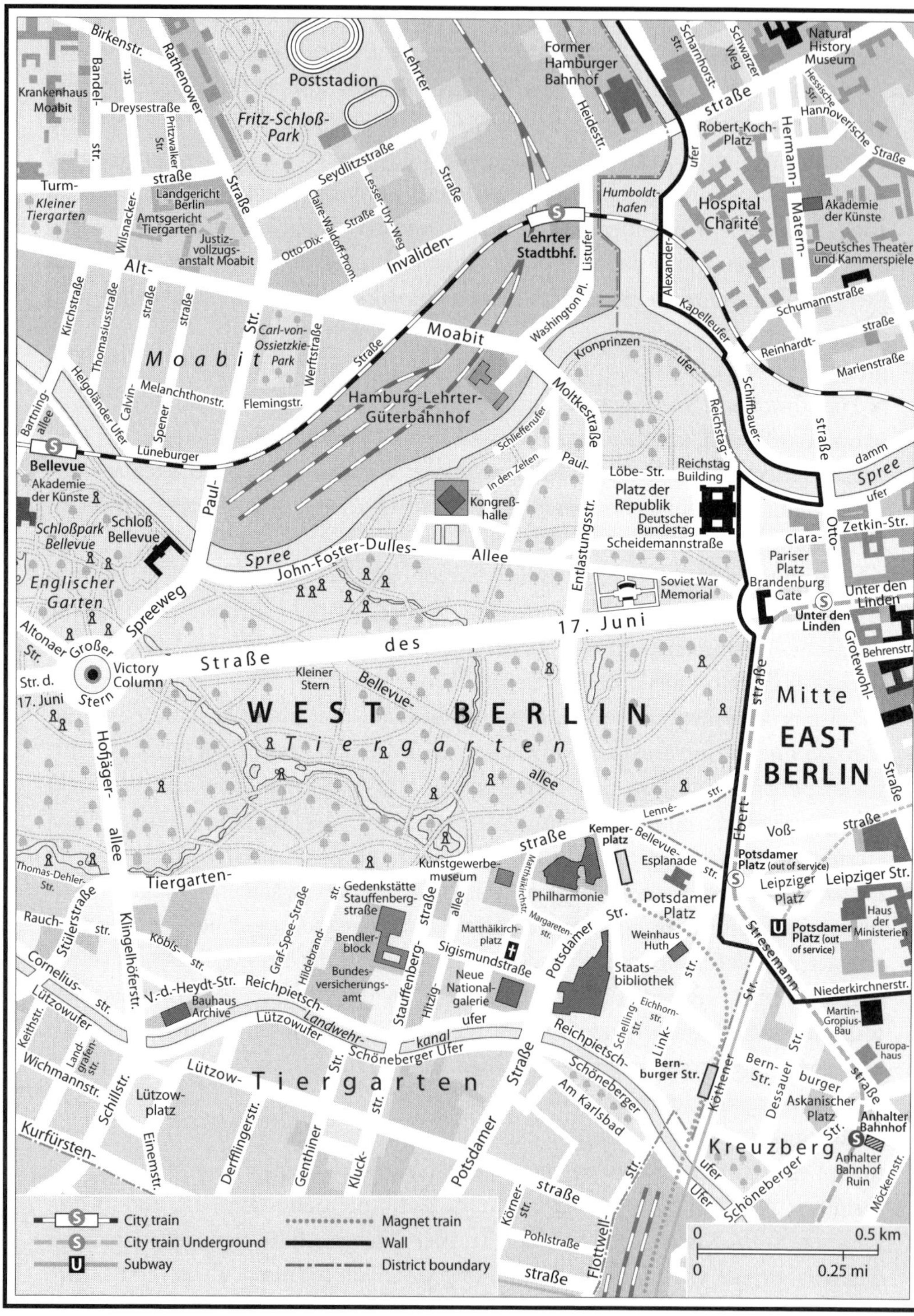
Birkenstr.
Bandel-
str.
Rathenower
Straße
Poststadion
Fritz-Schloß-
Park
Lehrter
Straße
Former
Hamburger
Bahnhof
Heidestr.
Scharnhorst-
str.
Schwarzer
Weg
Natural
History
Museum
Hessische
Str.
Hannoversche
Straße
Krankenhaus
Moabit
Dreysestraße
Pritzwalker
Str.
Turm-
straße
Kleiner
Tiergarten
Wilsnacker-
str.
Landgericht
Berlin
Amtsgericht
Tiergarten
Justiz-
vollzugs-
anstalt Moabit
Seydlitzstraße
Lesser-Ury-Weg
Claire-Waldoff-Prom.
Otto-Dix-
Straße
Invaliden-
straße
Humboldt-
hafen
Lehrter
Stadtbhf.
Listufer
Robert-Koch-
Platz
Hermann-
Matern-
Straße
ufer
Hospital
Charité
Akademie
der Künste
Deutsches Theater
und Kammerspiele
Schumannstraße
Reinhardt-
straße
Marienstraße
Alexander-
ufer
Kapelleufer
Alt-
Moabit
Kirchstraße
Thomasiusstraße
Calvin-
straße
Moabit
Str.
Carl-von-
Ossietzkie-
Park
Werftstraße
Washington Pl.
Kronprinzen
ufer
Helgoländer Ufer
Melanchthonstr.
Flemingstr.
Hamburg-Lehrter-
Güterbahnhof
Moltkestraße
Reichstag-
ufer
Schiffbauer-
damm
Bartning-
allee
Spener
Lüneburger
Bellevue
Akademie
der Künste
Schleifenufer
In den Zelten
Paul-
Löbe- Str.
Platz der
Republik
Reichstag
Building
Deutscher
Bundestag
Scheidemannstraße
Spree
ufer
Schloßpark
Bellevue
Schloß
Bellevue
Paul-
Kongreß-
halle
Entlastungsstr.
Clara-
Zetkin-Str.
Otto-
Pariser
Platz
Brandenburg
Gate
Unter den
Linden
Spree
John-Foster-Dulles-
Allee
Englischer
Garten
Spreeweg
Soviet War
Memorial
Altonaer
Str.
Großer
Stern
Victory
Column
Straße
des
17. Juni
Behrenstr.
Grotewohl-
Str. d.
17. Juni
Kleiner
Stern
Bellevue-
allee
WEST BERLIN
Tiergarten
Ebert-
straße
Mitte
EAST
BERLIN
Straße
Hofjäger-
allee
Lenné-
str.
Voß-
straße
Thomas-Dehler-
Str.
Tiergarten-
straße
Kemper-
platz
Bellevue-
str.
Esplanade
Potsdamer
Platz (out of service)
Leipziger
Platz
Leipziger Str.
Kunstgewerbe-
museum
Matthäikirch-
str.
Philharmonie
Potsdamer
Platz
Haus
der
Ministerien
Rauch-
str.
Stülerstraße
Klingelhöferstr.
Köbis-
str.
Graf-Spee-Straße
Hildebrand-
str.
Gedenkstätte
Stauffenberg-
straße
Bendler-
block
Stauffenberg-
straße
allee
Margareten-
str.
Matthäikirch-
platz
Sigismundstraße
Potsdamer
Str.
Weinhaus
Huth
Potsdamer
Platz (out
of service)
Stresemann-
str.
Niederkirchnerstr.
Cornelius-
str.
Lützowufer
V.-d.-Heydt-Str.
Bauhaus
Archive
Reichpietsch-
ufer
Bundes-
versicherungs-
amt
Hitzig-
Neue
National-
galerie
Staats-
bibliothek
Eichhorn-
str.
Schelling-
str.
Link-
str.
Martin-
Gropius-
Bau
Keithstr.
Land-
grafen-
str.
Landwehr-
kanal
Schöneberger Ufer
Reichpietsch-
ufer
Bern-
burger Str.
Köthener
Europa-
haus
Wichmannstr.
Schillstr.
Lützow-
platz
Lützow-
Tiergarten
Str.
Straße
Schöneberger
Am Karlsbad
Bern-
burger
Str.
Dessauer
Str.
Askanischer
Platz
Anhalter
Bahnhof
Kurfürsten-
Einemstr.
Derfflingerstr.
Genthiner
Kluck-
str.
Potsdamer
Kreuzberg
ufer
Schöneberger
Ufer
Anhalter
Bahnhof
Ruin
Möckernstr.
Körner-
str.
straße
Pohlstraße
straße
Flottwell-
str.
City train
City train Underground
Subway
Magnet train
Wall
District boundary
0
0.5 km
0
0.25 mi

Berlin 1987.

3

VIRTUALITY

Cinema, Archive, and the Interactive Map of Potsdamer Platz

A LAYERED VISION

At the Berlin International Film Festival in February 2001, a large display screen flanked the entrance to the Berlinale Palast, located at the point where Alte Potsdamer Straße runs into Marlene-Dietrich-Platz. At the top of the frame, journalists, festival guests, and fans encountered the simple question, "Do you remember?" Beneath the text was the still image of a construction site, labeled "Potsdamer Platz, 1994." Despite the square's widely circulating associations with the traffic and cosmopolitan entertainments of the Weimar metropolis and the urban rupture of the Berlin Wall, the city marketing firm Partner für Berlin GmbH was not asking passersby to recall these. Rather, its promotional montage initiated the festival's local and out-of-town visitors into a myth of architectural rebirth and invited them to marvel at the rapidity (only seven years!) with which a landscape of empty lots, death-strip scars, lone prewar buildings, and construction cranes had yielded the finished, new Potsdamer Platz beneath their feet.

Just one year earlier, the festival had relocated from its Cold War headquarters in (West) Berlin to Potsdamer Platz's more symbolic centrality, and only one month prior, Till Schneider and Michael Schumacher's giant, rectangular red INFO BOX (1995–2001), an information center dedicated to the past and future of the site, had been dismantled. If Potsdamer Platz had become "the primary visual symbol" in the New Berlin's place marketing strategies in the crucial years surrounding the government's move from Bonn to Berlin,[1] it was finally time for the remade square to begin functioning in its current built guise, without the crutches of mediated spatial memories and simulated, modeled futures.

Though Partner für Berlin's question may have been celebratory, its juxtaposition with postmodern surroundings also betrayed a perhaps latent cultural

Promotional montage from Partner für Berlin at the Berlinale. Video frame courtesy of the author, 2001.

anxiety regarding the sheer speed of Potsdamer Platz's and, for that matter, the city's transformation, one that recast sudden urban change and spatial disorientation as triumphal progress rather than traumatic loss. That year, the Berlinale itself provided the narrative glossing that the sleek, corporate, glass-and-metallic facades lacked. While Hubertus Siegert's *Berlin Babylon* (FRG 2001) probed the mystique of Berlin's 1990s construction sites *(Baustellen)* in the Panorama section, Manfred Wilhelms's six-hour documentary *Die Legende vom Potsdamer Platz* (*The Legend of Potsdamer Platz,* FRG 2001) explored the square's history in the International Forum of New Cinema. Two months later, just down the road, the Neue Nationalgalerie opened its exhibition, *Der Potsdamer Platz: Ernst Ludwig Kirchner und der Untergang Preußens* (Potsdamer Platz: Ernst Ludwig Kirchner and the downfall of Prussia). The new square hardly had to speak for itself.

Far more than any other place in Berlin, Potsdamer Platz has come to embody the city's dual ambivalence toward erasure and memory, the forgotten or selective pasts versus the overabundance of documentation that characterize its significant locations. At the turn of the millennium, and in the face of the city's construction boom, Paul Virilio and Andreas Huyssen reiterated, respectively, two of Berlin's popular descriptors: the "Tabula Rasa" and the "palimpsest." While Virilio invoked the mythical clean slate of 1945's zero hour *(Stunde Null)* as an ironic, retrospective convenience of aerial warfare for postwall urban planning and development, Huyssen's formulation of a "disparate city-text" with a "complex web of historical markers" attributed Berlin's singularity to its excessive and obsessive preservation of traces of the past amid all that was new.[2]

Even before the *Wende* of 1989–90, the period of political change that precipitated and followed the fall of the Berlin Wall, Potsdamer Platz and the adjacent, octagonal Leipziger Platz connoted histories that were only partially, if at all, visible in the marginal terrain and "disruptive power of an edge" separating East and West Berlin.[3] From the mid-eighteenth century onward, a western entrance to the recently expanded city limits, Potsdamer Platz could, a century later, boast its own train station, the Potsdamer Bahnhof, as well as the nearby Anhalter Bahnhof. By the late 1800s, hotels and cafés had helped to concretize the square's autonomy as a place, situated between the old city and its new West. A crowded bane of Berlin's traffic chaos in the 1920s, the bustling square nearly succumbed to Adolf Hitler's plans for "Welthauptstadt Germania," which included a massive north–south axis that would have diminished the Platz's importance as an intersection. Already in 1938, demolition crews began tearing down numerous buildings to clear the way.[4] While wartime destruction further altered the square's prewar built form, the initial 1961 construction and later reinforcement of the Wall effectively ended its continued function in the 1950s as a point of convergence, commerce, pleasure, and ideological exchange.

The gradual disappearance of Potsdamer and Leipziger Plätze's architectural infrastructure along and within the uncompromising Cold War boundary zone paradoxically accounted for the area's utility as a place of virtual and layered urban projections. As artist and architectural historian Matthias Pabsch has put it, the square's reputation increasingly relied on memory and images "no longer dependent on the effects of time."[5] Though Potsdamer Platz, with its Wall architecture, viewing platforms, border patrols, and flea markets, was never quite empty, devoid of purpose, or free of contemporary political symbolism, its notable absences and physical dissimilarity to the prewar square invited collective bouts of urban nostalgia for the 1920s. These filmic, photographic, and literary celebrations, which must also be understood as acts of mourning and convenient detours around responsibility for the square's destruction and bisection, emphasized lost architecture and tempo; the six hundred streetcars that used to run through the square each hour; the tourists arriving at Potsdamer Bahnhof; and the rich sensory experience of modern urban life.[6]

Potsdamer Platz in 1930, including, diagonally from the upper left, Anhalter Bahnhof, Haus Vaterland, Potsdamer Bahnhof, and Pschorr-Haus. Photograph by Ewald Gnilka. Courtesy of Landesarchiv Berlin.

At the same time, Potsdamer Platz's alignment with the Wall, another surface for projection as well as a persistent reminder of the two-world political standoff, ensured that the square would remain in the critical sights of West Germany's young, leftist filmmakers of the 1960s and 1970s, Eastern filmmakers during and after the *Wende,* and those wishing to draw attention to the clash of postwall xenophobia and nationalism with the influx of foreign labor, employed, sometimes illegally, to build this emblem of a new, united Germany. A line might be traced from Ulrich Schamoni's *Es* (*It,* FRG 1966), whose male protagonist, real estate agent Manfred (Bruno Dietrich), makes light of selling incongruous urban patches of land, to Helke Sander's *REDUPERS—Die allseitig reduzierte Persönlichkeit* (*The*

Potsdamer Platz in 1966 (photograph by Hans Seiler) and 1969 (photograph by Ludwig Ehlers). Some architectural skeletons were still visible then; intact images of the 1920s square supplied missing information. Courtesy of Landesarchiv Berlin.

All-Around Reduced Personality, FRG 1978), in which a group of female photographers hope to render the Wall and its implications more visible to apathetic West Berliners. In turn, the projections of archival footage of imperial, National Socialist, and Cold War militarism onto the Wall's western surface between Potsdamer Platz and the Brandenburg Gate in Jürgen Böttcher's *Die Mauer* (*The Wall,* GDR 1990) share concerns with Hito Steyerl's *Die leere Mitte* (*The Empty Center,* FRG 1998), which unearths, in Europe's largest construction site of the 1990s, the hidden, conflicting stories of Berlin's ethnic diversity and racism. The Wall's undeniable presence and unequivocal cartographic legibility could counteract Potsdamer Platz's erasures and voids; with its removal, the site lost one of its few temporal and spatial anchors. While the new Platz under construction would also catalyze competing strains of nostalgia and critique, planners, marketers, politicians, and builders selected what they considered the more appropriate historical continuities for the location: a combination of Weimar allusions and Cold War footnotes.

The events of the *Wende* quickly altered the future of Potsdamer Platz, as the square's voids and Cold War relegation to the eastern edge of West Berlin became its greatest postwall assets. After the opening of the East German border on November 9, 1989, and the unification of East and West Germany on October 3, 1990, the Bundestag decided, on June 20, 1991, to return the government to the unified capital of Berlin. In these years, Potsdamer Platz's now coveted real estate was sold to corporations such as Sony, Asea Brown Boveri, and Daimler-Benz subsidiary Debis, while the Berlin Senate's official planning competition for the area invited new, three-dimensional fantasies of what this undeveloped space could become.

Tasked with fulfilling an all-German *(gesamtdeutsch)* desire "for the revival of the city's traditional urban development, for merging together the sides of the Wall path, for a shared future in a city center capable of fostering a new identity,"[7] city planners and architects faced particularly high expectations for how the new Potsdamer Platz should relate to its preferred prewar legacy. Much scholarly criticism and public sentiment condemned the global, corporate, and Americanized aesthetic as well as the brazenly capitalist values of the square's emerging architecture.[8] At the same time, this resentment, shared among many of the city's inhabitants and visitors, arose in large part from a certain wistful conviction that the new Potsdamer Platz would "never match the myth of the square as an emblem of Weimar modernity."[9]

Conversely, Volker Hassemer, Berlin senator for urban development and environmental protection from 1991 to 1996, advised skeptics to get used to Berlin's new role as an important European capital. "The move of the parliament and the government to Berlin does not simply mean relocation," he warned. Far more, "the practices of a capital in the largest city in the country will be unlike those in the previous, very different location," the modest Rheinland city of Bonn. Hassemer predicted that citizens, organizations, German and international politicians, and financial representatives would have more opportunities in Berlin.[10] In his new capacity as chairman of the managing board of Partner für Berlin from 1996 to 2002, he could be explicit about the need to market and stage the city's future functions. Potsdamer Platz, with its conspicuous high-rise skyline of rounded facades and acute angularity designed by internationally renowned architects, could model these articulated urban aspirations in built space.

Poised between widespread attachment to an irrecoverable authenticity and bold promises of the city to come, the new Potsdamer Platz combined a selective acknowledgment of the past with the exhibition of big capital's architectural feats, an attraction for tourists. The square lies along the "memory district," a north–south route that leads from American architect Daniel Libeskind's Jewish Museum to the Topography of Terror at the Walter-Gropius-Bau, past the site of Hitler's former Reich Chancellery and the Monument to the Murdered Jews of Europe (designed by another American, Peter Eisenman) up to the Brandenburg Gate and the new government district.[11] Despite this proximity to Third Reich topographies, Potsdamer Platz itself predominantly cites events, places, objects, and names reminiscent of the Weimar era. While city building director Hans Stimmann advocated the controversial urban planning model of "critical reconstruction," meant to maintain visible, spatial continuities with Berlin's traditional, prewar planning and development, architects of the Debis complex hired a team of researchers to investigate the Platz's historical significance. The architects of Potsdamer Platz may have had some leeway with Stimmann's requirements, particularly with respect to building height, but even this uncharacteristic verticality resonated with a Weimar fascination with skyscrapers, captured in Fritz Lang's *Metropolis*. Predictably, the findings of the Debis Projektgruppe Potsdamer Platz generated a concept for future use, "life all around the clock," that could just as easily describe the 1920s square.[12]

Architects' choices, too, reflected this earlier incarnation of the location. Giorgio Grassi, working on the Asea Brown Boveri complex, retained the rounded form of a building on the site of the legendary entertainment venue Haus Vaterland, which once housed an array of culturally themed bars and cafés, a dance hall, and a cinema. Helmut Jahn incorporated the remains of the Kaisersaal of the grand Hotel Esplanade, built in the early twentieth century, into the Sony Center, while Renzo Piano's team attempted to minimize the abrupt stylistic transition between Richard Rodgers's Potsdamer Arkaden shopping mall and the contiguous, prewar Weinhaus Huth. The long, narrow Mendelssohn–Bartholdy Park marked the absence of Potsdamer Bahnhof as well as the still-present S-Bahn lines running through tunnels below.

Today a place predominantly of commerce, but also of culture, education, and tourism, Potsdamer Platz can easily be disregarded as "a mini-Vegas, a citational package,"[13] that merely speaks of history rather than revealing an organic clash of temporalities. Analyzed, however, as a physical expression of desired associations, of cultural political duty, and of cartographic commemoration of absence, the square becomes a far more nuanced exemplar of what might be termed Berlin's real *urban virtuality,* the multitemporal conflicts and moments of historical awareness yielded by quotidian, mobile encounters with the built city.

A replica of the original traffic tower, erected on the square in 1924, keeps time in five directions, even if it no longer regulates traffic. The streets bear the names of Weimar figures (the actress and émigré Marlene Dietrich, the Jewish writer Gabriele Tergit, and former Reich chancellor and foreign minister Gustav Stresemann) and noted antifascists like the American journalist Varian Fry. A monument to communist leader and antimilitarist Karl Liebknecht, assassinated in 1919, now occupies the space before the former site of the Haus Vaterland. A block away, at the entrance to Leipziger Platz, a hanging synthetic facade advertises a building that (still) does not yet exist. Over its faux entryway for many years read the words "Potsdamer Tor," a mnemonic gesture toward the stone guard and customs houses, vestiges of the western gate to the city, that suffered great damage during the Second World War and were eventually removed. The Cold War is visible in a modest line, the width of two cobblestones, cutting indiscriminately across sidewalks and streets until it runs into several segments of the Berlin Wall, repurposed props for touristic snapshots but also testaments to the dimensions, materials, and textures of decades of German and European division and to the symbolic point of departure for German unity. One might think of the current Platz as having concretized some of the invisible or mediated virtuality inherent in both the late Cold War square and the 1990s construction site.

Before and after the *Wende,* moving image media played an essential role in shaping public opinion and collective memories of Potsdamer Platz. This close alliance of place and audiovisual representation during a parallel technological turn—the rise of the personal computer; the Internet; and novel, digital means of organizing and storing data—suggests a productive disturbance between cinematic and new medial approaches to the square and to the problem of giving aesthetic form to profilmic urban virtuality. Between the release of Wim Wenders's *Der Himmel über Berlin* (*Wings of Desire,* FRG/France 1987), a narrative, cinematic attempt to depict (West) Berlin's "'double images' in time and space,"[14] and the earliest versions of Joachim Sauter and Dirk Lüsebrink's multimedia cartographic, architectural, and film archival project *The Invisible Shape of Things Past* (1995 to present), the imaginative exigencies of new construction discussed earlier dramatically changed the space in front of the camera and what exactly moving images of the square were recording, depicting, and preserving.

While Wenders's tale of urban angels, eternity, and the search for love premiered under the auspices of the city's 750th anniversary celebrations, which had seemed, at the time, an ultimate expression of East and West Berlin's political and geographic status quo, *The Invisible Shape of Things Past* appeared at a moment in which architectural simulations were remapping urban space and thus allowing virtual, imagined New Berlins to exist alongside sites of transformation. With the 1991 mandate to make the city "completely functional as the seat of parliament and government in ten to twelve years at the latest,"[15] the Bundestag effectively challenged Berlin's decision makers to gain control of its urban virtual contradictions. The historical proximity of Sauter and Lüsebrink's film archival maps of Potsdamer and Leipziger Plätze to Wenders's emotional, Cold War itinerary along the East–West border illustrates the fragility, but also the endurance, of Berlin's virtualities. These spatial myths, memories, and traditions have increasingly migrated from built space and even cinematic space and virtual reality to what Lev Manovich has termed "augmented space," physical space enhanced by an often multimedia realm of "dynamically changing information" usually "localized for each user."[16]

Cinematographic indexicality, the resemblance of the recorded image to the person, object, or place before the camera, links profilmic space to a variety of uses and means of contextualization from film narratives to larger informational structures of which moving images are only one element. Together Wenders's film and Sauter and Lüsebrink's project reflect a shift in virtual perceptions of Potsdamer Platz, one with long-term implications for how this controversial place is archived, remembered, and experienced.

URBAN VIRTUALITY AND MOVING IMAGES

Even before profilmic space is recorded and manipulated in postproduction, urban planning and development as well as sub- and countercultural movements bestow new uses and values on a given location and contribute to variously fluid and abrupt transitions in a place's cultural and political significance, popularity, or marginality. Owing to both the acceleration and the gravity of changes to its outward appearance in the twentieth and early twenty-first centuries, Potsdamer Platz has come to exhibit a paradigmatic, but also unusually dense, urban virtuality. The present place's perpetual concern with its past and future versions also foregrounds three competing, yet interlinked, antidotes to virtual clashes and conflicts in the cityscape: acquired knowledge, personal memory, and selective motion.

The first of these recalls Sigmund Freud's urban analogy for the human mind in his 1930 rumination on culture in *Civilization and Its Discontents.* Effectively imagining the mind as a collection of data in which "nothing which has been formed can perish" and in which "everything is somehow preserved," he suggests that, under certain conditions, earlier memories and behaviors can once again "be brought to light." To conceptualize this internal, multitemporal landscape of the mind, he turns to the palimpsest of Rome and asks what an informed observer might be able to deduce about the ancient city from contemplating its current guise. This ideal observer, armed with more insight than "present-day archaeology," should then be able to superimpose "the whole course of that [Servian] wall and the outline of Roma Quadrata" onto the contemporary cityscape. Despite these talents for reading into the ruins and reconstructions of the multilayered metropolis, the observer's abilities must necessarily fall short. After all, as Freud laments, "there is certainly not a little that is ancient still buried in the soil of the city or beneath its modern buildings."[17] That is to say, the built city has limitations as a metaphor for the mind's coexistent plethora.

Freud then posits a second, revised urban analogy, a city in which nothing, once built, can disappear. In this case, it is not the observer who must be knowledgeable about the past but rather the city that must display the simultaneous presence of all its architectural pasts. The observer need only shift his or her perspective "in order to call up the one view or the other." Freud ultimately abandons this imagined city as well by claiming, "If we want to represent the historical sequence in spatial terms we can only do it by juxtaposition in space," and then concluding, "the same space cannot have two different contents." Finally, he rejects his very notion of the city as an explanation for the mind, because even the most "peaceful" of cities experiences "demolitions and replacement of buildings."[18] Freud's recourse to the logic of physical reality in 1930 can obscure, however, the value of his insights for the later dawn of virtual and augmented reality.

Both versions of Rome—one requiring an erudite observer and the other defying the laws of space and time—imagine an interface between a visitor and a place in which historical knowledge is either brought to or gleaned from the encounter. While the tourist or archeologist of the analog era learned to interpret the signs of a place and of its history, today's digital database and emphasis on mobility both collect (centralize) and move (distribute) information. The Internet archive that now intersects and even communicates with place (particularly via GPS and a ubiquity of Quick Response codes) as a user moves through the city began, in the 1990s, to store historical images of place for access at a moment's notice on a desktop computer. Freud's impossible urban models harbor fantasies of unlimited access to past views—a knowledge of place that transcends temporal distance and personal experience. Like a mindscape, his Rome can never be lost.

A second approach to apprehending and managing urban virtuality is far more subjective. Contrary to an informed visitor, equipped with the objective facts of guidebooks and guided tours, or a site that bears legible traces of its own history, Walter Benjamin articulates the "native" flaneur's unique emotional and haptic relation to urban space in his review of Franz Hessel's 1929 collection *Spazieren in Berlin* (Strolling in Berlin). Importantly, it is motion *through* space that awakens memories in the subject. Unlike the tourist, the local flaneur, Benjamin suggests, travels "into the past, rather than to foreign parts," to construct an image of the city. Walking becomes a form of time travel as Hessel's footsteps "create an astounding resonance on the asphalt." Benjamin extends the temporal duality of this sound to the street lamps' "ambiguous light," shining on "this double floor." Invested with personal geography, individual memories linked to specific places in time, the city "conjures up more than" the flaneur's "childhood and youth, more than its own history."[19] Equipped with a sense of "having been there" and experiential, affectual knowledge of "how it feels," the native city dweller develops a far more intuitive and intimate understanding of place. In turn, this familiarity of subject and milieu allows the city to function as both "landscape" and "parlor," exterior and interior, endless extension and protective enclosure, for the flaneur, who would trade "all his knowledge of artists' quarters, birthplaces, and princely palaces for the scent of a single weathered threshold or the touch of a single tile."[20]

While Freud's visitor to Rome seeks ways to gather and preserve all of its material forms simultaneously, Benjamin's sketch of Hessel champions the immateriality of urban memories as much as the concrete edifices, materials, and locales that occasion them. As Frances Yates has observed in her work on the art of memory, architecture has as much to do with the immateriality of the architect's imagination and the subjective memory of its perceivers as with actual, three-dimensional buildings. Bound up with quotidian repetition, the spaces and objects of lived experience lend themselves to a "visual memorization" that can survive changes in a place's outward appearance.[21] The more rapid the change, the more intensely city dwellers might preserve memories of place.[22]

Potsdamer Platz, both in 1987 and after the *Wende,* was one of those Berlin places that had to be intuited, felt, remembered, and narrated. Full of strategies for remembering lost places, Vladimir Nabokov's reflections on emigration and his youth in Russia read like an instruction manual for cases of incurable nostalgia such as Berlin's. Like the mnemonic process by which his mother "cultivated an extraordinary consciousness of the various time marks distributed throughout" their "country place," personal and collective memories of the Weimar capital and the Cold War front city could be transferred between generations and stored "for the endurance of later losses" or, in the case of the Third Reich, as cautionary tales. The "intangible property, unreal estate" of these spatial memories could counteract erasure, demolition, restoration, renovation, and construction with selective urban virtualities, even where these were no longer legible ("a bunker," "the Wall," a "checkpoint").

Finally, the physical markers of history, combined with knowledge and memories of place, suggest degrees of desire and chance, but also of choice and manipulation, in the way that city dwellers move through the urban virtual landscape. To set out on a stroll is to open oneself not only to crowds, traffic, and new information but also to sudden, unexpected encounters with past autobiographical and civic events. Benjamin's flaneur is a particular kind of pedestrian, one with an insatiable interest in "images, wherever they lodge,"[23] but this hunger to discover the modern, visible world, to be attracted and acted upon, also risks unpredictable emotional revelations just around the corner.

Alternatively, walking can be a means of controlling (or regaining control of) urban space, of selecting routes for their particular histories, and of reviving or shunning others. Michel de Certeau has compellingly opposed walking and other "urban practices" to "discourses that ideologize the city."[24] Understanding walking as a "pedestrian speech act," he identifies three major outcomes of a subject's movement: "a process of *appropriation* of the topographical system," "a spatial acting-out of the place," and an implication of "*relations* among differentiated positions." In both the choice of route and the stylistic idiosyncrasies of its execution, the pedestrian "condemns certain places to inertia or disappearance and composes with others spatial 'turns of phrase' that are 'rare,' 'accidental,' or illegitimate."[25] In this way, city dwellers may opt for routes and spatial performances that disrupt, disregard, or recontextualize official acknowledgments of urban virtuality (e.g., running through or picnicking upon the stelae of the Monument to the Murdered Jews of Europe; skateboarding on or along communist monuments; or using the city's physical elements as a parkour course).

Both the flaneur's specific nostalgic tours and the pedestrian's control and potential repetition of routes activate a pleasure in pathways that can also be considered narrative. Just as one chooses a preferred genre based on its recurrent, anticipated features, one might select a route for its familiar sights and sensations. The subject's motivation may be "topophilic" in Yi-Fu Tuan's formulation of "all the human being's affective ties with the material environment." Preferred pathways might promise "aesthetic" and "tactile" enjoyment or comfortable, familiar patterns of home or the commute to work.[26] Each repetition of the route also, however, includes unforeseen details, requiring physical reactions and eliciting emotional responses: store displays, newspaper headlines, billboards, construction, traffic, playgrounds, and any number of unexpected obstacles. A mastery of the genre or route may still yield unique narrative characteristics, variations in plot and expression.

At first glance, the new Potsdamer Platz, with all its conspicuously choreographed self-reflection, seems to exemplify what M. Christine Boyer has termed the "City of Spectacle." In these thoroughly planned environments, "appropriations of historical styles and restaged scenographic allusions now become bounded nodes within an urban composition criss-crossed by highways and invisible electronic circuitry." Replete with simulations, the "posed and theatrically staged compositions" of such "designed milieus" can, with massive, eye-catching advertisements, reduce urban locations to "pure visual displays." City dwellers, caught in complicated articulations of time and space, "[travel] nostalgically backward through historic reconstructions" and project their "vision forward in futuristic travel adventures."[27] Certainly the large display screen in the immersive courtyard of the Sony Center; advertisements on the square's high buildings; the concentration of cinematic pasts and futures at the Filmhaus, the Berlinale, and the square's several cinemas; and the INFO BOX of the late 1990s would support this conclusion, though Potsdamer Platz hardly achieves the urban production values of New York's Times Square, Los Angeles's Staples Center, or the Las Vegas strip.

Making this comparison, however, assumes that the square's urban virtuality is only synthetic, only posed and re-created. During the late 1990s and early 2000s, Potsdamer Platz functioned, rather, as a lesson in urban rupture and incongruity and as a transient space of continuously morphing appearance and use. The walk or drive to the square from Leipziger Straße in the former East, from the Anhalter Bahnhof ruin up Stresemannstraße, or from Hans Scharoun's Kulturforum, an ensemble including the concert hall of the Berlin Philharmonic (1960–63) and the Staatsbibliothek (1967–78), required passage through a vaguely defined historical terrain that included a hodgepodge of architectural styles and remnants of the inner-Berlin border. Potsdamer Platz was a difficult place to get to, to maneuver past, and to loiter in, though the cinemas, the Potsdamer Arkaden, and one of the world's premiere film festivals provided incentives for cultural and recreational visits to this corporate node even before construction had ended and its new buildings were fully occupied.

More than Boyer's City of Spectacle, Potsdamer Platz, a place where dynamic change and contradictory "double floors" run into and up against efforts to control historical associations and merge divergent districts, enacts her "City of Collective Memory." Recognizing older "architectural residues" as "important sites of pleasure," Boyer suggests that "spectators" of a city must "establish a constant play between surface and deep structured forms, between purely visible and intuitive or evocative allusions," to "read across and through different layers and strata."[28] The City of Collective Memory combines the objective approach of Freud's observer with the more subjective vision of Benjamin's flaneur, all the while encouraging mobile perceivers of urban life to become (collectively) adept at reading between the buildings, at navigating temporal indeterminacy, or, for that matter, at remembering earlier stagings of a given site.

Motion through Berlin activates urban virtuality in a spatial and temporal sequence, much the way that moving images of a city activate the virtual urban experience of a stationary film spectator. Cinema's relationship to urban virtuality has numerous inflections, beginning with the camera's ability to record profilmic space and film and video's capacity for archiving these places in time. In addition, films can rescreen, in real time, places, buildings, and objects that no longer exist for a range of audiences in diverse formats and circumstances long after their moment of recording. These revivals reintroduce spectators to lost architecture and outmoded ideological framings as well as to the former social contexts and geographies of particular urban spaces.

Cinema's approximation of urban virtuality becomes clearest, however, in a film's discrete, unfolding route, a pathway of aesthetic logic and causal chains leading through on-screen spaces and diegetic worlds. Reconceptualizing cinema haptically, Giuliana Bruno refers to film as "a house of moving pictures" that is "as habitable as the house we live in."[29] What she seeks to establish is that films, like architecture, can be "tactilely apperceived by way of habit," an experience that relies on itineraries, a subject's mobility, and elements of texture.[30] Like Benjamin's flaneur, for whom the city is both landscape and living room, Bruno's spectator moves through an immersive, filmic map of emotional coordinates. "Viewing" a film thus becomes a means of acquiring mediated, multisensory spatial memories of imaginary places, real places never visited, and even places that have vanished. Lighting, focus, framing, sound, and editing construct unique atmospheric conditions for buildings, the characters who pass and inhabit them, and the spectators who encounter them virtually.

Excerpted from profilmic space, on-screen architecture and its formal presentation, whether in panoramic wide shots, in a rapid series of close-ups, or in slowly panning and tilting frames, concentrate spectators' attention on specific details and spatial passages. The architectural historian Anthony Vidler puts forth a provocative extension of Benjamin's claim, in "The Work of Art in the Age of Its

Technological Reproducibility," that architecture is consumed in a state of distraction, cinema in a state of critical reception. By this logic of modernity, Vidler suggests that architecture can only be made critical again by removing it from "its uncritically observed context, its distracted state," and returning it "to a now attentive public—that is, to make a film of the building."[31] As spectators wend their way through Bruno's emotional itineraries, they also attend to their temporary environment, the filmed buildings or landscapes, for that matter, that orient them in diegetic space and historical time, not only for the duration of the film but also in the greater world.

Because places and buildings are subject to processes of urban change, their filmed counterparts function as archives of location, preserved in duration, at a specific moment in history. These images thus participate in a triangulation of competing spatial information between constantly changing built space, the historically specific profilmic space cited in the film, and other, equally referential footage of the place from a variety of periods in the history of moving images. The resulting *aura of discrepancy* that much narrative, but also archival nonfiction footage, of Berlin acquires is crucial to the city's repeated grand choreographies of collective loss and longing as well as its performances of rebirth and cultural advancement.

Berlin films' depictions of Potsdamer Platz have rarely been neutral, neither as reflections of cultural political aspirations at the time of production nor in the various political contexts of their revival. This makes it all the more important to approach Wenders's frequently revived *Der Himmel über Berlin,* the first of this chapter's case studies, as a unique document of West Berlin's edge and to situate the film's constructed familiarity with Potsdamer Platz and its environs within the 750th anniversary's apotheosis of late–Cold War cultural policy and complex, all-German cultural topographies. As divergent theories for the representation and perception of the square, *Der Himmel über Berlin* and *The Invisible Shape of Things Past* illustrate the role of changing technological frameworks in the politicization of spatial memories of place.

RETROSPECTIVE POLITICS

Berlin's 750th anniversary challenged the city's eastern and western halves both to reaffirm their political differences and, much like the Prussian Year (Preußen-Jahr) of 1981, to revisit and narrate shared urban histories that predated the 1949 establishment of the two German states and the East's 1961 closure of the border. Despite efforts to distinguish their new architectural projects and yearlong cultural programs, the East's "City of Peace" (Stadt der Frieden) and the West's "City of the Present" (Stadt der Gegenwart) once again brought "national" and international attention to the division of Germany, of which Berlin bore the geopolitical, symbolic, and psychological brunt. What's more, by carrying on a tradition initiated in 1937 by Joseph Goebbels, the Third Reich's minister of propaganda and public enlightenment, the two Berlins were inadvertently engaging in a dialogue about the past, present, and future of *one* city.[32]

Predictably, public rhetoric surrounding the anniversary reiterated entrenched Cold War viewpoints, many of which ignored the growing spirit of reform in the Eastern bloc. While politicians in the West strategically emphasized the commonalities of all Germans, with an eye to eventual though seemingly unlikely reunification, those in the East continued to justify the separation of a German socialist state from the capitalist one, the alleged heir of the Third Reich. A *Festschrift* titled *750 Jahre Berlin* and edited by West Berlin mayor Eberhard Diepgen, a Christian Democrat, exemplified the West's encouragement of widespread nostalgia for a united, organically whole city and country. In his contribution, Louis Ferdinand, Prince of Prussia and son of Wilhelm II, invoked not the democratic, interwar Weimar Republic but the longer period of the *Kaiserreich* (1871–1918) to justify Berlin as "the spiritual capital of all Germans."[33] For former West German chancellor Willy Brandt, West Berlin's mayor at the time the Wall was built, the celebrations only made more apparent the absurdity of a structure "dividing much that belongs together." The "gaps left behind by the old city center," he hoped, would remind people of the "demands" facing the next generations.[34] Both the destructive path of the Wall and the remaining voids of the Second World War functioned, for Brandt, as built (or unbuilt) virtual bookmarks of indivisible German nationhood.

The GDR, for its part, countered West Berlin's calls for reconciliation and reunification with renewed, though equally hollow, rationalizations of its "antifascist protective rampart." In a 1985 treatise on the impending 750th anniversary, Erich Honecker, chairman of the Central Committee of the SED, reasoned, "The more than 50 million casualties of the Second World War are an eternal reminder and warning for peace. No one has the right to dismiss this reminder and warning and to call today's existing borders, borders of peace, into question."[35] Despite the geographical inflexibility of the SED dictatorship's unequivocal party line, the city's dual celebrations implicitly invited real and metaphorical glances across the Wall.

The comparative topographies of East and West Berlin's building and renewal efforts, exhibition landscapes, and cultural capital created a dialogue of presence and absence, visibility and invisibility, access and denial. Throughout the planning phase, both sides carefully monitored each other's progress and spending, and Karl Heinz Krüger, editor of the West German weekly news magazine *Der Spiegel*, even feared that the year would devolve into "an absurd exhibition fight between the systems," one in which the West might come up short.[36] The East, usually preoccupied with modern, mass-housing projects, pointedly invested in Old Berlin locations such as the Nikolaiviertel, the Gendarmenmarkt, and Friedrichstraße.

Bereft of these sites reminiscent of Berlin's founding and its Prussian heritage, West Berlin planned a similarly provocative route of exhibitions along the neglected path of the Wall between the Anhalter Bahnhof ruin and the Hamburger Bahnhof, which the East's Reichsbahn had just relinquished to the West Berlin Senate in 1984. Cutting straight through Potsdamer Platz along this north–south axis, the walk encouraged each visitor "to actively participate as a seeker and reader of traces, so that historical locations could, once again, be made to speak."[37] Participants could find an exhibition titled *Mythos Berlin* on the grounds of the former Anhalter Bahnhof, encounter the conflicting National Socialist and Cold War spatial histories of the *Topographie des Terrors* and *Mauer-Grenze-Teilung* (Wall-border-division) and the exhibits *Berlin-Berlin* and *Ich und die Stadt* (The city and I) at the Martin-Gropius-Bau, and contemplate a historical *Reise nach Berlin* (Trip to Berlin) at the Hamburger Bahnhof. Like East Berlin's renovations, West Berlin's Wall path must be understood as a spatial acknowledgment of all-German history (see the map at the beginning of this chapter).

Paradoxically, East Berlin's cartographic and rhetorical disavowals of West Berlin as well as its museal advantages only improved the communicative potential of the two programs. If (as was the practice in GDR cartography) the East's official program guide represented West Berlin as a block of solid color at its periphery, the West Berlin guide both traced the path of the Wall with a thin, pink line and included the names of streets and U-Bahn stations in the East. The location of the lion's share of royal architecture, prestigious museums, and eighteenth-century art objects in the GDR capital may have frustrated Western curators unable to borrow items subject to "jubilee competition," but the West's guide had a solution for this as well.[38] Ulrich Eckhardt, director of West Berlin's festivities, urged West Germans, West Berlin residents, and international visitors to "consciously see and perceive both sides together and to synthesize these different images in their minds."[39] Though East Berliners could not cross the border, the 750th anniversary provided additional incentive for West Berliners and tourists not only to spend money and time in the East but also to familiarize themselves with its geography. Even if asymmetrical, this targeted border crossing increased opportunities for all-German cultural contact and exchange. Beyond this, the socialist bent of the East's exhibitions, events, and film retrospectives could not fully forego the Weimar era and the prewall 1950s, let alone the similarly binding, if rejected, shared legacy of the Third Reich.

Voices from the West were quick to meet these conciliatory appearances halfway. Diepgen embraced the cultural political rivalry between East and West Berlin as a means of renewing discussions of "national unity." Unsettling a general apathy toward the inner-German border, the 750th anniversary would convey, he hoped, the idea that a "free Berlin" was "sustainable" and that reunification was still possible.[40] Eckhardt similarly interpreted the GDR's preservation of historical neighborhoods and judicious avoidance of construction projects that might inhibit the future "merger of both half-cities" as a will to unity, a commitment to "historical awareness, national feeling, a sense of homeland, and . . . identity."[41]

Still, Western cultural politicians' pragmatic, hermeneutic optimism was at odds with West Berliners' quotidian experience of noncontiguity with the FRG, of enclosure, and of subsidized and occupied freedom. By 1987, the Berlin Wall was an architectural fact, taken for granted by the populations it separated. West German chancellor Helmut Kohl may have criticized GDR authorities for not capitalizing on the jubilee as an occasion to remove "this horrendous monument of inhumanity" (a sentiment similar to U.S. president Ronald Reagan's appeal to Mikhail Gorbachev at the Brandenburg Gate that June), but it is important to remember that the Wall and the spatial logic, dual infrastructure, restricted mobility, and political impasse that it legitimized appeared permanent.[42] In Diepgen's anthology, former West Berlin mayor and Social Democrat Hans-Jochen Vogel, when given the chance to prophesy Berlin's future, could not even be certain whether the Wall would disappear by 2037. Even in the ideal, faraway future sketched in his political fantasy, Berlin remained divided, albeit peacefully. Vogel's solutions centered instead on the restoration of intersector mobility, the FRG's recognition of East Berlin as the capital of the GDR, and the official addition of West Berlin as the eleventh state *(Bundesland)* of the FRG.[43] These imagined, long-term accommodations with the Cold War and its unique spatial articulation in Berlin provide insight into the horizons of expectation that inform the representational challenges and cinematic spaces of *Der Himmel über Berlin.*

In 1986, as Wim Wenders was "attempting" a description of "an Indescribable Film," he was also reading an early catalog of concepts for the 750th anniversary's *Mythos Berlin* exhibit. Both this preliminary publication and the show's official catalog promised a perceptual history of the industrialized metropolis on the vast grounds of the former Anhalter Bahnhof. Like the works of art to be displayed, the catalogs emphasized Berlin's layered urban mythology of real and imagined, past and future cityscapes. At the same time, they approached the ruins as an archaeological site, harboring traces of the train station's own missing structure as well as buried wartime relics.[44] By eventually concentrating much of *Der Himmel über Berlin*'s narrative action along West Berlin's exhibition trail in the Kreuzberg and Tiergarten districts, Wenders insisted on Berlin's capacity as "a historical site of truth" in opposition to the rest of West Germany. Born in Düsseldorf in summer 1945, this proponent of the New German Cinema of the 1970s was well aware of the Federal Republic's preference for coming to terms with the past by "getting over" it *(Vergangenheitsbewältigung),* which risked neutralizing the legacy of National Socialist ideology, the perpetration of the Holocaust, the widespread war trauma of German civilians, and the more immediate state of Cold War. Berlin, by contrast, equipped Wenders with his "only genuine experiences of Germany" because "the (hi)story that elsewhere in the country is suppressed or denied" was "physically and emotionally present" there. Indeed, Wenders argued, the landscape of division endowed Berlin with "more reality than any other city."[45]

Wenders's choice of words in his fragmentary treatment is telling, particularly as he sought, in his new project, to translate urban virtuality into an audiovisual register. The qualities that he admires in the Berlin of 1986—its historical truth, the physical and emotional presence of its pasts, the excessively visible reality of its politics, and its singularity among other German cities—acknowledge both the three-dimensional features of the built city and the lost architecture implied by its voids. In tentative, poetic language, he hypothesizes a cinematic city that would combine Berlin's postwar history with a haptic sense of place, "something that seems to be so palpably there when you arrive: a feeling in the air and under your feet and in people's faces, that makes life in this city so different from life in other cities."[46]

Turning a purely referential camera on Berlin would not suffice; rather, Wenders imagines a mode of filmmaking that can transgress spatial and temporal barriers, fiction and nonfiction. Even his proposed title, *Der Himmel über Berlin,* provokes existing Cold War boundaries by subverting the title of celebrated GDR writer Christa Wolf's 1963 East–West novel *Der geteilte Himmel (Divided Heaven).* As "maybe the only thing / that unites these two cities, / apart from their past / of course," Wenders's "skies" over Berlin suggest the empowering vantage point of eternity, a position that reduces the earthly function of the Berlin Wall to a two-dimensional cartographic abstraction and its duration to a mere moment in time.

Not content, however, with a film that hovers, figuratively, above the city, Wenders insists as well on the "in, with, for, about Berlin," an urban intimacy that also works at ground level.[47] His research blended the study of old photographs and archival film images with the practice of walking, "a street-by-street recce" through Berlin. Effectively re-creating the "double floors" of Benjamin's flaneur, who understands pathways and places through memory, Wenders develops a representational strategy in which the visual archive and profilmic present can coexist. Choosing angels as protagonists, he imagines beings with the ability to see just as easily the ruins of the Second World War and the heightened ideological warfare of the 1950s front city as the divided Berlin of the present. Their access to Berlins of different eras could initiate the spectator into a past that is "still present everywhere, as a 'parallel world.'"[48] Much like Wenders's earlier claim that films both emerge from memories and produce new memories,[49] the revival of archival footage of place confirms and corrects the memories of those who knew the location at the time of recording but also supplies a new place memory for those who did not. By making archival images and the profilmic West Berlin of 1986–87 co-dependent in *Der Himmel über Berlin*'s diegetic world, Wenders in effect mirrors, via a discrete film narrative, the 750th anniversary's dual film preoccupations with retrospection and new production, with the careful custodianship of the city's cultural capital (here its audiovisual likenesses) as well as assurances of its urban future (the sustainability of its politics, institutions, and remaining industries).

Both the East and West Berlin jubilee programs featured numerous Berlin-themed retrospectives that activated new and existing exhibition topographies while reactivating the geographies of revived films. Unlike DEFA, which had taken over the Ufa studios, the most prominent site of Weimar and National Socialist film production located just south of Berlin in Potsdam-Babelsberg, much of West Berlin's film industry had relocated to the Federal Republic. While the state-run DEFA studios routinely celebrated the postwar achievements of its production plan in East Berlin and in traveling retrospectives throughout the GDR, West Berlin required its own cultural political interventions to maintain a foothold in the larger West German film landscape. If East German film scholars, curators, and archivists acknowledged only proto-socialist strains of Berlin's predivision filmography in the 750th anniversary retrospectives, West Berlin's retrospectives staged a *Gesamtkunstwerk* of urban mourning and film industrial prowess, covering all epochs of the city's film history. In the larger framework of the West's cultural events, *Der Himmel über Berlin* served both as an autumnal, "reflective" response to the "prelude" of Walter Ruttmann's *Berlin. Die Sinfonie der Großstadt* (*Berlin: Symphony of a Great City,* Germany 1927), which had opened the main festivities in April 1987, and as a reassurance that West Berlin could still produce world-class films.[50] For this reason, *Der Himmel über Berlin*'s narrative contribution to Berlin's urban virtuality cannot be separated from its role in this larger cultural political production and reception context.

In 1978, the West Berlin Senate had instituted the Berliner Filmförderung (BFF), a film funding board, in an effort to bolster the local film economy and combat declining box-office returns. Although successful abroad, the aesthetically rigorous, political, and often self-reflexive films of the New German cineastes had alienated West German audiences. One West Berlin theater owner complained,

"But what do [these filmmakers] bring to the screen? Permanent self-expression, schizophrenic masturbation, that, after the second film (at the very latest), no longer betrays any evidence of artistic potency." Continuing his hand-wringing lament, he attributes the problem to the auteurs' disregard for "the art of entertaining" in the manner of Ernst Lubitsch.[51] Related in film politician Hans Borgelt's timely 1979 book on Berlin's past and future as a film city, these sentiments suggest that German cinema's inimitable Weimar heyday was a retrievable model for West Berlin film production. After all, Borgelt argued, it was the duty of the West Berlin Senate both to protect Berlin's archival past and to foster its new productions, "to look after and support film as if it were a precious inheritance."[52]

To be considered for a discounted production loan, film projects either had to spend a significant portion of their budget in Berlin or had to be "in the cultural political interest" of the city.[53] In 1979, senator for economics Wolfgang Lüder all but dismissed the latter, proclaiming, "It doesn't come down to titles and content, but to the effective profit and advantage for the Berlin economy."[54] By 1983, however, once the BFF began to review the box-office and festival successes of its films, it became perfectly clear that "a completely undervalued side effect" of its production support was the dissemination of a new "Berlin image."[55] Anticipation of a new film's amendments to (West) Berlin's spectral identity was a logical consequence of a city image so uniquely dependent on film archival pasts.

Wenders proved an ideal candidate for a film commemorating Berlin's 750-year history. Combining international coproduction experience with a following in the GDR and in the FRG, he was one New German auteur who managed to appeal to art house and mainstream audiences at home and abroad, particularly with *Paris, Texas* (FRG/France/United Kingdom/United States 1984), which was shot in the United States.[56] His dissatisfaction with Hollywood's stifling of creative freedom and decision to return to West Germany were instrumentalized both by the West Berlin film industry, which could reclaim his talent, and by East German film culture, which could hail his rejection of American capitalist values.[57] The West Berlin Senate not only pledged to subsidize *Der Himmel über Berlin*; Volker Hassemer, culture senator at the time, took a personal interest in the project and even accompanied it to the 1987 Cannes International Film Festival (where Wenders won the award for best direction) as part of a promotional campaign for "Location Berlin." On October 27, the film premiered in West Berlin's large and centrally located Zoo-Palast cinema. Mayor Diepgen hosted an after-party for prominent guests on the rooftop garden of the fashionable Inter-Continental Hotel.[58] As the apex of the jubilee events, *Der Himmel über Berlin* provided the last word or, more aptly, privileged last images in a final bout of collective urban nostalgia before West Berlin resumed its Cold War routine.

A PLACE IN TIME(S)

In the film, the angels Damiel (Bruno Ganz) and Cassiel (Otto Sander) keep watch over (West) Berlin, listening to and easing the thoughts of its melancholic population. The past is ubiquitous in fictive re-creations, voice-over memories, and archival footage. While the American *Columbo* star Peter Falk arrives in town to play a detective in a period piece set in 1945, the elderly Homer (played by Weimar entertainer Curt Bois) wanders through the city contemplating human history and urban change. Nonfictional inserts repeatedly interrupt, cling to, or shadow *Der Himmel über Berlin*'s Cold War present. Tired of the angels' eternal realm, portrayed in black and white in the film, Damiel longs for mortality and a quotidian existence of physical consequences and sensations. He falls in love with the French trapeze artist Marion (Solveig Domartin), who is also searching for greater spiritual and romantic fulfillment. As Cassiel looks on, Damiel relinquishes his heavenly armor and thus enters the world of color and human finitude. There he meets Falk, a former angel, and, finally, Marion. The consummation of Damiel and Marion's love begets the film's final promise, "to be continued," written across Berlin's skies as Homer's voice offers the reassurance, "Nous sommes embarquées" (We have left port)—the city, the characters, and the spectator—on a collective journey.

Cold War Berlin's perpetual state of division and desire permeates the film's formal and narrative concerns. Fearing that overpreparation would reduce *Der Himmel über Berlin*'s radical effect, Wenders assembled much of the story from fragments that included Peter Handke's poetic dialogue, the actors' improvised lines, archival footage, literary citations, rock music, and his own stockpile of ideas for shots.[59] The result attempts to represent both the horizontal cross section of the built city and its population and the vertical relation between heaven and earth. Early scholarly criticism discussed the film's tension between dispersal and unity as postmodern, typically in reference to the construction of its narrative, which, after establishing a diverse social context of anonymous individuals, gradually comes to center on the love story between Damiel and Marion. This emphasis on the film's reflexive process of becoming a single narrative (and a single aesthetic object) obscures, however, its complex emotional and historical urban topographies as well as Wenders's careful mobilization of the unique properties of the film medium to create and overcome longing.[60]

Der Himmel über Berlin invites spectatorial longing for impossible spatial and temporal reunions through its delineation of territory and performance of mediated familiarity. The first of these identifies a specifically West Berlin terrain of iconographic architecture: sweeping helicopter shots over Charlottenburg, Damiel atop the Kaiser Wilhelm Memorial Church, the Radio Tower broadcasting

American Forces Network, and the International Congress Center seen out a window. Despite the angels' occasional return to West Berlin's central shopping and entertainment strip along Kurfürstendamm or the location of Falk's film shoot in the bunker in Pallasstraße, the spaces of narrative action begin to concentrate along the path of the Wall, whose western face repeatedly enters the frame. The Staatsbibliothek at Potsdamer Platz serves as the meeting point of the angels, who soothe scholars and bless their preservation of human knowledge. The Prussian Victory Column, located along the Strasse des 17. Juni, which commemorates all-German sentiment (via the 1953 uprising of GDR workers), provides Damiel and Cassiel with an omniscient perch from which to glance East or West. Peter Falk wanders across the grounds of the Anhalter Bahnhof. Damiel meets Marion at a Nick Cave concert in the remains of the Hotel Esplanade, which would later house the Deutsche Kinemathek's 750th anniversary exhibit, *Film in Berlin*, featuring set pieces from *Der Himmel über Berlin*.[61] Staging the film as closely as possible to the border and taking up the spatial politics of the anniversary celebrations, Wenders orients characters and spectators alike toward East Berlin. It is as if the film's diegetic world is straining to overcome a limited visibility.

After articulating this border region, the film offers a cinematic means of transgressing it. With the help of Henri Alekan's mobile camera and of trick cuts and dissolves, Damiel and Cassiel possess the extraordinary ability to fly over and pass through the Wall. One shot in which they walk straight toward and dissolve into the concrete edifice yields phantom rides (shot clandestinely by DEFA cinematographer Thomas Plenert) of a Prenzlauer Berg street lined with the GDR's telltale, diminutive Trabant cars. In this sequence, not only does *Der Himmel über Berlin* demonstrate the spatial and visual contiguity of the two Berlins; it performs cinema's potential to actualize the West's rhetoric of "keeping together what belongs together." Moreover, this elegant joining of film material flaunts the subversive camaraderie of West and East German cineastes, who, by collaboratively breaking GDR law, enabled these edits of authentically Eastern material in the first place.[62]

Just as the film relieves spatial longing by crossing the border, it provides a means of seeing beyond the built city's current form, of crossing the temporal chasm that separates Cold War voids from their former content. To ensure that spectators feel and understand the absence of this architecture, Wenders invests referential images of the city with mediated memories. In the case of archival footage, matches on action link the present to the past as Cassiel glances out the window of an old car, a Nazi era prop for the film within a film, only to see an archival tracking shot of soldiers and civilians clearing the streets of rubble after a bomb raid. Wenders repeats this device through the front windshield as pedestrians

The Berlin Wall and the East beyond it. *Der Himmel über Berlin* (cinematography by Henri Alekan, *above*, and Thomas Plenert, *below*). Frame stills.

make their way past an exploded streetcar, black figures against a hazy white mist. Elsewhere it is the sound of an air raid siren that links a contemporary child's cry to wartime airplanes overhead and burning apartment houses below. Falk's film set, a fictional re-creation of a concentration camp, supplies the Nazi uniforms and yellow stars of another of Berlin's missing pasts, the Holocaust.

These examples literalize and concretize relationships between profilmic space and the city's invisible histories, but at other moments Wenders conveys past geographies far more subtly through shots and sequences that evoke, but do not show, those from earlier films. Spectators lacking a familiarity with a specific Berlin location might nonetheless know or sense its mediated history, even where Wenders's images refuse to cite exact compositions.[63] There is nothing innocent about Falk's arrival by air in the opening minutes of the film, not alone because of his voice-over reverie about the city nor merely because of Jürgen Knieper's string-led orchestral score. The cut from Falk glancing out the airplane window to a floating aerial shot of the city and clouds carries with it an entire filmography of aerial approaches to Berlin, including the opening of Billy Wilder's *A Foreign Affair* (United States 1948) and the U.S. Signal Corps's long, overhead survey of the devastated city in Jost von Morr and John Lionel Bandmann's compilation film *Ein Tag im Juli, Berlin 1945* (One day in July, Berlin 1945, FRG 1975), which supplies some of the archival material seen elsewhere in the film. Behind these filmic flights lurk yet others, such as military documentation of the destructive missions of U.S. and British bombers in the Second World War or Adolf Hitler's grandiosely choreographed descent on Nuremberg in Leni Riefenstahl's *Triumph des Willens* (*Triumph of the Will*, Germany 1935).

Whereas *Der Himmel über Berlin*'s spatial longing incites the desire for unrestricted motion across the city's two halves, the temporal longing of what might be termed Wenders's déjà vu effect arises in part from the knowledge, suspicion, or feeling that a profilmic place has an unseen filmic predecessor. While passing the Anhalter Bahnhof ruin, Falk reflects on his motion and the station's history, "Spazieren . . . , walking, looking and seeing. I wish you were here, Grandma! This must be the station they told me about, with the funny name. Not the station where the trains stopped, but the station where the stations stopped." When a group of young workers wonder whether they have just seen Columbo, one concludes of the former train yard's dirt-filled vista, "He wouldn't be running around here in the boondocks. Are you crazy?" Though Anhalter Bahnhof's jagged entryway is already legible as a ruin, Falk's vantage point aligns him with the position of an arriving train and thus further suggests the discrepancy between past and present. His gaze toward the station and narration of its history recall a sequence that seems an impossible contradiction of this barren setting: the dynamic and triumphal locomotive approach to Weimar Berlin in Walter Ruttmann's *Berlin.*

Die Sinfonie der Großstadt. Neither the 1920s metropolis nor its film archival proxy comes to the rescue of this site's profilmic virtuality.

More than any other scene in *Der Himmel über Berlin,* Cassiel and Homer's stroll through Potsdamer Platz illustrates the film's complicated relationship to urban nostalgia. Indeed, Wenders's play of revealing, limiting, or withholding views across space and time can be understood as a means of conditioning spectators' perception of urban virtuality and of designing or manipulating their emotional responses.

Der Himmel über Berlin's only conspicuously named place, Potsdamer Platz appears after the film demarcates its specific geography of longing. Damiel glances West, then East, from the shoulder of the Victory Column's gilded statue of winged Viktoria. To the East, the Brandenburg Gate marks a border already established in Cold War films such as Franz Cáp's *Die Spur führt nach Berlin* (*International Counterfeiters,* FRG 1952/1958), Victor Vicas's *Weg ohne Umkehr* (Path of no return, FRG 1953), and Billy Wilder's *One, Two, Three* (United States 1961); East Berlin's space-age Television Tower (Fernsehturm) punctures the distant skyline. Homer, taking up the concerns and storytelling modus of his ancient Greek namesake, sits in the nearby Staatsbibliothek contemplating humanity's failure in "singing an epic of peace." He opens a copy of photographer August Sander's book of portraits, *Menschen des 20. Jahrhunderts (People of the 20th Century),* as the film cuts to archival wartime footage of Berlin civilians and soldiers examining

Peter Falk glancing at what remains of Anhalter Bahnhof in *Der Himmel über Berlin.* Frame still.

the dead after a bomb raid. They cover their noses at the stench and stare in disbelief at the corpses (including some bodies of children) as Homer questions the imperialist narratives of the past in voice-over. Cassiel, who has been observing the old man, presses his head to Homer's. Regaining his optimism, humanity's epic narrator determines "not to give up" because humanity would lose its religious "sonship" without its storyteller, the guardian of its history. A cut back to Damiel on the Victory Column and the Column's roundabout as well as the score's increasing emphasis on a lamenting string and piano motif align these thoughts with Homer's subsequent search for Potsdamer Platz.

In the next shot, Homer and Cassiel reappear, framed by two symmetrically curved Cold War structures, the Berlin Wall and the elevated platform of the West's magnetic train (Magnetbahn), a prototype conveniently set to begin operation in May 1987. Proceeding toward the camera along a ground of dirt, brush, and puddles, Homer muses in internal monologue, "I can't find Potsdamer Platz." As the mobile camera tracks their progress and dynamically reframes their relation to the Wall and the platform, they occupy a (pro)filmic space of heightened indexicality; the sequence is referential beyond doubt. A second framing stacks the location's geographical determinants as if they were part of a unique archaeological record: the blank ground that reveals no secrets; the Wall whose (Western) graffiti betrays, however, the ideological loyalties of its visible surface; the vague, bulbous outline of the Television Tower on its other side; and the newly built, top layer of the M-Bahn, whose tracks came closest to the Wall at Potsdamer Platz. It is not only the irony of Homer's confusion that locates the spectator. To take in all four of these elements at once, the camera or a contemporary observer had to stand on the site of the square.

As the camera presents one Potsdamer Platz, Homer begins to narrate the one he remembers. Like Benjamin's flaneur, he recounts his personal geography of the 1920s square, all the while maintaining that the visible world (the one also available to the spectator) could not be the one he seeks:

> Because the Café Josty was on Potsdamer Platz . . . in the afternoons I used to amuse myself there and drink coffee, looking at the people. . . . Before that I'd smoke my cigar at Loeser & Wolff, a well-known tobacco shop, just across the way here. So this can't be it, can't be Potsdamer Platz!

Homer's vivid descriptions of the square, like Falk's conspicuous blocking at Anhalter Bahnhof later in the film, recall Ruttmann's montage of a modern Berlin of traffic and tempo, but Wenders refuses to integrate these older images into his portrait of Berlin. Instead, the discrepancy between sound and image, between

Damiel (Bruno Ganz) looks east from the Victory Column. *Der Himmel über Berlin.* Frame stills.

"I can't find Potsdamer Platz." The square and its Cold War architecture in *Der Himmel über Berlin*. Frame still.

Potsdamer and Leipziger Plätze in Walter Ruttmann's *Berlin. Die Sinfonie der Großstadt*. Frame still.

the remembered place and its Cold War guise, initiates and denies a desire to participate in Homer's reverie. Because filmic border crossing and intertemporal matches on action prove that such metaphysical leaps are possible in *Der Himmel über Berlin,* the inaccessibility of the Weimar film archive stands out as a limitation to mobility and as a warning to overindulged fantasies.

The design of this mediated irretrievability becomes clearer as the scene progresses. Homer laments, "You don't run into anyone that you . . . can ask" and looks off-screen. His gaze is met with a reverse shot of faded color footage of bombed-out facades. This ghostly apparition of the iconic rubble landscape of the wartime and early postwar years floats by in a slow tracking shot, consistent with Homer and Cassiel's direction of motion. The absence of human life in the archival material subverts Homer's insistence that Potsdamer Platz "was a lively square!" In the following medium close-up, he and Cassiel seem to be contemplating a collective vision, but which one? At first, Homer squints to see more clearly. He could be looking toward the archival footage or beyond it. Then he closes his eyes altogether as if only able call forth the 1920s "streetcars, omnibuses with horses, and two automobiles, mine and chocolatier Hamann's" in his own mind. Whereas Wenders had imagined in his treatment that only the angels could see the city's "latent past" and only humans the world of color, conventions of analytical editing situate the color insert of skeletal architecture in a logic of causal chains, spatial relations, and spectatorial identification that transcends the subjective vision of either figure.[64]

Homer's motivated point of view may indeed (and convincingly) claim the archival shot and posit it as a memory or flashback at odds with both the physical space of the present and the narrated space of the past. But the shot's disjunction with these other temporalities suggests, rather, its function as a nondiegetic insert and a filmic provocation of urban nostalgia. Homer's description of Weimar Berlin awakens longing not merely for the lost Platz but also for its missing, withheld images. By juxtaposing the old man's oral history of a bustling intersection with the bleak profilmic space of 1986–87, Wenders forces his spectators to become aware of the aura of discrepancy and invites them to mourn the Weimar cityscape without asking how it came to disappear. Precisely at the moment when classical narrative and editing paradigms demand the representation of the 1920s (through fictional reconstructions or archival views), Wenders substitutes footage from the 1940s. Intercepting the potential reprieve of Homer, Cassiel, and the spectator's film archival time travel, the hollow ruins of the 1940s shot bear witness to a third temporality, one that must also remain "in the picture."

By thus inducing, then catching, nostalgia in the act, *Der Himmel über Berlin*'s Potsdamer Platz scene reinserts the Third Reich and its aftermath into an otherwise selective mode of urban retrospection. The disruptiveness of the ruins

"It was a lively square." *Der Himmel über Berlin.* Frame stills.

catalyzes a shift in the tone of Homer's recollections. Potsdamer Platz becomes the site of sinister, though still virtual, continuities as he acknowledges the square's indifference to the rise of National Socialism: "The Wertheim department store was also here. And then, suddenly, flags were hanging, over there. . . . The whole square was full of them . . . and people weren't at all friendly anymore. . . . Neither were the police." Homer's embodiment by the Jewish actor Bois, who left Germany in 1933, lends these sentiments a dual legitimacy: that of the native flaneur and that of the disoriented outsider. After navigating an expanse of tall grass, he settles into an abandoned armchair and vows not to stop searching until he has found the square. What he does not know is that he has already found what he will never find; the square's geographical location does not add up to the bygone place, architecture, and atmosphere of memory.

In 1920, the *Vossische Zeitung* asked journalist and art critic Karl Scheffler to predict how Potsdamer Platz would look twenty-five years later. His essay presents four possibilities, the most fanciful of which offers a hauntingly accurate description of Potsdamer Platz (and Berlin) after the Second World War:

> In twenty-five years, even Josty won't exist anymore. The buildings around the square will be ravaged, robbed of their usable materials; they will be ruins. Grass and shrubs will grow out of the cracked asphalt. Not a single train will run, seldom will a car be visible, and only a few people will timidly scurry about. The place will be teeming with rats and mice from the overgrown Tiergarten.[65]

In the midst of Berlin's expansion and modernization, this sketch surely strove for the antithesis of expectation. By the 1980s, it was the square's past that seemed just as unlikely. As architectural historian Alan Balfour has observed of a 1980 photograph of Potsdamer Platz, "this is a nondescript place, without distinction, and only through the use of words and the telling of stories can it be given significance."[66] In less than three minutes, *Der Himmel über Berlin* performs an audiovisual solution to this gap in urban narration. The Potsdamer Platz scene teaches spectators to perceive the virtuality of place, to become emotionally invested in profilmic space and urban change, to desire impossible sights, and, importantly, to question the medium's mechanisms of nostalgic manipulation in the very moment of their deployment.

INVISIBLE SHAPES

By the early 1990s, Potsdamer Platz's desolation was undergoing a profound shift in meaning. No longer the edge, the limit, or the border, the square had become, during the *Wende*, a representative site of literal and figurative all-German rapprochement. Wall-chipping tourism, infrastructural mergers, and the promise of new construction transformed the Cold War's "nondescript place" of retrospective narration into a dynamic space of collective, if critical, anticipation.

Wenders had faced the problem of defining Berlin's virtuality and West Berliners' spatial and temporal longing against the Wall's permanence. Nostalgia would always run into concrete in the Potsdamer Platz of 1987. Gradually relieved of its death strip walls and fences, antivehicle barricades, and floodlights, the postunification square invited a new, more fluid perception of its past and future virtualities. While *Der Himmel über Berlin* demonstrated a cinematic and narrative means of reinvesting the contemporary cityscape with its physically irretrievable past, the personal computer, the Internet, and database structures of the digital era could reinvent the virtuality of place as an inventory of past images, independent of narrative. In Wenders's film, cinematographic indexicality, the medium's photochemical claim of resemblance between moving images and their profilmic place, person, or object, forms the technological, but also emotional, basis of meaningful relationships among characters, recorded setting, archival views, and the world of the spectator. The resulting aura of discrepancy stages cinematographic indexicality as a tension or contradiction of beliefs about place. How could *this* profilmic space correspond to *that* archival image? How could *that* memory of a bustling street scene speak of *this* field of grass?

After the Wall, Berlin had to prepare to function as the capital of a united Germany and to serve residents socialized in divergent political systems. Given East and West Berliners' very different memories and uses of the city during the Cold War, proponents of the new (and new medial) Potsdamer Platz did well to avoid exclusionary narratives of place. At the same time, the prospect of new, all-Berlin building projects inspired skepticism about the future of the square's controversial legacy. In 1990, Balfour expressed trepidation toward the "flaw" or "chronic weakness" of new architecture that would be tasked with forging "on such a disturbed base, bridges across the wound of the future."[67]

The prevalence of digital, simulated representations of Berlin throughout the construction phase must thus be understood as a means of mastering uncertainty, manipulating expectations, and managing historical associations. At the INFO BOX, for example, visitors to Potsdamer and Leipziger Plätze could both survey this transitional landscape from a rooftop observation deck or virtually forego its temporary chaos via a pristine computer simulation of the finished site in the year 2000. Whereas the cinematographic indexicality of *Der Himmel über Berlin* involved spectators in a narrative process of coming to terms with place, the interactive media of the 1990s and early 2000s could, as Lev Manovich put it at the time, cast the subject in the oscillating "roles of viewer and user, shifting between perceiving and acting, between following the story and actively participating in it."[68] Or, as was the case in projects such as *The Invisible Shape of Things Past,* narrative contexts for images and the control of images may have been absent altogether. "Walk-in" simulations of historical and future environments were already a popular area of early virtual reality research and development, but anxieties surrounding erasure, memory, and new functions and forms made this cartographic and architectural turn in the virtual life of cities particularly attractive for Berlin.[69]

Media artist Joachim Sauter and computer programmer Dirk Lüsebrink of Art+Com, an architectural design group specializing in new media, were at the forefront of these explorations in Berlin in the early 1990s. When the collective was asked to participate in the planning competition for Potsdamer Platz in 1991, Sauter and Lüsebrink developed their own application for virtually navigating the city's historical center. Concerned with both temporal and spatial mobility as well as the organization of "interactively accessible multimedia information," they created a three-dimensional model of Berlin that could be manipulated with a data glove.[70] Unlike the INFO BOX application, which envisioned the pedestrian's experience of the future built square, Art+Com's simulation allowed users to navigate the city's historical built conditions. Rather than limiting these streetscapes to the bland, grayscale reinstatement of lost buildings and spatial relations, Sauter and Lüsebrink supplemented their graphics with archival film material shot at that specific location in time. Indeed, the "interactive information" that users gleaned in virtual strolls through the city came in the form of digitized single takes of place. Clicking on a still frame would activate the shot in duration. The film image, with all its detail, would then be mapped onto the architectural backdrop, paradoxically bringing the virtual world to life.

Art+Com's early deference to cinematographic indexicality as a higher historical truth of place than architectural blueprints and computer-simulated buildings migrated into *The Invisible Shape of Things Past* and represents an important step in cartographic approaches to postwall urban virtuality. Conceived as both an interactive map and a film archive of Potsdamer and Leipziger Plätze, the project's initial goal was a distributed VRML Web application to which Internet users and institutions could contribute their own film material according to the location and time of its recording.[71] This intersection of cinematographic and virtual cartographic representational tools in the service of educational time travel reassigns film images the primary task not of witnessing and revivifying lost spaces and times but of regaining indisputable geographical and historical coordinates.

The Invisible Shape of Things Past transforms film material into mappable data points by anchoring a shot's origin within the application's larger organizational structure. Just as film viewers at the time might first encounter the film's medium of storage (a reel of celluloid, a VHS tape, or, later, a DVD) before seeing the film, the application's users could access film footage through the abstraction of unique three-dimensional shapes or "interactive virtual objects" generated by the spatialization of a mobile shot's consecutive frames. Run through a projector, these same frames would produce moving images in duration; stacked one after the other along a horizontal axis, however, they yield an abstract filmic architecture. These complex icons, which Sauter and Lüsebrink call "film objects," both mark the external space of a shot's cartographic journey and offer virtually navigable, habitable interiors of these cinematic routes through urban space.[72] Only when activated by a mouse click do the objects perform the more traditional function of "playing" the shot, and even when that shot plays, its compositional elements (horizontals, diagonals, and verticals) align seamlessly with the features of the map. Receding in space as they proceed in time, the activated shots cover the 3-D map with a cinematographic patina. It is as if each section of the frame were being welded to the line of a street or the outline of a building.

One might think of these moving images as informational and cultural wallpaper that, given the right density and spatial distribution of archival data, could cover Sauter and Lüsebrink's Platz completely.[73] A virtual three-dimensional map welded to cinematic images from a specific historical moment already suggests the retrievability of lost cityscapes, but *The Invisible Shape of Things Past* does not stop at spatial contiguity. Rather, it aims to conquer the continuity of time. Through spatial morphing, spatial layering, and the "rupture" of "time-space linearity," Sauter and Lüsebrink extend user control to the temporal dimension. While morphing allows one historical city layout to transition smoothly into another, layering stacks the changing layout and built structures of Potsdamer and Leipziger Plätze vertically in time. Whereas film spectators relinquish control of what happens on-screen for a fixed duration, Sauter and Lüsebrink's users select a particular historical configuration with a time-slider and can even customize "a time-space environment in accordance with what interests them" (e.g., how the former path of the Wall relates to postwall urban planning).[74] Assured of their uninhibited mobility through time and space, they might explore all the film objects present in a given year or organize multiple layers of historical information as a kind of archeological record, visible, simultaneously, in varying percentages of transparency. Through their manipulation of time and a place's spatial conditions, users can supplement and rediscover the palimpsest of archival film objects in all

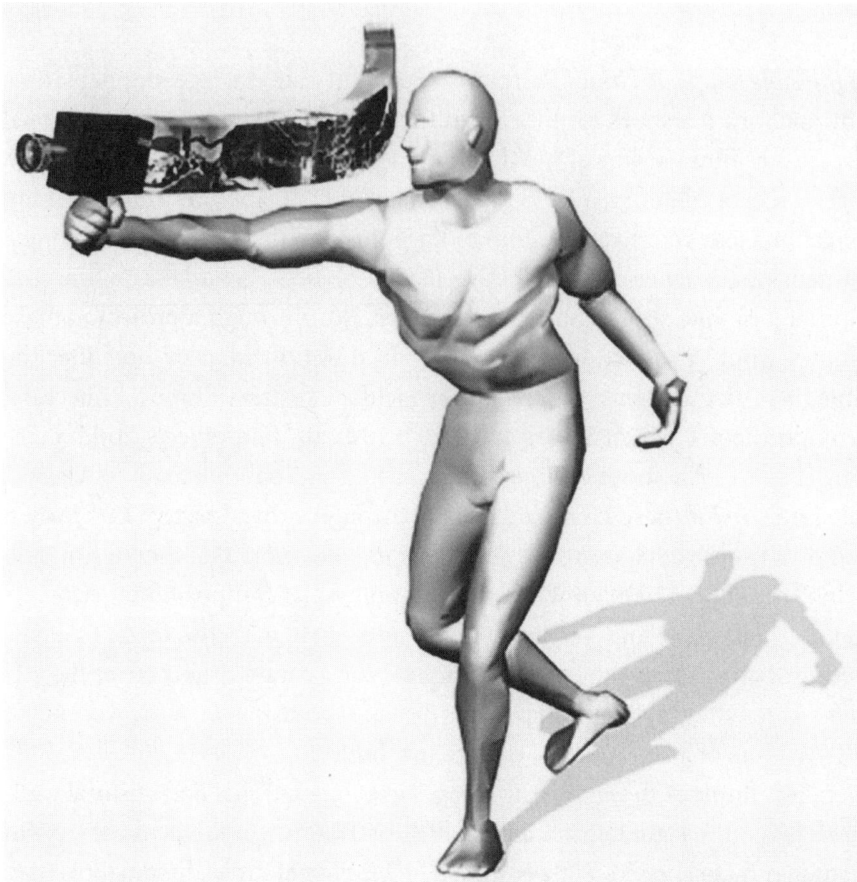

Transforming film sequences into digital film objects and returning a shot to its cartographic coordinates. Courtesy of Art + Com, 1996.

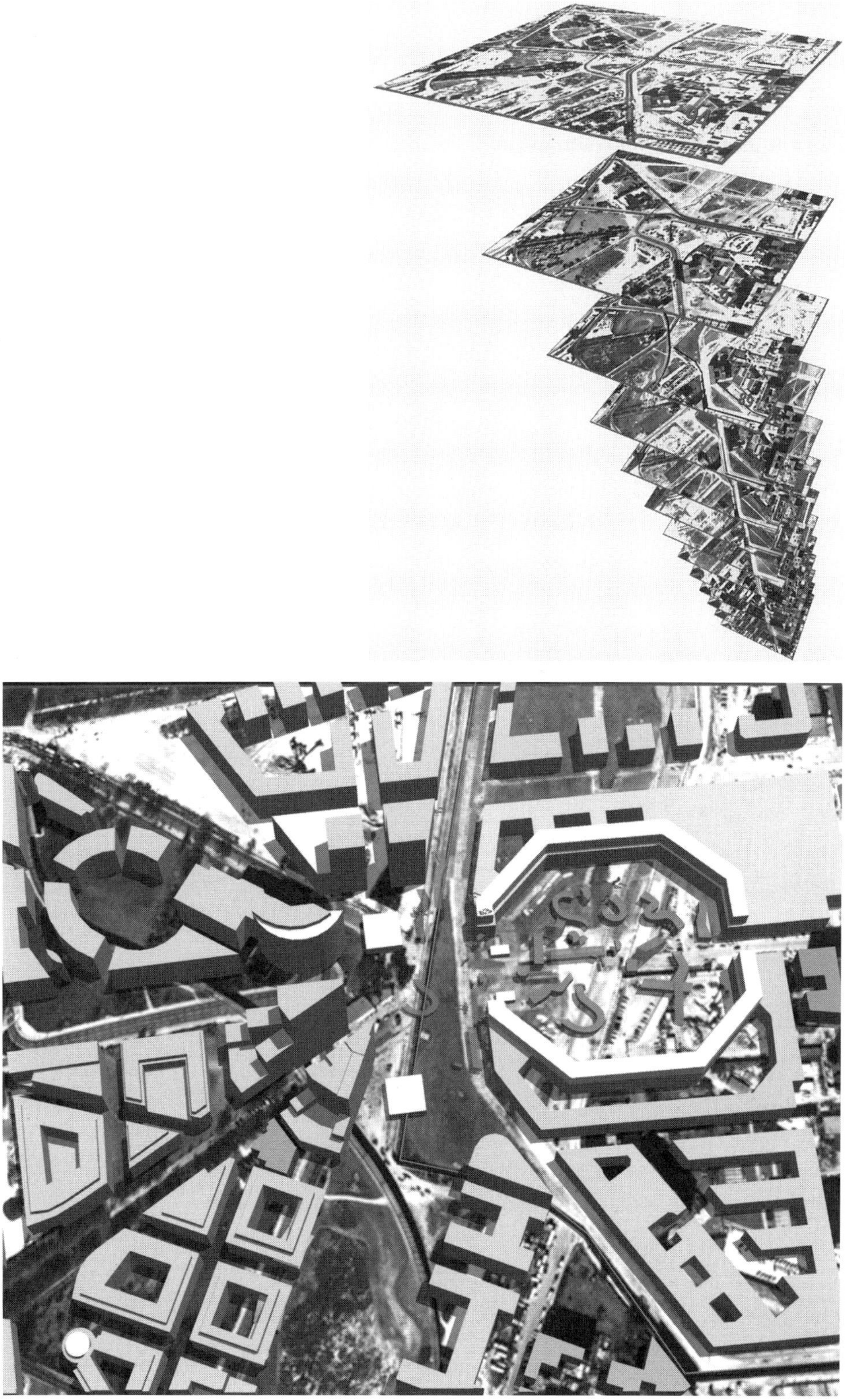

Time layers by year and a customized time–space environment. Courtesy of Art+Com, 1996.

directions and dimensions. Freud's once impossible urban analogy for the mind has found its ideal representation.

The application's conceit is to fill virtual urban space with the shapes generated by its filmic archive but also to achieve a densely packed endlessness of cinematographic views of Berlin. Though the design and conceptualization of *The Invisible Shape of Things Past* depend on the tools of new media, the primacy of the project's film material posits film's representational superiority to the abstractions of the city map and even to virtual, historically accurate three-dimensional architecture. In 1998, Philip Rosen suggested that the "digital demonstrates its radically new capabilities and superior representational powers through its capacity to appropriate the old" and through its performance of "hybridity."[75] Certainly one might think of digital video cameras and nonlinear editing programs this way. Sauter and Lüsebrink's appropriation of cinema, particularly in the referential capacity of its mapped shots, hardly makes the case for virtual reality or dynamic cartography's more faithful representation of Potsdamer and Leipziger Plätze *in* a given temporal horizon, despite the new versatility this hybridity creates *throughout* historical time.

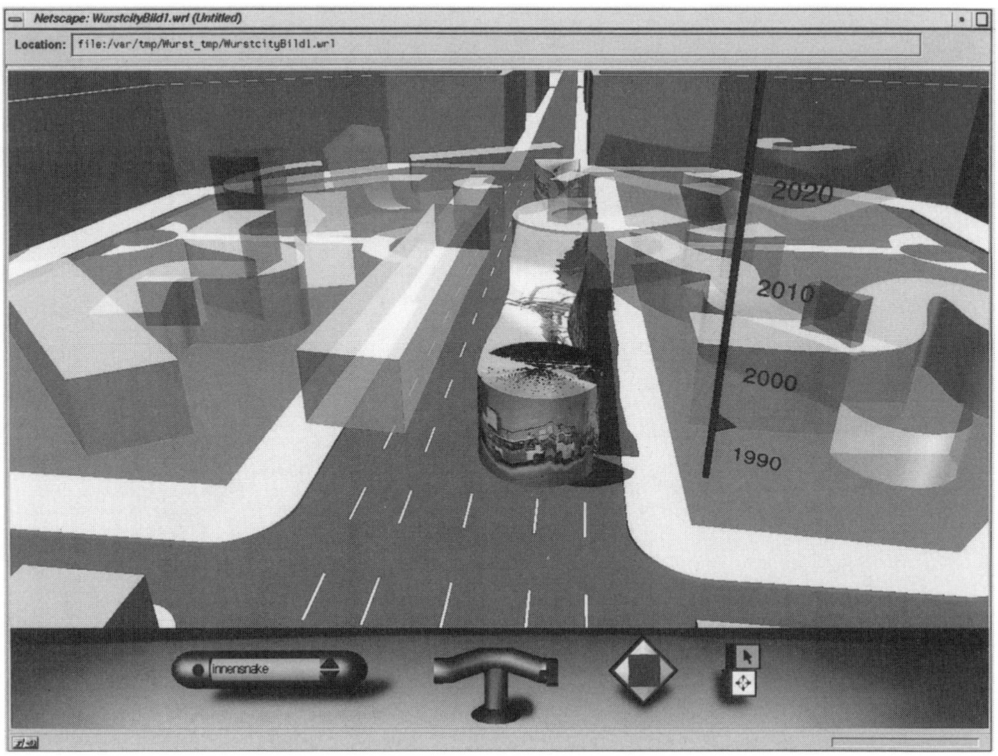

The Invisible Shape of Things Past's palimpsest of film objects. Courtesy of Art+ Com, 1996.

These additional representational contexts enabled by new media change the function of the film material, but they also maintain the authority of its relation to place. In a 2001 analysis of the project, Manovich refers to Sauter and Lüsebrink's return of "the records of cinematic vision" to their "historical and material context" as a devirtualization of cinema. Understanding cinema's virtuality as its postrecording independence from its profilmic origins, he interprets the application's location and solidification of ephemeral film footage as a "virtual monument to cinema," a respectful salute from digital media's new virtuality to that of a dry-docked analog predecessor.[76] Although this observation recognizes the project's new, spatial contextualization of the film medium, it ignores the effects of this cartographic embeddedness on the representation of Berlin.

The Invisible Shape of Things Past elevates and enhances cinema's relationship to Berlin's geography. By foregrounding a new, cartographic strain of indexicality, it shares concerns with Thom Andersen's later emphasis on films' often neglected, peripheral depictions of place in *Los Angeles Plays Itself* (United States 2003) and Tom Conley's insistence, in his 2007 study *Cartographic Cinema,* that "films *are* maps" in their capacity to locate the spectator.[77] In a city in which profilmic space changes so drastically between recording and reception, discrepancies between film images and the built city invite comparison. As *Der Himmel über Berlin* demonstrates, the built present does not always triumph over the archival past. To privilege cinematographic resemblance is to reveal something irrevocable: that the Potsdamer Platz of the 1920s existed, no longer exists, and may never exist again. What might be termed *cartographic indexicality,* conversely, prioritizes images' fidelity to unchanging geographical coordinates over their resemblance to a real, evolving profilmic space.

A postwar cinematic prototype for this image mapping occurs in an extended chase sequence in the prewall Cold War crime film *Die Spur führt nach Berlin,* whose German title already alludes to a pathway ("the trail leads to Berlin"). As the gangsters flee the West Berlin police in their getaway car, officers back at headquarters chart their progress on a massive wall map. Intercutting between city streets and the map, the sequence makes clear that postwar reconstruction is also a matter of reconstructing Berlin's real and filmic spatial relations. Reinforced via radio communication on the sound track, the criminals' route advances along a West–East axis of prominent landmarks. From Bahnhof Zoo to Wittenbergplatz, from the Victory Column to the Brandenburg Gate, location names correspond to cartographic representations, which in turn correspond to shots of the built city. While the corners of the frame might offer hints of rubble, destroyed buildings, and suspiciously blank plots of land, the cartographic and aural reassurance of these images' place identities legitimizes their changed appearance. This well-known, albeit defamiliarized, path not only maintains geographical continuity in a cityscape of altered surfaces; it traces the new spatial order of Cold War division. The chase stops, because it must, at the Brandenburg Gate, the edge of West Berlin's authority.

Cartographic indexicality posits location as a constant, a fixed origin to which contradictory images (the "lively square" and the desolate one) may be mapped with equal impartiality. Furnishing the indisputable continuity that Berlin's architecture and surfaces lack, *The Invisible Shape of Things Past* stores and restores the visible evidence of these structures in the one context they share with contemporary urban space. In the midst of Potsdamer Platz's transformation, the virtualization of such an archive countered uncertainties surrounding the new square's built outcome and East–West integration with the digital era's promise of ever-increasing storage. A virtual place to gather, return, sift through, and explore film fragments of place, Sauter and Lüsebrink's map of Potsdamer and Leipziger Plätze celebrated Berlin as a virtual reconstruction, the antithesis of loss. Finally, the application would seem to argue, there could be a Berlin immune to destruction.

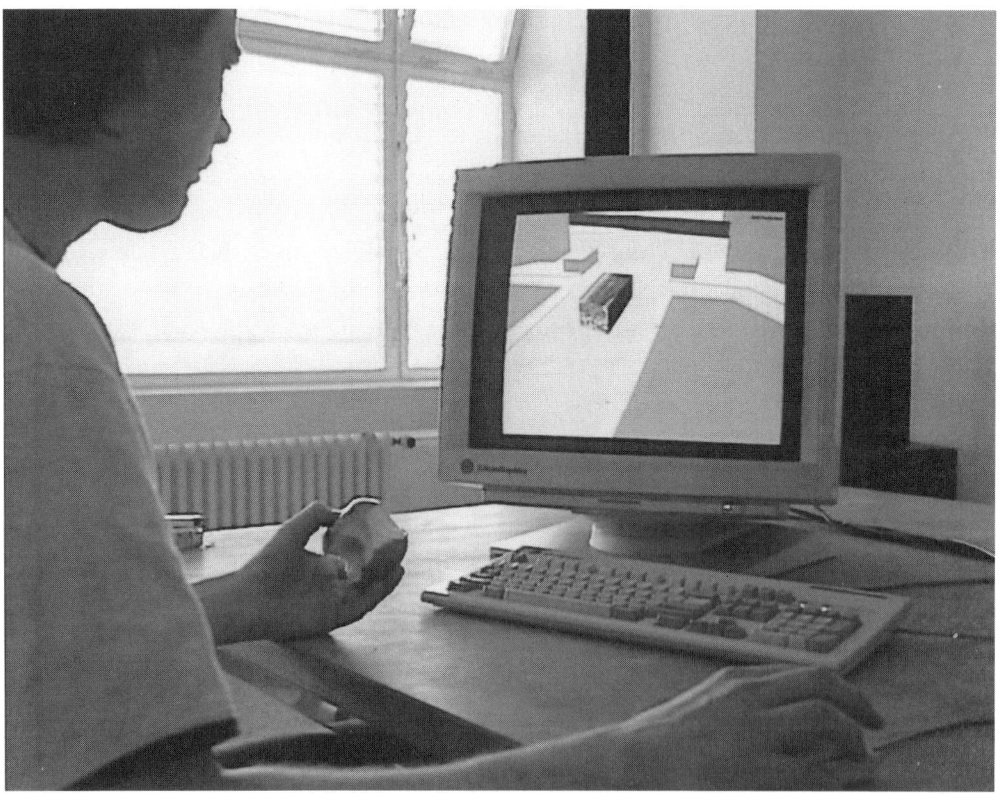

User interface. *The Invisible Shape of Things Past.* Promotional DVD, 1996.

Staged as the pinnacle of the application's information economy, a reward for the successful navigation of its interface, Berlin's historical film material and the power to activate it lay at the fingertips of the user.

Of course, the project's ideals of access and infinity, of individual navigation and collective archiving, and of unfettered revivification of the cityscape in space and time run up against numerous conceptual limitations. First, the history of cinema restricts the range of years that the application can represent. The density of film objects would likely correspond to limiting factors such as the availability of film or video cameras at a given historical moment or the changing interest in specific Berlin locations like Potsdamer and Leipziger Plätze over time. Was *The Invisible Shape of Things Past*'s claim to infinity no more than digital hubris in 1995?

Second, the film fragments that generate Sauter and Lüsebrink's visible shapes require either shifts in focal length or the camera's movement through space. While phantom rides, pans, tilts, zooms, or some combination of these yield complex three-dimensional architecture, a tracking shot parallel to a street would produce nothing more than a line. A static take, the basis for many of the first cinematographic views of urban space, would have no depth at all and would hardly draw attention to its single plane.

If recorded, uploaded, or selected only for their outlandish shapes, the shots and their historical import risk becoming secondary. This leads to a final concern that the images, extracted from their function in the aesthetic logic of larger films and further obscured by the abstract forms of film objects, might be too far removed from the narrative and historical contexts that give their existence meaning.

The computer's ability to represent "space independently of the observer's viewpoint" may have afforded Sauter and Lüsebrink's imagined users of the mid-1990s the chance to leap through Berlin's spatial history without the moral responsibilities and emotional entanglements of cinematic spectatorial identification.[78] *The Invisible Shape of Things Past* may, too, have sidestepped unpleasant pasts unearthed in Potsdamer Platz's construction in favor of a rationalized, cartographic interface. It did not, however, provide users with the memories, facts, descriptions, and details that could translate cartographic spatial relationships and found, excerpted, or newly recorded film footage into a cultural and political narrative of place. The human agents of change were as absent in the interface as film archivists' and film historians' knowledge of provenance and production conditions. These limitations to Art+Com's archive expose the opposition of two competing trends of 1990s computer culture—"data structure" and the more narrative "algorithm" found in video games. Referring to the "anti-narrative logic of the Web," Manovich articulates this conflict between the overwhelming and constantly changing "collection" of information and efforts to forge "a coherent narrative or any other development trajectory through the material."[79]

Certainly Sauter and Lüsebrink's early conceptualization of the project must be evaluated in relation to the technological questions of its time.[80] Just a few years later, "database narratives" of place, such as Norman Klein's interactive DVD-ROM *Bleeding Through: Layers of Los Angeles* (United States 2003), would combine film and photographic images, sound files, and text in various configurations of fictional and nonfictional storytelling and approximations of memory. This production of the University of Southern California's experimental Labyrinth Project, run by Marsha Kinder, represented interactive narrativity's new development toward database cinema.[81] As Kinder explains, database narratives invite the user to be "a 'performer' of the narrative—like an actor interpreting a role, or a musician playing a score, or a dancer performing traditional moves, contributing her own idiosyncratic inflections and absorbing the experience into her personal archive of memories."[82]

Users of *The Invisible Shape of Things Past* do not perform narratives but rather act out their own spatial curiosity. What's more, this curiosity must be formed in dialogue with information that can only be found beyond the application: through knowledge of Berlin's history and significant events, places, and personages, exposure to its depictions in films and other media, or the firsthand experience of its physical space. A tool that makes urban virtuality both visible and navigable, Art+Com's interactive cartographic archive can be understood as an electronic appendix to the built city. In 1992, media artist and theorist Peter Weibel could make the once provocative claim that urban life was increasingly taking place in virtual space "because we no longer live exclusively in streets, but also in cable channels, telegraph wires, fax machines, and in the digital ethernet."[83] By 2006, this idea of immersion into the world of data needed to be historicized. The "previous icon of the computer era—a VR user traveling in virtual space," had, Manovich argued, "been replaced by a new image: a person checking his or her email or making a phone call using a PDA/cell phone combo while at the airport, on the street, in a car, or any other actually existing space." Theorizing that an augmented physical space that extracts data from the physical world via surveillance provides "mobile physical space dwellers" with constant access to cellspace data, and populates the built city with public monitors, he acknowledges the degree to which this perpetual exchange of information between place and mobile users began to transform one's physical surroundings.[84]

Today, mobile applications, mobile networks, online social networks, and smart phones' and tablets' convergence of image-making, mapping, and data-distributing technologies coproduce and continually update mediated images of place. In the age of Facebook's geographical tracking of posts and photographs, the online biography of each user generates a unique map. It is not hard, in retrospect, to imagine a future for *The Invisible Shape of Things Past* of 1995 as a social-networking website to which city dwellers and visitors upload images according to their geographical coordinates. Or perhaps they must simply do a QR scan of their coded environment to call up invisible urban pasts. Or maybe they just don their Google glass to see what is not there.[85] Beyond the confines of the movie theater and the desktop computer, mobile urban virtuality returns the archive to the streets in the hands and pockets of moving humans, who watch and read the city's layout, its screens, and their own on the go.

ARCHIVES OF IMPERMANENCE

In the twentieth and twenty-first centuries, Berlin has repeatedly reinvented its virtuality and the choice of historical layers to be displayed. As a result, urban virtual representations such as *Der Himmel über Berlin* and *The Invisible Shape of Things Past* and their strategies for making temporal multiplicity palpable have also become dated, found new reception contexts, and gained cultural value with the passage of time. Understanding their process of historicization reveals a longer entwinement (not only the intersection) of Berlin's real and mediated urban virtualities.

When, over time, films become historical objects, their revival in rereleases and retrospectives can invite new engagement with past cityscapes, with former aesthetic priorities, with the political conditions of their production, and with the imagination of their makers. Today some are remembered through public film exhibition, television broadcasts, DVD home entertainment, and online streaming and through migration to new formats of storage and dissemination. Others are forgotten because they are no longer circulated, no longer migrated, or because their material base (or digital file) is lost or corrupted. They are also forgotten when there is no longer a cultural need to remember them.

Cinema shares this tension between permanence and transience with the digital era's burgeoning online archive. The Internet's capacity to host ever more information and the increasing digitization of analog archives convey the sense that "everything" is online and will always be "there." At the same time, the pace of the computer industry's research and development has so far assured that, after a few generations, old hardware cannot read new software, that new hardware cannot read old software. Digital eternity, too, has its practical and material limitations. Still, the long reception of *Der Himmel über Berlin* and the continued modification of *The Invisible Shape of Things Past* attest to the ongoing adaptation of their questions about urban space to the development of New Berlin and new technology.

In 1987, Wenders engineered the cinematic illusion of figures who could walk through and float over the Berlin Wall. Critic, actor, and filmmaker Friedrich Luft observed that, "following this punchline," the audience at the film's premiere "moaned with longing." Prompting an ovation, the virtuosity of the border crossing edits and mobile cinematography manifested, in Luft's view, the bittersweet optimism that the "skies over Berlin are wide open (at least on the film screen)."[86] Released in eighty-five West German cinemas in its first week (an unusually high number for an art house feature), *Der Himmel über Berlin* was hailed by one critic as "the greatest optical-acoustic evocation not only of Berlin, but of the modern metropolis par excellence (since Ruttmann's *Symphonie einer Großstadt*)."[87] Well aware of the film's "effort to sell Berlin cinematically," another critic lauded Wenders's portrayal of "a place of fantasy, melancholy" and "a city of dreams and dreamers."[88]

Through films like *Der Himmel über Berlin,* but also *Alice in den Städten* (*Alice in the Cities,* FRG 1974), *Tôkyô-ga* (*Tokyo-Ga,* FRG/United States 1985), *Yamamoto—Aufzeichnungen zu Kleidern und Städten* (*Notebook on Cities and Clothes,* FRG/France 1990), and *Lisbon Story* (FRG/Portugal 1994), Wenders has since come to be seen as an authority on cities, especially Berlin. At a panel on cinema's role in "metrobranding" at the 2007 Berlinale Talent Campus, he reminded the audience of young filmmakers that films often safeguard the "soul of the city" more effectively than urban planners. Over the years, *Der Himmel über Berlin* has achieved cult status and become canonized not only in Berlin's repertory and art house cinemas but also at cinemathèques, film academies, and universities around the world.[89]

In 2007, the year of the film's twentieth anniversary, the distribution company Neue Visionen released new 35mm and digital prints in acknowledgment that *Der Himmel über Berlin* was a "pearl of European cinema and film art that should absolutely be preserved on the big screen."[90] The film reopened across Germany on May 5, but one of the most significant screenings was its premiere in Berlin's Kino in der Kulturbrauerei—far from Kurfürstendamm—in the eastern district of Prenzlauer Berg. While students at the GDR's film academy, the HFF, and surely a few DEFA filmmakers had been able to see a smuggled video copy of the film before the *Wende,* the average East German filmgoer only encountered the film in 1990, when real borders had already been transgressed.[91] Inhabitants of the New Berlin could finally watch and remember the film together in cinemas throughout the city.

One way to fly over walls: to rebuild No-Man's-Land as a set in *Der Himmel über Berlin*. Production still courtesy of the Deutsche Kinemathek.

Homer could not find Potsdamer Platz in 1987, but how well would he fare today? In the postwall era, his search for the Weimar square has been supplanted by the tourist's hunt for the Cold War one. The new Café Josty in the courtyard of the Sony Center pays homage to its namesake but no longer attracts Berlin's cultural elite. Instead its patrons are visitors who come to admire the square's architecture. Filmgoers en route to and from the Cinestar, a first-run multiplex known for its original language versions, must dodge the incredulous busloads, who stare in awe at the center's funnel-shaped cupola, shimmering walls, and massive infoscreen—the city of the future in the present.[92]

Potsdamer Platz has changed, and so has *Der Himmel über Berlin*. By the early 2000s, the film had become "an architectural document of a city that no longer exists," one that, "with the passage of time," was increasingly becoming "a work of mourning."[93] The spectator's dual displacement from the squares of the 1920s and the 1980s has also altered the function of Wenders's cinematic nostalgia-trap in the Potsdamer Platz scene. Just as humans experience emotions either through

Looking north from Potsdamer Platz during the 2009 Berlinale from a viewing platform commemorating the twentieth anniversary of the fall of the Berlin Wall. Courtesy of the author.

direct sensory engagement or through remembered images, the film presents the Cold War square both as a contemporary sensory experience of space in duration and as an audiovisual approximation of recollection.[94] Homer's walk once implicated the spectator in uncritical nostalgia, in a rejection of the profilmic square, and in a longing for withheld views. Now, it is the film's referential present, its documentation of the stark Platz of 1987, that induces feelings of loss. Nostalgia is not tempered but enhanced by this additional, unplanned spatial and temporal discrepancy.

After unification, Wenders made good on his "to be continued" with a sequel *In weiter Ferne, so nah!* (*Faraway, So Close!*, FRG/United States 1993). This time it is Cassiel who enters the human world, a bitter place after the *Wende*. The actor Horst Buchholz, once West Berlin's iconic postwar rebel, returned to his hometown as the film's Americanized Tony Baker, a corrupt businessman, weapons dealer, and former profiteer of the Third Reich. Finding cultural continuities and common, if shameful, German pasts amid the new political transition, the second film hovers more closely to the ground. Unification had not solved the urban longing portrayed in *Der Himmel über Berlin*; it had created new problems for the city's inhabitants, who had to reorient themselves politically, culturally, economically, and geographically in the process of the merger.

Der Himmel über Berlin remains a preferred, mediated entrée into Berlin in any era. In 2003, MGM released it on an English-language DVD that included an interactive map of the film's major locations. In 1987, Luft had praised the film's ability to make "historical Berlin, now broken in pieces . . . intimately familiar in an almost enjoyable way."[95] Certainly West Berlin audiences would have responded to the spatial relations of these broken pieces most keenly, whereas general West German audiences would have gained familiarity with Berlin's topography through the film's audiovisual performance of spatial intimacy. By marketing the emotional content of the film along with knowledge of its principal locations, the MGM DVD effectively invites international spectators to map personal experience to urban space and civic history. Like Benjamin's native flaneur, these interactively enabled spectators know the routes and the places where urban nostalgia congregates. Or perhaps this DVD extra must be understood as a geographical augmentation of film space and, by extension, the built city, a liaison between the diegetic world and the real one.

Since their early experiments with the online film archive, Sauter and Lüsebrink have continued to develop *The Invisible Shape of Things Past* primarily as an artwork. Their initial emphasis on virtual reality and interactive cartography has given way to an architectural preoccupation with the forms of film objects and with their representation in urban space. In a 2002 exhibit at the Zentrum

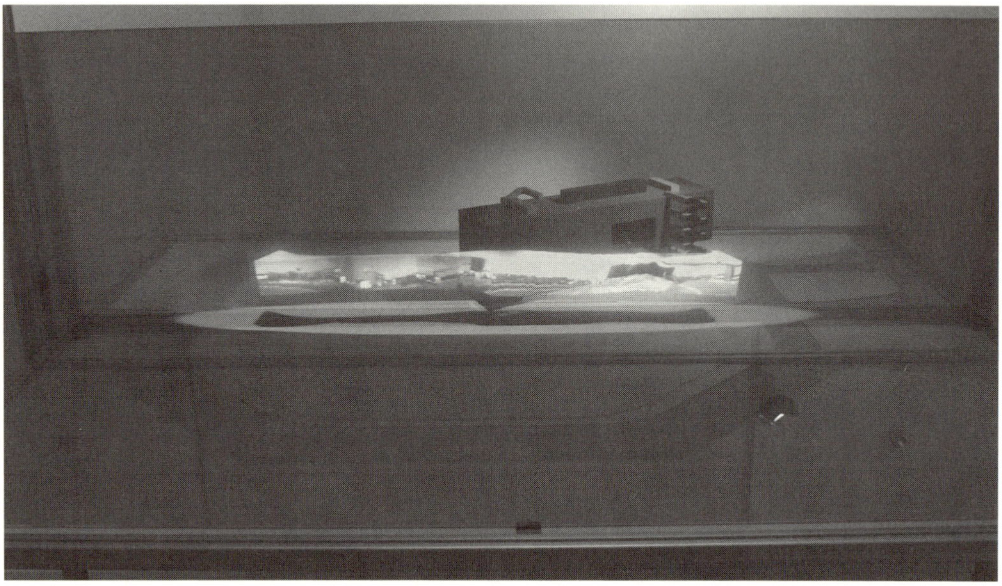

A model of the INFO BOX and a film object of Leipziger Platz resurrected through an optical illusion, 2007. Courtesy of Art+Com.

für Kunst- und Medientechnologie in Karlsruhe, they used video projection and Pepper's Ghost, a nineteenth-century mirror illusion, to place a "real" virtual film object in physical space.[96] Thus visualizing the haunting presence of unseen architecture, they "augmented" urban space.

Subsequent iterations of the project have put forth increasingly abstract architectural and sculptural articulations of original film footage. In the Martin-Gropius-Bau's new media exhibit *Vom Funken zum Pixel* (From transmission to pixel, 2007), film objects yielded two-dimensional prints of the forms and their interiors as well as small three-dimensional models. In a self-reflexive twist, Sauter and Lüsebrink transformed the exhibition space itself into a film object. Profilmic space could become film space, which could in turn be converted into a piece of sculpture or new, habitable architecture. Film footage no longer mapped the past to unchanging geographical coordinates throughout historical time. Instead, as Art+Com reframed the goals of the now plural *Invisible Shapes of Things Past* in 2011, "time becomes space and film becomes architecture"; the designers were well aware of the irony of this pathway from virtual reality back to tangible, analog objects.[97]

In 1995, Sauter and Lüsebrink's dream of a cartographic film archive of Berlin proved too costly and depended on technologies that did not yet exist. Since then, video portals such as YouTube and Vimeo have encouraged amateurs and professionals to upload personal and archival material, to identify the dates and profilmic locations of their footage, and to embed these images in e-mails and other websites or to post them in the streams of their social networking accounts. Place and time are just two of the properties that users can search. While a search for "Potsdamer Platz" generates a seemingly endless list of thumbnails and descriptions, these images and titles lack the spatial contextualization and cultural political application of Sauter and Lüsebrink's vision. In 2007, Sauter recognized that the interest in mapping images to place was evolving; he was eagerly anticipating the further development of Microsoft's Photosynth Research Lab, a project that reconstructed space in time via tourist photos and their GPS coordinates and that has since been adapted for criminal investigations.[98]

The objects at the Martin-Gropius-Bau provided little evidence of *The Invisible Shape of Things Past*'s origins. At the very end of the exhibition, a small model of the INFO BOX stood behind a projected and reflected film object recorded at Leipziger Platz in the mid-1990s. This contradictory pairing of virtualities and presences called up by the three-dimensional model of an absent building and the illusionary repetition of the film object's intangible, yet visible, return was the only reminder of the project's former foundation on the layers of Potsdamer and Leipziger Plätze. Asked about the future of the film archive, Dirk Lüsebrink shrugged, "I was using my own computer. Today those old machines are outdated. We cannot recreate the old project."[99] The application that posited a permanent cityscape through cartographic indexicality can no longer be displayed. Art+Com's short video documentation has, at least, preserved its concept.

Nostalgia had no place in Freud's Roman palimpsest. Why, after all, should emotions be necessary in a city where nothing is ever lost? *The Invisible Shape of Things Past* of 1995 hides an illusion that, if revealed, could encourage emotion in the database.[100] Sauter and Lüsebrink's ideal Berlin is a continuous one—a city that morphs into itself, is layered upon itself, and accommodates the data of multiple temporalities in a single view. Had Homer been a computer user shortly after the *Wende,* he would not have had to seek Potsdamer Platz's missing surfaces. The interactive, endless map of film fragments was, for a moment, an antidote to experience, to the affectual ties between mobile city dwellers and the built city, between the spectator and *moving* images. When confronted with all the information it contained, one could forget that there were gaps in the record—films that were lost, invisible films, films never made.

1. German Parliament and Reichstag Building
2–5. Federal Buildings
6. French Embassy
7. Akademie der Künste
8. British Embassy
9. Future Holocaust Memorial Site
10. Russian Federation Embassy
11. Temporary United States Embassy
12. Deutsche Staatsbibliothek
13. Humboldt Universität
14. Neue Wache
15. Deutsches Historisches Museum
16. Maxim-Gorki-Theater
17. Bodemuseum
18. Pergamonmuseum
19. Neues Museum
20. Alte Nationalgalerie
21. Altes Museum
22. Bebelplatz
23. Französischer Dom
24. Konzerthaus
25. Deutscher Dom

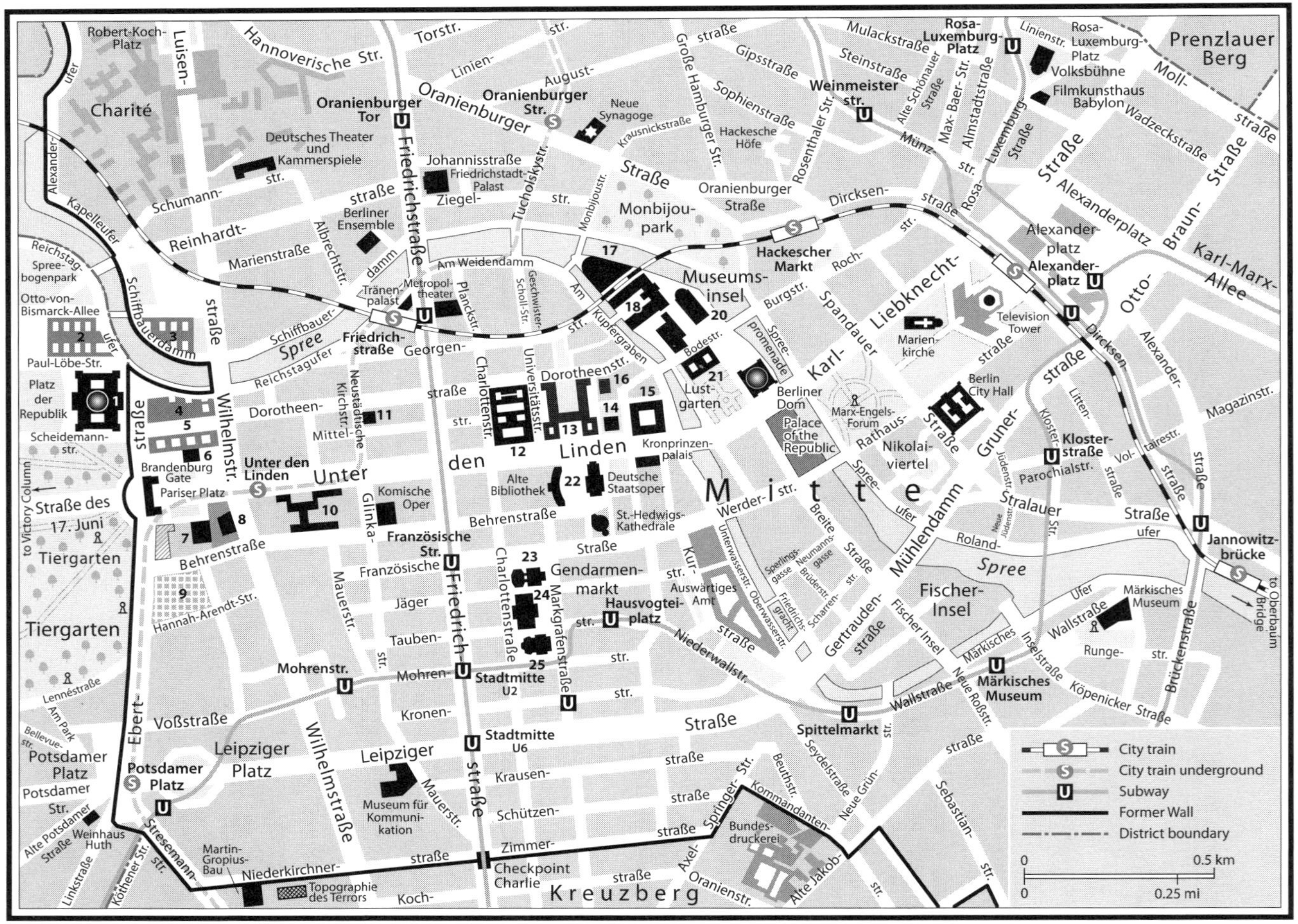

Berlin 2001

4

ORIENTATION

Geographical Didacticism and the X-Films of New Berlin

A REINSTATED CAPITAL

In 2003, capital marketing firm Partner für Berlin issued a promotional DVD titled *Location Berlin–Brandenburg.* In one of its short films, the renowned cinematographer Michael Ballhaus guides potential film producers through the many sites and sights of the New Berlin. As a figure who began his career in New German Cinema before working in Hollywood, this regular collaborator of Rainer Werner Fassbinder and Martin Scorsese was uniquely positioned to introduce the international film community to the merits of shooting in his "hometown": Studio Babelsberg, Potsdamer Platz, Alexanderplatz, and the Brandenburg Gate.

The same DVD, while extolling Berlin–Brandenburg as a production location, also features two additional shorts, *Ready for Business* (FRG 2002) and *Young Berlin* (FRG 2000), both produced by city government and tourism interests.[1] As the DVD's alignment of cinema, business, and youth culture makes clear, filmmaking in the unified German capital *(Hauptstadt)* was integral to urban image politics. Already in the business of forging screen realities, the film industry was being called on not only to enrich the regional economy but also to construct and circulate new visions of Germany's largest city.

In 1995, film critic Jan Gympel could wonder whether the unfinished Berlin of permanent construction sites *(Baustellen)* would ever again prove an impressive film location *(Schauplatz).* Lamenting the loss of Berlin's Cold War cachet, especially of the Berlin Wall, "its greatest tourist attraction," he doubted whether the city "would ever regain the glamour and status that the division of the world had once removed from it." Accordingly, postwall Berlin paled in comparison to the ubiquitous urban filmography, particularly to the Weimar era's *Berlin. Die Sinfonie der Großstadt* (*Berlin: Symphony of a Great City,* Germany 1927). Missing,

Michael Ballhaus walks through Alexanderplatz in *Location Berlin–Brandenburg.* Frame still.

Gympel argued, were not merely the new Berlin films but elements of the built city that they might portray: "pulsing squares, productive chaos, extreme oppositions." For Gympel, Berlin still lacked the true markers of an important cosmopolitan center:

> Where are the glass palaces, the elegant arcades, the swank boulevards, expensive shops, upscale restaurants, dignified villas, and country homes? Where are the decision makers from politics, business, journalism, and culture, whose reputations reach beyond Berlin and whose names aren't already unknown in Hamburg?[2]

He was not alone in criticizing the discrepancy between marketed promises and quotidian experiences of urban metamorphosis and occasional stasis. Politician Wolfgang Schäuble, a member of the conservative CDU, expressed a widespread sentiment that Berliners, still trapped in Cold War provincialism, were short on the requisite "courage for vision and perspective."[3]

Both Germanys had bolstered the representative status of the divided city. The FRG's subventions for its democratic outpost in West Berlin and East Berlin's prominence as the capital of the GDR had ensured a steady flow of resources to the Cold War's beleaguered urban front. Unification suddenly exposed the city's inhabitants to economic competition from other regions. Without the Wall to justify spatial practices, worldviews, and financial support, West and East Berliners found themselves disoriented both in the new market economy and in their altered geopolitical relations.[4] Neither West Berlin's island culture and political exceptionalism nor the ideological postures of the East German capital would suffice in the all-German *(gesamtdeutsch)* city, which had to display convincingly the emergent symbolism of the unified Federal Republic.

With the border reopened and access to the "other" Berlin assured, locals found that familiar places were taking on different meanings, particularly in the East and along former border zones. "Amid the city's fragile and contested urban traditions," Brian Ladd observed of 1990s Berlin, "the prospect of so much that is new raises fears of losing whatever historical identity remains." In the midst of architectural feats that included the new Potsdamer Platz, a revamped Friedrichstraße, and the Reichstag's modern glass cupola, traditionalists were calling for the reconstruction of the Hohenzollern City Palace on the site of the East's Palace of the Republic (Palast der Republik), the shimmering copper building that had housed both the GDR parliament (Volkskammer) and numerous cultural venues.[5]

The postwall capital had to serve a diverse population; its new political guise also had to persuade the greater Federal Republic and the world at large that the city could once again exhibit the cosmopolitan energies of the Weimar Republic while carefully contextualizing and containing its associations with Germany's National Socialist past.[6] If Gympel feared that Berlin would never achieve the filmic appeal of Frankfurt am Main ("Mainhattan"), with its skyscrapers and global financial district, just two years later, Partner für Berlin would make a virtue of Berlin's skyline of construction cranes and scaffolding. While Gympel suggested that architecture "disseminated through moving images" would be the best advertisement for Berlin, the marketing firm transformed the *Baustelle* into a proto-cinematic attraction in its own right: the *Schaustelle* (place to look and look at).[7] Undermining Gympel's claims, several films, including Wolfgang Becker's *Das Leben ist eine Baustelle* (*Life Is All You Get,* FRG 1997), Hussi Kutlucan's *Ich Chef, Du Turnschuh* (Me boss, you sneaker, FRG 1998), and Hito Steyerl's *Die leere Mitte* (*The Empty Center,* FRG 1998), took advantage of Berlin's transitional milieu, a place where building the future went hand in hand with unearthing the past and discovering oneself.

Between Gympel's 1995 indictment of Berlin as a failed profilmic space and Ballhaus's 2003 reassurance that "this area offers the largest variety of possibilities for shooting a movie," the postwall capital region and the German film industry experienced parallel pressures to display their renewal and economic potential. Starting in 1998, Partner für Berlin began promoting the city, which needed to be a functional seat of government by the end of the decade, under the title "The

New Berlin" (Das neue Berlin). Using several media and purposely "blurring" the "boundaries between political communication, city marketing and private advertising," the campaign, as urban planner Claire Colomb has argued, could simultaneously claim the rejuvenation of the built city, its symbolic entities, and its businesses.[8] Meanwhile, homegrown cinema in Germany and in Europe more generally was struggling to maintain its share in markets dominated by Hollywood imports and to increase foreign exports, particularly to the United States. At the time of Gympel's writing, German productions accounted for only 9.4 percent of domestic ticket sales, in contrast to American cinema's 80 percent share of the German market.[9] The industry, like the city, was in need of a boost to its local, national, and international image.

To live up to the expectations raised by Partner für Berlin, Berlin required new moving images, but who would make these? The (West) German film industry was undergoing generational realignment following the reign of New German Cinema's aesthetically and politically provocative, yet economically unviable, auteurism of the 1970s and 1980s. East German directors, once protected by a planned economy, secure positions at the DEFA studios, and the despised but predictable proscriptions of state censorship now found themselves competing for limited film funding reserves in a commercial industry dominated by their savvy Western counterparts. Local (West) Berlin filmmakers suffered, according to one funding board official, from a "subvention mentality" and were perceived to be ill-adept at justifying their esoteric projects for the market.[10] Relying on federal and regional funding as well as television coproduction coffers, German cinema of the 1990s pursued a combination of quality and popular appeal. One of the signature regional funding slogans of the period underscored this backlash against auteurist experimentation: "No more support without audience interest!"[11]

The industry's elevation of mass entertainment and profit above aesthetic complexity favored genre films that dealt uncritically with the German past and present. Critics, scholars, and film professionals from the generation reared on the political and social engagement of figures like Fassbinder, Volker Schlöndorff, and Alexander Kluge decried this shift in the priorities of Germany's national cinema. Labeling the popular films of the early 1990s a "New German Cinema of Consensus," film historian Eric Rentschler was wary of "characters whose primary sense of person and place" so soon after the *Wende* of 1989–90 was "rarely an overt function of their national identity or directly impacted by Germany's difficult past."[12] Screenwriter Jochen Brunow lauded the 1968 generation for its role in disseminating a differentiated image of postwar (West) Germany abroad, which, he implied, the more isolationist postwall cinema would do well to emulate. "We will not be able to avoid it," he argued, "we will have to talk about our self-image and our feeling of self-worth as Germans."[13] In turning away from the country's specific history and geopolitics, the German industry was jeopardizing its international standing exactly at a moment when it could have been circulating representations of the nation and the capital abroad.

In 1994, the convergence of urban and cinematic location politics *(Standortpolitik)* began preparing the ground for postwall Berlin's new cinema. In August, Klaus Keil, a professor of production and media economics at Munich's commercially oriented University of Television and Film, assumed the directorship of the new, regionally consolidated Filmboard Berlin-Brandenburg. Just one month earlier, a quartet of film professionals born in the 1950s and 1960s had founded X-Filme Creative Pool in Berlin as an antidote to the stagnation of the homegrown industry. Producer Stefan Arndt (Sputnik Film GmbH) and filmmakers Tom Tykwer, Wolfgang Becker, and Dani Levy espoused a programmatic production concept that would combine "an ambitious independent auteur cinema" with "authentic subject matter that takes place in Germany or has something to do with Germany but can also work internationally."[14] More than any German films shepherded by the FBBB between 1994 and 2004, Tykwer's *Lola rennt* (*Run Lola Run*, FRG 1998) and Becker's *Good Bye, Lenin!* (FRG 2003) successfully bridged domestic and foreign markets.

Shot in Berlin, X-Filme's popular exceptions to consensus cinema engaged in complex ways with the city's spatial and temporal anxieties, its clashing uses and memory cultures. While *Lola rennt,* in a play of determinate and indeterminate geographies, confounds cartographic indexicality, the mapping of cinematographic images to their place of profilmic origin, *Good Bye, Lenin!* manipulates urban space in all-German commemoration of a vanishing East German capital. Produced before and after the federal government's relocation to the city in 1999, the films explore urban change through youth culture, the demographic driving Berlin's millennial "hype."[15] Mobilizing discourses on urban identity, regional funding, location shooting, fictional setting, city and cinematic marketing, international distribution, and, ultimately, tourism, the films reveal the interdependence of profilmic and filmic spaces. The Berlin topographies put forth by *Lola rennt* and *Good Bye, Lenin!* imagine strategies for postwall spatial *re*-orientation.

THE POLITICS OF *HAUPTSTADT*

When the Bundestag met to choose the future seat of government in June 1991, a preference for Berlin was hardly universal. Politicians were weighing various divisions of labor between Berlin and the West German capital of Bonn against a complete relocation to Berlin. From the outset, voices for and against Berlin made recourse to national symbolism and symbolic geographies. At stake were competing notions of Germany's past and hopes for its future. Berlin's geographic location within unified Germany and within the boundaries of the new Europe, along with the city's contested historical topographies, dominated not only the twelve-hour debate; these factors shaped discussions of Berlin throughout the 1990s.[16] Popular acceptance of the new coordinates of German power would depend on the successful dissemination of a positive, more inclusive city image, one that would promote East–West integration while neutralizing reminders of national shame.

Particularly in the West, the return to Berlin challenged long-held associations of Bonn with postwar democracy, transparency, and modest national articulations. Opponents to relocation invoked the cautionary tale of National Socialism's unrealized utopia of world capital *(Welthauptstadt)* Germania. The legacy of the Third Reich still loomed, for most Westerners, over the former *Reichshauptstadt* of, as leftist politician Ulrich Briefs put it, "the most inhumane political terror system in all of human history." In his contribution to the Bundestag debates, Briefs argued that "respect for the suffering that was inflicted, from Berlin, on the people of Europe and beyond demands that we say: 'Never again Berlin!' just as we must also say: it must never again come to the aggressive, brutal, authoritarian Germany of the past."[17] The old Federal Republic had not only rejected the Nazi capital's symbiosis of urban and political ambition by opting for a provincial seat on the Rhein; it had also encouraged, like the GDR, the projection of National Socialist wrongdoing onto the "other" Germany. The possibility of a capital in unified Berlin forced Westerners to reconcile Bonn's rhetoric of democratic freedom with East Berlin's totalitarian continuities. The majority of German citizens (roughly three Westerners to every Easterner) would have to be persuaded that the capital could indeed evoke enough positive national imagery to counteract negative perceptions within and beyond Germany.

Prussian achievements and Weimar creative capital provided two rallying points for collective German pride in Berlin; the future offered another. The conservative Schäuble, at mid-decade, favored the cherry-picking of urban attributes and associations. With so many histories from which to choose, it was up to Berlin "to decide what its role in the past was, what its future role in the reunified Germany, in a unified Europe will be."[18] Berlin's new city image did not have to be predetermined by pasts that the FRG had already disavowed. Daimler-Benz CEO Edzard Reuter (son of the Berlin mayor Ernst Reuter, who had, in 1948, implored the international community to intervene in the Soviet Blockade) compared the business opportunities of the New Berlin not to the 1945 zero hour *(Stunde Null)* but to "a new Wilhelmine era" *(Gründerzeit)* in which large, lucrative enterprises might be undertaken.[19] Despite the city's enduring architectural evidence of the

National Socialist and SED regimes, CDU Mayor Eberhard Diepgen would suggest that Berlin had no future as a "monument mile or massive Wall museum." Instead, he urged all Germans to participate "in building our shared capital."[20] By late summer 1999, weekly news magazine *Der Spiegel* would declare Berlin "the workshop in which the Germany of the twenty-first century is already and intensively being constructed." From this "laboratory of the future," a new "Germany-feeling" could emerge.[21]

Proponents of a Berlin Republic also shone their optimism on the lingering stigma of National Socialism. Inverting the argument of Berlin's opponents, they claimed that the city was the ideal site for a confrontation with German history: "Only he who acknowledges his past and doesn't get rid of it through repression and forgetting gains the future!" With some careful reinterpretation, Berlin might even prove to be the better token of the FRG's allegiance with its Western allies.[22] Nazi blights on collective and prosthetic memory, such as the 1933 book burning at Bebelplatz, the anti-Semitic violence of Kristallnacht in 1938, or the 1942 Wannsee Conference, could be tempered by references to the Allied cooperation of the Berlin Air Lift, the Cold War speeches of American presidents, and the initial euphoria of November 9, 1989. With so many versions of Berlin available, federal and municipal politicians as well as urban marketers only needed to reactivate the right ones.

The geopolitics of unified Germany and postcommunist Europe ultimately trumped any concern with Berlin's past. Far more pressing was the city's utility in managing new local, regional, national, and transnational articulations of space and belonging. While Easterners *(Ossis)*, many experiencing unification as second-class citizens, found themselves living in the euphemistically titled "new states" *(neue Bundesländer)* of the Federal Republic, Westerners *(Wessis)* resentfully shared their welfare state and comparative wealth with their former ideological foes. As the most visible site of Cold War division, but also of peaceful revolution, Berlin was a place to which both groups could lay claim and where the intermingled histories of the two Germanys were most universally recognized. The Christian Democrat Horst Eylmann was one of several politicians eager to exploit the city as the cradle of German unity. As he put it, "the greatest political task before us is to become one people again," and "the name Berlin" was essential to this "feeling,"[23] which could be closely monitored and encouraged in the city itself. As Mayor Diepgen later echoed, "Germany's process of growing together could be directly experienced and shaped" in this urban "microcosm of German unity.[24]" Berlin could thus function both as a mediated symbol, consumed by the nation from afar, and as a local Petri dish, available for regular microscopic inspection by the federal government.

The move to Berlin also strategically repositioned the FRG's decision makers within the former territory of the GDR. Though unification had required much political, social, economic, and cultural adjustment, even sacrifice, by Easterners, the West's value system remained largely intact. Schäuble touted relocation as proof of the willingness "of us in the West" to "make our contribution to German unity."[25] Since Easterners had continually experienced Berlin as their capital, this gesture of the federal government would, governor of Mecklenburg–Vorpommern Bernd Seite argued, reassure them of "one constant" in all the "reorientation" of unification. Demanding from the Federal Republic a commitment to a more equitable understanding of the Eastern perspective, he maintained that a "capital in the Eastern part of Germany stands for a bit of adaptation of the West to the East in comparison to the wholesale takeover of the East by the West." Only with the West's acknowledgment that unification was more than the acquisition of citizens and territory could the two sides truly collaborate on forging "a new shared German identity."[26] Some of this all-German identity would result from the gradual disappearance of the architectures of division: the Wall, its swaths of no-man's-land, and the interruptions to urban planning that it had occasioned; some would develop with efforts to link the infrastructures of Berlin and the surrounding state of Brandenburg. Spatial prejudices, such as the vestigial "Wall in the head" *(Mauer im Kopf),* and their existing visual representations had to be overcome if the city was to address Germany's multiple constituencies.

The countdown to relocation pressed Germans and Berliners to begin thinking differently about themselves, the city's built environment and mediated images, and the many functions that a unified capital would have to fulfill nationally, but also globally as a central economy of the European Union. Berlin's proximity to the countries of the former Soviet bloc assured Germany a leading role in the balance of Eastern and Western European powers and promised more traffic through the economically depressed states of the former GDR. Seite, whose own state stood to benefit from the development of the capital region, championed the north–south and east–west axes that intersected in Berlin: "Copenhagen–Prague–Vienna–Budapest" and "Paris–Berlin–Warsaw–Moscow."[27] No longer a first world island in the communist East, Berlin's access to emergent Eastern European markets was a boon for capitalism. Reuter went so far as to compare Berlin and its surroundings to "metropolitan regions and globally successful mega-centers" like Dallas and Hong Kong.[28]

Despite the city's constant construction, financial difficulties, and physical ruptures, politicians joined architects, cultural institutions, artists, and businesses in fostering a temporary Berlin that was all potential, "a projection surface for desires and expectations," a cityscape-as-screen, showcasing progress and anticipated outcomes.[29] A concerted advertisement for all that had not yet happened, projects like Potsdamer Platz resembled alien impositions on the built city's modest, self-contained neighborhoods *(Kieze)*. An architectural expression of wishful thinking, the square asserted a new corporate internationalism *(Weltoffenheit)* at the city's geographic center, one that both marketed Location Berlin–Brandenburg to global investors and set a new standard for inhabitants' sense of place.

Over larger distances, the New Berlin could begin acting the part of the capital on television. The staging of its mediated city image in the nightly news domesticated official representations of Germany's center of political power in households throughout the country. As common markers of place, the Brandenburg Gate, Potsdamer Platz, the new Chancellery, and the new Reichstag cupola exposed viewers regularly to an updated political presentation of the city, one that far exceeded "everyday perceptions of the Bonn Republic."[30]

Reviving film production in the capital after the setback of the industry's postwar division and the privatization and sale of DEFA's former studios in Babelsberg was also paramount. On one hand, cinema had always remained a crucial point of contact and differentiation between East and West German culture, as

In summer 1995, visitors to the Panorama Exhibition *Berlin 2005* imagine Potsdamer Platz's future. Photograph by Barbara Esch-Marowski. Courtesy of Landesarchiv Berlin.

evidenced by the Berlin International Film Festival's 1951 origins in Cold War competition. On the other hand, filmmaking in Berlin had a long tradition that predated, but also accompanied, both the armed and ideological conflicts of the twentieth century. With studio lots, postproduction facilities, important archival holdings, two major film academies, an extensive exhibition landscape, and one of the premiere film festivals in the world, the East and West German film industries had effectively preserved an investment opportunity for the utopian, unlikely event of reunification. Quite apart from the cultural reception of individual features, filmmaking was a business that could thrive quickly in the New Berlin, especially under effective leadership.

Federal and regional film funding in the FRG had protected West German cinema's domestic market share by ensuring that German films, despite their limited box-office draw and competition with television, would continue to be made for theatrical release. In 1968, the Film Funding Law (Filmförderungsgesetz) established the FFA, the German Federal Film Board, and required exhibitors to pay a tax *(Filmabgabe)* on all tickets sold. This revenue in turn supported new productions. Since 1974, television stations have partnered with production companies and funding boards, often to the financial and aesthetic detriment of the films they sponsor.[31] With production financing spread among such diverse sources and often attached to incompatible interests, film teams compete for limited resources and struggle to assemble their budgets from numerous sources; in turn, regional funding boards must fight to attract producers, filmmakers, and screenwriters.

Institutional film subvention in West Berlin began as a defensive measure to maintain the visibility of the city's hobbled industry among West German film production's more affluent, postwar centers in Munich, Hamburg, Frankfurt, and Cologne. Founded in 1978, the Berliner Filmförderung was initially preoccupied with existential matters. In the sober assessment of film politician Hans Borgelt, "the basic survival" of "the film economy" was at stake. At the time, he believed neither that West Berlin was "on the verge of a new Ufa epoch" nor that "a newly discovered 'Berlin style' would captivate the world." Though his study of "film city Berlin" did indeed affirm continuities with Weimar cinema, Borgelt insisted on the purely financial "Berlin effect" that the BFF's subventions were to have. The film board was wagering that film crews would spend more in the city than the local banks would provide in credit.[32] Considerations of how new images of West Berlin might affect perceptions of the Cold War city were secondary.

This changed when, after five years, the BFF had amassed a number of culturally valuable (*wertvoll* and *besonders wertvoll*) "Berlin films" and "films made in Berlin." From Ulrich Edel's *Christiane F.—Wir Kinder vom Bahnhof Zoo* (*Christiane F.,* FRG 1981) to Andrzej Zulawski's *Possession* (*The Night the Screaming*

Stops, FRG/France 1981), and from Volker Schlöndorff's *Die Blechtrommel* (*The Tin Drum,* FRG/France/Poland/Yugoslavia 1979) to Margarethe von Trotta's *Die bleierne Zeit* (*Marianne and Juliane,* FRG 1981), the BFF's filmography charted a route from specific urban backdrops or local studio facilities to festival accolades and international distribution. Detlef Stronk, West Berlin's secretary of the economy and transportation at the time, recognized the potential of "an artistically well made film" to "solicit sympathy for our country, even if it deals critically with history or the present." The Berlin films of the FRG's postwar generation might probe the darker themes of the Third Reich, the Holocaust, 1970s leftist terrorism, Cold War malaise and anxiety, and urban neglect, but they also provided national and international film culture with new and varied representations of West Berlin at a moment of ennui in the city's reunification prospects. The films that "unpretentiously portrayed the city and its particular spirit and conveyed a positive Berlin image without false commercialism" recalled for Stronk the realist appeal of Munich in "the Schwabing films of the 1960s." The BFF may not have demanded that "*Buletten* be eaten in every film" or that "the Radio Tower or Memorial Church be visible onscreen," but those features shot in the city could ensure, even subtly, that West Berlin remained in the geopolitical picture of the greater FRG and its allies.[33]

The FBBB inherited the BFF's distinction between the financial and cultural values of funded films as the "Berlin effect" became a regional effect. Berlin and Brandenburg's politicians and industry interests were keen, however, to construct a far more commercially competitive business model for regional film production. Klaus "Kommerz" Keil, who controlled all final decisions on funding allocation in the limited liability company (GmbH), approached films as financial investments in which artistry and production values served the larger project of establishing a location brand name.

Form and content were reduced to a streamlined notion of quality that was to assure the future of the "production location" by attracting new films. These in turn would "secure and create jobs, strengthen the film economy, exploit production capacities, further bolster the location's qualifications."[34] Known for his phrase "away with indiscriminate subsidies, no more shelved films," Keil instituted start-to-finish supervision *(geschlossene Förderung)* of a range of development, production, distribution, marketing, and exhibition projects that both maximized a film's chances to be seen (regardless of its budget) and connected the finished product to its place of manufacture.[35] Though Keil insists that he made no special efforts to promote cinematic visions of the new capital, his policies contributed to the glitz of Berlin's urban performance.[36] Not only did films made in Berlin and Brandenburg revive local star culture and generate regional and national press during shooting; they were contractually obligated to premiere in the city, often, in the early 2000s, at Potsdamer Platz, by then also the headquarters of the Berlinale.[37]

Keil's innovations, moreover, reeducated film professionals in Berlin to produce toward the market and, with the help of the city's reputation for creativity and young ideas, convinced both established industry figures and newcomers to relocate. His later description of 1990s Berlin as "a crystal" shining outward and a "magnet" drawing talent inward might just as well apply to the FBBB itself after its first few years in operation.[38] From screenwriting master classes to a requirement that producers raise 30 percent of the production budget themselves, have a distribution contract in hand, and repay the FBBB from a film's profits within five years of its release, the Filmboard's policies were meant to hone the professionalism of regional film culture while encouraging its practitioners to continue developing their careers in Berlin and Brandenburg.[39]

As a Berlin company with plans to produce *x* films (which in German signals an indefinite, large number) and with a common financial interest in each member's productions, X-Filme was uniquely positioned to benefit from the FBBB's financially and geographically circular policies. Success in Keil's system guaranteed future support. If a film sold enough tickets to repay the Filmboard, the revenue could be used toward a new project, provided that this was also produced in Berlin–Brandenburg. The revolving funds of this reference principle *(Referenzprinzip)* gave producers incentives, if implicitly, to seek material set in the capital region.

In 2006, the daily digest *Welt Kompakt* proclaimed, "There's hardly a German film these days that doesn't take place in Berlin." In the popular imagination, *Good Bye, Lenin!* was still, along with *Lola rennt,* considered the definitive Berlin film of the postwall era.[40] Generously supported by the FBBB and additional federal, regional, and television partners, Stefan Arndt and his directors modeled the standard for what might be termed a new German Cinema of International Quality, one that transported a rejuvenated Berlin image to audiences around the world.[41]

AN UNRELIABLE BACKDROP

In 1997, X-Filme needed a hit. As one of the Filmboard's returning beneficiaries, the company was taking advantage of Keil's "jump-start financing" *(Anschubfinanzierung),* designed to furnish a limited number of established production houses with funds to develop several new projects at once. Keil had decided to sponsor Arndt's cohort of promising filmmakers generously to "stabilize" their firm.[42] While the vote of confidence effectively assured that X-Filme would have projects overlapping in various stages of production and exhibition throughout the FBBB's tenure, the company had already had one box-office flop, Dani Levy's *Stille Nacht* (*Silent Night*, FRG 1996). After producing Levy's film, Wolfgang Becker's generation-X Berlin drama *Das Leben ist eine Baustelle*, and Tom Tykwer's alpine thriller *Winterschläfer* (*Winter Sleepers*, FRG 1997) consecutively, Arndt was seeking a project that could be developed quickly to secure "the survival of the company."[43] With domestic theater admissions climbing from 1996 to 1998 because of the widespread construction of multiplexes and the expansion of FRG film exhibition in the eastern states, new masses were in place for the few German films that could compete with American blockbusters.[44]

With only four months to write the screenplay and fewer than two months to shoot, Arndt and Tykwer turned to the city where X-Filme's "united artists" already lived.[45] *Lola rennt* was conceived from the start as a Berlin film, one that had to prove the company's economic viability at box offices farther afield. Though images of the city were ubiquitous in the German public sphere and could evoke the location's myriad historical associations and future projections for domestic audiences, global art house audiences would have required different degrees of conspicuousness in the naming, framing, and presentation of place. Far from indisputably identifying the film's setting with the built city, Tykwer emphasized youthful mobility (action) over legible cultural and historical topographies (setting). His trademark spatial and temporal dexterity, accentuated by the kinetic cinematography of Frank Griebe and rapid editing of Mathilde Bonnefoy, drew attention to striking formal innovations that were unusual in the well-made and formulaic features favored by funding boards and television stations.[46] The film's resulting geographical ambiguity constructs an aesthetic mechanism for spatial play. This alternation between referential, determinate geographies of place (those that combine cinematographic and cartographic indexicality) and fictionalized, indeterminate urban space changes the built city—but how?

Lola rennt's eponymous red-haired heroine (Franka Potente) receives a frantic payphone call from her boyfriend Manni (Moritz Bleibtreu), a petty gangster who has just lost the one hundred thousand marks he was transporting to his boss after successfully completing a challenge: the smuggling of a fleet of Mercedes to Eastern Europe in exchange for diamonds. Because Lola's moped gets stolen and her taxi driver gets lost between East and West Berlin, she is not able to meet Manni, who instead takes the U-Bahn. When ticket controllers enter the train, he flees, accidentally leaving behind the plastic bag of cash, which a homeless man (Joachim Król) finds. With only twenty minutes to come up with the sum or else face the wrath of his boss, Manni threatens to rob a nearby supermarket. Lola urges him to stay put, promises to procure him the funds, and sets off on a techno-fueled race through the city. Presented in three consecutive versions, Lola's run is beset by contingency and obstacles; the first two variations end in death, first of Lola, then of Manni. Between narrative segments, the couple lies in bed, contemplating love and free will. Choosing to live, they finally manage a happy outcome and walk into the future with cash to spare.

Millennial commentators were struck by what they perceived as the film's ambivalence toward German culture, its perplexing international success in the absence of German cinema's export hallmarks: brooding *Vergangenheitsbewältigung* (coming to terms with the past) and period pieces. Seen as poised between American (popular) and German (high) culture, global and local diegetic elements, and universal and culturally embedded appeal, *Lola rennt* navigated a mixed scholarly reception.[47] While some voices distrusted the film's minimizing of national identity, which could resemble the denial of history, others celebrated its sophisticated cultural hybridity. In retrospect, they echo the turns of skepticism and enthusiasm with which foreign governments, German politicians, national and international observers, and Berliners initially greeted the prospect of a Berlin Republic.[48] What's more, the discomfort they betrayed toward the new capitalist orientation of German cinema recalls the bafflement of some Berlin filmmakers in the face of Keil's controversial restructuring of the regional film industry.

As a film that arose from new location-based funding practices mandated by capital region politicians, *Lola rennt* must be understood as an audiovisual dialogue with place and memories of place in two senses: (1) in its broader institutional dependence on Berlin's city marketing and (2) in its cinematographic approach to profilmic space. Tykwer's extreme cinephilic formalism both maps urban space, rendering it visible and structuring its unique relations between shots, and remembers Berlin's film history, its previous spatial interpretations. What might be called the film's spatial attitude or behavior *(Einstellung),* a particular means of framing the world, of reconstituting it for the camera and future screens, is crucial to the way *Lola rennt* imagines a New Cinematic Berlin, a city of youth, dynamism, and forward motion. Hardly a film that turns its back on Germany, it performs and reinterprets urban space for the postwall generation.

Lola rennt's title sequence takes up the central concerns of the Federal Republic and the New Berlin in the 1990s. In a voice-over that is at once ominous and soothing, Heinz Paetsch, the well-known (West) German narrator of children's stories, asks, "Who are we? Where do we come from? Where are we going?" These questions posit a line, a pathway, a trajectory—in short, the motion between the past and the future and between geographical points. From the outset, the film announces, however, the cyclical rules of its cinematic game. Two epigraphs, foreshadowing its narrative structure, emphasize the impossibility of separating beginnings from endings:

> We shall not cease from exploration
> And the end of all our exploring
> Will be to arrive where we started
> And know the place for the first time.
>
> T. S. Eliot[49]

> After the game is before the game.
>
> S. Herberger

A ticking clock punctuates the electronic score as its pendulum wipes the screen between company, funding board, and directorial credits. This acoustic and visual evocation of unrelenting temporal progression is paired with continued references to the tension between repetition and singularity. Passage through the demonic mouth of the clockface reveals a throng of anonymous people, moving at accelerated speed in desaturated blues and grays. Handheld at chest height, Griebe's camera rushes through the crowd, occasionally focusing, at normal speed, on a figure in full color. All the while, Paetsch contemplates humanity's eternal search for meaning, its perpetual generation of new questions. Much like Eliot, he concludes, "But isn't it always the same question . . . and always the same answer?" To this, one of the highlighted characters, a uniformed guard (reprised by Armin Rohde from X-Filme's modest art house success *Das Leben ist eine Baustelle*), offers a film industrial variation on another famous quip of Sepp Herberger, the national soccer coach responsible for the FRG's 1954 "miraculous" World Cup win. Looking into the camera, he explains, "The ball's round. The game lasts ninety minutes. That much is clear. Everything else is theoretical." He kicks a soccer ball into the air as the camera rises above the masses, whose bodies form the sentence *Lola rennt.* Having thus proclaimed its desired continuities, the film now displays its novelty.

This extended prelude to the film's further animated credits already alludes to film and urban histories. In using Paetsch's "soothing, warm," yet "ironic" voice, Tykwer hoped to convey that *Lola rennt* itself was something of a modern "fairytale."[50] The narrator's omniscience and philosophical tone clearly revive the poetic register of Peter Handke's refrain, "When the child was a child," at the beginning of Wim Wenders's *Der Himmel über Berlin* (*Wings of Desire,* FRG/France 1987). While Wenders's film reflects on the whole of Berlin history, lingers on the melancholic spaces and specific architectures of division, and explores love as a vehicle between eternity and human finitude, *Lola rennt* rehearses the New Berlin's preoccupations: (1) the repetition of history; (2) ends and new starts (1871, 1918, 1919, 1945, 1949, 1961, 1989); (3) the countdown to government relocation, which was also publicly choreographed by the "New Berlin" campaign;[51] and (4) the merging of the East and the West.

In the first diegetic shot, two halves of the city bounce into view at the top and bottom of the frame. Their collision produces the clap of a production slate as the two parts settle into a coherent aerial perspective. It is as though the film is granting permission to the urban and narrative space it is forming. The resultant "map," though betraying the unmistakable curve *(Bogen)* of the River Spree, rebukes cartographic convention by turning the city on its side. With respect to the frame, East and West assume the positions of North and South, and the river runs vertically rather than horizontally. Though the two pieces come from the geographical, rather than filmic, East and West, their composite topography yields the former Eastern border district of Mitte, the principal site of postwall construction, international diplomacy, and cultural heritage, but also the center of postwall Berlin's new all-German youth culture.

Just as this initial view of Berlin both establishes and defamiliarizes the film's setting, it evokes and then abandons Wenders's motif of the "skies over Berlin." If *Der Himmel über Berlin* approaches the city gradually in a series of sweeping aerial shots, *Lola rennt* quite literally cuts to the chase. No sooner does the image

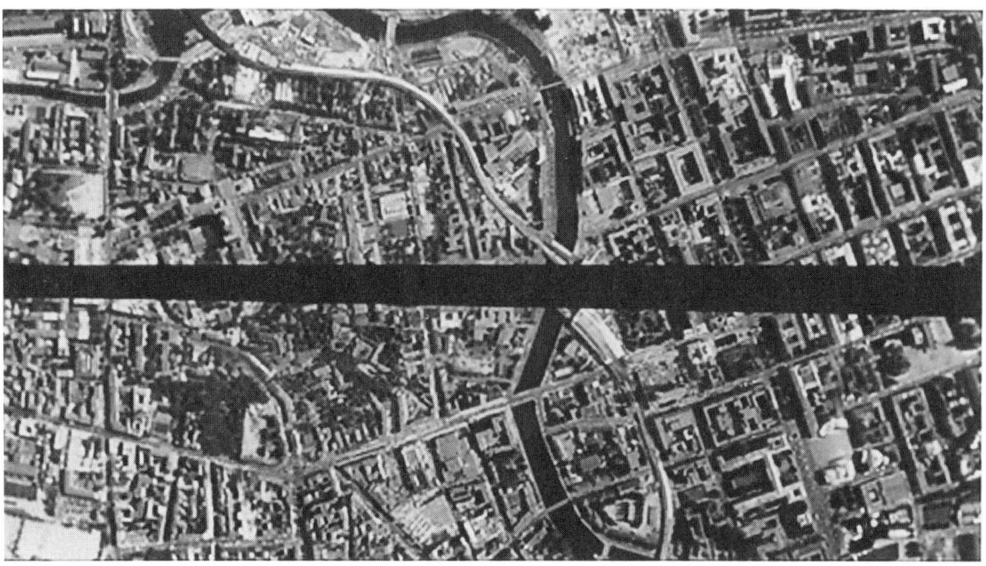

Berlin-Mitte bounces into view with East and West in the positions of cartographic north and south, respectively, in *Lola rennt*. Frame still.

of the city form than the camera accelerates to earth, traveling into a courtyard, through a window, and straight to Lola's predicament. In *Der Himmel über Berlin,* Henri Alekan's mobile camera remains observational in the passage from exterior to interior and elegantly scales the Berlin Wall with the best tools of analog cinematography and editing, for example, crane shots and dissolves. Tykwer's digitally enhanced velocity compresses the distance between cartographic abstraction and concrete events at ground level without betraying "the exact place where the transition happens."[52] There is no time to get one's bearings in a single, limited vantage point.

Between his screenplay and the finished film, Tykwer made numerous adjustments to the city's degree of conspicuousness. In the script's third version, he still envisioned the words "Berlin" and "Summer" drifting horizontally into view just prior to the aerial shot, referred to the setting as "Berlin-Mitte," and described the presence of construction cranes in the distance. Curiously, however, he also added the qualification "actually looks more like London here." Aside from brief allusions to the Polish border and Lola's more extensive rendition of her taxi driver's confusion of East and West Berlin, the screenplay, like the film, avoids further mention of the city.[53]

Domestic publicity materials, in contrast, capitalized on *Lola rennt*'s affiliation with Berlin. Neither X-Filme nor distributor Prokino Filmverleih shied away from opportunities for the cross-promotion of place and product, and the film's official press kit included the shooting location in many of its slogans: "Berlin. Now . . ."; "a woman runs through the streets of Berlin"; and "Berlin. Lola. 100,000 DM. Manni. 20 minutes. A pair of lovers . . ." Indeed, many of the formulations suggested to the press, festival programmers, and film buyers presented *Lola rennt* as a *Gesamtkunstwerk* of the music video era, a veritable postwall heir to Walter Ruttmann's *Berlin. Die Sinfonie der Großstadt*:

> With a pulsating contemporary soundtrack, an exciting, unusual visual aesthetic, and the tempo of the big city, *Run Lola Run* celebrates the triumph of a love that captures the breathless feeling of life in the late 1990s. . . .
>
> A story as old and new as life itself. The heartbeat of a metropolis, that echoes in the pulsating, pop-oriented soundtrack. Images full of power and dynamism: *Run Lola Run* portrays the exciting feeling of life in the late 1990s. Forceful, current, breathless—and larger than life.[54]

Deploying catchphrases of Weimar modernity in the service of 1990s youth culture, these descriptions align Ruttmann's virtuoso audiovisual experiments in optical music with Tykwer's feature-length extension of the music video, a format

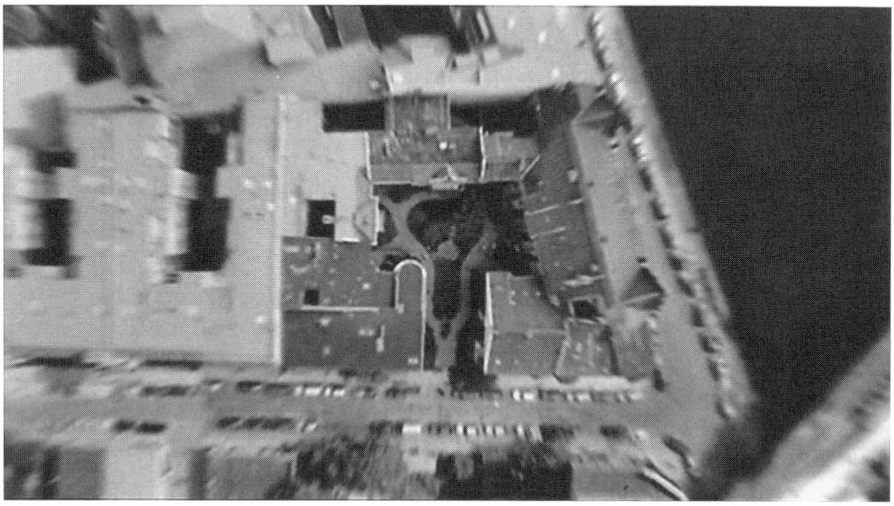

From the heavens to earth in *Lola rennt*. Frame stills

driven by innovations in editing. Tykwer and his team were steeped in contemporary music culture. While Mathilde Bonnefoy, an early proponent of the Avid digital, nonlinear editing system, had previously cut music videos for Rammstein, Udo Lindenberg, and White Wooden Horses, Tykwer designed the film's technopop score with Johnny Klimek and Reinhold Heil, known for their electronic music in the 1980s. In the weeks leading up to the film's release in August 1998, German MTV broadcast sequences from *Lola rennt* in the form of a music video for "Wish," the sound track to Lola's first run.[55]

With Lola's "flaming red shock of hair" lighting the way "right through the Republic on posters and in televised music videos," her run through Berlin publicly recast the contested spaces of German history as an anonymous urban backdrop *(Kulisse)*.[56] Ruttmann's Berlin symphony had synthesized urban experience through montage and a grand score requiring an orchestra of seventy-five. Tykwer's Lola, a beacon of postwall cinema, navigated the uncharted terrain of Berlin's construction sites, paying homage to all the filmic Lolas before her: those of Josef von Sternberg (Marlene Dietrich), Alfred Hitchcock (evoked in the German title of *Stage Fright,* United Kingdom 1950), Max Ophüls (Martine Carol), and Fassbinder (Barbara Sukowa). In routes of repetition and variation, much like Tykwer's own turns of emulation and differentiation, Lola's mobility was choreographed to the

Lola running past a wall in *Lola rennt.* Publicity still courtesy of Deutsche Kinemathek.

beats of the Love Parade generation, for whom Mitte had become "a kind of massive adventure playground."[57]

Launched into each of her three runs by her animated alter ego (reminiscent of a video game avatar), she traverses the same series of spaces en route first to her father's bank and then to Manni's phone booth. In jump cuts and tracking shots, in a variety of shot scales, and in alternations of slow motion and normal speed, Lola dashes past buildings, walls, and fences, across streets and over bridges—a cinematic parkour course. Arms pumping and hair flying, she encounters a procession of obstacles (a woman with a baby, a group of nuns, a man on a bicycle, an ambulance, etc.) that affect her timing and choices and, ultimately, the outcome of the segment. The pure spectacle of Lola's movement is occasionally interrupted by narrative elements: rapidly cut still photo flash-forwards of people she passes, video footage of her father (Herbert Knaup) and his mistress (Nina Petri) discussing their relationship, and Manni's parallel frustrations of immobility. These intrusions heighten the suspense of Lola's progress.

Tykwer credited his strong "cinematic socialization" for *Lola rennt*'s origin in an image of a woman running rather than in a story. As he put it, "this image is cinema: movement and emotion."[58] Much like Tom Gunning's concept of an early "cinema of attractions" that reveled in nonnarrative visual demonstrations unique to cinematographic technology, Tykwer's film rediscovers the visual pleasures of motion itself.[59] As a result, Lola's body becomes a red and blue-green graphic element, whose mobile articulations (particularly in the extended first sprint, when the spaces and destinations are new) "reduce" the city to "walls that zip by, streets quickly rushed through, dangerous intersections, and action-filled interiors."[60] With fluid motion their imperative, Tykwer and Griebe employed all matter of roving vehicles: "jeeps, cranes, even tricycles or carts . . . anything with wheels."[61] Their efforts to keep Lola in view and in focus effectively limit depth of field and blur the background in lateral tracking shots. Likewise, their camera positions and framing conspire to withhold information about the film's shooting locations, many of them significant sites in Berlin's history.

Lola's first run to her father's bank includes a case in point, her photogenic race across Oberbaumbrücke from Kreuzberg in the West to Friedrichshain in the East. Built in 1895, the year of cinema's first public screenings in Berlin, the bridge staged a grand entrance into the Wilhelmine city's Northern Spree shore. Partially destroyed by the Nazi regime in 1945, the bridge would subsequently divide the two neighborhoods during the Cold War. Reopened in 1994, the restored route embodied politicians' promises to unite the city's East–West infrastructure. Though locals would surely still recognize the curve of the elevated U-Bahn tracks between Schlesisches Tor in the West and Warschauer Straße in the East,

Lola dashing across Oberbaumbrücke. *Lola rennt.* Frame still.

Lola's passage occurs without the help of an establishing shot. Instead, the bridge's unmistakable architectural features—its two decorative towers—are nowhere to be seen. As Lola runs through the arcades below the U-Bahn tracks, the bridge is reduced to a series of red brick columns and an ornate banister, whose regular intervals might recall, for the cinema-socialized, the view from Ruttmann's Berlin-bound train, tearing across a bridge in the German countryside. The Spree provides a glistening white and yellow background for Lola's profile as the camera moves into close-up. Rapid cuts between lateral and frontal slow-motion shots of her head all but obscure the surrounding space, and a final long shot of Lola in the arched walkway abruptly gives way to the next scene.

Later, en route to Manni, Lola sprints across the Gendarmenmarkt, a square not only known for its Huguenot history, its eighteenth-century German and French cathedrals, and its Konzerthaus but also meticulously restored by the GDR government for the city's all-German 750th anniversary in 1987. Lola's first and second runs present the square from a bird's-eye perspective, yet none of these buildings is visible. In her initial crossing, she runs diagonally through a square pattern of dark gray cobblestones. The statue on the right of the frame is unrecognizable as the eighteenth-century poet, dramatist, and intellectual Friedrich Schiller. In the second variation, the camera zooms out to reveal Lola running along the straight edge of the pattern, which has now been placed at a diagonal. In the final run, the camera tracks along Gendarmenmarkt at ground level as Lola passes in front of the French Cathedral and Konzerthaus. A reverse establishing

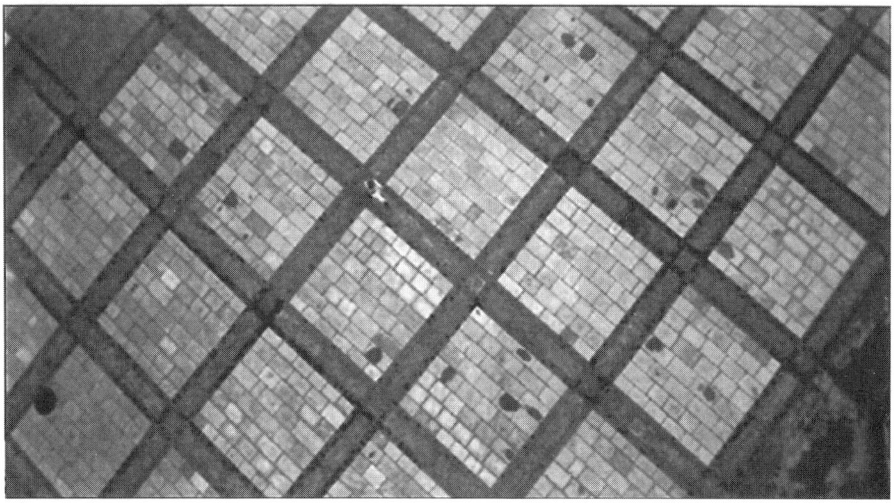

Run 1, run 2, and run 3 across Gendarmenmarkt. *Lola rennt.*

shot, this final framing of the square inverts classical cinematic conventions for portraying place while also making sure that initiated spectators might catch the gesture. It *is* possible, this variation suggests, to see Berlin anew.

Tykwer's reluctance to confirm specific locations and landmarks remains conspicuous throughout the film. Even when signage comes into view, it appears, often blurred, at the edge of the frame or in the background and disappears quickly in editing transitions. Just as the film's initial cartographic clarity was too soon abandoned to be interpreted, the barely acknowledged signs for Friedrichstraße, Behrenstraße, Tauroggener Straße, Deutsche Oper, and Hinter dem Gießhaus make no overt claims to the space of narrative action. What's more, when historical buildings such as the Hotel de Rome opposite Bebelplatz and the Kronprinzenpalais on Unter den Linden are shown, it is in their respective fictive guises as the Deutsche Transfer Bank (where Lola's father works) and a casino (where she eventually wins one hundred thousand marks).[62]

For those who know Berlin, Lola's runs create a series of impossible spatial relations between Mitte (East), Kreuzberg (West), Friedrichshain (East), and Charlottenburg (West). When urban planner Kevin Lynch asked in 1960 how the "image of the city" is perceived by its inhabitants, he found that "familiar observers can store up a vast quantity of point images in familiar sequences" but that "recognition may break down when the sequence is reversed or scrambled." He also discovered that some inhabitants would construct their visual memories of urban space as a cinematic, "continuous organization employing unrolling interconnections instead of static hierarchies" of various urban elements, including paths, edges, districts, nodes, and landmarks.[63] What Lynch's suggestions of reversed or scrambled places and cinematic spatial memory make clear is the extent to which films can reinterpret and obscure profilmic space. Unlike classical cinema's usual analytical spatial leaps through cuts on action, consistent screen direction, and narrative logic, *Lola rennt*'s running sequences activate two contradictory forms of continuity: the (illogical) spatial contiguity of the built city and (perfectly logical) matches on action. As one commentator later put it, the capital comes across as a "puzzle that is impossible to put together."[64] Tykwer's reassembly of Berlin's misshapen pieces does construct, however, a coherent filmic cityscape, "a truly unified Berlin," from its fusion of Eastern and Western locations.[65] Just as early chase films were the genre par excellence of continuity, linking spaces through action, Lola's runs naturalize a proximity of locales that was both imagined and real but unrealized in 1990s Berlin, where increasingly invisible borders were becoming internalized.[66]

Within national film culture, Tykwer consciously positioned *Lola rennt* as a cinematic urban response to *Das Leben ist eine Baustelle,* in which Jan (Jürgen

Vogel) struggles in life and love amid the uncertainties of German unity. Cowritten by Tykwer and Becker, the film presented "a realistic, nearly extinct Berlin on the move and in upheaval, still in the maelstrom of the fall of the Wall and the *Wende*." In its historical, realist guise, Berlin portended darker contemporary themes of unemployment, the housing shortage, and the risk of AIDS. *Lola rennt* was to offer "another" Berlin of pure potentiality, not one that would "isolate the Memorial Church" or "add in Alexanderplatz," but one that was "in an exciting synthetic state between building the new and demolishing the old."[67] In keeping with Tykwer's irreverence toward Berlin's landmarks, both the Reichstag and the Palace of the Republic appear merely as blurred backgrounds amid the debris of construction. Whereas Jan grows depressed at the intersection of adulthood and Berlin's new social challenges, Lola's trajectories and repetitions demonstrate a mastery of change, an ease of navigation through the city's building sites and detours. Indeed, the pop heroine, whom Tykwer described with Pippi Longstocking's phrase "I create the world as I like it," traces new, unexpected pathways through Berlin's video-game-like "battleground."[68]

As politicians and business leaders complained of Berlin's transitional traffic problems, Lola performed unfettered movement in spaces once known for their Cold War limitations to mobility.[69] In the weeks after *Lola rennt*'s release, Social Democratic member of parliament and former Easterner Thomas Krüger defined what success meant for a new generation of young, creative Berliners in his anthology *Die bewegte Stadt* (City on the move): "The experiment, the spontaneous and unconventional, the weird and the wild, in short the individual is in demand." In what he termed "a post-ideological era," a figure like Lola could run indiscriminately over old ground and the temporarily marginal spaces of Berlin's new center.[70] From the distance of the FRG's new and old states, Tykwer's Berlin departed from Cold War media representations. Instead, Lola's hair, tank top, and bell-bottom pants highlighted the colors of a city in the process of renewal: the reds, whites, and yellows of construction barriers; the yellows of construction cranes; the pinks, yellows, and whites of pipes; the blues of containers; and the browns of unsettled earth.

Tykwer's revisions of the city cast off predetermined historical and political associations with Berlin's specific places and buildings, but his didactic spatial shorthand over the three runs also trained spectators to mistake Berlin for other locations. Contrary to his statements in Germany, the director emphasized the global interchangeability of *Lola rennt*'s urban backdrop for the North American market: "The film could just as easily be set in Peking, Helsinki or New York, the only thing that would change is the scenery, not the emotional dimension. I think everyone, truly everyone, can identify with Lola."[71] The flexibility of Lola's Berlin, its utility for the film's simple adventure and romance plot, may have resulted from limited visual access to the city's unique urban features. But it also helped the film to flaunt something that both X-Filme and the FBBB had championed: a kind of filmmaking that could keep pace with American and other successful national cinemas.

Lola rennt's flamboyant exploitation of new technological possibilities located it alongside a series of millennial art house productions that self-reflexively experimented with editing and the sequence of story information. While Hal Hartley's *Flirt* (United States 1996) repeated the same script with different casts in New York, Berlin, and Tokyo, Peter Howitt's *Sliding Doors* (United Kingdom/ United States 1998) explored, like *Lola rennt,* contingency and parallel lives.[72] Mike Figgis's *Time Code* (United States 2000) employed digital editing to sync four perspectives of the same plot in simultaneous, quadruple split screen. With its hyperstylized cuts, contemporary sound track, saturated color palette, and young protagonists, *Lola rennt* achieved a cult status comparable, in 1990s youth culture, to Quentin Tarantino's *Pulp Fiction* (United States 1994), Baz Luhrmann's *Romeo + Juliet* (United States 1996), and Danny Boyle's *Trainspotting* (United Kingdom 1996), all of which had premiered in Germany before Tykwer completed his screenplay.

With its box-office success in Germany (two million tickets in four months) and mounting prospects for international distribution, *Lola rennt,* a project that had initially divided the votes of Keil and his team, now embodied the Filmboard's ambitions.[73] By the end of 1998, the FBBB director would take stock of the board's achievements, concluding that Berlin–Brandenburg had indeed improved its national and international credentials as a "production location."[74] As the government feted its arrival in Berlin the following year, news weekly *Der Spiegel* would playfully invoke the rhetoric of motion and adaptation: "New capital, new government, new millennium and everyday a new detour—in a 5-kilometer-range surrounding the Brandenburg Gate, one searches in vain for Germany's darkest trademark, stagnation."[75] From Mayor Eberhard Diepgen's reelection campaign, "Diepgen rennt" (which depicted the Mayor sprinting past a finished Potsdamer Platz),[76] to Berlin's new influx of young Germans and expats, Germany's red Lola helped to set the tempo of the Berlin Republic.

When the Filmmuseum Berlin opened its doors in September 2000, its exhibit on more than a century of German film history ended with a life-sized statue of Lola in a runner's pose. Located in the Sony Center Filmhaus on Potsdamer Platz (home to the German Film and Television Academy as well as the Deutsche Kinemathek), Lola's likeness quite literally bridged the past and future of German cinema on one of Berlin's most contested sites.

An Eberhard Diepgen campaign postcard from 1999. Courtesy of the author.

RETROSPECTION AND THE BERLIN COMPASS

In the months following the release of *Lola rennt,* Keil would observe, "They're not here yet, the 'local stories for the global market.' Maybe they're not yet ripe, not yet."[77] He was referring to films that might convey the political and social complexities of the postwall city, including residual conflicts between Easterners and Westerners, to the world at large. *Good Bye, Lenin!* was X-Filme's answer to this omission in the Filmboard's catalog. After years of receiving proposals for films addressing the *Wende,* Arndt finally landed on Bernd Lichtenberg's treatment, an appropriate entrée into the dramatic potential of that period. The "ten year distance" between historical events and their fictional representation, the producer would later reflect, had been "necessary."[78] Though Becker and Lichtenberg's film did not explicitly confront the city's conflicted historical present, it did legitimize the rapid changes of 1989–90 as the New Berlin's all-German origin.

Lola rennt taught spectators to perceive the city anew; *Good Bye, Lenin!* reconstructed the spaces of (East) Berlin's recent past. Throughout the 1990s, urban planning and bitter popular and political battles over the GDR's buildings, monuments, and street names had so transformed the remnants of "Berlin, capital city of the German Democratic Republic" that twenty-first-century location scouts increasingly struggled to "find the GDR" in the city's streets.[79] As traces of the Cold War disappeared, so, too, did the hallmarks of postwall youth culture's Berlin-Mitte vanguard: cheap rents, abandoned apartments, and improvised clubs. By the time *Good Bye, Lenin!* began shooting in late summer and fall 2001, construction sites were finally yielding long promised alterations to the built city and threatening Berlin's reputation as a "place of indeterminacy." A new "concretization" of what had been long-term, collective projections brought fears of lost, transitional freedom.[80]

Several films had already revisited East Berlin as the site of (1) inner-German trauma in Margarethe von Trotta's *Das Versprechen* (*The Promise,* FRG 1995); (2) coming of age under socialism in Leander Haußmann and Sebastian Peterson's respective adaptations of Thomas Brussig, *Sonnenallee* (*Sun Alley,* FRG 1999) and *Helden wie wir* (*Heroes Like Us,* FRG 1999); and (3) postwall ideological disorientation in Oskar Roehler's *Die Unberührbare* (*No Place to Go,* FRG 2000) and Hannes Stöhr's *Berlin Is in Germany* (FRG 2001). *Good Bye, Lenin!,* a tragicomedy combining aspects of all of these, restored the unified city's built and topographical continuities with the GDR capital. Emphasizing architecture and cultural topographies that persisted after unification, the film domesticated the Eastern portion of the city for a broader spectatorship within the expanded Federal Republic. Whereas politicians from the East and the West had long warned against ostalgia *(Ostalgie),* an Eastern nostalgia for the securities and familiar social structures of everyday life in the GDR's planned economy, Becker's film staged a more inclusive retrospection, one that could reconcile the East and West German experience of the *Wende* through a shared revival of the GDR past.[81]

In *Good Bye, Lenin!,* which begins in the idyllic late 1970s, Alex Kerner (Daniel Brühl) and his sister Ariane (Maria Simon) are raised in East Berlin by their mother Christiane (Katrin Saß) after their father (Burghart Klaußner) escapes to the West. A fervent, progressive socialist with a penchant for subtle, epistolary critiques of household items, Christiane works to improve the daily lives of GDR citizens. By October 1989, Alex, a TV repairman, has grown disillusioned with the government and takes part in a peaceful demonstration that turns violent. En route to a state award ceremony, Christiane witnesses not only the brutality of the SED regime but the arrest of her own son. She has a heart attack, falls into a coma, and sleeps through November 9 and its aftermath. In the meantime, Alex falls in love with his mother's Russian nurse, Lara (Chulpan Khamatova), and Ariane abandons her university studies for a job at Burger King and a *Wessi* boyfriend, Rainer (Alexander Beyer). When Christiane reawakens, she is at risk for a relapse; for this reason, Alex determines to shield her from the shock of imminent German unification.

With the help of his new *Wessi* colleague, the amateur videomaker Denis (Florian Lukas), he reconstructs the GDR—complete with simulated episodes of the evening news show *Aktuelle Kamera* (Current camera)—in the family's seventy-nine-square-meter prefabricated high-rise flat. The ruse becomes increasingly complicated to maintain, and Alex begins to create an ideal version of the GDR, the one "he would have wished for himself." Christiane dies, aware of her son's efforts, but Alex believes that he has allowed the GDR to survive "until her last second."

Contrary to planners' efforts to erase Berlin's socialist markers, the film reintroduced "spaces of Eastness" that were identifiable in the cityscape before and after 1989 and that could be easily recognized across generations. Appearing at a moment in which Berlin's young Westerners and international youth culture were ensconced in the central Eastern districts of Mitte, Prenzlauer Berg, and Friedrichshain, *Good Bye, Lenin!* participated in a more widespread fascination with both East German popular culture and 1970s West German terrorist chic. T-shirts and messenger bags bore the emblems and slogans of the communist bloc (CCCP, Interflug, Aeroflot, Che Guevara, and the GDR car manufacturer Trabant), while numerous films glamorized the leftist ideals and violence of the West's Rote Armee Fraktion (Red Army Faction).[82] Heiner Carow's cult DEFA feature *Die Legende von Paul und Paula* (*The Legend of Paul and Paula*, GDR 1973), a Berlin film championing love and personal happiness over conformity, screened regularly in the city's revival houses. Through its youthful protagonist, *Good Bye, Lenin!* addressed a generation for whom "the history of unified Germany" was "exactly as long as that of the divided country."[83] Beyond *Ostalgie* and more positive inflections of the *Ossi* (Eastie) stereotype, a new demographic of non-*Ossi* residents of the former East Berlin took pride in the socialist history of its neighborhoods.

The film's principal locations in and around Alexanderplatz mapped the lost GDR onto architectural ensembles still familiar in the New Berlin. Just as the *Ostalgie* maps and guidebooks of the early 2000s listed new and old street names side by side, explained socialist architecture, and reinstated earlier spatial relations, *Good Bye, Lenin!* prepared spectators to perceive the past in the present cityscape.[84] By historicizing spaces of contemporary use, the film proffered an East Berlin that would resonate with those who had lived in the GDR as well as with those who had no organic, personal memory of the East German capital. With its iconic Television Tower (Fernsehturm), massive square, World Time Clock (Weltzeituhr), and train station, Alexanderplatz had not yet undergone its capitalist facelift and still evoked the dimensions of the GDR's symbolic architectural and space-age ambitions, as run-down as these might have been.[85]

Critics questioned the legitimacy of a GDR story developed by a trio of West Germans because assuming the right to speak artistically for the East German experience could seem like an extension of the West German political and cultural arrogance perceived in other aspects of unification. The public rhetoric of Arndt, Becker, and Lichtenberg deflected such accusations, instead reclaiming GDR history as an all-German one and therefore an appropriate source of narrative inspiration for (West) German film production. Recalling their own memories of the GDR and the *Wende,* they insisted on West as well as East German losses in the process of unification. Arndt saw the film as a chance for the West to mourn its hasty rejection of Eastern values, "from constitutional change to the good conditions for single mothers, from recycling to social interaction." Westerners, he maintained, "really missed an opportunity" and "paid out billions without getting anything for it."[86] Becker cited his decades as a resident of West Berlin, "right in the midst of things," where he could observe "frightening parallels between the bourgeois narrow-mindedness of West and East Germans."[87] While Arndt and Becker volunteered their "Westalgic" take on mutual loss and thus invited a more dialogical approach to postwall retrospection, Lichtenberg offered the year of the *Wende,* which he had "experienced first-hand," as a Western point of empathetic access to and entrance into GDR history.[88]

X-Filme's casting choices, for instance, assured the film's broad East–West and intergenerational appeal. *Good Bye, Lenin!*'s reconciliation politics deliberately united GDR actors with their Western counterparts, rising stars of the postwall era with their pre-*Wende* predecessors. While older Eastern viewers could recognize the familiar faces of Katrin Saß, Michael Gwisdek, Christine Schorn, and Jürgen Holtz from East German film and television of the 1970s–1980s, Burghart Klaußner had gotten his start in the films of New German cineaste Helke Sander and was equally present in West German television. The GDR-born younger actors Florian Lukas, Alexander Beyer, and Maria Simon were already, respectively, populating critically acclaimed features like *Absolute Giganten* (*Gigantics,* FRG 1999), *Sonnenallee,* and *Mein langsames Leben* (*Passing Summer,* FRG 2001); their FRG peer, Daniel Brühl (later named a 2003 European Shooting Star), was already an established lead in contemporary coming-of-age tales such as *Schule* (*No More School,* FRG 2000) and *Nichts bereuen* (*No Regrets,* FRG 2001). Even cameos by Ernst-Georg Schwill, the iconic, pudgy "Kohle" of *Berlin—Ecke Schönhauser* (*Berlin—Schönhauser Corner,* GDR 1957), and Jürgen Vogel (who reprised both Jan's arrest and chicken costume from *Das Leben ist eine Baustelle*) contributed to interfilmic affinities between the historical East Berlin of DEFA classics and the reconstructed and contemporary Berlins of X-Filme's growing filmography.

What's more, *Good Bye, Lenin!*'s opening credits encouraged an all-German nostalgia for place by way of familiar, outdated media common to memories of both Germanys. As Yann Tiersen's simple piano score repeats a melody that will return and grow more complex later in the film, a small-gauge projection of Super 8mm footage appears on a black background; the clatter of an unspooling film reel is just audible. Beneath the frame, a caption reads, "Our dacha, summer '78," and a young boy pushes a girl in a wheelbarrow through a lush, green garden. The children laugh, and an adult male voice, presumably that of the camera operator, implores them to look in his direction. The frame expands to fill the background, thus further emphasizing the graininess and soft focus of the images. While the boy lounges on a hammock, the girl sneaks up behind him and begins to rock it violently. Laughing, the boy cries out, "Papa! Help me!" and the adult male voice warns, "Alex, hold on!" In the next shot, the boy (Nico Ledermueller) stands, smiling, in front of East Berlin's Television Tower at the square known affectionately to Berliners by his own name, "Alex." His shirt bears the letters "CCCP" and "DDR" and displays a rocket ship blasting into space. A Trabant asserts authenticity at the corner of the frame, and a saturated red title card is gradually superimposed over the image of the child, who is now framed by the hammer and sickle insignia of the East German flag. The symbols of state authority may discolor and invade the universality of nuclear family life, but East Berlin, for its part, is presented with a wistfulness analogous to that of the Kerners' private celluloid memories.

In synthetic, digital movements, the camera glides across and zooms into and out of old postcards of famed GDR buildings, sculptures, and squares: the Palace of the Republic, Alexanderplatz, the World Time Clock, Strausberger Platz, the Mokka-Milch-Eisbar, the Kino International, Leninplatz, and the Haus des Lehrers und Kongresshalle. With the exception of Strausberger Platz, these structures were built or modernized in the 1960s and 1970s, and the postcards reflect an East Berlin of astral aspirations and leisure. Brightly dressed crowds fill Alexanderplatz, and the saturated 1970s color film stock presents the GDR, quite literally, in the best light. The film's title appears as a rotating bust of Lenin gives way to a rocket launch. The camera pulls back to reveal a television set, before which a young Alex and Ariane proudly watch the takeoff of the Sojus 31. An adult Alex explains in voice-over, "On August 26, 1978, we were world-class. Sigmund Jähn, citizen of the German Democratic Republic, was the first German to fly into outer space."

Speaking from the postwall present, Alex invokes a polysemic "we." Jähn's space travel was, after all, both a triumph for East Germany and, in retrospect, an all-German achievement. Just as the postcards feature spaces of pop cultural resonance in the GDR, from "Erich's light shop" (Palace of the Republic) with its numerous public entertainment venues to Mokka-Milch-Eisbar's subversive disco and concert space, they also attest to the presence and evolving meaning of these buildings in the New Berlin's united cityscape. Aside from Leninplatz (renamed

The young Alex at Alexanderplatz with the Television Tower in the background and the title sequence's use of GDR postcards of the square. *Good Bye, Lenin!* Frame stills.

Platz der Vereinten Nationen and stripped of its Lenin statue in 1991), the architectural ensembles of *Good Bye, Lenin!*'s title sequence still adhered to the spatial expectations of Berlin's millennial residents. Despite the removal of the Lenin statue and the controversial decision, in 1993, to close and eventually demolish the asbestos-ridden Palace of the Republic, both "touchstones of Ossi resentment," the palace remained a commanding presence in one of the New Berlin's major tourist districts.[89] By 2003, Partner für Berlin had succeeded in reopening the building for tours and concerts; by 2004, it began to serve an official temporary cultural function *(Zwischennutzung),* which rendered every stage of the edifice's gradual dismantling a spectacle.

By establishing a topography of cultural and architectural landmarks in the blocks surrounding Alexanderplatz, the postcards invite reflection on urban change. Darius Ghanai, who designed the sequence, hoped the camera movements would evoke a search for truth "as if the eye wanted to look behind the curtain," but his technique of matting and dissolving between postcards also suggests loss and disappearance.[90] While some of the buildings had indeed been sacrificed to post-*Wende* urban planning and development, sites of urban continuity often became palimpsests of urban nostalgia amid the city's geographic realignments of power and commerce. If the Super 8mm footage solicits emotional identification with one family's history, the concentration of visual remnants of the East German state broadly disseminates and validates the New Berlin's GDR heritage.

Whereas Tykwer sought to maintain Berlin's ambiguity as a location, Becker opted for a duality of landmarks that could point forward and backward in time. More than any other single structure in *Good Bye, Lenin!,* the ubiquitous Television Tower elicits multiple associations. A silver globe resting on a long, thin, concrete base and topped with a red-and-white-striped antenna, the tower fulfills the conditions Lynch required for a structure to become a significant landmark of the city image: (1) clear form, (2) contrast with the background, and (3) prominence of location. The importance of a landmark may further result from its visibility "from many locations" and its "location at a junction involving path decisions," such as a major train station linking subway, city, regional, and long-distance train service with tram and bus lines.[91] The Television Tower is at once a demonstrable height of the SED's aggrandizing socialist rhetoric, the most recognizable feature of Berlin's skyline by land and by air, and an urban compass forever pointing eastward, much like the Freedom Tower (and formerly the Twin Towers) of New York City's World Trade Center used to signal Manhattan's downtown tip. In West German Berlin films of the Cold War era, the Television Tower's distant presence warned of the "other" Berlin and the "other" Germany across the Wall.

In Becker's film, the tower is recast as a guarantor of authenticity. It often anchors the setting or else bears silent witness to the layered truths that Alex constructs for his mother. While archival television footage and Alex's narration mark the passage of historical time, Christiane's bedroom window, which looks out onto the tower, should substantiate the GDR's ongoing sovereignty. Instead, it repeatedly betrays the rapidly changing world outside. On one hand, the window faces the same gray, concrete high-rises of pre-*Wende* East Berlin. On the other, it endangers Alex's mission when advertisements from the West enter its frame.

Christiane's birthday presents one such danger. Alex gathers family members, neighbors, his mother's former colleague (played by Gwisdek), and two fake Young Pioneers to simulate a birthday celebration in the GDR. He stands with his back to the window, orchestrating the performances and rounds of well-wishing. Just then, a bright red Coca-Cola banner unfurls on the facade of a nearby building, behind his head, but in Christiane's line of sight. Even when Alex and Denis create their own window on the world in the form of forged installments of *Aktuelle Kamera,* the view from Christiane's window continues to threaten the illusory GDR microcosm. Just as the real *Aktuelle Kamera* responded to West German reports on the GDR and worked in turn to generate negative images of the FRG, Alex's news program must fabricate explanations for contradictory information gleaned from Christiane's window. In this way, the two young men cleverly spin an unlikely historical reversal, one that reinvents Coca-Cola as a socialist soft drink.[92]

On another occasion, Alex falls asleep in his mother's room, and Ariane's daughter Paula, who cannot yet speak, points to the window. She walks toward it with her arm raised while Christiane, immobile in bed, marvels at her granddaughter's first steps. A cut to the window reveals a blimp for West Cigarettes passing in front of the Television Tower. This unrestricted knowledge that the spectator then wields over Alex creates suspense as Christiane determines to walk. By the time she reaches the window, the blimp has disappeared behind a building. Once ambulant, however, she keeps moving, leaves the apartment, and encounters the inexplicable: a swastika and pornographic graffiti in the elevator, a new neighbor from the western industrial city of Wuppertal, an IKEA advertisement, and a parking lot filled with West German cars. Alex awakens to find his mother gone. In the meantime, Christiane wanders, dazed, past billboards for Western goods. If she has not already caught on that something is amiss in the socialist state, an army helicopter emerges in the distance, carrying a statue of Lenin. The scene intensifies with cuts between Alex's frantic search for his mother, Christiane's awe, and the statue's westward journey from Strausberger Platz along Karl-Marx-Allee.

The bedroom window betrays the changing times. *Good Bye, Lenin!* Frame still.

In a climactic, emotional sequence underscored by Tiersen's music, Lenin floats by with his arm outstretched toward Christiane as she looks on in slow motion, positioned between an underwear ad and the composite image of a car that is part Mercedes, part "Trabi." Alex runs past mounds of abandoned GDR furniture as Ariane exits the subway. Both race toward their mother, who stands, disoriented, in the middle of the street. The helicopter continues its journey, flying between the Television Tower and the Haus des Lehrers into the setting sun. All three objects of the old East Berlin are partially silhouetted in the background, while, in the foreground, the banners of the used car lot, harbingers of the West's influx and influence, blow in the wind.

The GDR's architectures of power no longer secure its former citizens in a social logic and worldview. Before the Television Tower where Alex, the boy, once stood smiling, Alex, the young adult, now expresses post-*Wende* rage. On the rooftop of his building, he throws the family's worthless East German marks to the winds. With the long base of the tower lit up in the background, he gives voice to his frustrations: "I felt like the commander of a submarine of the North Sea Fleet, whose battle-worn steel surface had a leak. No sooner had I stopped one leak than another started." Alexanderplatz's momentary betrayal of Alex does not, however, last long. Urged by Lara to scream, he lets out a cathartic, apelike cry in the direction of the square. As he faces the soaring architectural triumph of his youth, his scream is drowned by the jubilation of Germany's 1990

Lenin flies by, disappearing behind Alexanderplatz. *Good Bye, Lenin!* Frame stills.

World Cup soccer victory. As fireworks, cheers, and flags emerge from the surrounding high-rises, *Good Bye, Lenin!* effectively recasts both Alex and Alexanderplatz as participants in the construction of a new German identity.

By the end of the film, Alexanderplatz becomes the representative site of East–West reconciliation. Alex prepares his last *Aktuelle Kamera* broadcast to coincide with the eve of German unification in October 1990. After watching a Sigmund Jähn look-alike announce the opening of the GDR's borders to eager West German masses, Christiane dies in the hospital. The film's ensemble of characters gathers on the rooftop of the Kerners' building to watch Alex launch his mother's ashes in a rocket much like the one he had launched as a boy in the film's Super 8mm footage: "She had wished that we would scatter her ashes in all the winds. This is illegal in Germany. In the West as well as the East. But we didn't care." The "we" to which Alex refers has come to include East–West friendships, East–West lovers, East–West families, and Ariane and Rainer's future "all-German baby."[93] After all, this scene would suggest, it takes Western participation to properly memorialize the end of the GDR, both the historical one and the ideal one that died with Christiane. The rocket explodes into a brief fireworks display, and the group on the roof stares upward at the evening skies over (East) Berlin. As Alex imagines his mother looking down on them, "exactly as Sigmund Jähn did back then," the film cuts to archival footage of Jähn in outer space with dolls from the popular East German stop-motion animation series *Unser Sandmännchen*

Alex screams, the base of the Television Tower visible in the background. *Good Bye, Lenin!* Frame stills.

(Our little sandman), which had its counterpart, *Das Sandmännchen* (The little sandman), in the West.[94] Berlin's new filmic angels were the heroes—official, pop cultural, and private—of the GDR, but in *Good Bye, Lenin!,* former West Germans and those too young to remember were initiated into the brand names, locales, and in-jokes of a once exclusionary *Ostalgie.*[95]

In its final images, the film resumes the nostalgic tone of its opening sequence in a return to the melody and archival textures of Alex's youth, a socialist garden of Eden. Elegiac, historical tracking shots of drab East Berlin streets give way to fictional Super 8mm footage of the young Alex and Ariane at the beach with their mother. The spectator, now educated emotionally, is invited to mourn an irretrievable country, parent, and childhood. As Alex concedes in voice-over that his invented GDR was a country "that had never really existed," the Television Tower is visible in the gray distance, its sphere and antenna rising modestly above a prewar building at the end of a Trabi-lined street. *Good Bye, Lenin!*'s parting views offer the ever accessible film archive in place of the lost East German capital. The updated "street furnishings" and lively colors of the New Berlin may have posed problems to the film's production designer and required optical compromises. The Lenin statue may have been digitized. The once underground art and cultural squat, Tacheles, may have been relocated to a less renovated ruin. In contrast, the Television Tower and Alexanderplatz could function not just as a point of orientation in urban space but as a point of orientation between archived moments.[96] Their presence in the film's multiple temporalities is one of reassurance: yes, Berlin was the capital of the GDR, and yes, the GDR lives on in postwall Berlin and in German cinema.

In the first four days following its premiere in Competition at the Berlinale, *Good Bye, Lenin!* ("after *Lola rennt* the second Berlin Blockbuster by the X Filmmakers"[97]) sold more than 360,000 tickets and roughly 45,000 in Berlin alone.[98] By the end of 2003, the viewer totals climbed to nearly six and a half million, almost twice the box-office yield of the year's second most successful German film, *Das Wunder von Bern* (*The Miracle of Bern,* FRG 2003), a father–son drama set in the Adenauer era.[99] Indeed, *Good Bye, Lenin!* ranked third among all the films shown in Germany in 2003 after *Finding Nemo* (United States/Australia 2003) and *The Lord of the Rings III: The Return of the King* (United States/New Zealand 2003). Newspapers reported "a state of emergency" in Berlin cinemas (long lines, full houses, and people turned away at the door) and marveled that the film was attracting equal numbers of Easterners and Westerners, something *Sonnenallee* had failed to do.[100] As the East-oriented newspaper *Berliner Kurier* put it, spectators "in the East and the West wanted to experience the GDR again." While the Adlershof Studios made the Kerner living room and other East German

The Television Tower, Berlin's compass, "now" and then. *Good Bye, Lenin!* Frame stills.

props available for visitors and parties, some former GDR citizens wore their old FDJ uniforms and brought along Eastern Rotkäppchen champagne to the cinema.[101] That summer, nearly ten thousand spectators gathered to watch the film in (West) Berlin's outdoor amphitheater, the Waldbühne, a venue that had, in the 1950s, attracted East Berlin border crossers, eager to keep up with cultural life in the West.

Reviewers were quick to distinguish between *Ostalgie* and *Nostalgie* and suggested that the film marked a shift in the all-German approach to GDR history.[102] One critic even compared the film's reception across Berlin's exhibition landscape. While he found a weeping audience in the southeast, the "cinemas of the East-West meeting ground of Berlin-Mitte" yielded a similarly moved but more upbeat response. In the Colosseum on Schönhauser Allee, the audience experienced "the pleasures and pains of recognition without the troublesome interference of false nostalgia or sweat-inducing coming to terms [with the past]." In an audience that brought together "generations, regions, milieux, and subcultures," the author noted "a constant soft rustle" of questions and explanations, "an all-German whisper," in Germany's new "melting pot" of Prenzlauer Berg. *Good Bye, Lenin!* had become not a "curiosity show of real existing socialism" but rather a "film about a shared German history."[103]

So significant was the film's cultural currency that government organizations began to take note. Not only did the film, which did "so much all-German good," bring together nearly one-third of Germany's parliament (including politicians from both East and West) in a special screening at the Kino International in a ploy to get a new Film Funding Law passed;[104] it also became a central cultural text both for teaching GDR history in schools and for a new program of national film pedagogy. Whereas Wolfgang Schäuble admitted to tears and "goose bumps" during the screening, federal minister for family affairs Renate Schmidt observed, "From this we *Wessis* in particular can learn: a lot in the former GDR was pretty good."[105] Brandenburg's minister of education Steffen Reiche attended the film with high school students and immediately understood its utility for intergenerational dialogue: "The post-*Wende* generation is in the process of taking a new look at the GDR of their teachers, parents, and grandparents."[106] At the same time, Thomas Krüger, by then president of the Federal Agency for Civic Education (Bundeszentrale für politische Bildung, BPB), was calling for a new "intersection between cinema and school." In his foreword to the BPB's official *Good Bye, Lenin!* workbook, Krüger urged both a national recognition of film as cultural heritage and the improved profile of "media literacy" in German schools.[107]

The film and its retrospective geographies helped to revise local, regional, and national perceptions of the GDR past. As a cultural object of official sanction, collective access, and private, personal reflection, the film became a celluloid monument to East Berlin—its study, an act of urban commemoration.

FILMS THAT TRAVEL

The domestic and festival successes of *Lola rennt* and *Good Bye, Lenin!* piqued the interest of international, particularly American, distributors. Just weeks after *Lola rennt*'s premieres in Germany and at the Venice International Film Festival, Sony Pictures Classics purchased the North American rights to the film as well as those for Australia, New Zealand, the United Kingdom, and Latin America. While Tom Tykwer proclaimed that Sony Pictures Classics and X-Filme "share the same philosophy" on how films "should be brought to audiences," Stefan Arndt recognized the Sony Pictures Classics acquisition as a "worldwide" advertisement for the "high standard of uniqueness and quality" of X-Filme's products.[108] Known for bold marketing strategies of American independent and international films in the 1990s, Sony Pictures Classics started the film in just a handful of U.S. theaters and then gradually increased the number of screens nationwide as more interest developed.[109] Despite initial concerns that American audiences would have to overcome their preconceptions of German cinema and that the film's "youthful target aud in the U.S. normally wouldn't be caught dead within a mile of a subtitled movie," *Lola rennt* earned more than twenty-three million dollars worldwide by fall 1999.[110] When X-Filme and Sony Pictures Classics reunited in 2003 for the U.S. distribution of *Good Bye, Lenin!*, the goal for both was "to try to exceed our mutual U.S. success of 'Run Lola Run.'"[111]

Though Becker, like Tykwer, emphasized the universality of his film and claimed in the *New York Times* that *Good Bye, Lenin!*'s mother–son story "could have happened anywhere," this degree of intercultural caution proved unnecessary.[112] Not only had the *New York Times* reported regularly on developments in the New Berlin in the years between *Lola rennt* and *Good Bye, Lenin!*; U.S. reviews of the films hardly shied away from referencing the German capital.[113] Rather, critics made it clear that Lola was running "like hell through the streets of Berlin" and that Alex Kerner was "[re-creating] Communist East Berlin."[114]

Even Tykwer modified his global rhetoric for the *New York Times*: *Lola rennt* "could take place in any major city of the world. But Berlin is the perfect match, because Lola is someone who is running between times and Berlin itself is a city between eras. The whole center of town is a construction site."[115] Like the Berlin clubgoer who, in 1999, euphorically predicted to Roger Cohen, the newspaper's Berlin Bureau chief, that "this place is going to be to Germany as New York is to the United States," Tykwer's acknowledgment of the film's location identified Berlin globally as the capital of German cool. Lola's urban backdrop, through geographic and cultural analogy, became an advertisement for the New Berlin, which was beginning to acquire the reputation of a "new" New York.[116] If, in one critic's estimation, *Lola rennt* was "probably the hippest movie of the year in any language," the possibility existed that Berlin, by extension, was the hippest city in the world.[117]

In fall 2003, the *New York Times* was already discussing *Good Bye, Lenin!* (which would not open in the United States until February 2004) in relation to international *Ostalgie* tourism. Describing the alternative city tour concept of "Trabi Safari," in which visitors could rent a Trabant and a guide for rides through the "Wild East" or "Classic Berlin," the article credits Becker's film with reviving an interest in "old East German products."[118] Though Arndt denied that X-Filme was promoting a specific Berlin image, he noted that Japanese publicity for *Lola rennt* featured a map of the city; young Japanese tourists were also seeking out *Good Bye, Lenin!*'s locations, such as Karl-Marx-Allee.[119] The German print media began to tout Berlin's accomplishments as a center of film production, and, in 2006, X-Filme producer Manuela Stehr would proclaim that "international buyers have a great deal of confidence in films that take place in Berlin."[120] The new German capital was attracting film professionals, viewers, and tourists alike.

In 2003, the *Production Guide Berlin-Brandenburg* encouraged international filmmakers to "realize" their "visions" in the region and included a map of major world cities and their flying times to Berlin.[121] By the time Keil stepped down from the Filmboard (which was subsumed by the more expansive, multimedia Medienboard Berlin–Brandenburg) in 2004, the region had become a destination for countless international and domestic productions. By 2006, the *Production Guide* could proudly list not only a series of international titles, such as Roman Polanski's *The Pianist* (France/FRG/United Kingdom/Poland 2002) and Frank Coraci's *Around the World in 80 Days* (United States/FRG/Ireland/United Kingdom 2004), in which Berlin had "played the world," but also several successful German films in which the city had played itself. X-Filme's features were singled out as heralds of Berlin–Brandenburg's "bright future" of "cinema film production."[122] With a location database of more than eight hundred sites and thirteen thousand images, the Berlin–Brandenburg Film Commission could offer the national and international film communities diverse spaces in time—a Berlin and non-Berlin of pasts, presents, and futures.[123]

Berlin is once again a desirable film *Schauplatz,* even if urban marketing rhetoric continues to aggrandize achievements of the built city (such as the debacle of the delayed Berlin Brandenburg Airport in 2012–15) long before they are realized. Since the arrival of the MBBB, the revamped film city has continued to change local, regional, and national, but also European and global, perceptions of the real

Weekly news magazine *Der Spiegel* declares the city's comeback to world-class status in 2007. Courtesy of *Der Spiegel*.

Berlin. In 2007, three new guidebooks revealed the locations of celebrated Berlin films and placed *Lola rennt* and *Good Bye, Lenin!* alongside the classics of Weimar, DEFA, and New German Cinema.[124] Urban continuity, it would seem, is also a matter of film history, of knowing where to look for the city's profilmic residues, how to find familiar and lost places in the moving image archive, or how to create these anew with unexpected reframings. The montage of famous film scenes in the region's 2003 promotional DVD ends with an image of Lola running and the slogan "To be continued. Welcome to Berlin and Brandenburg." Writing a tongue-in-cheek plea for the inclusion of more Berlin films in the BPB's recommended school filmography, a critic from the left-leaning *tageszeitung* perhaps best captured and lovingly mocked the optimistic spirit of Germany's film and capital region revival in his summary of the didactic merits of *Good Bye, Lenin!,* winner of several Lolas (the name of the German Film Award statuette since 1999): "We're back on top. The city, the cinema, and the audience."[125]

EPILOGUE

BERLIN RETURNS, AGAIN

In 2009–10, Berlin's municipal authorities and residents alike had reason once again to take stock of urban change. Commemorating the twentieth anniversary of the fall of the Berlin Wall and German unification, they could examine the city anew and very consciously separate the immediate postwall era from what would follow. By then Berlin was a functioning capital of a country at the center of European Union politics. It had, with several other German cities, successfully hosted the 2006 World Cup, a feat that had restored confidence in the capital's and country's ability to pull off peaceful internationalism despite the specters of the 1936 Berlin and 1972 Munich Olympic Games, marred, respectively, by Nazism and terrorism. The building sites of the 1990s and early 2000s, which had demanded so much imagination from Berlin's inhabitants and visitors, were yielding completed structures with national, civic, cultural, and business functions. There were new, global dimensions to urban space and belonging as the city absorbed creative expats fleeing the 2008 world economic crisis and refugees seeking asylum in one of Europe's strongest economies and liberal democracies.

Today Berlin has hardly retired its habit of retrospection. As the Internet and social-networking sites and apps have revolutionized the outsider's access to local information, there is a new ubiquity of cultural portals into the city's past and present. Cinematographic and cartographic indexicality provide the foundation for myriad public encounters between images and the geographical location of their profilmic space. Photographic and filmic comparisons between "here now" and "here then" have become as commonplace as images on the walls of Berlin's renovated subway stations, an enlarged photograph covering the wall of a discount supermarket in Kreuzberg, or the projected spatial memories in the gallery of the West's new "concept mall," Bikini, opened in 2014 just opposite the Kaiser

Wilhelm Memorial Church. As tourists take to bicycles and Airbnb rentals, and more neighborhoods gentrify, it is sometimes difficult to tell who actually lives in Berlin, who has a stake in its past and future. Moving images continue to supply evidence of what Berlin has been and to fascinate those encountering the city for the first time. In a moment of heightened simultaneity across vast distances, Berlin has become something of a beacon, not just a place in physical space but a virtual geography of desired urban congruence. The restaurant Berlyn in Brooklyn's Fort Greene neighborhood advertises its "Regional German/New Brooklyn Cuisine" with an urban skyline of global longing: a painting that seamlessly links landmarks like the Brooklyn Bridge to the Television Tower and the Brandenburg Gate. There is no ocean in sight.[1]

What will be the hallmarks of Berlin's *post*-postwall era? Summers accompanied by surveys of Berlin's filmography, such as Babylon Mitte cinema's 2014 retrospective *Best of Berlin*? The new geographies of global belonging promised by the completion of Berlin Brandenburg Airport? The continued marketing of the city as a place for play and innovation? This book ends as new questions begin. The following parting glances, final frames of cinematographic and cartographic reference, present just some of the ways that film was returned to the physical space of the city on the cusp of this new period.

TIME TRAVEL AND TOURISM (2008)

Nearly two decades into the New Berlin, many of the once inconceivable building projects of the 1990s have been realized. There is a new government district and a Central Train Station, a revamped Potsdamer Platz and a Holocaust Memorial. Once marginal neighborhoods have become central, and the Palace of the Republic has been stripped to its steel frame.[2] There are state visits and visits from *Provinzler,* organized pub crawls in Mitte and locations crawling with international tourists. One such spot is Unter den Linden, the East Berlin boulevard between the Brandenburg Gate and the Schloßplatz. Toward the grounds of the Hohenzollern and GDR palaces, the street boasts the Staatsoper, the Deutsches Historisches Museum, and Humboldt University, but in the blocks just east of the gate, it features endless shops full of Berlin kitsch. Tour buses park at the curb to pick up new passengers or else to allow their existing busloads some time for snapshots.

One company called Zeitreisen (Time Travels) parks its bus in front of Berlin Story, the connoisseur's Berlin store. Passengers who have made their reservations weeks in advance board a bus with four television monitors, and tour guide Arne Krasting—pioneer of the Videobustour format—rewards early birds with a film sequence from *Menschen am Sonntag* (*People on Sunday,* Germany 1930) "to get them in the mood." No ordinary tour of the city, Krasting's rolling cinema promises to introduce its guests to the "film city Berlin." Bracketing the small rupture of National Socialist cinema, the tour sets out to prove Berlin's positive cinematic legacy through the empirical reunion of images and their referents.[3]

As the bus pulls into the Saturday tourism traffic, a promotional montage cuts between Berlin images past and present—among them sequences from *Lola rennt* (*Run Lola Run,* FRG 1998), *Good Bye, Lenin!* (FRG 2003), *Die Legende von Paul und Paula* (*The Legend of Paul and Paula,* GDR 1973), *Berlin—Ecke Schönhauser* (*Berlin—Schönhauser Corner,* GDR 1957), *Emil und die Detektive* (*Emil and the Detectives,* Germany 1931), *Christiane F.—Wir Kinder vom Bahnhof Zoo* (*Christiane F.,* FRG 1981), and the adventures of James Bond and Jason Bourne. Following this preview of imminent attractions is a list of Zeitreisen's film partners, to whom the company pays dear sums for one-minute film clips: X Verleih, Chronos, DEFA-Stiftung, Progress Film-Verleih, Universum Film, and Studio Babelsberg. Other logos—Bundeszentrale für politische Bildung, Deutsches Historisches Museum, Radioeins, Spiegel TV, and Rundfunk Berlin-Brandenburg—testify to the convergence of educational and entertainment interests.

With stops at Old Berlin's Gendarmenmarkt, Bebelplatz, and Lustgarten, at East Berlin's Alexanderplatz and West Berlin's Kreuzberg, Krasting impresses the spectator–tourist with "Berlin's variety" and "all the locations that Berlin can play"—its imitations of other times and places. With one eye to the window and the other to the screen, passengers compare the London and Paris of *Around the World in 80 Days* (United States/FRG/Ireland/United Kingdom 2004) and the Moscow of *The Bourne Supremacy* (United States/FRG 2004) to today's Berlin. They seek out the artificiality and authenticity in the 1980s of *Herr Lehmann* (*Berlin Blues,* FRG 2003) and the 1940s of *Mein Führer—Die wirklich wahrste Wahrheit über Adolf Hitler* (*My Führer,* FRG 2007) and marvel at the "real" 1970s of *Hostess* (GDR 1976) or the still convincingly drab facades of Friedrichshain's Wedekindstraße, where *Das Leben der Anderen* (*The Lives of Others,* FRG 2006) was filmed. The "illogicalness" of Lola's "bizarre route" is demonstrated on a map.

But the Videobustour is not only informational. Its route through Berlin stages unexpectedly moving encounters between cinematic space and the built city. An ornate prewar edifice visible on-screen has been replaced by the supermarket seen from the window. In place of Cold War intrigue at Checkpoint Charlie, tourist families pose with fake border guards. Opposite the window, a massive ad for Nivea hair products dwarves the quadrilingual sector sign, now a Cold War vestige, at the center of *Octopussy*'s (United Kingdom/United States 1983) frame. The path of the Berlin Wall runs unobtrusively along the gutter at Zimmerstraße; it is marked by the modest width of two cobblestones.

At other moments—either through careful timing or by chance—the motion of the bus and that of the films coincide. Riding down Karl-Marx-Allee from Alexanderplatz to Strausberger Platz, the passengers move toward a statue of Lenin that, in turn, moves toward them. They approach the very architectures that recede on the monitor and, in a sense, push back against the inevitable onward march of the post-*Wende* era.

When the bus turns into Potsdamer Straße, a scene from *Emil und die Detektive* presents the fabled square of Weimar tempo. The traffic tower at the center of the frame corresponds to the replica seen from the window, and passengers looking up at the representative structures of the New Berlin can judge for themselves whether the postwall city has captured the spirit of the interwar metropolis and its filmic projections.

After a quick passage through the government district, the bus rests on the Straße des 17. Juni just opposite the Soviet War Memorial. Krasting plays a sequence from Billy Wilder's *A Foreign Affair* (United States 1948) in which, thanks to rear

Potsdamer Platz then and now in Zeitreisen's Videobustour. Photograph courtesy of the author.

projection, a jeepload of visiting Americans tours the rubble landscape of postwar Berlin. A sequence from Wilder's *One, Two, Three* (United States 1961), made during the construction of the Wall, follows, tracing East–West geographies interrupted by the Brandenburg Gate. Just in front of the bus, the renovated gate glistens in the afternoon sunlight. It has ceased to be a border.

One would think that a tour of Berlin's film locations would attract scores of people unfamiliar with the city—those who know it only from its images—but as the bus draws up to the curb outside Berlin Story, Krasting asks his guests where they come from. The majority are Berliners.

BORDER CROSSING AT THE SALON (2010)

Salon Populaire is located in a still seedy corner of Northern Schöneberg, in the former West. Not far from its gallery and performance space in a roomy, renovated *Altbau* at Bülowstraße 90, the gargantuan sex shop LSD pierces the summer dusk with pink neon promises of "Love . . . Sex . . . Dreams." Around the corner, prostitutes await the occasional customer, a car creeping away from the otherwise unrelenting flow of east–west and north–south traffic. These are just the kinds of marginal zones where Berlin's burgeoning art scene thrives—in discarded buildings, forgotten districts, in, on, and along the crevices, strips, courtyards, basements, rooftops, and ruins overlooked by development capital. Given the proclivities of the neighborhood, it is perhaps fitting that the Salon's first season should feature "conversations and activities on the subjects of SPACE & LOVE."[4]

On a warm Wednesday in June, film curator and artist Florian Wüst visits the Salon with the second in a series of programs that he calls Film City Berlin. The theme, this evening, is the rather cryptic "Escape Forward." By 8:00 P.M., when the show is supposed to start, the room designated for performance events is overflowing with art kids on casually arranged plastic garden chairs. Nimble bodies seem to meld with and mold around a large wooden installation piece and a small television monitor looping scenes from early Helke Sander and Christian Ziewer films. Enthusiastic eyes strain forward to the event's screen, which is not a screen but a wall rendered cinematic by the light of a digital projector perched on a black ladder. Equipped with beer and wine, the young audience chatters in all languages but German. Wüst is prepared for this international crowd, one for whom Berlin is the gateway to creative thought and for whom Berlin's film history is exotic terrain in new or ongoing love affairs with the city. In English, he briefly introduces Jürgen Böttcher's *Jahrgang 45* (*Born in '45*, GDR 1965–66/1990), famously banned during the Eleventh Plenum of the Central Committee of the Socialist Unity Party, and released after the fall of the Wall, and Ulrich Schamoni's *Es* (*It*, FRG 1966), an early exemplar of the West's Young German Cinema.

"Escape Forward"—Film City Berlin no. 2. Photograph courtesy of Florian Wüst and Salon Populaire.

The Salon is not a cinemathèque, and though Wüst has recently coedited a volume on the underground film scene in 1980s West Berlin, he is there neither to pontificate nor to show the films in their entirety.[5] Rather, he takes seriously the Salon's call to "break the hierarchical forms of traditional presentations" and to experiment with the hybridity of "semi-public space." In this public parlor of experimental communication, films become a "series of mises-en-scène."[6] This is Wüst's art: to bring films into dialogic relation, to make them mean something to each other here and now, in the moment of comparison. His method fluctuates between playful and pointed revelations about the frustrations of young adults in the divided city. At times Wüst resembles a low-tech VJ, irreverently recombining images into a live performance; then suddenly he channels the earnest film professor, presenting carefully selected sequences for classroom analysis. In either mode, it is Wüst's retelling of the city and its inhabitants that counts.

The films' mises-en-scène, editing, and cinematography bear the markings of emergent European new waves as the postwar couples, Al and Li in East Berlin and Manfred and Hilke in the West, face off against each other and the social strictures that suffocate them. Shot in black and white with mobile cameras, the films navigate private and public space with a similar lightness of touch that betrays a generational restlessness. Cuts willfully weave together personal and urban conflicts in *Es.* Manfred sells real estate and land left vacant by the war and German division, while Hilke contemplates, then receives, an abortion. In *Jahrgang 45*, Al and Li's separation bespeaks auto mechanic Al's larger dissatisfaction with expected behaviors and norms within socialist society. If there is a postwar dream on one or the other side of the German–German border, neither couple attains it.

This seems to be exactly the point that Wüst, the *metteur-en-scène* of East–West juxtapositions, is trying to make. In one such comparison, Manfred's cheeky speculation about the future value of a plot of undeveloped land near Potsdamer Platz is offset by the vague hopefulness of Al and Li and Al and his friends in the face of new socialist construction. In both cases the future of the built city rests on a destructive past and the architectural violence and urban violation of the Berlin Wall. Individually, the films recount the ambivalent and uncertain fates of young people in a specific time and place. Together, in alternating sequences, they perform their aesthetic relationship, which is also a relationship of spatial longing.

In comparative retrospection, the Berlins of *Jahrgang 45* and *Es* are more alike than different. One has the sense that Al and Li and Manfred and Hilke are bound up in the same generational, professional, and gendered conflicts. Indeed, just a few years earlier, they were one border-crossing generation of Berliners.

Wüst's spectators, predominantly postmillennial arrivals, may search in vain for increasingly rare evidence of the border zone. Sailing the city in search of its "off" and equally intrepid in Spandau and Schöneweide, they hardly realize that they themselves are harbingers of Cold War erasure. The new border crossers are eager to learn about the city's past, and the story Wüst chooses to tell them is one of Berliners belonging together. It is a cinematic argument made possible by integrating East and West German film history. It is also an argument that becomes more persuasive the more one escapes forward.

THE LONGEST CINEMA IN THE WORLD (2010)

Berliner Fenster, which translates as "Berlin window(s)," are the dual television monitors that were installed in the cars of the city's U-Bahn system in 2000. Providing a combination of cultural, political, sports, and entertainment news, these underground windows into the city and world above have become both a mundane, "ambient" visual backdrop to urban mobility and a focal point for passengers avoiding eye contact and passing time between stations.[7] It is not uncommon, in a longer cross-town ride, to learn all the latest soccer scores, celebrity gossip, and political scandals in concise bullet points furnished by the news agency N-24 and the boulevard newspaper *BZ*. Interspersed with this content are advertisements for concerts, film screenings, and new and annual Berlin cultural events. The screen to the left conveys text, the one to the right images. Eyes dart from one monitor to the other. Throughout the day, stories are updated.

Subsequent initiatives like the international short film festival Going Underground and Foto des Tages (Photo of the Day) have explored subway television's potential as a venue for original film art and interactive spectatorship.[8] Boasting 3,768 adjacent monitors in 1,106 train cars and reaching a daily audience of up to 1.13 million, Berliner Fenster links passengers of varying ages, genders, classes, ethnicities, religions, professions, and neighborhood affiliations in a simultaneous, mediated reception of their city.[9]

In July 2010, the Babylon Mitte cinema (located just across from the Volksbühne at Rosa-Luxemburg-Platz in the former East) partnered with Bologna's Il Cinema Ritrovato on Berlin's first StummfilmLIVEfestival. Curator Friedemann Beyer hoped to reach a new, wider, and younger audience through innovative presentations and an emphasis on modern and live musical accompaniment to silent films.[10] For weeks, posters with an iconic image of Marlene Dietrich in gender-bending Weimar drag could be seen throughout Berlin. They announced not only the support of the office of Mayor Klaus Wowereit but also the patronage of filmmaker Volker Schlöndorff, who had overseen Studio Babelsberg in its post-DEFA transition. The opening night included a free outdoor screening of the 2010 *Metropolis* (Germany 1927) restoration, while the capital's *ur*-representation, Walter Ruttmann's *Berlin. Die Sinfonie der Großstadt* (*Berlin: Symphony of a Great City,* Germany 1927), was to screen the following night, for the first time, in the U-Bahn; the screening would transform Berlin's subway system, Berliner Fenster proclaimed, into "the longest cinema in the world."

Eagerly, my friend Max Hirsh, a transportation and architecture scholar and Berliner Verkehrsgesellschaft aficionado, and I boarded the U7 line at Hermannplatz on July 17 at 8:00 P.M. If the U-Bahn was Berlin's newest and the world's longest cinema, this was something we had to see. Outfitted with a still camera, an iPhone, and a video camera, we were prepared to document this underground happening—the live transmission of a feature-length film across sixteen and a half kilometers' worth of train cars.[11] Indeed, the gimmick had the potential to attract, not passengers, but spectators to the U-Bahn, to convert even this quotidian network of urban pathways into a cultural destination in its own right.

As we rode into the southeastern depths of Neukölln, the monitors flickered and went blank. There was no city symphony. Even Berliner Fenster's usual silent newsfeed had failed. We waited tensely as the other passengers, absorbed with their routine routes, reading material, mp3 players, and travel companions, barely registered the absence of their infotainment. Suddenly the film's title and the screening's sponsors appeared on the left monitor, but instead of Ruttmann's rushing engine and speed-inducing montage, the right monitor displayed a still image of a twenty-first-century U-Bahn train arriving at an underground station, just above the slogan "Television on the whole line." We were nearly in Rudow by then.

Still optimistic, we caught a train back to Hermannplatz and transferred to the northbound U8. In the modern cars on this line, there are no barriers, and one looks infinitely from one end of the train to the other. We were that much closer to "the longest cinema." A few images appeared, but instead of moving, they froze into film stills. A streetcar. The facade of a prewar building. At Kottbusser Tor, we made a final switch, to the U1, eastbound to Warschauer Straße. Over the Oberbaumbrücke, along Lola's West–East route, connecting Kreuzberg to Friedrichshain, were the same static images.

Only when we finally boarded the westbound train, having given up and resigned ourselves to return to Kotti, did the film begin to play smoothly between

Berlin. Die Sinfonie der Großstadt playing on the U-Bahn's Berliner Fenster. Photograph courtesy of the author.

stations. In a car full of tourists and suburban and intra-European weekend revelers picked up from the city's S-Bahn ring and regional train service, our attention to the small monitors drew stares and whispers, "What are they looking at? *Berlin.* Berlin?" The late sunset of a long summer evening shimmered in the windows of Kreuzberg's *Altbauten* seen through the real windows of an elevated train carrying Ruttmann's vision of urban modernity on monitors called "windows." Ruttmann filmed a train. His film was playing in a train that I was filming playing the film of a train rushing toward the camera(s). "Meta," Max said as we exited the car and left our fellow passengers glancing thoughtfully from one set of windows to the other. Maybe some of them would continue on to Babylon Mitte later that night for electronic musical duo Tronthaim's live accompaniment of Ruttmann's film. For others, we had been the happening—those people filming the television screens in the U-Bahn.

One year later, I was doing some research at the library of Potsdam-Babelsberg's Hochschule für Film und Fernsehen Konrad Wolf. I had been regaling the librarians, many of whom had been there since Babelsberg's DEFA days, with stories of *Berlin. Die Sinfonie der Großstadt*'s postwall ubiquity. The retrospectives; the museum exhibitions; the television documentaries; the restorations; the DVDs; the techno concerts and VJing; the tour buses. "Really? *Is* the film everywhere? We don't see as much of that Berlin emphasis here in Potsdam." The next week, I returned for some photocopies, and there, on the front door of the building, was a bright yellow poster announcing a performance by twelve students from the film academy's master's program in film music. The event? A live accompaniment of Walter Ruttmann's city symphony at the Filmmuseum Potsdam. Even the glass walls of the library displayed the image. As I entered, the librarians greeted me, smiling, "Frau Dr. Wagner, you would never guess our surprise . . ."

In Berlin the longest cinema in the world is, perhaps, neither the longest in distance nor the longest in duration, but the film or films and, also, merely the images that recur most often in the city's story of itself.

ACKNOWLEDGMENTS

Berlin Replayed began with the simple question of how moving images relate to place, particularly in a city whose built form was in the midst of redefinition. Exploring this question has been the work of years, and I am grateful to a number of institutions for generously supporting my research: the Alexander von Humboldt Foundation, the College of Arts and Humanities Institute and Office of the Vice President of International Affairs at Indiana University, the Mahindra Humanities Center and the Minda de Gunzburg Center for European Studies at Harvard University, the Fulbright Commission, the Andrew W. Mellon Foundation, the Dartmouth College Alfred K. Priest Fund, DAAD (German Academic Exchange Service), and Berlin's Center for Metropolitan Studies.

Berlin and Potsdam-Babelsberg's wealth of film resources and brilliant and meticulous archivists and librarians were indispensable in this endeavor, notably the Bundesarchiv-Filmarchiv (Babette Heusterberg and Ute Klawitter), the Deutsche Kinemathek (Regina Hoffmann, Wolfgang Theis, Peter Latta, and Anke Hahn), the DEFA Foundation (Ralf Schenk, Helmut Morsbach, Juliane Haase, Dorothée Basel, and Manja Meister), the Deutsches Rundfunkarchiv (Dr. Jörg-Uwe Fischer), the Hans-Helmut-Prinzler Bibliothek, the Landesarchiv Berlin (Barbara Schäche), and the Library of the Hochschule für Film und Fernsehen "Konrad Wolf" (Lydia Wiehring von Wendrin and Renate Göthe).

The programming of several Berlin cinemas in the early and mid-2000s was instrumental to the evolution of this book: Adria, Arsenal Institut für Film und Videokunst, Babylon Mitte, Blow Up, BrotfabrikKino, Börse, Central, FSK, Hackesche Höfe, Lichtblick, Moviemento, Nickelodeon, and the Deutsches Historisches Museum's Zeughauskino. Some of these theaters continue to contribute to the city's culture of urban retrospection today.

Conceptualizing a larger project between disciplines benefits from constructive feedback from a variety of scholarly perspectives. I am thankful to Eric Rentschler for his early support of this book and for sharing his vast insight into German film history in careful readings throughout my writing process. Svetlana Boym, Giuliana Bruno, Gerd Gemünden, Gertrud Koch, and Kristin Kopp were likewise welcome and generous interlocutors in discussions of space, place, cinema, nostalgia, architecture, and Berlin. At Indiana University, the Departments of Germanic Studies and Communication and Culture provided a supportive, interdisciplinary home for my research. Often, turns that one takes as a writer and researcher, scholarly epiphanies, are the result of a conversation, a challenge, or just the right question. A number of these events contributed to my work, but I am particularly indebted to conversations with Dominique Bluher, Claire Colomb, Robin Curtis, Tom Gunning, Anton Kaes, Despina Kakoudaki, Jennifer Kapczinski, Frank Kessler, Barbara Klinger, Johannes von Moltke, Volker Pantenburg, David Rodowick, Jörg Schweinitz, Christina Svendsen, Maria Tatar, Karen Till, Katie Trumpener, William Uricchio, and Linda Williams.

Several astute colleagues in German film studies have helped me to sharpen my arguments in workshops and at conferences, and I am particularly appreciative of discussions with Marco Abel, Eric Ames, Barton Byg, Roger Cook, Michael Cowan, Jaimey Fisher, Frances Guerin, Sabine Hake, Sara Hall, Lutz Koepnick, Tobias Nagl, Brad Prager, and Mike Richardson.

My understanding of Berlin's film culture and its implications for local, regional, national, and international spectatorship has been greatly enriched through discussions and correspondence with Michael Barker, Jeanpaul Goergen, Jan Gympel, Klaus Keil, Wolfgang Kohlhaase, Arne Krasting, Dirk Lüsebrink, Sascha Moser, Eva Riehl, Joachim Sauter, Thomas Schadt, Werner Schwarz, Amie Siegel, Philipp Stiasny, Wim Wenders, and Florian Wüst.

A book only becomes a book through the hard work of a production and design team. At the University of Minnesota Press, Danielle Kasprzak has been a thoughtful and rigorous editor.

And books are not written in cloisters; they are written in the midst of life. I was writing *Berlin Replayed* as the city was changing before my eyes. In years of absences and returns, I cannot thank Lihi, Holger, Per, Max, Naoko, and Franz enough for teaching me, again and again, that there was more to discover in the city I thought I knew.

Finally, I am grateful to my family, who brought me to Berlin in the first place. From them I learned to travel, to read maps (the ones in this book were furnished by my father, Bernhard H. Wagner), and to appreciate old films.

NOTES

INTRODUCTION

1. See the argument on Kaiser Wilhelm's use of film in Peter Schamoni's *Majestät brauchen Sonne* (His Majesty needs some sun, FRG/The Netherlands 1999).

2. Paul Steege, *Black Market, Cold War* (Cambridge: Cambridge University Press, 2007), 21. For a study of the rubble film, see Robert R. Shandley, *Rubble Films* (Philadelphia: Temple University Press, 2001).

3. Rürup Reinhard, ed., *Berlin 1945* (Berlin: Willmuth Arenhövel, 1995), 57, 62.

4. Otto Hagemann and Paul Ortwin Rave, *Berlin: Vor der Zerstörung aufgenommen*, 2nd ed. (Berlin: Deutscher Kunstverlag/Gebrüder Mann, 1949), 19, 26, and photographs 60 and 61. This and all other translations, unless otherwise specified, are my own. For an overview of the *Heimat* genre, see Johannes von Moltke, *No Place Like Home* (Berekely: University of California Press, 2005).

5. Claire Colomb, *Staging the New Berlin* (London: Routledge, 2012), 170.

6. This rich body of work spans literary, cultural, historical, architectural, geographic, and urban planning approaches. See, e.g., Brian Ladd, *The Ghosts of Berlin* (Chicago: University of Chicago Press, 1997); Matthias Pabsch, *Zweimal Weltstadt* (Berlin: Reimer, 1998); Kathrin Becker and Urs Stahel, eds., *Remake Berlin* (Göttingen, Germany: Steidel, 2000); Andreas Huyssen, *Present Pasts* (Stanford, Calif.: Stanford University Press, 2003); Karen E. Till, *The New Berlin* (Minneapolis: University of Minnesota Press, 2005); Jennifer A. Jordan, *Structures of Memory* (Stanford, Calif.: Stanford University Press, 2006); Andrew J. Webber, *Berlin in the Twentieth Century* (Cambridge: Cambridge University Press, 2008); Katharina Gerstenberger, *Writing the New Berlin* (Rochester, N.Y.: Camden House, 2008); and Janet Ward, *Post-Wall Berlin* (New York: Palgrave Macmillan, 2011).

7. The 1990s and 2000s have seen numerous anthologies and monographs on cinema, cities, space, and architecture, notably Dietrich Neumann, ed., *Filmarchitektur* (Munich: Prestel, 1996); David B. Clarke, ed., *The Cinematic City* (London: Routledge, 1997); François Penz and Maureen Thomas, eds., *Cinema and Architecture* (London: BFI, 1997); Mark Lamster, ed., *Architecture and Film* (New York: Princeton Architectural Press, 2000);

Mark Shiel and Tony Fitzmaurice, eds., *Cinema and the City* (Oxford: Blackwell, 2001); Stephen Barber, *Projected Cities* (London: Reaktion Books, 2002); Mark Shiel and Tony Fitzmaurice, eds., *Screening the City* (London: Verso, 2003); Linda Krause and Patrice Petro, eds., *Global Cities* (New Brunswick, N.J.: Rutgers University Press, 2003); Edward Dimendberg, *Film Noir and the Spaces of Modernity* (Cambridge, Mass.: Harvard University Press, 2004); John David Rhodes, *Stupendous, Miserable City* (Minneapolis: University of Minnesota Press, 2007); Andrew Webber and Emma Wilson, eds., *Cities in Transition* (London: Wallflower Press, 2008); Barbara Mennel, *Cities and Cinema* (New York: Routledge, 2008); Philipp Brunner, Anita Gertiser, Nathalie Jancso, René Müller, and Tereza Smid, eds., "Stadt," special issue, *Cinema* 54 (2009); and Richard Koeck, *Cine-scapes: Cinematic Spaces in Architecture and Cities* (New York: Routledge, 2012).

8. Giuliana Bruno, *Atlas of Emotions* (New York: Verso, 2002), 71; Tom Conley, *Cartographic Cinema* (Minneapolis: University of Minnesota Press, 2007), 5. See also cartographers' framing of these questions in Sébastien Caquard and D. R. Fraser Taylor, eds., "What Is Cinematic Cartography?," in "Cinematic Cartography," special issue, *The Cartographic Journal* 46, no. 1 (2009): 5–8.

9. John David Rhodes and Elena Gorfinkel, *Taking Place* (Minneapolis: University of Minnesota Press, 2011), xi. Because location studies of films intersect with touristic interests, numerous trade books and travel guides (but very few scholarly works) have treated Berlin as a film location: Claudia Hellmann and Claudine Weber-Hof, *On Location: Cities of the World on Film* (Munich: Bucher, 2006); Regina Aggio, *Filmstadt Berlin* (Berlin: Jena, 2007); Markus Münch, *Drehort Berlin* (Berlin: berlin edition, 2007); Michaela Schubert and Wolfgang Bernschein, *Berlin: Reisen—Ein Film* (Berlin: Wolbern, 2007); and Susan Ingram, ed., *World Film Locations: Berlin* (Bristol, U.K.: Intellect Books, 2012).

10. Though overt Nazi propaganda films are routinely studied and commercially available outside Germany, titles such as *Hitlerjunge Quex* (*Hitler Youth Quex,* Germany 1933), *Triumph des Willens* (*Triumph of the Will,* Germany 1935), *Der ewige Jude* (*The Eternal Jew,* Germany 1940), and *Jud Süß* (*Jew Süß,* Germany 1940) are banned for purchase within the Federal Republic, do not appear on television, and cannot be programmed in repertory cinemas without special permission and careful historical contextualization. When such works do screen publicly, it is usually in conjunction with an academic conference, a museum exhibit, a film school seminar, or a citation in a postwar documentary. Although a few milder entertainment films from the era, such as *Zwei in einer großen Stadt* (*Two in a Big City,* Germany 1942) and *Großstadtmelodie* (*Melody of a Great City,* Germany 1943), depict Berlin as a still-bustling home front and have been distributed on DVD, few of these films are known to younger audiences or programmed beyond, for example, venues such as the Deutsches Historisches Museum's Zeughauskino and film historians' groups such as Cinegraph. Many factors have blocked nostalgia for these films: laws; the threat of Neo-Nazi identification with these images; the divergent East and West German responses to the legacy of fascism in their memory cultures; Germany's postunification promotion of tolerance for diversity and multiculturalism; a sense of guilt and responsibility; the widespread public distaste for and shame toward Nazi ideology and the Holocaust; and the complexity of longing for a period in which many German civilians beyond the frame were actually suffering. The filmmaker and historian Felix Moeller provides a helpful overview of the remaining *Vorbehaltsfilme* (films subject to special

conditions and reservations), many of which toured in a special retrospective, in his documentary *Verbotene Filme* (*Forbidden Films,* FRG 2014). See also Hanns-Georg Rodek, "Wie viel Gift steckt noch in den 'Vorbehaltsfilmen'?," *Die Welt,* January 31, 2012, and Angela Müller, "Was tun mit NS-Propagandafilmen?," *Deutsche Welle,* March 10, 2014.

11. Hans-Georg Gadamer, *Truth and Method,* 2nd rev. ed. (London: Continuum, 2004), 305.

12. See "Ein historisches Filmkonzert im Friedrichstadtpalast," S-Bahn Berlin, September 23, 2007, http://www.s-bahn.de/aktuell/2007/281_sinfonie_der_grosstadt.htm.

13. The film's plot offers both Cold War conciliation and an effort to get over the past *(Vergangenheitsbewältigung)* through a young Soviet officer sent to work in a German POW camp in Siberia. Unlike the camp's brutal commander, the young man, whose Jewish wife survived a German concentration camp, attempts to treat the prisoners with human dignity.

14. Feuerhelm is known for his role in Rosa von Praunheim's cult gay film *Nicht der Homosexuelle ist pervers, sondern die Situation, in der er lebt* (*It Is Not the Homosexual Who Is Perverse, but the Society in Which He Lives,* FRG 1971).

15. For more on the film program, see the exhibition catalog *Flimmern auf dem Eisernen Vorhang: Berliner Grenzkinos, 1950–1961* (Berlin: Berliner Grenzkinos, 2011), 27.

16. Barbara Klinger, *Beyond the Multiplex* (Berkeley: University of California Press, 2006), 175; see generally 135–90.

17. Alison Landsberg, *Prosthetic Memory* (New York: Columbia University Press, 2004), 26. Though Landsberg's examples focus on contemporary films' depictions of the past as well as science fiction's imagination of prosthetic memory in the future, I find this concept particularly compelling in the age of increasingly digitized audiovisual heritage.

18. For a discussion of the transnational forces behind the Europeanization of films made in the post-DEFA Studio Babelsberg, see Randall Halle, *German Film after Germany* (Urbana: University of Illinois Press, 2008), 60–88.

19. The others included the FBBB, the German Federal Film Board (Filmförderungsanstalt, FFA), the Berlin International Film Festival, the formerly Eastern Hochschule für Film und Fernsehen "Konrad Wolf" (HFF) (renamed Filmuniversität Babelsberg Konrad Wolf in July 2014), the formerly Western Deutsche Film- und Fernsehakademie Berlin (DFFB), the Deutsche Kinemathek, and the Bundesarchiv-Filmarchiv.

20. For a general overview of the beginnings of the FBBB, see Dirk Lüneberg, *Filmförderung in Berlin und Brandenburg* (Berlin: Rubikon, 1999), 69–78.

21. *1994–2004: 10 Jahre Filmförderung in Berlin und Brandenburg* (Potsdam–Babelsberg: Medienboard Berlin-Brandenburg GmbH, 2004), 16. See also the MBBB's promotional booklet *Media. IT. Communication: Capital Region Berlin–Brandenburg* (Berlin: Königsdruck, 2004).

22. *Guideline Issued by the Federal Government Commissioner for Culture and the Media: "Incentive to Strengthen the Film Industry in Germany"* (Bonn: BKM, 2009), 4, 23–24. There are several additional categories under cultural content, though it is worth noting that "European" content, while acceptable, achieves a lower number of points. Additional sections of the test assign points for the nationality of the creative talents, for the level of narrative importance of characters played by German actors, and for the percentage of production and postproduction work completed in Germany.

23. Ibid., 23.

24. Certainly the ramifications of the terrorist attacks of September 11, 2001, on the cinematic appearance and disappearance of the World Trade Center's Twin Towers offer one indication of how national politics may affect the use of CGI.

25. Lev Manovich, "Remixability," in *After the Digital Divide? German Aesthetic Theory in the Age of New Media,* ed. Lutz Koepnick and Erin McGlothlin (Rochester, N.Y.: Camden House, 2009), 48, 50.

26. "Workshop," *rePLACE BERLIN,* February 5, 2012, http:/berlin.re-place.info. For more on the projects that resulted from the workshop, see Daniel Berndt et al., eds., *rePLACE BERLIN* (Berlin: rePLACE Project, 2011).

1. REMAKE

1. The installation was shown at KW Institute for Contemporary Art as part of the 2006 Berlin International Film Festival's new video art program, *Forum Expanded.* The films include Wolfgang Staudte's *Die Mörder sind unter uns* (*The Murderers Are among Us,* SOZ 1946), Jürgen Böttcher's *Jahrgang 45* (*Born in '45,* GDR 1965–66/1990), and Peter Kahane's *Die Architekten* (*The Architects,* GDR 1990).

2. Amie Siegel, "Berlin Remake," in *International Forum of New Cinema Catalogue* (Berlin: 56. Internationale Filmfestspiele, 2006), 215.

3. Ibid.

4. See Brian Ladd, *The Ghosts of Berlin* (Chicago: University of Chicago Press, 1997), 1; Karen E. Till, *The New Berlin* (Minneapolis: University of Minnesota Press, 2005), 8; and Claire Colomb, *Staging the New Berlin* (London: Routledge, 2012), generally.

5. Svetlana Boym, *The Future of Nostalgia* (New York: Basic Books, 2001), xiii–xiv.

6. Corey Ross and Deborah Smail, "New Berlins and New Germanies: History, Myth, and the German Capital in the 1920s and 1990s," in *Representing the German Nation,* ed. Mary Fulbrook and Martin Swales (Manchester: Manchester University Press, 2000), 64.

7. See, e.g., Irmgard von zur Mühlen's television film *Weltbühne Berlin—Die Zwanziger Jahre* (World stage: The 1920s, FRG 1986). See also comments by Berlin film historian and Ruttmann scholar Jeanpaul Goergen in an e-mail to the author, March 24, 2007: "You are absolutely right. Ruttmann's Berlin film is constantly used as 'archival footage' for the 1920s, but also for the turn of the century, the 1910s, and the 1930s! All films that deal with the first half of the twentieth century hark back to Ruttmann!" This and all subsequent translations in this chapter, unless otherwise noted, are my own. I am thankful to Lihi Nagler and Maya Barzilai for bringing to my attention the misuse of Ruttmann's footage in the Yad Vashem Museum in Jerusalem. The exhibit recontextualizes the film's opening sequence—a train rushing to Berlin—as a train en route to a concentration camp. This further ahistorical appropriation of the film's images inverts their more positive Weimar associations in present-day Germany.

8. Till, *New Berlin,* 44–45.

9. Anton Kaes, "History and Film: Public Memory in the Age of Electronic Dissemination," in *Framing the Past,* ed. Bruce A. Murray and Christopher J. Wickham (Carbondale: Southern Illinois University Press, 1992), 314.

10. John Berger, *Ways of Seeing* (London: BBC and Penguin Books, 1972), 33. Berger is referring to images' predominance over and independence from original artworks, but this extraction of mobile images from immobile, historically and culturally rooted objects might also apply to the representation of place.

11. This argument is laid out in Walter Benjamin, "The Work of Art in the Age of Its Technological Reproducibility (Third Version)," in *Walter Benjamin: Selected Writings*, ed. Howard Eiland and Michael W. Jennings, vol. 4 (Cambridge, Mass.: Belknap Press of Harvard University Press, 2003), 254.

12. See William Uricchio, "Ways of Seeing: The New Vision of Early Nonfiction Film," in *Uncharted Territory: Essays on Early Nonfiction Film*, ed. Daan Hertogs and Nico de Klerk (Amsterdam: Nederlands Filmmuseum, 1997), 129. For Uricchio, natural scenes, containing very little intrusion of historicity in the frame, not only indicate "a late nineteenth century concern for 'liveness'" but also act as precursors to notions of "simultaneity" across spatial distance. This is quite different from urban views, replete with historical information and implications of change and development.

13. Benjamin, "Work of Art," 270.

14. Berger, *Ways of Seeing*, 10.

15. "New Berlin," *Der Spiegel*, September 6, 1999, front cover.

16. Jochen Thies, "Berlin als Medienereignis," in *Berlin: Die Hauptstadt*, ed. Ralf Rytlewski and Werner Süß (Bonn: Bundeszentrale für politische Bildung, 1999), 703.

17. Till, *New Berlin*, 38.

18. Boym, *Future of Nostalgia*, xiii.

19. See, e.g., a discussion of *The Missing House* in Große Hamburger Straße in John Czaplicka, "History, Aesthetics, and Contemporary Commemorative Practice in Berlin," *New German Critique* 65 (Spring/Summer 1995): 159–73.

20. Mary Ann Doane, *The Emergence of Cinematic Time* (Cambridge, Mass.: Harvard University Press, 2002), 223.

21. Ibid.

22. Lesser known Berlin films include Adolf Trotz's *Die Stadt der Millionen: Ein Lebensbild Berlins* (The city of millions: A living portrait of Berlin, Germany 1925); the short by Wilfried Basse, *Wochenmarkt auf dem Wittenbergplatz* (Weekly market at Wittenbergplatz, Germany 1929); and László Moholy-Nagy's *Berliner Stilleben* (*Berlin Still Life*, Germany 1931); as well as numerous informational films and newsreels.

23. Vladimir Nabokov, "A Guide to Berlin," in *The Stories of Vladimir Nabokov* (New York: Vintage, 1995), 157.

24. Boym, *Future of Nostalgia*, 195. See also Paolo Cherchi Usai, *Silent Cinema: An Introduction* (London: BFI, 2000), on the difficulties of archiving, identifying, and preserving silent films and anonymous fragments.

25. André Bazin, "The Ontology of the Photographic Image," in *What Is Cinema?*, ed. and trans. Hugh Gray (Berkeley: University of California Press, 2005), 1:14–15.

26. Ibid., 1:15, 12.

27. Ibid., 1:13–14.

28. Siegfried Kracauer, *Theory of Film* (Princeton, N.J.: Princeton University Press, 1997), 28.

29. Ibid., 71–72.

30. Roland Barthes, *Camera Lucida,* trans. Richard Howard (New York: Hill and Wang, 1981), 77. For Barthes's argument on the differences between cinema and photography, see also 55–57.

31. Ibid., 80.

32. Jeff Hopkins, "A Mapping of Cinematic Places: Icons, Ideology, and the Power of (Mis)representation," in *Place, Power, Situation, and Spectacle,* ed. Stuart C. Aitken and Leo E. Zonn (London: Rowman and Littlefield, 1994), 53. Hopkins, a geographer, also considers the way that the same filmed skyline can function, in Peirce's terms, as an icon, index, or symbol.

33. Doane, *Emergence of Cinematic Time,* 16.

34. Walter Ruttmann, "Berlin als Filmstar," *B.Z.*, September 20, 1927, qtd. in Jeanpaul Goergen, ed., *Walter Ruttmann: Eine Dokumentation* (Berlin: Freunde der Deutschen Kinemathek, 1987), 79.

35. Barthes, *Camera Lucida,* 27.

36. Ibid., 55.

37. Ibid., 96; see also 55–59. Though Barthes does make an effort to distinguish between photography and cinema by way of photography's lack of a "blind field" of life and possibility beyond the frame (as compared to the continuity of life beyond the film's screen), he suggests that the "punctum" provides a photograph with exactly such a blind field: "The *punctum,* then, is a kind of subtle *beyond*—as if the image launched desire beyond what it permits us to see," he writes of the erotic photograph. Barthes's differentiations of photographic and cinematographic images actually end up connecting cinema even more deeply to photography's "noeme" of the former existence of the person or object before the camera.

38. Rudolf Arnheim, *Film as Art* (Berkeley: University of California Press, 1957), 12. See also Hugo Münsterberg, *The Photoplay: A Psychological Study, Hugo Münsterberg on Film,* ed. Allan Langdale (New York: Routledge, 2002), 69: "*we are fully conscious of the depth, and yet we do not take it for real depth.*"

39. Giuliana Bruno, *Atlas of Emotion* (New York: Verso, 2002), 250–51. See also Benjamin, "Work of Art," 268–69, for his related discussion of film as a perceptual "training ground" for the modern subject, who must increasingly perceive the world in a state of "distraction."

40. Marianne Hirsch, *Family Frames* (Cambridge, Mass.: Harvard University Press, 1997), 22.

41. Benedict Anderson, *Imagined Communities,* rev. ed. (New York: Verso, 1991), 6 and 37.

42. Maurice Halbwachs, *On Collective Memory,* ed. and trans. Lewis A. Coser (Chicago: University of Chicago Press, 1992), 40.

43. Alison Landsberg, *Prosthetic Memory* (New York: Columbia University Press, 2004), 20–21.

44. Thomas Schadt, *Berlin: Sinfonie einer Großstadt* (Berlin: Nicolai, 2002), 14.

45. See, e.g., the comparisons of Berlin to London and Paris in English-language Baedeker travel guides from the 1920s. Karl Baedeker, *Berlin and Its Environs,* 6th ed. (Leipzig: Karl Baedeker, 1923), 48–49: "With improved means of locomotion the inner town has

now gradually become the commercial nucleus of Berlin, like the City in London"; "Just as in London, in Paris, and other capitals, so in Berlin, the upper classes tend on the whole to live at the W. end of the town while the E. is given over to factories and workers"; and "The [Unter den] Linden is to Berlin what Bond Street and Picadilly are to London" (51). Comparisons to American cities reflected a much wider German and European discourse on Americanism in the interwar period.

46. For an overview of German–American film relations in Weimar Germany, see Thomas J. Saunders, *Hollywood in Berlin.* (Berkeley: University of California Press, 1994).

47. Peter Fritzsche, *Reading Berlin, 1900* (Cambridge, Mass.: Harvard University Press, 1996), 1.

48. Erhard Schütz, "Beyond Glittering Reflections of Asphalt: Changing Images of Berlin in Weimar Literary Journalism," in *Dancing on the Volcano: Essays on the Culture of the Weimar Republic,* ed. Thomas W. Kniesche and Stephen Brockmann (Columbia, S.C.: Camden House, 1994), 123, and Janet Ward, *Weimar Surfaces* (Berkeley: University of California Press, 2001), 10. General anthologies of Weimar feuilleton articles include Anton Kaes, Martin Jay, and Edward Dimendberg, eds., *The Weimar Republic Sourcebook* (Berkeley: University of California Press, 1994), and Christian Jäger and Erhard Schütz, eds., *Glänzender Asphalt* (Berlin: Fannei and Walz, 1994).

49. For a history of Potsdamer Platz's architecture and planning, see Matthias Pabsch, *Zweimal Weltstadt* (Berlin: Reimer, 1998).

50. Michael Bienert, *Die eingebildete Metropole* (Stuttgart: Metzler, 1992), 97–98; Colomb, *Staging the New Berlin,* 43–44; Ross and Smail, "New Berlins and New Germanies," 65–66.

51. Ewa Gossart, "Berlin wird Weltstadt: Lichtreklame als Medium der urbanen Selbstinszenierung," in *Berlin im Licht,* ed. Franziska Nentwig (Berlin: G+H Verlag Berlin/ Stiftung Stadtmuseum Berlin, 2008), 51; Colomb, *Staging the New Berlin,* 45; Ward, *Weimar Surfaces,* 107–10.

52. Ward, *Weimar Surfaces,* 111; and Frances Guerin, *A Culture of Light* (Minneapolis: University of Minnesota Press, 2005). Guerin lays out her intriguing argument about the political importance of light in silent German fiction films in her first chapter on "The Electrification of Light, Cinema, and Art," 1–47.

53. Erich Kästner, "Besuch vom Land," in *Berliner Gedichte* (Berlin: Rütten and Loening, 1987), 84. The original quotation reads, "Sie stehen verstört am Potsdamer Platz. / Und finden Berlin zu laut. / Die Nacht glüht auf in Kilowatts, / Ein Fräulein sagt heiser: 'Komm mit, mein Schatz!,' / Und zeigt entsetzlich viel Haut."

54. Of course, the cinematic fascination with Berlin persisted into the Third Reich in the uncharacteristically poetic and Weimar-inflected work of Werner Hochbaum in *Morgen beginnt das Leben* (*Life Begins Tomorrow,* Germany 1933), in Hans Cürlis's nonfiction short *Berlin bleibt Berlin* (Berlin remains Berlin, Germany 1935), and in wartime entertainment films. For more on German city films and Berlin films of the 1920s, see Anton Kaes, "Sites of Desire: The Weimar Street Film," in *Film Architecture: Set Design from Metropolis to Blade Runner,* ed. Dietrich Neumann, 26–32 (New York: Prestel, 1996); Kaes, *M* (London: BFI, 1999); Karl Prümm, "'Dynamik der Großstadt': Berlin-Bilder der Zwanziger Jahre," in *Berlin . . . Blicke auf die deutsche Metropole,* ed. Gerhard Brunn and Jürgen Reulecke, 105–23 (Essen: Reimar Hobbing, 1989); and Brigitta B. Wagner, "Urban Representation

and (Inter)national Film Style in the Case of Weimar Berlin," in *Lo stile cinematografico/Film Style,* ed. Enrico Biasin, Giulio Bursi, and Leonardo Quaresima, 292–307 (Udine: Forum, 2007). For a discussion of inflation and *Dr. Mabuse, der Spieler,* see Bernd Widdig, *Culture and Inflation in Weimar Germany* (Minneapolis: University of Minnesota Press, 2001), 113–33. For more on women, gender, and sexuality in Weimar cinema, see Richard W. McCormick, *Gender and Sexuality in Weimar Modernity* (New York: Palgrave, 2001), and Patrice Petro, *Joyless Streets* (Princeton, N.J.: Princeton University Press, 1989).

55. See Klaus Kreimeier, *The Ufa Story,* trans. Robert and Rita Kimber (New York: Hill and Wang, 1996), 127, and Saunders, *Hollywood in Berlin,* 69–71. For a transcultural approach to the Americanization of the European film industry generally in the 1920s–1930s, see Andrew Higson and Richard Maltby, eds., *"Film Europe" and "Film America"* (Exeter: University of Exeter Press, 1999). Ufa also made a separate, smaller deal with Universal.

56. For a Social Democratic approach to the excessive Americanization of Germany's youth through film imports, see Hans Feld, "Film, Filmpolitik und politische Parteien," *Der Film-Kurier,* October 12, 1927.

57. "Was ist ein deutscher Film?" *Lichtbildbühne,* January 1, 1929. This article goes on to point out the absurdity of the legal "Germanness" of a Portuguese film shot in Germany by a crew of mixed nationality.

58. Ernst Jäger, "Der deutsche Spezial-Film wird sich stets in Amerika durchsetzen," *Der Film-Kurier,* November 5, 1927.

59. For more on city films, see William Uricchio, "Ruttmann's 'Berlin' and the City Film to 1930," PhD diss., New York University, 1982, and Helmut Weihsmann, "The City in Twilight: Charting the Genre of the 'City Film' 1900," in *Cinema and Architecture,* ed. François Penz and Maureen Thomas, 8–27 (London: BFI, 1997).

60. Fox-Europa's more experimental projects included Berthold Viertel and Béla Balázs's *Die Abenteuer eines Zehnmarkscheins* (*Adventures of a Ten Mark Note,* Germany 1926).

61. Walter Ruttmann, "Wie ich meinen BERLIN-Film drehte," *Lichtbildbühne,* October 8, 1927, 80. Owing to a loss of records and a reliance on interviews, much of the information regarding the involvement of various members of *Berlin. Die Sinfonie der Großstadt*'s production team has been obscured. Discrepancies occur in the accounts of Carl Mayer, Karl Freund, and Ruttmann. Two extensive studies, by Uricchio and by Goergen, privilege Ruttmann as the principal force behind the shooting and the montage. For an overview of the controversy, see Uricchio, "Ruttmann's 'Berlin,'" 152–59; Siegfried Kracauer, *From Caligari to Hitler* (Princeton, N.J.: Princeton University Press, 1947), 182–88; and Goergen, *Walter Ruttmann,* 25–27. In this case, see Carl Mayer, "Wie ich zur Idee des BERLIN-Films kam," *B.Z.,* September 27, 1927, in Goergen, *Walter Ruttmann,* 115; and Edmund Meisel, "Edmund Meisel über seine BERLIN-Musik," *Film-Kurier,* September 20, 1927, in Goergen, *Walter Ruttmann,* 116. Ruttmann credits the invention of the low-light film stock to camera operator Reimar Kuntze in Ruttmann, "Wie ich," 80.

62. Walter Ruttmann, "Der neue Film," *Spielplan des Tauentzien-Palast,* September 23–29, 1927, in Goergen, *Walter Ruttmann,* 80.

63. Ruttmann, "Berlin als Filmstar," in Goergen, *Walter Ruttmann,* 79. These sentiments echo Karl Scheffler's often quoted (and decontextualized) 1910 observation that

Berlin is a city that is always becoming without ever·being. See Karl Scheffler, *Berlin—Ein Stadtschicksal* (Berlin: Fannei and Walz, 1989), 219.

64. Ruttmann, "Wie ich," 80.

65. Ruttmann, "Der neue Film," 80; Ruttmann, "Wie ich," 80. Also see Georg Simmel's 1903 discussion of urban stimuli and perception of the modern city dweller in "The Metropolis and Mental Life," in *Georg Simmel: On Individuality and Social Forms,* ed. Donald N. Levine, 324–39 (Chicago: University of Chicago Press, 1971). In Simmel's parlance, the assault on the urban subject's perception causes the individual to develop a "blasé attitude" toward his or her surroundings, to create a personal, reactive distance to the flattening of individual identity. Benjamin's take on cinema as a training ground for the modern subject's ability to process information in a state of distraction (see Benjamin, "Work of Art," 268–69) is also useful in considering spectators' perceptual relationship to the filmed and edited city.

66. Around the time of *Berlin. Die Sinfonie der Großstadt*'s premiere, the Tauentzienpalast had more than one thousand seats. With a facade typical of early-twentieth-century department stores, it was fittingly located near the busy Kurfürstendamm and the Kaiser Wilhelm Memorial Church. In 1929, Berlin had 381 cinemas and a total of 180,662 seats. See Heinz Udo Brachvogel, "Mit dem R.K.A. durch Gross-Berlin!," *Lichtbildbühne,* March 8, 1929. For more on cinemas in Berlin, see Peter Boeger, *Architektur der Lichtspieltheater in Berlin* (Berlin: Willmuth Arenhövel, 1993); Sylvaine Hänsel and Angelika Schmidt, eds., *Kinoarchitektur in Berlin 1895–1995* (Berlin: Reimer, 1995); and Esther Sabelus and Jens Wietschorke, eds., *Die Welt im Licht* (Berlin: Panama, 2015).

67. Außenberg's expectations for this experiment in German film art *(Filmkunst)* bear this out as he claims that *Berlin. Die Sinfonie der Großstadt* will remind the world "of the uninterrupted German strength and indefatigable German diligence" that "have made Berlin a stronghold of labor." See Julius Außenberg, "Das Experiment," *Illustrierter Film-Kurier* 658 (1927), in Goergen, *Walter Ruttmann,* 116.

68. See Willy Haas, "Berlin, Die Symphonie der Großstadt," *Der Film-Kurier,* September 24, 1927, and Schauburg am Hauptbahnhof, advertisement, *HE,* October 20, 1927, in Mappe 424, Schriftgut, Deutsche Kinemathek (DK). In fact, one Hamburg newspaper even mentioned the presence of a film barker, who explained the shorts as in "those days" at the Hamburg premiere: "Sinfonie der Großstadt," *HE,* October 19, 1927, in Mappe 424, Schriftgut, DK.

69. TZ, "Berlin eine Sinfonie der Großstadt," *Der Film,* September 24, 1927, in Mappe 424, Schriftgut, DK.

70. See "'Berlin' in der Provinz," *Der Film-Kurier,* October 31, 1927; "Berlin Kino-Kurier," *Der Film-Kurier,* October 2, 1927; "'Berlin' in New York," *Der Film-Kurier,* October 4, 1927; and Goergen, *Walter Ruttmann,* 114.

71. See Rudolf Kurtz, "Berlin. Die Sinfonie der Großstadt," *Lichtbildbühne,* September 24, 1927, and Hans Feld, "Das 'größte grundsächlich witchtige Filmereignis seit Jahren,'" *Der Film-Kurier,* September 24, 1927.

72. See *Das Reichsfilmblatt,* October 1, 1927; Kurtz, "Berlin. Die Sinfonie der Großstadt"; *Der Kinematograph,* September 25, 1927; Leo Hirsch, "Tauentzien-Palast: 'Berlin,'" *Berliner Tagesspiegel,* September 24, 1927; and *HE,* October 24, 1927, all in Mappe 424, Schriftgut, DK.

73. The speed of this sequence recalls a "Jeder Einmal in Berlin" poster, depicting an engine rushing toward the image's point of convergence on the city. Bearing the slogan "Nach Berlin!," the poster was also a collaboration between the tourism board and the Deutsche Reichsbahn. See Colomb, *Staging the New Berlin,* 46.

74. See Wolfgang Schivelbusch, *The Railway Journey* (Berkeley: University of California Press, 1986), 174: "The station functioned as a gateway which had to connect two very different kinds of traffic and traffic space with one another: the traffic space of the city, and that of the railroad." For additional analyses of *Berlin. Die Sinfonie der Großstadt*'s opening sequence, see Sabine Hake, "Urban Spectacle in Walter Ruttmann's *Berlin, Symphony of the Big City,*" in *Dancing on the Volcano: Essays on the Culture of the Weimar Republic,* ed. Thomas W. Kniesche and Stephen Brockmann (Columbia, S.C.: Camden House, 1994), 136; Anton Kaes, "Leaving Home: Film, Migration, and the Urban Experience," *New German Critique* 74 (Spring/Summer 1998): 179–84; and Uricchio, "Ruttmann's 'Berlin,'" 221–33.

75. Joseph Roth, "Some Reflections on Traffic," in *What I Saw,* trans. Michael Hoffmann (New York: W. W. Norton, 2003), 103, 97.

76. Lion Feuchtwanger, "Herr B.W. Smith besichtigt die Leipziger Strasse," in *Berliner Gedichte* (Berlin: Rütten and Loening, 1987), 67. In contrast, guidebooks of the 1920s represented Leipziger Straße as a tourist attraction. See, e.g., Baedeker, *Berlin and Its Environs,* 127: "It [Leipziger Straße] is now the chief artery of traffic in Berlin and is distinguished by the number of its handsome buildings, some of which show that the Renaissance style is being succeeded by more modern forms."

77. Kracauer, "Wir schaffens," *Frankfurter Zeitung,* November 17, 1927. It is worth noting the delay in the release of certain Soviet montage films in Germany, e.g., *Bronenosets Potyomkin* in 1930. This is important to understanding how novel montage might have appeared to German audiences in 1927, though Kracauer, as a film critic, may have had opportunities to see earlier Soviet examples.

78. Joseph Goebbels, "Around the Gedächtniskirche," in Kaes et al., *Weimar Republic Sourcebook,* 561.

79. Siegfried Kracauer, "Film 1928," in *The Mass Ornament,* trans. and ed. Thomas Y. Levin (Cambridge, Mass.: Harvard University Press, 1995), 318.

80. Uricchio, "Ruttmann's 'Berlin,'" 111. See also a defense of Ruttmann's approach to his Berlin material in Goergen, *Walter Ruttmann,* 30. Another defense comes from Ruttmann's contemporary Béla Balázs, who at once champions the role of inanimate objects in film and New Objectivity *(Neue Sachlichkeit)* and reminds the film community that "artists such as Ruttmann, Freund, and Mayer were never as radical as their critics and never thought that such Objectivity would represent the only future of cinema." In this way, he returns the discussion to the team's avant-garde experimentation with the film medium. See Balázs, "Nebenbei," *Der Film-Kurier,* October 15, 1927. For more on Moholy-Nagy's plans for *Dynamik der Großstadt,* see László Moholy-Nagy, *Malerei Fotografie Film,* ed. Hans M. Wingler (Berlin: Gebr. Mann, 1986).

81. Kracauer, *From Caligari,* 185–86. The following scholarly contributions use Kracauer's critique either as a point of departure or as a point of contention: Martin Gaughan, "Ruttmann's Berlin: Filming in a 'Hollow Space,'" in *Screening the City,* ed. Mark Shiel and Tony Fitzmaurice, 41–57 (New York: Verso, 2003); Hake, "Urban Spectacle"; and

Wolfgang Natter, "The City as Cinematic Space: Modernism and Place in *Berlin, Symphony of a City*," in Aitken and Zonn, *Place, Power, Situation, and Spectacle*, 203–27.

82. Kracauer, *Theory*, 207, 64.

83. Ernst Blass, "'Berlin' und Berlin," *Berliner Tagesspiegel*, July 22, 1928, in Mappe 424, Schriftgut, DK.

84. See Uricchio, "Ruttmann's 'Berlin,'" 222: "Berlin as a city is not presented as a series of monuments or grand vistas; rather, a vital and active complex of activities, emotions and forces is created and organized around time."

85. See the discussion of the editing "cluster" in Uricchio, "Ruttmann's 'Berlin,'" 223, and the analysis of "bracket syntagma," based on Christian Metz's term, in Matthew Bernstein, "Visual Style and Spatial Articulations in Berlin, Symphony of a City (1927)," *The Journal of Film and Video* 36 (Fall 1984): 7.

86. Siegfried Kracauer, *Travel and Dance*, ed. and trans. Thomas Y. Levin (Cambridge, Mass.: Harvard University Press, 1995), 65–66.

87. Kurt Pinthus, "Der Berlin-Film," in *Kurt Pinthus: Filmpublizist*, ed. Rolf Aurich und Wolfgang Jacobsen (Munich: Edition Text + Kritik, 2008), 237.

88. Guntram Vogt, *Die Stadt im Kino: Deutsche Spielfilme 1900–2000* (Marburg: Schüren, 2001), 177. Conversely, Vogt quotes a rather lengthy 1936 article in praise of Ruttmann's city film as a cinematographic challenge to both the American and Soviet film industries.

89. The films, *Kleiner Film einer Grossen Stadt . . . der Stadt Düsseldorf am Rhein* (Small film of a great city . . . the city Düsseldorf on the Rhein, Germany 1935), *Stuttgart, die Grosstadt zwischen Wald und Reben* (Stuttgart, the great city between woods and vines, Germany 1935), *Stadt Stuttgart: 100 Cannstatter Volksfest* (The city of Stuttgart: The 100th Canstatt Folk Festival, Germany 1935), and *Weltstrasse See-Welthafen Hamburg* (Street to the world: World-class harbor Hamburg, Germany 1938), showcase aspects of these cities that are critical to the National Socialist agenda: German cultural heritage and, in the case of Hamburg, Germany's importance in the world. See Goergen, *Walter Ruttmann*, 144–47 and 153. For a critical account of Ruttmann's Nazi film career, see William Uricchio, "Ruttmann nach 1933," in Goergen, *Walter Ruttmann*, 59–65. For an account of Ruttmann's involvement in *Triumph des Willens*, see Jeanpaul Goergen, "Walter Ruttmann: Ein Porträt," in Goergen, *Walter Ruttmann*, 17. For accounts of Ruttmann's entire oeuvre, also across media and film modes, see Leonardo Quaresima, *Walter Ruttmann: Cinema, pittura, ars acustica* (Calliano: Manfrini, 1994), and Michael Cowan, *Walter Ruttmann and the Cinema of Multiplicity* (Amsterdam: Amsterdam University Press, 2014).

90. See Goergen, *Walter Ruttmann*, 140 for an annotated filmographic entry. Neither articles on the film's production nor those following its release mention Ruttmann's participation and the use of material from *Berlin. Die Sinfonie der Großstadt.* Officially Ruttmann is credited on the film for cinematography and sound. See Cowan, *Walter Ruttmann and the Cinema of Multiplicity*, 118–32, for a more recent account of *Blut und Boden* and Ruttmann's participation in its making. Cowan argues that Ruttmann's technical expertise and established reputation as well as the use and reediting of footage from *Berlin. Die Sinfonie der Großstadt* point to the filmmaker's more central involvement in the film and sees this early Nazi cooption of the left-leaning Ruttmann as "a testimony to

the malleability of the interwar avant-garde" (118). Despite Ruttmann's cooperation, much evidence suggests that the Nazi Party still viewed him with skepticism (216).

91. Vogt, *Die Stadt im Kino,* 398–99. In a 1977 personal account, Laforgue claimed that the film was banned due to its avoidance of the Nazi presence, but Vogt could not find additional corroboration for this story.

92. *Symphonie einer Weltstadt/Berlin, wie es war* screened regularly in weekend matinees at the Adria cinema in Berlin-Steglitz in the early 2000s. The film was also distributed on video and DVD.

93. Filmbegutachtungskommission für Jugend und Schule, *Protokoll 19.10.62* (Landesbildstelle, 1962), 3, in Mappe 424, Schriftgut, DK.

94. The film was shown at least nine times between 1969 and 1988 on six different West German television stations, according to OPAC "Kinofilme im TV." The Deutsches Rundfunkarchiv had no evidence on record of television broadcasts of the film in the GDR. The Bundesarchiv-Filmarchiv possesses a short, Super 8mm version of the film, labeled "Heimkino," that DEFA's central processing laboratory delivered to the State Film Archive in 1984. Because the material has not been conserved in a second copy and thus cannot be seen, and because the film comes with no clarifying information, archivists are reluctant to acknowledge it as evidence of the film's availability for private home use in the GDR.

95. See Dorothea Becker, *Zwischen Ideologie und Autonomie: Die DDR-Forschung über die deutsche Filmgeschichte* (Münster: Lit, 1999), 110–12, for more on GDR film history's evaluation of Ruttmann's *Berlin. Die Sinfonie der Großstadt.* As Becker notes, film scholars were often able to find ways to construe formalist decadence as somehow in keeping with socialism. In Ruttmann's case, New Objectivity could be linked to documentary realism or else function as a legitimate means of social critique: Jerzy Toeplitz, *Geschichte des Films* (Berlin: Henschelverlag, 1984), 1:430–32. Indeed, early GDR scholarship dealing with the film placed it in dialogue with Soviet filmmaking of the 1920s or with a socially productive, if immature, stage of modernist experimentation. See Werner Wallroth, "Walter Ruttmann: *Berlin—Die Symphonie einer Großstadt* Dsiga Wertow: *Der Mann mit der Kamera:* Eine vergleichende Studie," Diplomarbeit, Deutsche Hochschule für Filmkunst, 1959; Rolf Liebmann, "Dramaturgie und Montage in Ruttmanns 'Berlin—Symphonie einer Großstadt,'" *Film* 1 (1965): 127–41; and Thomas Kuschel, "Die Darstellung des Menschen und seiner Gesellschaft in den Filmen 'Berlin—Symphonie einer Großstadt' von Walter Ruttmann und 'Vorwärts, Sowjet!' von Dsiga Wertow unter Berücksichtigung der künstlerisch-formalen Gestaltungsmittel," *Film* 1 (1965): 142–53.

96. See Staatliches Filmarchiv, "Verleihprogramm 1964/65," *Film* 1 (1964): 23, and Staatliches Filmarchiv der DDR, *Dokumentarfilm im Zeitalter Lenins* (Leipzig: Internationale Leipziger Dokumentar- und Kurzfilmwoche für Kino und Fernsehen, 1970), 9.

97. Eckhart Jahnke, "Berlin—Symphonie einer Großstadt," *Film-Blätter,* March 15, 1977, in Mappe 1495, Schriftgut, Bundesarchiv-Filmarchiv (BArch).

98. Günter Schulz, "Berlin—Sinfonie der Grosstadt," in *Internationale Dokumentarfilme* (Berlin: Staatliches Filmarchiv der Deutschen Demokratischen Republik, 1962), 19.

99. See the explanatory text "Anmerkungen zur Wiederaufführung '82 von 'Berlin. Die Sinfonie der Großstadt'" in Mappe 424, Schriftgut, DK.

100. Michael Schwarze, "Asphalt-Zauber," *Frankfurter Allgemeine Zeitung,* February 17, 1982.

101. See Jeanpaul Goergen, "Ein wertvolles Fundstück," *Der Tagesspiegel,* April 26, 1987. Goergen explains that the Library of Congress print was the same version as a Museum of Modern Art (MoMA) print that Lothar Prox found via a private collector. As it turns out, the original MoMA print was a copy of a print originally found in the Reichsfilmarchiv in Berlin. Thus the reconstruction of *Berlin. Die Sinfonie der Großstadt*'s score and image also served to reclaim German cultural capital that had been seized by the Allies.

102. For accounts of these events, see Bernd Feuchtner, "Im Rausch des Tempos," *Frankfurter Rundschau,* December 16, 1987; Andreas Bomba, "Sinfonie der Großstadt," *Die Welt,* December 17, 1987; and Jeanpaul Goergen, "Malerei mit Zeit," *Frankfurter Allgemeine Zeitung,* December 28, 1987.

103. See Komitee der Deutschen Demokratischen Republik zum 750jährigen Bestehen von Berlin, *750 Jahre Berlin* (Berlin: VEB Tourist, 1986), 283–89; *Sonntag* 28 (1987), in Mappe 1459, Schriftgut, BArch.; *Camera* 3 (1987): 3; and *Camera* 4 (1987): 3. Not only did the film play in the Babylon with live piano accompaniment in October but it returned by popular request in November.

104. See *Film und Fernsehen* 6 (1987). For more on the scholarly results of the symposium, see *Beiträge zur Film- und Fernsehwissenschaft* 34 (1988): 87–220.

105. Rudolf Freund, "'Augenmusik' über einen Frühlingstag," *Berliner Zeitung,* December 5, 1987, and "Das Berlin von einst im Film," *Kölnischer Anzeiger,* April 16, 1987.

106. Ian Brown, qtd. in "Stummfilmklassiker als Brücke zwischen Europas Metropolen," *Berliner Morgenpost* 25 (August 1995); State secretary of the cultural senate Winfried Sühlo, qtd. in Kathi Seefeld, "Trilaterale Enthemmung in Noten," *die tageszeitung,* August 25, 1995.

107. "Stummfilmklassiker."

108. Frank Schoser, "Berlin im Wettstreit der europäischen Zentren," in *Hauptstadt Berlin,* ed. Werner Süß (Berlin: Berlin, 1996), 3:232.

109. For more on the events, see the Film Concert brochure (in French), *Projections* 3, in Mappe 424, Schriftgut, DK.

110. Several of these *Programmkinos* were located in the Eastern parts of the city as well as in the East–West border regions, where youth culture was concentrated in the 1990s and early 2000s. Typical would be the Kino Arsenal at Potsdamer Platz (to which it had moved from Viktoria-Luise-Platz in the West), Filmkunsthaus Babylon (now Babylon Mitte) and Central in Mitte, and the Kino Blow Up in Prenzlauer Berg.

111. "Tronthaim," June 10, 2006, http://www.tronthaim.de/English/GB Index.htm/. The current website describes the "ecstasy of the pictures in 1927" and a "reborn city of Berlin."

112. Tronthaim, *Berlin. Die Sinfonie der Großstadt,* perf. Daniel Dorsch and Sascha Moser, Kino Blow Up, Berlin, January 26, 2001.

113. See Hans-Jörg Rother, "Ruttmann steht mir bei," *Frankfurter Allgemeine Zeitung,* May 15, 2001, and Birgit Galle, "Zehn Stunden, zwei Bilder," *Die Zeit* 33 (2001). See also Schadt, *Berlin,* 165: funds were provided by Südwestrundfunk, Sender Freies

Berlin, Arte, Telepool, the Bundesfilmstiftung, Filmboard Berlin-Brandenburg, and MFG Baden-Württemberg.

114. See Hans-Günther Dicks, "Das Erlebnis des Augen-Blicks—an Orten, wo doch gar 'nichts los ist,'" *Neues Deutschland,* June 12, 2001.

115. "Berlin: Sinfonie einer Großstadt," lobby card, in Mappe 48883, Schriftgut, DK.

116. Galle, "Zehn Stunden, zwei Bilder."

117. Lasse Ole Hempel, "Das lädierte Gesicht von Berlin," *Berliner Zeitung,* May 31, 2001. See also Schadt, *Berlin,* 11.

118. Schadt, *Berlin,* 13.

119. Boym, *Future of Nostalgia,* 49–50.

120. Hempel, "Das lädierte Gesicht."

121. For more on Schadt's approach to documentary filmmaking, see Thomas Schadt, *Das Gefühl des Augenblicks* (Bergisch Gladbach: Bastei Lübbe, 2002). Particularly important to Schadt is the "authenticity" of his images. It should also be noted that his companion book to the film showcases a series of still photographs isolated from several of the film's sequences. In their composition, the images function equally as photographs, which suggests a notion of movement, camera mobility, and montage quite different from Ruttmann's. See Schadt, *Berlin,* 19–131.

122. Manuel Brug, "Das ganz alte im immer neuen Berlin," *Die Welt,* April 10, 2002.

123. Thomas Schadt, personal interview, Ludwigsburg, Germany, June 22, 2006. Schadt also discussed his interest in making a film that would stand the test of time.

124. Ibid.

125. In the first group, see, e.g., "Eine Liebeserklärung an Berlin," *Die Welt am Sonntag,* April 7, 2002, and Eckhard Fuhr, "Berlin zum kuscheln," *Die Welt,* April 12, 2002. In addition, Brug writes scathingly, "The new Berlin. Not much different from the old," and calls Schadt's Berlin "a feel-good metropolis." In the second group, see Björn Gottstein, "Die Stadt ohne Eigenschaften," *die tageszeitung,* April 12, 2002, and Klaus Georg Koch, "Der Grund unserer Ruhe," *Berliner Zeitung,* April 12, 2002. For additional scholarly reception of the film, see Sabine Hake, *Topographies of Class* (Ann Arbor: University of Michigan Press, 2008), 271; Evelyn Preuss, "The Collapse of Time: German History and Identity in Hubertus Siegert's *Berlin Babylon* (2001) and Thomas Schadt's *Berlin: Sinfonie einer Großstadt* (2002)," in *Berlin: The Symphony Continues,* ed. Carol Anne Costabile-Heming, Rachel J. Halverson, and Kristie A. Foell, 119–41 (New York: Walter de Gruyter, 2004); and Andrew J. Webber, *Berlin in the Twentieth Century: A Cultural Topography* (Cambridge: Cambridge University Press, 2008), 179–87.

126. Lasse Ole Hempel, "Recht offizielles Bild," *die tageszeitung,* May 16, 2002.

127. Schadt, personal interview.

2. GENERATION

1. The series was directed by Thomas Kufus and Jan Schütte. *Unsere 60er Jahre (Our 1960s),* directed by Thomas Kufus and Michael Wulfes, appeared on ARD in 2007. See also Claudia Tieschky, "Traum aus Palisander: Acht ARD-Anstalten erkunden die 60er Jahre," *Süddeutsche Zeitung,* November 12, 2007: 3.5 million viewers tuned in to *Unsere 50er Jahre.*

2. See, e.g., the front jacket cover of Rudolf Großkopff, *Unsere 50er Jahre* (Frankfurt/ Main: Eichborn, 2005). This and all subsequent English translations in this chapter are, unless otherwise noted, my own.

3. See Klaus Wiegrefe, "Blühende Landschaften," in "Die 50er Jahre: Vom Trümmerland zum Wirtschaftswunder," special issue of *Der Spiegel* 1 (2006): 6; "Inhalt," ibid., 4.

4. Chancellor Gerhard Schröder (born in 1944) and a number of his prominent cabinet members were born just before or during the Second World War or else in its immediate aftermath, e.g., Franz Müntefering (1940), Hans Eichel (1941), Reinhard Klimmt (1942), Heidemarie Wieczorek-Zeul (1942), Herta Däubler-Gmelin (1943), Oskar Lafontaine (1943), Walter Riester (1943), Peter Struck (1943), Rudolf Scharping (1947), and Joschka Fischer (1948).

5. Wiegrefe, "Blühende Landschaften," 9. This teleology was also reflected in the West's Cold War reunification rhetoric. See Edgar Wolfrum, *Geschichtspolitik in der Bundesrepublik Deutschland* (Darmstadt: Wissenschaftliche Buchgesellschaft, 1999), 356. Wolfrum discusses the way in which Helmut Kohl's government revived the anniversary of June 17, 1953, the day of the workers' uprising in the East, in 1983 as "a first democratic impulse in the socialist camp" and as "the beginning of the historical emancipation process of GDR society." While North American scholars had begun to design projects that integrated the two histories, many German accounts of the 1950s continued to subsume the social, political, and cultural experiences of the decade under Western rubrics. See Jeffrey Herf, *Divided Memory* (Cambridge, Mass.: Harvard University Press, 1997); Uta G. Poiger, *Jazz, Rock, and Rebels* (Berkeley: University of California Press, 2000); and John Davidson and Sabine Hake, eds., *Framing the Fifties* (New York: Berghahn, 2007). Two anthologies that emphasize the FRG's history are Werner Faulstich, ed., *Die Kultur der fünfziger Jahre* (Munich: Wilhelm Fink, 2002), and Eckhard Siepmann, ed., *Bikini: Die fünfziger Jahre* (Reinbeck bei Hamburg: Rowohlt, 1983).

6. For more on heritage cinema, emotion, nostalgia, and German suffering, see Lutz Koepnick, "Reframing the Past: Heritage Cinema and the Holocaust in the 1990s," in "Postwall Cinema," ed. Eric Rentschler, special issue of *New German Critique* 87 (Fall 2002): 47–82; Johannes von Moltke, "Sympathy for the Devil: Cinema, History, and the Politics of Emotion," *New German Critique* 102 (Fall 2007): 17–43; the contributions of Jaimey Fisher, Jennifer M. Kapczynski, Elisabeth Krimmer, Anna M. Parkinson, and Wilfred Wilms in *The Collapse of the Conventional: German Film and Its Politics at the Turn of the Twenty-First Century,* ed. Jaimey Fisher and Brad Prager (Detroit, Mich.: Wayne State University Press, 2010); and Mattias Frey, *Postwall German Cinema* (New York: Berghahn, 2013).

7. Paul Steege, *Black Market, Cold War* (Cambridge: Cambridge University Press, 2007), 56.

8. Ernest Renan, "What Is a Nation?," in *Becoming National,* ed. Geoff Eley and Ronald Grigor Suny (New York: Oxford University Press, 1996), 52.

9. See Rolf Fröhner, *Wie stark sind die Halbstarken?* (Bielefeld: Maria von Stackelberg, 1956), 145–46, 360. Fröhner's study of West German and West Berlin youths reveals that 62 percent were filmgoers. While 1955 saw 34 percent of all youths from the FRG visiting the cinema three or more times each month, this number jumped to 44 percent in West Berlin. Fröhner explains this higher number as a reflection of the urban milieu. See as

well Heinz Kersten, *Das Filmwesen in der Sowjetischen Besatzungszone Deutschlands,* Bonner Berichte aus Mittel- und Ostdeutschland (Bonn: Bundesministerium für Gesamtdeustsche Fragen, 1963), 1:385. Though not specifically referring to youth statistics and filmgoers' articulation of their own viewing habits, Kersten's table shows that the number of film screenings per filmgoer in the GDR in 1955 was 14.8 (or a little more than one cinema visit per month, assuming that spectators regularly visited the cinema).

10. Helmut Schelsky, *Die skeptische Generation* (Düsseldorf: Eugen Diederichs, 1957), 127–28.

11. The *Halbstarkenproblem* refers to a phenomenon of social unrest and delinquency among predominantly working-class East and West German teenagers and young adults. The trouble seemed to arise from both postwar German social realities and the influence of American popular culture. There has been much discussion of how widespread this social attitude was and to what extent its exaggerated importance in the media signaled a larger anxiety about social and cultural change. The term *Halbstarke* came into use around the turn of the century. See Mark Fenemore, *Sex, Thugs, and Rock 'n' Roll* (New York: Berghahn, 2007); Thomas Grotum, *Die Halbstarken* (Frankfurt: Campus, 1994); Wiebke Janssen, *Halbstarke in der DDR* (Berlin: Ch. Links, 2010); Kaspar Maase, "Establishing Cultural Democracy," in *The Miracle Years,* ed. Hanna Schissler, 428–50 (Princeton, NJ: Princeton University Press, 2001); and Poiger, *Jazz, Rock, and Rebels,* generally. At the time, West German sociologists in particular were addressing the problem in book-length studies. In addition to Schelsky and Fröhner, see Günther Kaiser, *Randalierende Jugend* (Heidelberg: Quelle and Meyer, 1959).

12. For more on the cinematic ideals of socialist realism, see Hermann Axen, "Für den Aufschwung der fortschrittlichen deutschen Filmkunst. Aus dem Referat von Hermann Axen auf der Konferenz der Filmschaffenden in Berlin," in *Das Filmwesen in der Sowjetischen Besatzungszone Deutschlands,* ed. Heinz Kersten, Bonner Berichte aus Mittel- und Ostdeutschland (Bonn: Bundesministerium für Gesamtdeustsche Fragen, 1963), 2:12–18. For general overviews of German film production in the 1950s, see Sabine Hake, *German National Cinema,* 2nd ed. (London: Routledge, 2008), 92–126; Wolfgang Jacobsen, Anton Kaes, and Hans Helmut Prinzler, eds., *Geschichte des deutschen Films* (Stuttgart: Metzler, 1993), 171–210, 323–64; Klaus Kreimeier, "Die Ökonomie der Gefühle," in *Zwischen Gestern und Morgen,* ed. Hilmar Hoffmann and Walter Schobert, 8–28 (Frankfurt: Deutsches Filmmuseum, 1989); and Ralf Schenk, "Mitten im Kalten Krieg," in *Das zweite Leben der Filmstadt Babelsberg, 1946–92,* ed. Ralf Schenk, 51–157 (Berlin: Henschel, 1994).

13. Since 1989, the 1950s productions of Klein-Kohlhaase and Tressler-Tremper have received much scholarly attention. For Klein-Kohlhaase, see, e.g., Horst Claus, "Rebels with a Cause: The Development of the *'Berlin-Filme'* by Gerhard Klein and Wolfgang Kohlhaase," in *DEFA: East German Cinema, 1949–1992,* ed. Seán Allan and John Sandford, 93–116 (New York: Berghahn, 1999); Joshua Feinstein, *The Triumph of the Ordinary* (Chapel Hill: University of North Carolina Press, 2002), 45–77; and Sabine Hake, "Anti-Americanism and the Cold War," in *Americanization and Anti-Americanism,* ed. Alexander Stephen, 148–65 (New York: Berghahn, 2005). For Tressler–Tremper, see Norbert Grob, "'Es gibt keine bessere Kulisse als die Straße . . .': Berlin-Filme von Gerhard Oswald und Georg Tressler in den fünfziger Jahren," in *Zwischen Gestern und Morgen,* ed. Hilmar Hoffmann and Walter Schobert, 206–22 (Frankfurt: Deutsches Filmmuseum, 1989), and

Robert Buchschwenter and Lukas Maurer, eds., *Halbstark* (Vienna: Filmarchiv Austria, 2003), 11–30, 69–99. For discussions of both director–writer teams, see Jürgen Felix, "Rebellische Jugend," in "Positionen deutscher Filmgeschichte," ed. Michael Schaudig, special issue of *diskurs film* 8 (1996): 309–28; Irina Jüngling, "Halbstarke vom Wedding und von der Schönhauser," in *Zwischen Bluejeans und Blauhemden,* ed. Ingelore König, Dieter Wiedemann, and Lothar Wolf (Berlin: Henschel, 1995), 69–75; and Poiger's second and third chapters.

14. Erika M. Hoerning, *Zwischen den Fronten* (Cologne: Böhlau, 1992), 43.

15. Ibid., 231. It should be noted that the number of West-to-East border crossers dropped significantly between 1952 and 1953 and declined gradually throughout the decade, while the number moving from East to West continued to rise from 30,990 in 1952. See also T. H. Elkins, *Berlin: The Spatial Structure of a Divided City* (London: Methuen, 1988), 55. Elkins estimates another twenty thousand border crossers engaged in domestic work or in a second job. For a historical perspective from the GDR, see Gerhard Keiderling and Percy Stulz, *Berlin, 1945–1968* (Berlin: Dietz, 1970), 471. They estimate an additional two hundred thousand to three hundred thousand East-to-West border crossers (possibly an inflated number) from East Berlin and Brandenburg beyond those officially registered.

16. Hoerning, *Zwischen den Fronten,* 53.

17. See, e.g., Peter Müller, "Counter-Architecture and Building Race: Cold War Politics and the Two Berlins," *GHI Bulletin Supplement* 2 (2005): 101–14; Regine Beckmann, Christoph Brachmann, and Karen Straub, "Der Ernst-Reuter-Platz als 'Symbol des freien Berlin,'" in *Die Technische Universität und ihre Bauten,* ed. Christoph Brachmann and Robert Suckale, 119–35 (Berlin: Bauwesen, 1999); and Diethelm Prowe, "Brennpunkt des Kalten Krieges: Berlin in den deutsch-amerikanischen Beziehungen," in *Die USA und Deutschland im Zeitalter des Kalten Krieges, 1945–1990,* vol. 1, ed. Detlef Junker, Philipp Gassert, Wilfried Mausbach, and David B. Morris, 260–70 (Stuttgart: Deutsche-Verlags-Anstalt, 2001).

18. See Prowe, "Brennpunkt des Kalten Krieges," 264.

19. Hoerning, *Zwischen den Fronten,* 107–10.

20. Katie Trumpener, "Border Cinemas: Mediascapes of the Cold War," in *The Divided Screen: The Cinemas of Postwar Germany* (Princeton, N.J.: Princeton University Press, forthcoming). This quote comes from the 2006 book manuscript.

21. See *Ausländische Spiel- und abendfüllende Dokumentarfilme in den Kinos der SBZ/DDR 1945–1966* (Berlin: Bundesarchiv-Filmarchiv and DEFA-Stiftung, 2001), 56–174. The number of revivals increases significantly with the addition of Austrian documentaries and features. According to a West German trade report, "Ostzonale Spielfilme 1945 bis 1958," *Filmblätter* 16 (1958): 419, there were 867 German and Austrian features shown in the East during this period, with 732 released in the immediate postwar years from 1945 to 1947 and 14 to 24 films screened annually until 1953. The West German films imported by Progress included features by Hans Deppe and Kurt Hoffmann. Among the few DEFA films that managed to reach a West German audience were Wolfgang Staudte's *Der Untertan* (GDR 1951), released in a shortened version there in 1957, and Konrad Wolf's *Lissy* (GDR 1957).

22. See "Ostzonale Spielfilme," 419, and Poiger, *Jazz, Rock, and Rebels,* 52. In addition to *Salt of the Earth* (United States 1953), imported in 1955, and *Marty* (United States 1955) and *Not as a Stranger* (United States 1955), both shown in 1957, the GDR screened several Chaplin shorts for a 1955 Chaplin festival titled Lachen Verboten (No Laughing). Reflecting the struggles of the downtrodden, all of these films espouse themes deemed appropriate for a socialist state.

23. Werner Löffler, "Berlin und der deutsche Film," *Die Filmwoche* 22 (1951): 271.

24. Axen, "Für den Aufschwung der fortschrittlichen deutschen Filmkunst," 17.

25. Hake, *German National Cinema,* 109–10. Border-crossing actors included the legendary silent star Henny Porten as well as Werner Peters and Wolfgang Kieling. See also Wolfgang Kohlhaase, "'Er suchte die Poesie, die in den Dingen steckt': Gespräch mit dem Autor Wolfgang Kohlhaase," in *Werkstatterfahrungen mit Gerhard Klein,* ed. Hannes Schmidt (Berlin: Betriebsakademie des VEB DEFA Studio für Spielfilme, 1984), 27. The cinematographer Wolf Göthe was living in West Berlin throughout the filming of *Eine Berliner Romanze* and *Berlin—Ecke Schönhauser.* In addition, the character actor Egon Vogel appeared both as a pharmacist in *Eine Berliner Romanze* and as a janitor in *Die Halbstarken,* while Ilse Pagé, the female lead of *Berlin—Ecke Schönhauser,* was a West Berliner.

26. *Der Tagesspiegel,* April 6, 1956, qtd. in Uta Berg-Ganschow and Wolfgang Jacobsen, eds., . . . *Film . . . Stadt . . . Kino . . . Berlin* (Berlin: Argon, 1987), 52.

27. See "Gedanken zur Wiedervereinigung," *Filmblätter* 32 (1957): 962; and Berg-Ganschow and Jacobsen, . . . *Film . . . Stadt . . . Kino . . . Berlin,* 49.

28. For accounts of the border cinema, see Ganschow and Jacobsen, . . . *Film . . . Stadt . . . Kino . . . Berlin,* 52–55; Michael Hanisch, *Um 6 Uhr abends nach Kriegsende bis High Noon: Kino und Film im Berlin der Nachkriegszeit 1945–1953* (Berlin: DEFA-Stiftung, 2004), 64–77; Hoerning, *Zwischen den Fronten,* 51–53; Poiger, *Jazz, Rock, and Rebels,* 54, 68–69, 84–85, 134–35; Trumpener, "Border Cinemas," 102–3; "Grenztheater: Kapitel Berliner Filmtheater-Geschichte," *Filmblätter* 40 (1958): 1218; *Flimmern auf dem Eisernen Vorhang: Berliner Grenzkinos 1950–1961* (Berlin: Berliner Grenzkinos, 2011).

29. Committee for German Unity, *250 Questions 250 Answers about the German Democratic Republic* (Berlin: Die Wirtschaft, 1956), 161. Regarding the youthful, musical atmosphere of the cinemas, see Ganschow and Jacobsen, . . . *Film . . . Stadt . . . Kino . . . Berlin,* 55.

30. Poiger, *Jazz, Rock, and Rebels,* 85, and "Ostkulturprogramm ohne Filmtheater," *Filmblätter* 19 (1957): 458.

31. See "Was westdeutsche Filme für Bewohner der Ostzone bedeuten?," *Filmblätter* 19 (1953): 458, and "Der DDR-Filter für Filmimporte," *Filmblätter* 5 (1957): 142.

32. Wolfgang Kohlhaase, personal interview, tape recording, Berlin, Germany, May 9, 2008.

33. For an account of the Berlinale's early years and festival organizers' consideration of a special screening of 1940s star Hans Albers's *Nachts auf den Straßen* (*The Mistress,* FRG 1952), see Heide Fehrenbach, *Cinema in Democratizing Germany* (Chapel Hill: University of North Carolina Press, 1995), 240.

34. See *Telegraf* 207 (1950), qtd. in Hanisch, *Um 6 Uhr abends nach Kriegsende bis High Noon,* 67.

35. Hanisch, *Um 6 Uhr abends nach Kriegsende bis High Noon,* 68.

36. See Bianca Schemel, *Die Geschichte der Berliner Grenzkinos 1950–1961* (The history of the Berlin border cinemas 1950–1961, Bianca Schemel, FRG 2011), installation video.

37. Kohlhaase, personal interview. He makes the point that the "B-movies" programmed at border cinemas did not appeal to people who carefully selected films on aesthetic grounds.

38. "'Berliner Kulturplan' läuft," *Filmblätter* 38 (1957): 1122.

39. "Ein Fanal!," *Filmblätter* 39 (1957): 1146.

40. "Berlins Aufgabe," *Filmblätter* 50 (1957): 1428.

41. "Grenztheater," 1218; see also "Zum Gesamtberliner Kulturplan," *Filmblätter* 33 (1958): 1024, and Poiger, *Jazz, Rock, and Rebels,* 68–69: West Berlin officials were already pressuring border cinemas to change their programs in 1955.

42. For a detailed account of the rise of the teenage marketplace and teen genres in postwar America, see Thomas Doherty, *Teenagers and Teenpics,* rev. ed. (Philadelphia: Temple University Press, 2002).

43. See Kohlhaase, "Er suchte," 11, and Wolfgang Fischer, "Herrscher über Licht und Schatten: Zur Fotografie in Pehlkes Spielfilmen," *Filmmaterialien* 7 (1995): 6.

44. Kohlhaase, "Er suchte," 9, and Georg Tressler, qtd. in Lukas Maurer, "Kleine Wirklichkeiten," in *Halbstark,* ed. Robert Buchschwenter and Lukas Maurer (Vienna: Filmarchiv Austria, 2003), 20–21. Maurer provides a useful biographical overview of Tressler's career. For more on Klein, see Ralf Schenk, "Keene Venus aus Pudding . . . ," *Neues Deutschland,* May 2, 1995. While Tressler had been a film officer for the American Economic Cooperation Administration, an Austrian office administering the Marshall Plan, from 1950 to 1954, Klein worked in the documentary division of DEFA before he began directing features. The screenwriters Tremper and Kohlhaase, born in 1928 and 1931, respectively, were roughly the same age as the male leads in all four films.

45. Will Tremper, "Ich sehe etwas und wir fangen sofort an zu drehen," in *Will Tremper—Filme eines Journalisten, Kinemathek* 80 (March 1993): 21.

46. For more on the complex triangulation of American, West German, and East German culture, see Poiger, *Jazz, Rock, and Rebels,* 31–70; and Hake, "Anti-Americanism," 153. See Felix, "Rebellische Jugend," 324, where he notes that the majority of 1950s West German youth films steered clear of rebellion.

47. See Will Tremper, "Die Kuh," in *Kalter Krieg,* ed. Helga Belach and Wolfgang Jacobsen (Berlin: Stiftung Deutsche Kinemathek, 1999), 122; güb, "'Halbstarke' soll er heißen!," *Volkstimme,* June 30, 1956; Thomas Heimann, *DEFA, Künstler und SED,* Beiträge zur Film- und Fernsehwissenschaft 46 (Berlin: Vistas, 1994), 292; Ekkehard Schall, ". . . hat mich der Regisseur Klein in eine Krise getrieben und mich dadurch erneut, verändert und auch entwickelt," in *Werkstatterfahrungen mit Gerhard Klein,* ed. Hannes Schmidt (Berlin: Betriebsakademie des VEB DEFA Studio für Spielfilme, 1984), 81; and Schenk, "Mitten im Kalten Krieg," 130. On the politics of *Deutschlandsender,* see Klaus Arnold, *Kalter Krieg im Äther* (Münster: Lit, 2002). For more on the history of RIAS: Herbert Kundler, *RIAS Berlin: Eine Radio-Station in einer geteilten Stadt* (Berlin: Reimer, 2002).

48. Kaiser, *Randalierende Jugend,* 102–5.

49. Committee for German Unity, *250 Questions 250 Answers,* 139. The committee's insistence on the small number of occurrences contradicts internal GDR discussion of

the growing gulf between FDJ leadership and critically distanced youth. See Ulrich Mählert and Gerd-Rüdiger Stephan, *Blaue Hemden, rote Fahnen* (Opladen: Leske + Budrich, 1996), 110.

50. Werner Fiedler, "Geschäfte mit Halbstarken?," *Der Tag,* July 15, 1956. This article, appearing before the film's release, expressed anxiety about its suggestive potential for Berlin teenagers. Parallel fears in the East German press can be found in the reception of *Berlin—Ecke Schönhauser,* e.g., in R. B., "Großstadtjugend auf Abwegen," *Thüringische Landeszeitung,* September 4, 1957: "In the big city Berlin, the youth problem is exacerbated through the absurdity of the zonal border, which far too easily appears to the uncertain and morally endangered as a tempting destination, as a sure way to a better existence."

51. For more on DEFA's tenth anniversary, see "10 Jahre-100 Filme," *Thüringer Landeszeitung,* May 17, 1956; Heinz Kersten, "Glanz und Elend der DEFA," *Der Tagesspiegel,* May 17, 1956; and "Rückblick und Vorschau," *Junge Welt,* May 17, 1956.

52. See "Eine Berliner Romanze," *DEFA-Pressedienst* 5 (1956): 4, in Mappe 2835, Schriftgut, DK; and *Eine Berliner Romanze* (East Berlin: VEB Progress Film-Vertrieb, 1956), handbill in Mappe 1454, Schriftgut, BArch.

53. See Hoerning, *Zwischen den Fronten,* 42–43. Whereas the favorable exchange rate brought much-needed capital into the GDR, West Berlin officials struggled to discredit the practice of shopping in the East.

54. The West in this sequence is often interpreted as Kurfürstendamm in the center of West Berlin. See, e.g., John Griffith Urang, "Realism and Romance in the East German Cinema, 1952–1962," *Film History* 18 (2006): 98. Klein and Kohlhaase had, however, a very specific trajectory in mind and elsewhere describe a route from Rosenthaler Platz in Mitte along Brunnenstraße up to Gesundbrunnen. See Gerhard Klein and Wolfgang Kohlhaas[e], *Eine Berliner Romanze* (Berlin: Henschelverlag, 1956), 10–11. See also Sylvaine Hänsel and Angelika Schmitt, eds., *Kinoarchitektur in Berlin, 1895–1995* (Berlin: Reimer, 1995), 145–46. There was an Astoria-Filmtheater in Reinickendorf from 1946 to 1965, though it was not near any of the major crossing points. It is likely that Klein was combining specific interstitial B-roll material with more generally evocative profilmic space. Kohlhaase recalls that the shots with the actors were probably filmed in the East (masquerading as the West) because of the difficulty of getting permission to shoot in West Berlin. See Wolfgang Kohlhaase's contribution to the panel "Competing Cold War Cultures: Crossing the Border" organized by Brigitta B. Wagner for the Minda de Gunzburg Center for European Studies in Berlin, February 18, 2008.

55. Siegfried Kracauer, *Theory of Film* (1960; Princeton, N.J.: Princeton University Press, 1997), 68–69.

56. Klein and Kohlhaas[e], *Eine Berliner Romanze,* 102.

57. On the reception of *Eine Berliner Romanze,* see Poiger, *Jazz, Rock, and Rebels,* 93; Schenk, "Mitten im Kalten Krieg," 130; and Heimann, *DEFA, Künstler und SED,* 196. While, as Poiger, notes, many East German newspapers complained of the film's weak differentiation between East and West Berlin, Schenk describes GDR film administration Hauptverwaltung Film's concern that the film made West Berlin too exciting and attractive for East German youths. As for *Berlin—Ecke Schönhauser*'s dialogue with *Die Halbstarken,* contemporary reviews of Klein and Kohlhaase's new feature were quick to contrast it with American and West German youth films that the critics had presumably

seen in West Berlin. While the reviews do not name the Tressler–Tremper collaboration, their allusions to the film are clear. See, e.g., Horst Knietzsch, "Wo wir nicht sind . . . ," *Neues Deutschland,* September 3, 1957.

58. Feinstein, *Triumph of the Ordinary,* 55. See also Dieter Borkowski, "Berlin—Ecke Schönhauser Allee," *Tribüne,* August 31, 1957. In his review of the film, Borkowski expressed disappointment that this opening shot conveyed sad, gray, and unrealistically empty streets.

59. H. Hell, "Die gütige Volkspolizei," *Die Zeit,* October 3, 1957.

60. Ibid.

61. For more on *Republikflucht* and *Rückkehrer* as well as the substantial rate of return for young people, see Peter Skyba, *Vom Hoffnungsträger zum Sicherheitsrisiko* (Cologne: Böhlau, 2000), 307–17. Skyba attributes their numbers both to individual disappointment and to a generally higher mobility of young people. In 1956, between one-fifth and one-quarter of young people who fled the GDR also returned.

62. Held in July 1958, the GDR's second Film Conference reassessed film production after the thaw. For an overview of the controversy, including a discussion of *Berlin—Ecke Schönhauser,* see Dagmar Schittly, *Zwischen Regie und Regime* (Berlin: Ch. Links, 2002), 91–100. For a contemporary, critical perspective on the film, see Manfred Herz, "Ostberlins 'Halbstarke,'" *Deutsche Volkszeitung,* June 7, 1958. Herz claims that the film employs a false ideology and overly psychologized characters reminiscent of Western films.

63. See Feinstein, *Triumph of the Ordinary,* 52, 265; and Heimann, *DEFA, Künstler und SED,* 344.

64. "Berlin—aus der Nähe gesehen," *Berliner Zeitung,* May 20, 1956. See also Ch. W., "Eine Berliner Romanze," *Die Union,* June 2, 1956; and "Die Kluft zwischen den Generationen," *Der Morgen,* August 31, 1957, which even acknowledges *Berlin—Ecke Schönhauser's* overly schematic portrayal of the West.

65. See "Für jeden ein Platz an der Sonne," *Junge Welt,* September 3, 1957; and Fbol, "Ostberlin modernisiert," *Filmblätter* 18 (1957): 433.

66. Dieter Borsche, "Berlin—Ecke Schönhauser," *Junge Welt,* September 13, 1957.

67. Anna Teut, "Unter den Torbögen Ostberlins," Die Welt, September 7, 1957. Interestingly, SPIO's *Filmblätter* reacted venomously to the two DEFA successes. See Irene, "Eine Berliner Romanze," *Filmblätter* 22 (1956): 607; and "Berlin Ecke Schönhauser . . . ," *Filmblätter* 39 (1957): 1145.

68. See Karolus Heinz Heil, *Das Fernsehen in der Sowjetischen Besatzungszone Deutschlands 1953–1963,* Bonner Berichte aus Mittel- und Ostdeutschland (Bonn: Bundesministerium für Gesamtdeustsche Fragen, 1967), 60, 32.

69. Hell, "Die gütige Volkspolizei."

70. Hans-Dietrich Weiss, "Neue DEFA-Filme werden sofort ferngesendet," *Filmpress* 7 (1956): 9–10. This new approach to film and television was announced just three months before *Eine Berliner Romanze* premiered. Because, however, the breadth of signal coverage was still being adjusted in the 1950s, it is hard to assess how idiosyncratically these films may have been seen beyond the inner-German border. For more on the race to improve the GDR's television signal, see Heather Gumbert, "Constructing a Socialist Landmark: The Berlin Television Tower," in *Berlin Divided City, 1945–1989,* ed. Philip Broadbent and Sabine Hake, 88–99 (New York: Berghahn, 2010).

71. See statistics from the SPIO/FSK/OPAC database "Kinofilme im TV" as well as the broadcast logs of the Deutsches Rundfunkarchiv (DRA). *Eine Berliner Romanze* even appeared on West German television in the late 1980s; *Berlin—Ecke Schönhauser* was shown on the East's DFF1 in spring 1990.

72. See Fiedler, "Geschäfte mit Halbstarken?"; and Poiger, *Jazz, Rock, and Rebels,* 85–89.

73. See "Tausend 'Halbstarke,' ein Bürgermeister und der Film diskutieren Jugendproblem," April 24, 1956, in Mappe 20267, Schriftgut, DK.

74. Fp, "Berliner Jugend-Senator nahm zum 'Halbstarken'-Film Stellung," *Filmpress* 19 (1956): 4; and DA, "Verleumdung der Berliner Jugend," *Der Abend,* May 3, 1956. See also Christa Rotzoll, "Gutwillige Erwachsen stören nur," *Die Welt,* July 28, 1956.

75. See K. H., "Bandenchef Freddy scheitert," *Telegraf,* July 22, 1956; and Gero Gandert, "Die 'halbstarke' Karin," *Abendzeitung,* September 1–2, 1956. For details on the casting of Sissy, see Will Tremper, *Meine wilden Jahre* (Berlin: Ullstein, 1993), 454–61. Tremper organized this Berlin-wide search for a German version of French star Marina Vlady. The Palladium event included a public vote to choose between two finalists.

76. Gandert, "Die 'halbstarke' Karin."

77. André Bazin, "An Aesthetic of Reality: Neorealism," in *What Is Cinema?,* ed. and trans. Hugh Gray (Berkeley: University of California Press, 1971), 2:24; and Gisela Huwe, "Die deutschen Marlon Brandos," *Der Tagesspiegel,* July 22, 1956.

78. K. K., "Ein deutscher Halbstarken-Film," *Frankfurter Allgemeine Zeitung,* October 8, 1956; Oskar Kalbus, *Filme der Gegenwart* (Heidelberg: Ewalt Skulima, 1957), 341.

79. Ponkie, "Die Halbstarken," *Filmblätter* 40 (1956).

80. Ibid.; R. P., "Die Halbstarken," *Kurier,* October 7, 1956.

81. Karena Niehoff, "Die Halbstarken," *Taggesspiegel,* October 7, 1956.

82. Huwe, "Die deutschen Marlon Brandos."

83. Poiger, *Jazz, Rock, and Rebels,* 118, 105.

84. Both films also employ the sexual motif of the girl's stained skirt and the young man's effort to retrieve *Fleckwasser* (liquid for removing stains).

85. See Tremper, "Ich sehe," 23. This title, as well as the narrative, is evocative of British writer Alan Sillitoe's "Angry Young Man" novel *Saturday Night and Sunday Morning,* published in 1958.

86. K. H., "Endstation Liebe," *Hamburger Abendblatt,* May 10, 1958; A. S., "Endstation wird neuer Anfang," *Deutsche Woche,* June 25, 1958.

87. See, e.g., *"Berliner Romanze," Film-Echo* 64 (1956): 2263.

88. Georg Herzberg, "Endstation Liebe," *Film-Echo* 12 (1958): 184.

89. Günter Groll, "Endstation Liebe," *Süddeutsche Zeitung,* June 12, 1958.

90. "Berliner Verband und Wiedervereinigung," *Filmblätter* 44 (1958): 1313. In this article, the VBF compiles several of its previous comments on reunification from 1954 to 1958 to illustrate the extent to which the organization had promoted German–German relations all along. This, of course, masks the economic motivations behind the discounted tickets.

91. "Tausend 'Halbstarke.'"

92. "Endstation Liebe," *Gloria-Kundendienst,* 4, in Mappe 29355, Schriftgut, DK.

93. Kaspar Maase, *Bravo Amerika* (Hamburg: Junius, 1992), 205–6.

94. Committee for German Unity, *250 Questions 250 Answers*, 136.

95. "Die Halbstarken," *Süddeutsche Zeitung*, August 5, 1956.

96. Will Tremper and Georg Tressler, *Die Halbstarken*, screenplay, 100–101, in Schriftgut, DK.

97. For more on Karin Baal and the character of Sissy, see Maya McKechneay, "Baal oder Das ewig Weibliche zieht uns hinab," in *Halbstark*, ed. Robert Buchschwenter and Lukas Maurer, 89–99 (Vienna: Filmarchiv Austria, 2003). McKechneay notes that the character of Sissy was diametrically opposed to Romy Schneider's star persona as a saccharin good girl (90).

98. See, e.g., Erhard Förster, "Vom großen Geheimnis der DEFA," *Volksstimme*, January 21, 1956; "Berlin—aus der Nähe gesehen," *Berliner Zeitung*, May 20, 1956; and "Barbara Frey: Es ist kein Traum . . . ," *Endstation Liebe—Presse Mappe*, in Mappe 29355, Schriftgut, DK. Bürger, though originally born in Berlin, had grown up in Saxony. Barbara Frey's discovery and pairing with Horst Buchholz was an ongoing topic in the West German youth magazine *Bravo* in 1957 and in Schnitzler, "Berlin." Although most East German film critics mentioned Ilse Pagé's status as a nonactor, they tended not to acknowledge that she was actually a West Berliner. See the exception of Wolfgang Joho, "Nachkriegsjugend vor der Kamera," *Sonntag*, September 8, 1957. Joho expresses an interest in having Pagé "over here with us again sometime." See also Schenk, "Mitten im Kalten Krieg," 130. DEFA even paid for Pagé's acting lessons—a cause for later critique. Claus, "Rebels with a Cause," 102, has noted the hypocrisy involved in the East's use of Western capitalistic marketing tactics in the case of Klein and Kohlhaase's Berlin films.

99. Irmgard Wilharm, "Der Quellenwert von Filmen für die doppelte deutsche Nachkriegsgeschichte," *Beiträge zur Film- und Fernsehwissenschaft* 58 (2001): 82.

100. Jutta Voigt, "Berlin—Ecke Schönhauser," *Sonntag* 15 October 1978.

101. Hannes Schmidt, "Poesie des Alltäglichen," *medium* 7 (1985): 40–41.

102. See, e.g., Claudius Seidl, *Der Deutsche Film der fünfziger Jahre* (Munich: Wilhelm Heyne, 1987), 46–51. In this section, Seidl considers the value of 1950s films for a 1980s audience.

103. Manuela Reichart, "Filmtips," *Die Zeit*, December 18, 1981.

104. Felix, "Rebellische Jugend," 328.

105. See information about Berlin's 750th anniversary celebrations in Mappe 220267, Schriftgut, DK; and Helmut Ullrich, "Berlin in bewegten Bildern: Auskunft von Progress-Direktor Wolfgang Harkenthal," *Filmspiegel* 26 (1986): 23.

106. For accounts of this process and its aftermath, see Leonie Naughton, *That Was the Wild East* (Ann Arbor: University of Michigan Press, 2002), 45–59; and Randall Halle, *German Film after Germany* (Urbana: University of Illinois Press, 2008), 60–88.

107. Rolf Richter, ". . . Ein historischer Augenblick," qtd. in "Die 'Verbotsfilme' der DDR aus den Jahren 1965/66 und das 11. Plenum des ZK der SED," *20. Internationales Forum des jungen Films Berlin 1990* 15 (1990): 5. For more on the impact of this delay, see Barton Byg, "Generational Conflict and Historical Continuity in GDR Films," in *Framing the Past*, ed. Bruce A. Murray and Christopher J. Wickham, 197–219 (Carbondale: Southern Illinois University Press, 1992).

108. Klaus Finke, "DEFA-Film als 'nationales Kulturerbe?' Thesen zum DEFA-Film und seiner wissenschaftlichen Aufarbeitung," *Beiträge zur Film- und Fernsehwissenschaft* 58 (2001): 106–7.

109. Jürgen Haase, "Haben Repertoirefilme noch eine Chance im Kino?," in *Der geteilte Himmel,* ed. Helmut Pflügl (Vienna: Filmarchiv Austria, 2001), 1:16.

110. See broadcast dates and channels in SPIO/FSK/OPAC database "Kinofilme im TV."

111. See Thomas Thieringer, "Der erste Freddy," *Süddeutsche Zeitung,* December 21, 1996. Buchholz explains, "As Freddy I was very decisively against my father, and the audience was behind me. So I can't suddenly expect the audience that saw me in that film to accept me as the father. I can imagine that they would have been horrified if I had played this role today." The remake was directed by Urs Egger for Constantin Film.

3. VIRTUALITY

1. See Colomb, *Staging the New Berlin,* 157.

2. See Paul Virilio, "Open Skies over Berlin," in Becker and Stahel, *Remake Berlin,* 153; and Huyssen, "After the War: Berlin as Palimpsest," in *Present Pasts,* 81.

3. Kevin Lynch, *The Image of the City* (Cambridge, Mass.: MIT Press, 1960), 64. Lynch defines edges as "linear elements not considered as paths: they are usually, but not quite always, the boundaries between two kinds of areas. They act as lateral references" (62).

4. See Pabsch, *Zweimal Weltstadt,* 55; and Alan Balfour, *Berlin: The Politics of Order* (New York: Rizzoli, 1990), 85.

5. Pabsch, *Zweimal Weltstadt,* 58. This and all subsequent translations of previously untranslated German texts are my own.

6. See, e.g., Lothar Müller, "Modernität, Nevosität und Sachlichkeit: Das Berlin der Jahrhundertwende als Hauptstadt der 'neuen Zeit,'" in *Mythos Berlin* (Berlin: Ästhetik und Kommunikation, 1987), 79–92. The latter essay uses images of the Platz's famous traffic tower, erected in 1924, to illustrate the frazzled nerves of the modern subject. For postwall accounts written in this vein, see Jörg Müller, *Der Potsdamer Platz in Berlin* (Berlin: Technische Universität Berlin, 1990), 45, and Hans Wilderotter, "Die Gegend vor dem Potsdamer Tor," in *Der Potsdamer Platz,* ed. Yamin von Rauch and Jochen Visscher (Berlin: Jovis, 2000), 14.

7. Hans Stimmann, "Städtebau und Architektur für die Hauptstadt," in Süß, *Hauptstadt Berlin,* 2:408.

8. Ingeborg Majer O'Sickey, "Cinematic Ciphers," *German Politics and Society* 19, no. 4 (2001): 67; Janet Ward, "Las Vegas on the Spree," in *Visual Culture in Twentieth-Century Germany,* ed. Gail Finney (Bloomington: Indiana University Press, 2006), 88; Ward, *Post-Wall Berlin,* 309; and Colomb, *Staging the New Berlin,* 166–67. Representations of the square in popular culture further emphasized Potsdamer Platz's interchangeability with other cities. See, e.g., the music video for Melanie Thornton's 2000–2001 hit "Love How You Love Me," in which Potsdamer Platz is intercut with skyscrapers from other urban nodes, including New York City's Times Square.

9. Huyssen, "After the War," 81.

10. Volker Hassemer, "Das neue Berlin," in *Berlin: Die Hauptstadt,* ed. Werner Süß and Ralf Rytlewski (Bonn: Bundeszentrale für politische Bildung, 1999), 536.

11. For more on the politics of the memory district, see Till, *The New Berlin,* generally.

12. See Stimmann, "Städtebau und Architektur für die Hauptstadt," 409. Critical reconstruction required architectural designs to adhere to specific guidelines: (1) to respect the city grid, (2) to limit building height, (3) to reserve a percentage of space for residential use, (4) to adjust building density to the type of use, and (5) to limit new constructions to land parcels no greater than a city block. See also Hans-Jürgen Ahlbrecht, "Der Potsdamer Platz," in Süß, *Hauptstadt Berlin,* 3:413–14.

13. Ward, *Post-Wall Berlin,* 309.

14. Wim Wenders, "An Attempted Description of an Indescribable Film," in *The Logic of Images,* trans. Michael Hofmann (Boston: Faber and Faber, 1992), 76–77.

15. See "Document 3: Bundestag Decision to Make Berlin the Capital, 20 June 1991," in *Uniting Germany: Documents and Debates, 1944–1993,* ed. Konrad H. Jarausch and Volker Gransow (Providence, R.I.: Berghahn, 1994), 238.

16. Lev Manovich, "The Poetics of Augmented Space," *Visual Communication* 5 (2006): 220.

17. Sigmund Freud, *Civilization and Its Discontents,* ed. and trans. James Strachey (New York: W. W. Norton, 1989), 16–18.

18. Ibid., 18–19.

19. Walter Benjamin, "The Return of the *Flâneur,*" in Eiland and Jennings, *Walter Benjamin: Selected Writings,* 2:262.

20. Ibid., 2:263.

21. Frances A. Yates, "Architecture and the Art of Memory," *Architectural Design* 38, no. 12 (1968): 573.

22. Elizabeth Wilson, "Looking Backward: Nostalgia and the City," in *Imagining Cities,* ed. Sallie Westwood and John Williams (London: Routledge, 1997), 129.

23. Benjamin, "Return of the *Flâneur,*" 264.

24. Michel de Certeau, *The Practice of Everyday Life,* trans. Steven Rendall (Berkeley: University of California Press, 1984), 95.

25. Ibid., 97–99.

26. Yi-Fu Tuan, *Topophilia* (New York: Columbia University Press, 1990), 93.

27. M. Christine Boyer, *The City of Collective Memory* (Cambridge, Mass.: MIT Press, 1994), 47–48.

28. Ibid., 19, 21.

29. Giuliana Bruno, *Atlas of Emotion* (New York: Verso, 2002), 251.

30. Ibid., 250.

31. Anthony Vidler, "The Explosion of Space: Architecture and the Filmic Imaginary," *Assemblage* 21 (August 1993): 53. For Benjamin's discussion of film and architecture, see Walter Benjamin, "Work of Art," 4:268.

32. See Karl Heinz Krüger, "Wat de kriegen kannst, det nimmste," *Der Spiegel,* January 5, 1987, 59. As Krüger explains, the Nazis based their 700th anniversary of Berlin on a convenient, though by no means conclusive, document dated October 28, 1237, "in order to stage another spectacle in August 1937, one year after the Olympic Games."

33. Louis Ferdinand, "Die geistige Hauptstadt aller Deutschen," in *750 Jahre Berlin,* ed. Eberhard Diepgen (Berlin: Nicolai, 1987), 240.

34. Willy Brandt, "Berlin, die Mauer, und der Prozess der Entspannung," in Diepgen, *750 Jahre Berlin,* 44.

35. Erich Honecker, "Erich Honecker auf der konstituierenden Sitzung des Komitees der Deutschen Demokratischen Republik zum 750jährigen Bestehen von Berlin," in *750 Jahre Berlin: Das Buch zum Fest* (Berlin: VEB Tourist Verlag, 1986), 9.

36. Krüger, "Wat de kriegen kannst," 55. See also his article on Friedrichstraße in the same issue: Karl Heinz Krüger, "Straße des Luxus und der Moden," *Der Spiegel,* April 20, 1987, 212–22. He repeatedly refers to the new cosmopolitan flair of the street as a challenge to West Berlin's Kurfürstendamm.

37. Ulrich Eckhardt, "Das doppelte Fest Berliner Geschichte(n) in West und Ost," in *750 Jahre Berlin: Stadt der Gegenwart,* ed. Ulrich Eckhardt (Berlin: Ullstein, 1986), 20.

38. Gottfried Korff and Reinhard Rürup, "Zur Ausstellung," in *Berlin, Berlin,* ed. Gottfried Korff and Reinhard Rürup (Berlin: Nicolai, 1987), 19.

39. Eckhardt, "Das doppelte Fest Berliner Geschichte(n) in West und Ost," 18.

40. Eberhard Diepgen, "Impulse für die Zukunft: Eine Stadt in der Mitte," in Eckhardt, *750 Jahre Berlin: Stadt der Gegenwart,* 8, 15.

41. Eckhardt, "Das doppelte Fest Berliner Geschichte(n) in West und Ost," 29, 27.

42. Helmut Kohl, "Unmittelbar erlebte Geschichte," in Diepgen, *750 Jahre Berlin,* 168.

43. Hans-Jochen Vogel, "Berlin in 50 Jahren," in Diepgen, *750 Jahre Berlin,* 332–33.

44. See Dietrich Riemann, "Vegetationsstruktur," in *Mythos Berlin,* 256. The preparations for the exhibition hall even unearthed "a rust-eaten steel helmet" from the Second World War. For the initial exhibition concepts, see Mythos Berlin Ausstellung GmbH, ed., *Mythos Berlin Concepte* (Berlin: Ästhetik und Kommunikation, 1986).

45. Wenders, "An Attempted Description," 74.

46. Ibid., 73–74.

47. Ibid., 75.

48. Ibid., 80. Related to Wenders's layered histories of place is Benjamin's fascination with a Paul Klee painting he owned before he left Germany: *Angelus Novus,* a central allegory of the philosopher's own understanding of history. For a description of the "angel of history," see Walter Benjamin, "On the Concept of History," in Eiland and Jennings, *Walter Benjamin: Selected Writings,* 392: "It shows an angel who seems about to move away from something he stares at. His eyes are wide, his mouth is open, his wings are spread. This is how the angel of history must look. His face is turned toward the past. Where a chain of events appears before *us, he* sees one single catastrophe, which keeps piling wreckage upon wreckage and hurls it at his feet. The angel would like to stay, awaken the dead, and make whole what has been smashed. But a storm is blowing from Paradise and has got caught in his wings; it is so strong that the angel can no longer close them. This storm drives him irresistibly into the future, to which his back is turned, while the pile of debris before him grows toward the sky. What we call progress is *this* storm." Not only does Wenders refer to this angel in "An Attempted Description" (77); he cites it in the thoughts of the Staatsbibliothek scholars in *Der Himmel über Berlin.*

49. Wim Wenders, "Film Thieves," in Hofmann, *Logic of Images,* 33–38. The original discussion took place in 1982.

50. For more on the anniversary's seasons, see Eckhardt, "Das doppelte Fest Berliner Geschichte(n) in West und Ost," 23. The "big festivities" took place in the summer. See also Wim Wenders, "Le souffle de l'Ange," in Hofmann, *Logic of Images,* 110. He wanted to shoot the film in fall 1986.

51. Qtd. in Hans Borgelt, *Filmstadt Berlin* (Berlin: Nicolai, 1979), 86.

52. Ibid., 221.

53. Ibid., 191–92.

54. Wolfgang Lüder, qtd. in ibid., 193.

55. Detlef Stronk, "Filme nach Berlin," in *Film in Berlin,* ed. Senator für Wirtschaft und Verkehr (Berlin: Colloquium, 1983), 13.

56. See Borgelt, *Filmstadt Berlin,* 86. *Der amerikanische Freund* (*The American Friend,* FRG/France 1977), e.g., ran for thirteen weeks in the West Berlin cinema Studio am Kurfürstendamm 71. *Paris, Texas* was released in Europe, the United States, South America, and Japan. Both films screened at international festivals and won and were nominated for several awards.

57. For an account of Wenders's difficulties in the United States, see Roger F. Cook, "Angels, Fiction, and History in Berlin: *Wings of Desire,*" in *The Cinema of Wim Wenders,* ed. Roger F. Cook and Gerd Gemünden (Detroit, Mich.: Wayne State University Press, 1997), 163–64. For accounts of Wenders's 1984 visit to East Berlin's Akademie der Künste, see Wolfgang Gersch, "Mit Filmen übers Filmen denken," *Filmspiegel* 8 (1984): 10–11, and Regina Köhler, "Hommage für das klassische Kino," *Neue Zeit,* July 4, 1984.

58. For more on the Cannes trip, see Der Senator für Kulturelle Angelegenheiten, "Wim Wenders dreht Berlin-Film," *Pressedienst,* July 11, 1986, in Mappe 11404, Schriftgut, DK, and "Unendliche Gnade," *Der Spiegel* 22 (1987): 218. On the film's premiere, see Angelika Kettelhack, "Ein Märchen vom Glauben und Wunder und die Stadt," *Volksblatt,* October 29, 1987, and Dieter Strunz, "Stadt der Träume und der Träumer," *Berliner Morgenpost,* October 29, 1987.

59. See, e.g., Wenders's accounts of working without a screenplay in "Le souffle," 134–35, and in *The Angels among Us, Wings of Desire,* DVD (MGM, 2003). For more on the importance of images over narrative for Wenders prior to 1987, see Thomas Elsaesser, "Spectators of Life: Time, Place, and Self in the Films of Wim Wenders," in Cook and Gemünden, *Cinema of Wim Wenders,* 240–56.

60. See Cook, "Angels," 171, for whom the lack of a "controlling narrative" causes spectators to long for meaning. See also Cesare Casarino, "Fragments on *Wings of Desire* (or, Fragmentary Representation as Historical Necessity)," *Social Text* 24 (1990): 167–81, and David Caldwell and Paul W. Rea, "Handke's and Wenders's *Wings of Desire:* Transcending Postmodernism," *German Quarterly* 64, no. 1 (1991): 46–54. Other texts discuss *Der Himmel über Berlin* as a city film but provide no sustained analysis of *how* urban space is constructed and presented in the film. See, e.g., Hanno Möbius and Guntram Vogt, *Drehort Stadt* (Marburg, Germany: Hitzeroth, 1990), 149–64; Martin Jesinghausen, "The Sky over Berlin as Transcendental Space: Wenders, Döblin and the 'Angel of History,'" in *Spaces in European Cinema,* ed. Myrto Konstantarakos (Exeter, U.K.: Intellect, 2000), 77–92; and Guntram Vogt, "Wim Wenders—*Der Himmel über Berlin* (1987)," in *Die Stadt im Film: Deutsche Spielfilme, 1900–2000* (Marburg, Germany: Schüren, 2001), 689–700. Numerous books on Wenders's oeuvre mention Berlin but surprisingly do not incorporate the city's geography into their larger arguments: Reinhold Rauh, *Wim Wenders* (Munich: Wilhelm Heyne, 1990), 110–17; Norbert Grob, *Wenders* (Berlin: Edition Filme, 1991), 258–65; Stefan Kolditz, *"Der Himmel über Berlin,"* in *Wim Wenders,* ed. Peter W. Jansen and Wolfram Schütte, 270–82 (Munich: Carl Hanser, 1992); and Robert

Phillip Kolker and Peter Beicken, *The Films of Wim Wenders* (Cambridge, Mass.: Cambridge University Press, 1993), 138–60.

61. The exhibit ran from May 22 to June 30, 1987. See Volker Baer, "Auch Engel kennen Sehnsucht," *Tagesspiegel,* October 29, 1987.

62. See "Engel, die durch Mauern gehen," *Filmspiegel* 22 (1990): 5. Wenders described a visit to the GDR's "Filmminister" Horst Pehnert, during which he asked for permission to film in the East and on the Brandenburg Gate's quadriga. The film minister asked if the angels could go through walls and then sent Wenders home. In a controversial memoir, Pehnert remembers the encounter differently. See Horst Pehnert, *Kino, Künstler und Konflikte* (Berlin: Das Neue Berlin, 2009), 166. He claims that he simply directed Wenders to the appropriate decision makers, who refused to let the filmmaker shoot in the real "military security zone." As for the shots of East Berlin that appear in *Der Himmel über Berlin,* Pehnert dismisses the game of "cat and mouse," claiming that Wenders could have obtained these images legally. In an e-mail to the author, August 1, 2011, cinematographer Thomas Plenert remarks that Wenders visited him in East Berlin in the editing phase (in a meeting engineered by Hanns Zischler), gave him three rolls of black-and-white film, showed him the desired streets, and described the images. Plenert then shot the material over two days with his assistant Michael Loewenberg. Ultimately, DEFA director Helke Misselwitz aided in the relaying process, and Zischler smuggled the film over the border and brought it to a West Berlin processing laboratory. See Peter Badel, "Ein Film mit Jürgen Böttcher ist wie ein Ritterschlag" in *Kamera läuft* (Berlin: Schriftenreihe der DEFA-Stiftung, 2007), 2:408–9, for an additional account from Plenert's perspective.

63. See also Elsaesser, "Spectators of Life," 248, for this more general observation of Wenders's oeuvre: "To make films is for Wenders in a sense to watch once more and remember the films one had already seen. Action could only be the retelling of action. The point was not to film something that had never been shown before but to show something in such a way that it appeared to be a memory of something one had already seen."

64. Wenders, "Attempted Description," 80, 82. Although Wenders insists that the color portion of the film does not necessarily indicate a greater degree of reality and truth, he sees it as an indicator of three-dimensional human life and of a new form of sensory perception for angels who become human. Because most of the film's archival footage is black and white, the color material stands out as a representation both of pastness and of human perception. Wenders does not comment on the distinction between these two kinds of archival footage.

65. Karl Scheffler, "Wie sieht der Potsdamer Platz in 25 Jahren aus?," in *Glänzender Asphalt,* ed. Christian Jäger and Erhard Schütz (Berlin: Fannei and Walz, 1994), 119. The article was originally published in the *Vossische Zeitung,* August 29, 1920. The other alternatives included a communist future; a further development, albeit more international, of the status quo; and a wait-and-see approach that would depend on the future of Germany, Europe, and the Western world.

66. Balfour, *Berlin: The Politics of Order,* 49.

67. Ibid., 253.

68. Lev Manovich, *The Language of New Media* (Cambridge, Mass.: MIT Press, 2001), 207.

69. See Oliver Grau, *Virtual Art* (Cambridge, Mass.: MIT Press, 2003), 173. Grau lists this kind of application as one of several attracting nonmilitary investments. A later example is the *Bundesrat's* panorama (actually a static bird's-eye view) of Potsdamer and Leipziger Plätze in which the user selects a year to see the spatial relations of various buildings and objects at that time. See "The Bundesrat Building in the Berlin Townscape from 1904 to 2004," Bundesrat, November 1, 2012, http://gsb.download.bva.bund.de/. Todd Samuel Presner has used new media and cartography as a means of teaching Berlin's historical layers. See UCLA's collaborative online research platform Hypermedia Berlin, March 15, 2008, http://www.berlin.ucla.edu/. For more on this project, see Todd Samuel Presner, "Hypermedia Berlin," *German Politics and Society* 23, no. 1 (2005): 171–88, and Todd Samuel Presner, "The City in the Ages of New Media: From Ruttmann's *Berlin. Die Sinfonie der Großstadt* to Hypermedia Berlin," in Koepnick and McGlothlin, *After the Digital Divide?*, 167–85.

70. Joachim Sauter, "Experiencing Virtual Reality," in *Cinema and Architecture*, ed. François Penz and Maureen Thomas, (London: BFI, 1997), 145–46. In fact, Art+Com had already worked to represent Potsdamer Platz as early as 1989 in the project "New Media and Town Planning," which was conceived as a historical and cartographic aid for "town planners, architects, citizens' initiatives, and planning authorities."

71. See Art+Com's promotional DVD for the project, *The Invisible Shape of Things Past* (Art+Com, Hochschule der Künste, 1996/DVD 2003).

72. Joachim Sauter and Dirk Lüsebrink, "Invisible Shape of Things Past," in *Future Cinema*, ed. Jeffrey Shaw and Peter Weibel (Cambridge, Mass.: MIT Press, 2003), 436. Sauter and Lüsebrink refer to the "outer pixel rows of the frames" as the "skin" of the film objects, which further casts them as habitable bodies or shells.

73. This could be considered the computer's virtual approximation of, e.g., the 1993–94 wrapping of the Palace of the Republic with a plastic facade of the old City Palace.

74. Sauter and Lüsebrink, "Invisible Shape of Things Past," 437.

75. Philip Rosen, *Change Mummified* (Minneapolis: University of Minnesota Press, 2001), 325.

76. Manovich, *Language of New Media*, 86–87.

77. Tom Conley, *Cartographic Cinema* (Minneapolis: University of Minnesota Press, 2007), 2. He refers to both as forms of "what cartographers call 'locational imaging.'"

78. Sauter, "Experiencing Virtual Reality," 144. One might consider both the ideological position of cinema's subject in the apparatus theory of the 1970s and the later emphasis on emotional involvement in narrative cinema and in cinema generally. See, e.g., Jean-Louis Baudry, "Ideological Effects of the Basic Cinematographic Apparatus," trans. Alan Williams, *Film Quarterly* 28, no. 2 (1974–75): 39–47, and Laura Mulvey, "Visual Pleasure and Narrative Cinema," *Screen* 16, no. 3 (1975): 6–18. Wolfgang Ernst has echoed Sauter's formulation of the larger shift in a user's perception in the transition from cinema to new media. See Wolfgang Ernst, "Dis/continuities," in *New Media, Old Media*, ed. Wendy Hui Kyong Chun and Thomas Keenan (New York: Routledge, 2006), 117. Referring to Knut Hickethier, he argues, "Whereas kinematographic forms of narrative still conform to human ways of perception by translating themselves into technical operations as instrumental extensions of human senses (ears and eyes), electronics directs images according to its own rules, only remotely connected to human perception."

79. Manovich, *Language of New Media,* 221, 226.

80. Dirk Lüsebrink and Joachim Sauter, personal interview, Berlin, October 26, 2007.

81. Norman M. Klein, *Bleeding Through: Layers of Los Angeles, 1920–1986,* DVD (ZKM Digital Arts Edition, 2003). See as well the accompanying novella: Norman M. Klein, *Bleeding Through* (Karlsruhe: ZKM Digital Arts Edition, 2003), and Norman M. Klein, *The History of Forgetting* (London: Verso, 1997).

82. Marsha Kinder, "Designing a Database Cinema," in Shaw and Weibel, *Future Cinema,* 351.

83. Peter Weibel, "Virtuelle Architektur," *Architese* 5 (1992): 66.

84. Manovich, "Poetics of Augmented Space," 221. This essay is the revised version of Lev Manovich, "The Poetics of Augmented Space," in *New Media,* ed. Anna Everett and John T. Caldwell, 75–92 (New York: Routledge, 2003).

85. See Google Glass, November 12, 2013, http://www.google.com/glass/start.

86. Friedrich Luft, "Nur Engel passieren die Mauer leicht," *Die Welt,* October 29, 1987. Luft had supplied the postwar voice-over to Leo de Laforgue's *Symphonie einer Weltstadt: Berlin, wie es war* (Symphony of a world city: Berlin, the Way It Was, Germany/FRG 1943/1950), originally a Third Reich response to Ruttmann's city symphony. Laforgue's film, which contains shots of Berlin before the Allied bombardments, was banned in Nazi Germany but finally premiered in West Berlin one year after the founding of the two German states.

87. The quote is from Wolfram Schütte, "Niederauffahrt zu den Menschen," *Frankfurter Rundschau,* October 29, 1987. See also Werner Mathes, "Unschuldsengel an der Mauer," *Stern,* October 29, 1987.

88. Strunz, "Stadt der Träume."

89. Wim Wenders, "Metrobranding," discussion moderated by Vinzenz Hediger, Berlinale Talent Campus, Hebbeltheater am Ufer, Berlin, February 11, 2007. Wenders also appeared in Hubertus Siegert's documentary *Berlin Babylon* and provided the foreword for Claudia Hellmann and Claudine Weber-Hof, *On Location: Cities of the World in Film* (Munich: Bucher, 2006). His own volume of essays on place and cinema is *A Sense of Place* (Frankfurt: Autoren, 2005). In the early 2000s, *Der Himmel über Berlin* was programmed regularly in Berlin's Lichtblick Kino, Central Kino, Filmkunsthaus Babylon (now Babylon Mitte), Freiluftkino Hasenheide, and Kino Arsenal (now Arsenal Institut für Film und Videokunst).

90. See *Der Himmel über Berlin,* press kit, 2007, 2, Neue Visionen, December 19, 2007, http://www.neuevisionen.de/.

91. Filmmaker Andreas Dresen described a screening among film students at the HFF. See Brigitta B. Wagner, "Not a Bad Heritage: An Interview with Andreas Dresen," in *DEFA after East Germany,* ed. Brigitta B. Wagner (Rochester, N.Y.: Camden House, 2014), 19. For East German responses to the film, see "Die Himmel ändern sich," *Filmspiegel* 22 (1990): 5, and Günter Sobe, "Die DEFA startete in die Neuzeit," *Berliner Zeitung,* October 8, 1990. In hindsight, Enk observes, "The angels succeed at that which humans were only allowed to do years later: to get over the Wall without a passport and visa." Sobe reflects, "In amazement you notice today how precisely the film feels like that time."

92. A JVC cinema commercial *(Kinowerbung)* from 2000–2001 represented Potsdamer Platz as a high-tech, futuristic space of various levels and doors. As in a video

game, a young man navigates the vertical and horizontal elements of the square's new architecture only to be rewarded, at the end of his quest, with the latest JVC gadget. This understanding of the square resonated throughout popular culture.

93. Bruno, *Atlas of Emotion,* 34.

94. Antonio Damasio, *The Feeling of What Happens* (New York: Harcourt Brace, 1999), 56: "Emotions occur in one of two types of circumstances. The first type of circumstance takes place when the organism processes certain objects or situations with one of its sensory devices—for instance, when the organism takes in the sight of a familiar face or place. The second type of circumstance occurs when the mind of an organism conjures up from memory certain objects and situations and represents them as images in the thought process—for instance, remembering the face of a friend and the fact that she has just died."

95. Luft, "Nur Engel passieren die Mauer leicht."

96. Sauter and Lüsebrink, "Invisible Shape of Things Past," 437.

97. See Joachim Sauter et al., eds., *Art+Com: Media Spaces and Installations* (Berlin: Gestalten, 2011), 25. Sauter remarked on this irony in a conversation with the author at Universität der Künste on July 12, 2011.

98. Lüsebrink and Sauter, personal interview. For more on this project, see http://research.microsoft.com/IVM/PhotoTourism.pdf.

99. Lüsebrink and Sauter, personal interview.

100. Like database cinema's interactive multimedia narratives in the 2000s, virtual reality research of the 1990s took interest in users' emotional engagement. See, e.g., Mike Goslin and Jacquelyn Ford Morie, "'Virtopia': Emotional Experiences in Virtual Environments," *Leonardo* 29, no. 2 (1996): 95–100.

4. ORIENTATION

1. *Location Berlin–Brandenburg,* DVD (Berlin: Deutsche Film- und Fernsehakademie Berlin, 2003). The DVD was commissioned by the Medienbüro Berlin–Brandenburg and the FBBB together with Partner für Berlin-Gesellschaft für Hauptstadt-Marketing. *Ready for Business,* produced by Partner für Berlin for the Senate Department for Economics, Labor, and Women's Issues, is made up of interviews with top representatives of corporate business and government. *Young Berlin* was produced by Partner für Berlin and Berlin Tourismus Marketing GmbH for the Senate Department for Economics and Technology and provides a montage of locations, cultural events, and shots of young people enjoying life in Berlin.

2. Jan Gympel, "Berlin—kein Schauplatz mehr für Filme?," in Süß, *Hauptstadt Berlin,* 2:589–91. Unless otherwise noted, this and all subsequent translations from German are my own.

3. Wolfgang Schäuble, "Veränderungen ertragen, Veränderungen bewältigen," in Süß, *Hauptstadt Berlin,* 1:37.

4. For a nuanced comparison of the effects of these changes in the former East and West Berlin, see Werner Süß and Heiko Rabe, "Was wird aus Berlin?," in Süß, *Hauptstadt Berlin,* 1:454.

5. See Brian Ladd, *The Ghosts of Berlin* (Chicago: University of Chicago Press, 1997), 226; see also 47–70 for an account of the controversy surrounding the two palaces.

6. By "containment," I am referring to efforts to acknowledge the Nazi past in the cityscape while limiting the negative effects of these spaces on the city as a whole. See Till, *New Berlin*, 202. Speaking of Berlin's "memory district," which includes the Topography of Terror, the Jewish Museum, and the Monument to the Murdered Jews of Europe, Till observes, "This new dramaturgic space of national commemoration will stage a hypervisible cosmopolitan Holocaust memory for citizens, politicians, foreigners, and a Western moral community of democratic nations." As a result, the very public nature of the space, still emerging in the 1990s, allows for a certain symbolic control over Germany's relation to its National Socialist history (203).

7. Gympel, "Berlin," 596. By 2000, Potsdamer Platz was emerging as an alternative urban backdrop to Frankfurt. A case in point is Melanie Thornton's 2000 music video for "Love How You Love Me," which cuts from a shot of Potsdamer Platz to the skyline of Frankfurt am Main and then to New York's Times Square. The editing implies that all three represent the same city.

8. Colomb, *Staging the New Berlin*, 172–73.

9. Otto Altendorfer, *Das Mediensystem der Bundesrepublik Deutschland* (Wiesbaden: VS Verlag für Sozialwissenschaften, 2004), 2:84–85. See also David Morley and Kevin Robins, *Spaces of Identity* (London: Routledge, 1995), 18. The American share of the European film market was around 75 percent in the mid-1990s, in contrast to the international share of the American film market at a mere 2 percent. For an overview of the European cinema crisis, see Mike Wayne, *The Politics of Contemporary European Cinema* (Bristol: Intellect Books, 2002).

10. Klaus Keil, personal interview, digital recording, Berlin, Germany, August 10, 2010.

11. Benedikt Berg-Walz, "Die Filmboard Berlin-Brandenburg GmbH," in *Visuelle Politik*, ed. Wilhelm Hofmann (Baden-Baden: Nomos, 1998), 51.

12. Eric Rentschler, "From New German Cinema to the Post-Wall Cinema of Consensus," in *Cinema and Nation*, ed. Mette Hjort and Scott Mackenzie (London: Routledge, 2000), 272.

13. Jochen Brunow, "Bündnis für Film," in *Szenenwechsel*, ed. Michael Töteberg (Reinbeck bei Hamburg: Rowohlt, 1999), 12.

14. Stefan Arndt, qtd. in X-Filme Creative Pool, "Eins, zwei, drei . . . x Filme," in Töteberg, *Szenenwechsel*, 41.

15. See, e.g., Heinz Bude, *Generation Berlin* (Berlin: Merve, 2001); Tanja Dückers, "Spaßhaus Mitte," *Der Spiegel* 6 (September 1999): 102–5; and Thomas Krüger, "Die bewegte Stadt," in *Die bewegte Stadt*, ed. Thomas Krüger, 21–26 (Berlin: FAB, 1998).

16. For a transcript of the debate, see Helmut Herles, ed., *Die Hauptstadt-Debatte* (Bonn: Bouvier, 1991). For a series of essays compiled on the eve of relocation, see Rheinische Post, *Streitfall Berliner Republik* (Düsseldorf: Droste, 1999), and for an overview of the relocation process, see Michael Sontheimer, *Berlin, Berlin* (Hamburg: Spiegel-Buchverlag, 1999).

17. "34. Sitzung," in Herles, *Hauptstadt-Debatte*, 258–59.

18. Schäuble, "Veränderungen ertragen," 33.

19. Edzard Reuter, "Regionale Potentiale, globale Chancen," in Süß, *Hauptstadt Berlin*, 2:47.

20. Eberhard Diepgen, "Berlin—die Hauptstadt des wiedervereinigten Deutschland in einem zusammenwachsenden Europa," in Süß, *Hauptstadt Berlin,* 2:60.

21. Jürgen Leinemann and Hajo Schumacher, "Labor der Zukunft," *Der Spiegel,* September 6, 1999, 33–34.

22. Bernd Seite, "Die Bedeutung der Hauptstadt für die neuen Länder," in Süß, *Haupstadt Berlin,* 1:183–84. See also Michael Staack, "Der Westen und die veränderte außenpolitische Rolle Deutschlands," in Süß, *Haupstadt Berlin,* 1:253.

23. "34. Sitzung," in Herles, *Hauptstadt-Debatte,* 181. Numerous scholars have discussed the asymmetrical relationship between the two populations in the unified Federal Republic. See, e.g., John Borneman, *Belonging in the Two Berlins* (Cambridge: Cambridge University Press, 1992); Patricia Hogwood, "After the GDR: Reconstructing Identity in Post-Communist Germany," *Journal of Communist Studies and Transition Politics* 16, no. 4 (2000): 45–67; and Paul Cooke, *Representing East Germany since Unification* (Oxford: Berg, 2005).

24. Diepgen, "Berlin," 50.

25. Schäuble, "Veränderungen ertragen," 28.

26. Seite, "Bedeutung der Hauptstadt," 180.

27. Ibid., 185.

28. Reuter, "Regionale Potentiale," 41.

29. Leineman and Schumacher, "Labor der Zukunft," 38. See also Colomb, *Staging the New Berlin,* 183: Berlin's "superlative 'global city imagery'" of the immediate post-*Wende* years continued to circulate even long after it became clear that the city's finances could not keep up with these projections.

30. Christine Lutz, *Berlin als Haupstadt des wiedervereinigten Deutschlands: Symbol für ein neues deutsches Selbstverständnis?* (Berlin: Logos, 2002), 94.

31. See Michael Böhme, "Wo steht heute die Filmförderung?," in *Filmproduktion-Filmförderung-Filmfinanzierung,* ed. Jan Berg and Knut Hickethier (Berlin: edition sigma, 1994), 22–24. Among his criticisms of television's role in feature film production, Böhme, a producer, lists (1) the copyright of cofinanced films, often exploited on television; (2) stations' failure to pay a tax on broadcasts of the films; and (3) the lack of regulation of film broadcasts on international cable television. See also Rentschler, "From New German Cinema," 267, for the adverse effects of television interests on the artistic values of the postwall film industry.

32. Borgelt, *Filmstadt Berlin,* 222, 191.

33. Stronk, "Filme nach Berlin," 14.

34. Berg-Walz, "Filmboard Berlin-Brandenburg GmbH," 50.

35. Christiane Peitz, "Im Jahr des Produzenten," *die tageszeitung,* February 9, 1995, 16.

36. Keil, personal interview.

37. See *Filmförderung in Deutschland und der EU 2003* (Berlin: Verlag für Wirtschaftskommunikation, 2003), 2:68.

38. Keil, personal interview.

39. Lüneberg, *Filmförderung in Berlin und Brandenburg,* 72–77.

40. Kai Ritzmann, "Good Bye, Fernsehturm!," *Welt Kompakt,* May 30, 2006, 28.

41. Both *Lola rennt* and *Good Bye, Lenin!* received support from the FFA, Filmstiftung Nordrhein-Westfalen, the Bundesministerium des Inneren (for *Good Bye, Lenin!*

the Beauftragter der Bundesregierung für Kultur und Medien), and the television stations WDR (Westdeutscher Rundfunk) and Arte.

42. Keil, personal interview. For more on jump-start financing, see Lüneberg, *Filmförderung in Berlin und Brandenburg,* 71.

43. *Lola rennt,* press kit (1998), 32, in Mappe 26631, Schriftgut, DK.

44. See Filmförderungsanstalt, *Geschäftsbericht 1998* (Berlin: Bundesanstalt des öffentlichen Rechts, 1998), 22–27. From 1996 to 1998, the number of multiplex visits jumped from 19,416,949 to 45,094,521, as did the numbers of spectators and available screens in the FRG's new and old states.

45. *Lola rennt,* press kit, 27.

46. For more on Tykwer's formalism, particularly his manipulations of space and time, see Lutz Koepnick, "Free Fallin': Tom Tykwer and the Aesthetics of Deceleration and Dislocation," *Germanic Review* 82, no. 1 (2007): 7–30.

47. See comments on the film from Christine Haase, "You Can Run, but You Can't Hide," in *Light Motives,* ed. Randall Halle and Margaret McCarthy (Detroit, Mich.: Wayne State University Press, 2003), 397; Helmut Krausser, "Lola. Ein Nachwort, viel zu früh," in Töteberg, *Szenenwechsel,* 35; Randall Halle, "German Film, *Aufgehoben*: Ensembles of Transnational Cinema," *New German Critique* 87 (2002): 42; David Clarke, "In Search of Home: Filming Post-Unification Berlin," in *German Cinema since Unification,* ed. David Clarke (London: Continuum, 2006), 153; and Margit Sinka, "Tom Tykwer's *Lola rennt*: A Blueprint of Millennial Berlin," *Glossen* 11 (2000), http://www.dickinson.edu/glossen/heft 11/lola.html.

48. See, e.g., Harold James and Marla Stone, eds., *When the Wall Came Down* (New York: Routledge, 1992).

49. T. S. Eliot, "Little Gidding," in *Four Quartets* (London: Faber and Faber, 1959), 48.

50. Tom Tykwer, "Ein romantisch-philosophischer ActionLiebesExperimentalThriller," in *Lola rennt,* ed. Michael Töteberg (Reinbeck bei Hamburg: Rowohlt, 1998) 130.

51. Colomb, *Staging the New Berlin,* 176. Choosing May 23, 1999, as the New Berlin's birthday, Partner für Berlin displayed advertisements, starting one year earlier, that emphasized the countdown and time running out. The phrase used was "Der Countdown läuft," approximately "The clock is ticking" or "Time is running out" or "10–9–8–7–6–5–4–3–2–1, blastoff!"

52. Tykwer, "Ein romantisch-philosophischer," 131.

53. See Tom Tykwer, *Lola rennt,* screenplay, version III, May 19, 1997, 5–6, in Mappe 8186, Schriftgut, DK.

54. *Lola rennt,* press kit, 9–11.

55. See ibid., 25 and 38; and Gudrun Holz, "Spellbound auf Speed," *die tageszeitung,* August 20, 1998, 15. For a critical discussion of the film music, see Caryl Flinn, "The Music That Lola Ran To," in *Sound Matters,* ed. Nora M. Alter and Lutz Koepnick, 197–213 (New York: Berghahn, 2004).

56. Tobias Kniebe, "Läuft und läuft und läuft," *Focus Magazin,* August 17, 1998, http://www.focus.de/panorama/boulevard/kino-lauft-und-lauft-und-lauft_aid_172334.html.

57. Dückers, "Spaßhaus Mitte," 102. See also Leinemann and Schumacher, "Labor der Zukunft," 38. By 1999 the decade-old Love Parade, a summer electronic music and dance parade in Tiergarten, was drawing "1.5 million fun-seeking kids" to the New Berlin. For a

brief history of the parade, see Oliva Henkel and Karsten Wolff, "Erst eins, dann zwei, dann drei . . . und schon ist der Spaß vorbei: Die Love Parade GmbH," in *Berlin Underground* (Berlin: FAB, 1996), 102–9.

58. Tykwer, "Ein romantisch-philosophischer," 129.

59. Tom Gunning, "The Cinema of Attractions: Early Film, Its Spectator and the Avant-Garde," in *Early Cinema: Space Frame Narrative,* ed. Thomas Elsaesser (London: BFI, 1990), 58.

60. Guntram Vogt, "Tom Tykwer—Lola rennt (1998)," in *Die Stadt im Kino: Deutsche Spielfilme 1900–2000* (Marburg: Schüren, 2001), 734.

61. Tykwer, "Ein romantisch-philosophischer," 133.

62. See ibid., 136. The interiors of these buildings were shot in the Oberfinanzdirektion von Berlin (bank) and the Rathaus Schöneberg (casino).

63. Lynch, *Image of the City,* 83, 89.

64. Markus Münch, "Der unmögliche Lauf," in *Drehort Berlin,* 119. See also *Lola rennt,* press kit, 27. The film's executive and line producer Maria Köpf also found it necessary to explain that "the routes make no claims to geographical accuracy."

65. Sinka, "Tom Tykwer's *Lola rennt.*"

66. Tom Gunning, "Non-Continuity, Continuity, Discontinuity: A Theory of Genres in Early Films," in Elsaesser, *Early Cinema,* 91–92. One might think, as well, of Buster Keaton's humorous exaggeration of continuity editing in *Sherlock Jr.* (United States 1924), in which the actor's movements keep transporting him to the most far-flung settings.

67. *Lola rennt,* press kit, 38. See also 27: the production team was explicit in its desire to show "an until now unknown side of Berlin" from "a youthful angle."

68. Ibid., 110; and Sandra Schuppach, *Tom Tykwer* (Mainz: Bender, 2004), 150.

69. Reuter, "Regionale Potentiale," 45. See also *Lola rennt,* press kit, 33. Even the production team had to overcome the challenge of location shooting amid the city's poor infrastructure and disruptive construction sites.

70. Krüger, "Bewegte Stadt," 22.

71. Tom Tykwer, "Director's Statement," Sony Pictures Classics, January 21, 2005, http://www.sonypictures.com/classics/runlolarun.html.

72. Forerunners to both *Lola rennt* and *Sliding Doors* include Krzysztof Kieslowski's *Przypadek* (*Blind Chance,* Poland 1981/1987) and Harold Ramis's *Groundhog Day* (United States 1993), both of which explore the contingency of repeated chances. Two of Tykwer's earlier short films, *Because* (FRG 1990) and *Epilog* (Epilogue, FRG 1992), experimented with similar narrative structures.

73. Filmförderungsanstalt, *Geschäftsbericht 1998,* 32; Michael Töteberg, "Run, Lola, Run," in Töteberg, *Szenenwechsel,* 44, which lists all countries, distributors, and start dates as of 1999; and Keil, personal interview.

74. Rolf Lautenschläger, "Geld und Erfolg für die Filme aus Berlin," *die tageszeitung,* December 14, 1998, 23.

75. Leinemann and Schumacher, "Labor der Zukunft," 34.

76. See Diepgen rennt, advertisement, postcard, winter 1999. On the reverse side, the postcard invites readers to run with Diepgen. One check box states, "Yes, I also run for this city. Please send me further information about Eberhard Diepgen and his goals for Berlin." The mayor's campaign headquarters were conveniently located in Friedrichstraße.

In response to this appropriation, Tykwer took action against the CDU on grounds of copyright infringement. See, e.g., "CDU will Streit um Diepgen-Plakat ohne Gericht lösen," *Welt am Sonntag*, January 10, 1999.

77. Keil, qtd. in Lautenschläger, "Geld und Erfolg," 23.

78. Stefan Arndt, "Das vergessene Jahr," in *Good Bye, Lenin!*, ed. Michael Töteberg (Berlin: Schwarzkopf und Schwarzkopf, 2003), 146.

79. Ritzmann, "Good Bye, Fernsehturm!," 28.

80. Dückers, "Spaßhaus Mitte," 105.

81. For politicians' take on ostalgia, see Schäuble, "Veränderungen ertragen," 27, and Rainer Eppelmann, "Die Rolle Berlins für die neuen Bundesländer," in Süß, *Hauptstadt Berlin*, 3:162. Both criticized this longing for the past as an irresponsible approach to the history of German division and SED dictatorship. Official rhetoric placed positive personal and collective memories and affirmations of experience in the GDR in opposition to the understanding of the postwall nation, as if the two could not coexist. A number of essays discuss the film's more complex relation to Eastern identity as well as its relation to nostalgia for the West *(Westalgie)* and a gradual process of mutual understanding. See, e.g., Seán Allan, "*Ostalgie*, Fantasy, and the Normalization of East-West Relations in Post-Unification Comedy," in *German Cinema since Unification*, ed. David Clarke (London: Continuum, 2006), 106, 117; Roger F. Cook, "Recharting the Skies above Berlin," *German Politics and Society* 23, no. 1 (2005): 43–44; Roger F. Cook, "*Good Bye, Lenin!*: Free-Market Nostalgia for Socialist Consumerism," *Seminar* 43, no. 2 (2007): 206–19; Cooke, *Representing East Germany since Unification*, 131–35; Mattias Frey, *Postwall German Cinema* (New York: Berghahn, 2013), 107–38; Nick Hodgin, "*Berlin Is in Germany* and *Good Bye Lenin!*," *Seminar* 12, no. 1 (2004): 25–45; Jennifer Kapczynski, "Negotiating Nostalgia: The GDR Past in *Berlin Is in Germany* and *Good Bye, Lenin!*," *The Germanic Review* 82, no. 1 (2007): 81–89; and Michael D. Richardson, "A World of Objects: Consumer Culture in Filmic Reconstructions of the GDR," in *The Collapse of the Conventional*, ed. Jaimey Fisher and Brad Prager, 216–37 (Detroit, Mich.: Wayne State University Press, 2010).

82. The sudden surge in these films included Volker Schlöndorff's *Die Stille nach dem Schuß* (*The Legend of Rita*, FRG 2000); Christian Petzold's *Die innere Sicherheit* (*The State I Am In*, FRG 2000); Andres Veiel's *Black Box BRD* (*Black Box Germany*, FRG 2001); Christopher Roth's *Baader* (FRG/United Kingdom 2002); Hans Weingartner's *Die fetten Jahre sind vorbei* (*The Edukators*, FRG/Austria 2004); and Bruce LaBruce's *The Raspberry Reich* (FRG/Canada 2004).

83. Dückers, "Spaßhaus Mitte," 104. The film's general audience rating for "six and above" even attempted to include children born after 1989. See Stefan Arndt in *Good Bye, Lenin!*, press kit (2003), 33.

84. The following, e.g., were published the same year as the film's release: *Ostalgie-Plan: Berlin Hauptstadt der DDR im aktuellen Stadtplan* (Berlin: Edition Gauglitz, 2003) and Anne Holper and Matthias Käther, *DDR-Baudenkmale in Berlin* (Berlin: Via Reise, 2003). Later Berlin's DDR Museum, opened in 2006, would represent the historical duality of street names through a hologram map.

85. For a detailed study of the postunification transformation of the square, see Gisa Weszkalnys, *Berlin, Alexanderplatz* (New York: Berghahn, 2010).

86. Arndt, "Das vergessene," 146.

87. Wolfgang Becker, "Bitte einmal ohrfeigen," *Hamburger Abendblatt,* February 13, 2003.

88. Bernd Lichtenberg, "Eine Familiengeschichte," in Töteberg, *Good Bye, Lenin!,* 148.

89. Ladd, *Ghosts of Berlin,* 198.

90. Darius Ghanai, qtd. in "Der Vorspann," in Töteberg, *Good Bye, Lenin!,* 144–45.

91. Lynch, *Image of the City,* 78–81. For an account of the Television Tower's genesis in 1950s Cold War competition for Berlin's and (East and West) Germany's airwaves, see Heather Gumbert, "Constructing a Socialist Landmark: The Berlin Television Tower," in Broadbent and Hake, *Berlin Divided City,* 88–99.

92. See Georg Schütte, "ABC-Berichterstattung—Das Bild der Bundesrepublik Deutschland in der 'Aktuellen Kamera,'" in *Die Bundesrepublik Deutschland im Spiegel der DDR-Medien* (Bonn: Bundeszentrale für politische Bildung, 1996), 17. Schütte notes that *Aktuelle Kamera* tried to find out the main themes of West German evening news ahead of time so that the editorial team could prepare appropriate responses.

93. In the original screenplay, the character of Denis was supposed to be a young Turkish-German man from Kreuzberg, though this multicultural dimension of postwall German identity remains absent from the film. See Jan Ole Gerster's documentation *Der Schmerz geht, der Film bleibt* (The pain goes away, the film remains, FRG 2004), about the making of *Good Bye, Lenin!*

94. Both versions included a bedtime greeting for children. See Volker Petzold, "Der Sandmann als Fabelfigur und Medienstar," *Volkskunde in Rheinland-Pfalz* 19, no. 1 (2004): 128–29, http://www.volkskunde-rheinland-pfalz.de/seiten/zeitschrift/2004 01/sandmann .pdf.

95. For a typical account of persistent East–West stereotyping in Berlin, see Karen Andresen, "Trotz und Vorurteil," *Der Spiegel,* September 6, 1999, 75. She describes an East German couple who cannot stand having more than a few *Wessis* at a Christmas party: "Usually there's still trouble. Like when the former GDR citizens indulgently remember their private happiness in the failed state and how much they had helped each other out, and the Westerners opinionatedly interrupt with comments about the Wall and the order to shoot to kill."

96. See Lothar Holler, "Filmaufbau Ost," *Die Zeit* 1 (2003), http://www.zeit.de/2004/01/12_2f07-2fHoller. Holler, an Easterner, tells of former GDR citizens looking on and critiquing the film team's location work: "Some people didn't understand that in cinema you're dealing with an art form. In every film you construct a unique world." For an account of the computer-animated statue, see Michael Töteberg, "Der digitale Lenin," in Töteberg, *Good Bye, Lenin!,* 154–55. For more on the Tacheles shoot, see Gerster, *Der Schmerz geht, der Film bleibt.*

97. See Stefan Arndt, "Der Leninist," *tip* 10 (2003): 40.

98. Nicole Dolif, "Lenin lässt die Kinokassen klingeln," *Die Welt* 41 (2003): 35.

99. Filmförderungsanstalt, *Geschäftsbericht 2003* (Berlin: Bundesanstalt des öffentlichen Rechts, 2003), 48.

100. See Oliver Michalsky, "Da musste erst ein Wessi kommen . . . ," *Die Welt* 41 (2003): 1; Dolif, "Lenin lässt die Kinokassen klingeln," 35; and Peter Körte, "Der Erfolg von 'Good Bye, Lenin!,'" *Frankfurter Allgemeine Zeitung,* February 20, 2003, 37.

101. Kathrin Finke, "Die DDR lebt weiter—79 qm im Studio B," *Berliner Kurier,* February 25, 2003, 8; and Georg Seitz, "Die DDR lebt—und lacht," *Bunte,* March 6, 2003, 84.

102. See, e.g., Körte, "Der Erfolg von 'Good Bye, Lenin!,'" 37; and Elmar Krekeler, "Nur im Falschen gibt es Wahres," *Die Welt* 48 (2003): 27.

103. Krekeler, "Nur im Falschen gibt es Wahres," 27.

104. For accounts of the screening, held on April 2, 2003, see "Bundestag nimmt Abschied von Lenin," *Spiegel Online,* April 3, 2003, http://www.spiegel.de/kultur/gesellschaft/0,1518,243206,00.html; and Holger Mehlig, "Kinoabend für den Bundestag," Associated Press Worldstream–German, April 3, 2003. Cultural minister Christina Weiss had just presented her new proposal for an updated *Filmförderungsgesetz* that would increase the federal funds available for film subsidy.

105. Mehlig, "Kinoabend für den Bundestag."

106. Johannes Frewel, "Die DDR ist abgewickelt, es ist vorbei," Agence France Presse–German, March 5, 2003.

107. Thomas Krüger, "Filmerziehung," in *Good Bye, Lenin!,* by Christina Moles Kaupp (Bonn: Bundeszentrale für politische Bildung, 2003), 2. See also Hannes Heine, "Die Kodes der bewegten Bilder," *die tageszeitung,* June 17, 2003, 24.

108. Thom Geier, "SPC Wins Race to Catch 'Lola,'" *The Hollywood Reporter,* September 16, 1998.

109. See Töteberg, "Run, Lola, Run," 48. The film eventually played in 172 theaters (by the time of Töteberg's writing). In contrast to Sony Pictures Classics's success with the film, the French distributor ARP Sélection attempted to release *Lola rennt* as a dubbed blockbuster, a strategy that ultimately failed. See as well Töteberg's summary of Sony Pictures Classics copresident Michael Barker's approach to the film.

110. David Rooney, "In Venice, U.S. Distribs Look at 'Lola,'" *Daily Variety,* September 8, 1998, 8; and Liza Foreman, "X-Filme Eyes Distrib: 'Run Lola Run' Producer Looking to Expand," *Daily Variety,* October 20, 1999, 5.

111. Scott Roxborough, "'Lenin!' Claims Nine Lolas," *The Hollywood Reporter,* June 9, 2003.

112. Nora Fitzgerald, "Berlin's Wall Is Down, but Try to Keep Mom from Finding Out," *New York Times,* April 2, 2003, E1. See also Wolfgang Becker, "Director's Note," Sony Pictures Classics, http://www.sonyclassics.com/goodbye/flash.html, in which Becker downplays the film's German content: "That's what's so wonderful about this topic. It's a slice of German history, but it's told incidentally and not placed in the forefront of the story." See Export-Union des Deutschen Films GmbH, *Filme der Bundesrepublik Deutschland 2003* (Polling, Germany: Esta Druck, 2003), 57. This annual publication (usually distributed at film festivals where world sales are conducted) similarly highlights the mother–son story over the film's historical context: "In a wonderful, touching and comic manner, *Good Bye, Lenin!* tells the story of how a loving son tries to move mountains and create miracles to restore his mother to health—and keep her in the belief that Lenin really did win after all."

113. See, e.g., Eve Schaenen, "Berlin, Young Again," *New York Times,* March 21, 1999; Roger Cohen, "The New Berlin: Building a Capital Where Triumph Is Taboo," *New York Times,* April 11, 1999; Thomas Ostermeier, "The New Berlin: Berliners," *New York Times,* April 11, 1999; Alan Riding, "The New Berlin: Building on the Rubble of History," *New*

York Times, April 11, 1999; Roger Cohen, "So In, So Very Berlin: A Capital Seeks Its Identity," *New York Times,* September 26, 1999; Roger Cohen, "Berlin in Search of Itself," *New York Times,* November 21, 1999; Alisa Roth, "In Chic New Berlin, Ugly Is Way Cool," *New York Times,* January 24, 2002; Steven Erlanger, "What's Doing In: Berlin," *New York Times,* July 14, 2002; William Murray, "Celebration Berlin," *New York Times,* March 2, 2003; and Eric Pfanner, "After Dark, East German Chic," *New York Times,* November 30, 2003. Many of these articles appeared in the "Travel" or "Arts" section.

114. Edward Guthmann, "Filmmaker on the Fast Track," *San Francisco Chronicle,* June 26, 1999, B1; and Ann Hornaday, "'Good Bye, Lenin!': Unification Blues," *Washington Post,* March 19, 2004, C05. On *Lola rennt,* see also Laura Winters, "A Rebel with Red Hair Rumples Stuffed Shirts," *New York Times,* June 13, 1999; Kristin Hohenadel, "How German Is It?," *L.A. Weekly,* June 18, 1999; J. Hoberman, "So Long a Go-Go," *Village Voice,* June 22, 1999, 149; Paula Span, "Hit and 'Run' Director," *Washington Post,* June 27, 1999, G04; and Carol Williams, "Wherever 'Lola' Runs . . . ," *Chicago Sun-Times,* June 27, 1999, 10. On *Good Bye, Lenin!,* see also V. A. Musetto, "Why Kids Keep Their Mom in Bed, Seeing Red," *New York Post,* February 27, 2004, 46; Elvis Mitchell, "Restoring a Berlin Wall to Comfort Dear Old Mom," *New York Times,* February 27, 2004, E8; and Ty Burr, "Mother May I . . . Stay a Communist?," *Boston Globe,* March 26, 2004, C1.

115. Tykwer, qtd. in Winters, "A Rebel with Red Hair."

116. In 2002, *New York Magazine* did a cover story on Berlin called "Where to Go Next: Why Berlin Is the New Hot Spot for New Yorkers." See Amy Larocca, "The New City: Berlin Calling," *New York Magazine,* October 28, 2002, 36–40. See also Ethan Brown, "The New Prague: Bohemian Rhapsody," *New York Magazine,* October 28, 2002, 41–42. Just a few years later, New York's admiration for Berlin was expressed through Carnegie Hall's Berlin in Lights Festival (November 2007); the Center for Architecture's exhibition *Berlin–New York Dialogues: Building in Context* (November 8, 2007, to January 26, 2008), which compared urban renewal projects in New York to those in Berlin; and the New York Foundation for the Arts's summer 2011 visit to Berlin to see how the organization might work together with New York's expat artist community in Berlin.

117. Lewis Beale, "Foreign Films Hit Home," *Daily News,* June 16, 1999, 46.

118. Richard Bernstein, "Old Cities, Full of Life: Berlin," *New York Times,* September 14, 2003. The film's official German website includes links to numerous websites for GDR products as well as a lexicon of "East German phrases." See http://www.good-bye-lenin.de/aktuelles.php.

119. Arndt, "Der Leninist," 41; and Ritzmann, "Good Bye, Fernsehturm!," 28.

120. Stehr, qtd. in Ritzmann, "Good Bye, Fernsehturm!," 28. For contemporary accounts of film production in Berlin, see, e.g., Reiner Fischer, "Die Hauptstadt Berlin ist die begehrteste Kulisse für den deutschen Film," *Die Welt,* February 20, 2003, 34; Bert Rebhandl, "Filmlabor Berlin," *Tip* 10 (2003): 34–37; Thomas Steiger, "Willkommen in einer anderen Welt," *Zitty* 4 (2005): 19–20; Christa Beckmann, "Filmstadt Berlin: 3000 Anfragen," *Berliner Morgenpost,* July 18, 2007, 16; and Tobias Kniebe, "Es wird gedreht wie wild," *Süddeutsche Zeitung,* July 24, 2007, 11.

121. *Production Guide Berlin–Brandenburg* (Berlin: Berlin Brandenburg Film Commission, 2003), 1, 11.

122. Berlin Brandenburg Film Commission, *Production Guide: Film and TV in Berlin-Brandenburg* (Berlin: KönigsDruck, 2006), 2.3–2.5.

123. *Film Funding Allocation Guidelines* (Berlin: Medienboard, 2006), cover.

124. See Münch, "Unmögliche Lauf"; Regina Aggio, *Filmstadt Berlin* (Berlin: Jena, 2007); and Michaela Schubert and Wolfgang Bernschein, *Berlin: Reisen—Ein Film* (Berlin: Wolbern, 2007).

125. Rolf Lautenschläger, "B—eine Stadt sucht ihren Film," *die tageszeitung,* July 17, 2003, 21.

EPILOGUE

1. See http://berlynrestaurant.com/.

2. Soon afterward, the building was removed completely, its grounds converted, temporarily, into a public park. In June 2013, the cornerstone was laid for the construction of the new City Palace, based on the facades and proportions of the prewar one.

3. What follows is based on Zeitreisen's Videobustour and a personal interview with Arne Krasting, Berlin, Germany, March 15, 2008.

4. Salon Populaire, program pamphlet, Berlin, April–June 2010.

5. See Stefanie Schulte Strathaus and Florian Wüst, eds., *Wer sagt denn, dass Beton nicht brennt, hast Du's probiert?* (Berlin: b_books, 2008).

6. Salon Populaire, program pamphlet.

7. For more on the effects of public monitors, see Anna McCarthy, *Ambient Television* (Durham, N.C.: Duke University Press, 2001). See also the discussion of Berliner Fenster in Lutz Koepnick, *Framing Attention* (Baltimore: Johns Hopkins University Press, 2007), 263–67.

8. While Going Underground allows passengers to vote for their favorite film, Foto des Tages encourages them to become producers of Berlin images, much as the city's "Be Berlin" campaign, launched in 2008, has encouraged inhabitants to participate in marketing the city.

9. *Fahrgastfernsehen in der U-Bahn: Mediadaten* (Berlin: Berliner Fenster GmbH, 2010), 2–4. Berliner Fenster GmbH also distinguishes the number of viewers from the number of "contact opportunities" that potential advertisers would have: 1.5 million.

10. Peter Zander, "Babylon bringt den Stummfilm zum Klingen," *Berliner Morgenpost,* June 17, 2010. In Berlin's contemporary film revival culture, Babylon Mitte's programming recalls the cinema's associations with both the silent film era and East German cinema. For more on the history of the theater, see Michael Hanisch, *Das Babylon* (Nuremberg: KDD, 2002).

11. A calculation provided by Zander, "Babylon bringt den Stummfilm zum Klingen."

FILMOGRAPHY

A Foreign Affair (Billy Wilder, United States 1948)
À propos de Nice (Regarding Nice, Jean Vigo, France 1930)
Abenteuer eines Zehnmarkscheins, Die (*Adventures of a Ten Mark Note,* Berthold Viertel, Germany 1926)
Absolute Giganten (*Gigantics,* Sebastian Schipper, FRG 1999)
Aimée & Jaguar (Max Färberböck, FRG 1999)
Alarm im Zirkus (*Alarm at the Circus,* Gerhard Klein, GDR 1954)
Alice in den Städten (*Alice in the Cities,* Wim Wenders, FRG 1974)
amerikanische Freund, Der (*The American Friend,* Wim Wenders, FRG/France 1977)
Am Tag als der Regen kam (*The Day It Rained,* Gerd Oswald, FRG 1959)
Architekten, Die (*The Architects,* Peter Kahane, GDR 1990)
Around the World in 80 Days (Frank Coraci, United States/FRG/Ireland/United Kingdom 2004)
Asphalt (Joe May, Germany 1929)
Baader (Christopher Roth, FRG/United Kingdom 2002)
Because (Tom Tykwer, FRG 1990)
Berlin, Alexanderplatz (Phil Jutzi, Germany 1931)
Berlin Babylon (Hubertus Siegert, FRG 2001)
Berlin bleibt Berlin (Berlin remains Berlin, Hans Cürlis, Germany 1935)
Berlin. Die Sinfonie der Großstadt (*Berlin: Symphony of a Great City,* Walter Ruttmann, Germany 1927)
Berlin—Ecke Schönhauser (*Berlin—Schönhauser Corner,* Gerhard Klein, GDR 1957)
Berlin Is in Germany (Hannes Stöhr, FRG 2001)
Berlin Remake (Amie Siegel, United States 2005, installation)
Berlin: Sinfonie einer Großstadt (Berlin symphony, Thomas Schadt, FRG 2002)
Berlin um die Ecke (*Berlin, Around the Corner,* Gerhard Klein, GDR 1965/1990)
Berliner Romanze, Eine (*A Berlin Romance,* Gerhard Klein, GDR 1956)
Berliner Stilleben (*Berlin Still Life,* László Moholy-Nagy, Germany 1931)
Big Lift, The (George Seaton, United States 1950)

Black Box BRD (*Black Box Germany,* Andres Veiel, FRG 2001)
Blackboard Jungle (Richard Brooks, United States 1955)
blaue Engel, Der (*The Blue Angel,* Josef von Sternberg, Germany 1930)
Blechtrommel, Die (*The Tin Drum,* Volker Schlöndorff, FRG/France/Poland/Yugoslavia 1979)
Bleeding Through: Layers of Los Angeles (Norman Klein, United States 2003, DVD)
bleierne Zeit, Die (*Marianne and Juliane,* Margarethe von Trotta, FRG 1981)
Blut und Boden: Grundlagen zum Neuen Reich (Blood and soil: Foundations of the New Empire, Rolf von Sonjewski-Jamrowski, Germany 1933)
Bourne Supremacy, The (Paul Greengrass, United States/FRG 2004)
Bronenosets Potyomkin (*Battleship Potemkin,* Sergei M. Eisenstein, USSR 1925)
Brug, De (*The Bridge,* Joris Ivens, The Netherlands 1928)
Chelovek s Kino-apparatom (*Man with a Movie Camera,* Dziga Vertov, USSR 1929)
Christiane F.—Wir Kinder vom Bahnhof Zoo (*Christiane F.,* Ulrich Edel, FRG 1981)
Comedian Harmonists (*The Harmonists,* Joseph Vilsmaier, FRG/Austria 1997)
Demolishing and Building Up the Star Theatre (Frederick S. Armitage, United States 1901)
Démolition d'un mur (*Demolition of a Wall,* Louis Lumière, France 1896)
Dr. Mabuse, der Spieler (*Dr. Mabuse, the Gambler,* Fritz Lang, Germany 1922)
Dresden (Roland Suso Richter, FRG 2006)
East of Eden (Elia Kazan, United States 1955)
Ein Tag im Juli, Berlin 1945 (One day in July, Berlin 1945, Jost von Morr and John Lionel Bandmann, FRG 1975)
Emil und die Detektive (*Emil and the Detectives,* Gerhard Lamprecht, Germany 1931)
Endstation Liebe (*Last Stop Love,* Georg Tressler, FRG 1958)
Epilog (Epilogue, FRG 1992)
Es (*It,* Ulrich Schamoni, FRG 1966)
ewige Jude, Der (*The Eternal Jew,* Fritz Hippler, Germany 1940)
fetten Jahre sind vorbei, Die (*The Edukators,* Hans Weingartner, FRG/Austria 2004)
Finding Nemo (Andrew Stanton, Lee Unkrich, United States/Australia 2003)
Flanagan Boy, The (Reginald Le Borg, United States 1953)
Flirt (Hal Hartley, United States 1996)
Frauenschicksale (*Destinies of Women,* Slatan Dudow, GDR 1952)
freudlose Gasse, Die (*The Joyless Street,* Georg Wilhelm Pabst, Germany 1925)
Frühling in Berlin (Springtime in Berlin, Arthur Maria Rabenalt, FRG 1957)
Germania anno zero (*Germany Year Zero,* Roberto Rossellini, Italy/SOZ/France 1948)
Geschichte der Berliner Grenzkinos 1950–1961, Die (The history of the Berlin Border Cinemas 1950–1961, Bianca Schemel, FRG 2011, installation video)
Gone with the Wind (Victor Fleming, United States 1939)
Good Bye, Lenin! (Wolfgang Becker, FRG 2003)
Großstadtmelodie (*Melody of a Great City,* Wolfgang Liebeneiner, Germany 1943)
Groundhog Day (Harold Ramis, United States 1993)
Halbstarken, Die (*Teenage Wolfpack,* Georg Tressler, FRG 1956)
Halbstarken, Die (The hooligans, Urs Egger, FRG 1996)
Hanna (Joe Wright, United States/United Kingdom/FRG 2011)
Helden wie wir (*Heroes Like Us,* Sebastian Peterson, FRG 1999)

Herr Lehmann (*Berlin Blues,* Leander Haußmann, FRG 2003)
Himmel ohne Sterne (*Sky without Stars,* Helmut Käutner, FRG 1955)
Himmel über Berlin, Der (*Wings of Desire,* Wim Wenders, FRG/France 1987)
Hitlerjunge Quex (*Hitler Youth Quex,* Hans Steinhoff, Germany 1933)
Hostess (Rolf Römer, GDR 1976)
I Vitelloni (The idlers, Federico Fellini, Italy/France 1953)
Ich Chef, Du Turnschuh (Me boss, you sneaker, Hussi Kutlucan, FRG 1998)
Impressionen vom alten Marseiller Hafen (vieux port) (*Impressions of the Old Marseille Harbor,* László Moholy-Nagy, Germany 1929)
In weiter Ferne, so nah! (*Faraway, So Close!,* Wim Wenders, FRG/United States 1993)
Inglourious Basterds (Quentin Tarantino, United States/FRG 2009)
innere Sicherheit, Die (*The State I Am In,* Christian Petzold, FRG 2000)
International, The (Tom Tykwer, United States/FRG/United Kingdom 2009)
Invisible Shape of Things Past, The (Art+Com and Hochschule der Künste, FRG 1996/DVD 2003)
Irgendwo in Berlin (*Somewhere in Berlin,* Gerhard Lamprecht, SOZ 1946)
Jahrgang '45 (*Born in '45,* Jürgen Böttcher, GDR 1965–66/1990)
Jud Süß (*Jew Süß,* Veit Harlan, Germany 1940)
Kandidat, Der (The candidate, Thomas Schadt, FRG 1998)
Kleiner Film einer Grossen Stadt . . . der Stadt Düsseldof am Rhein (Small film of a great city . . . the city Düsseldorf on the Rhein, Walter Ruttmann, Germany 1935)
Kuhle Wampe oder Wem gehört die Welt? (*Kuhle Wampe, or Who Owns the World?,* Slatan Dudow, Germany 1932)
Ladri di biciclette (*Bicycle Thieves,* Vittorio De Sica, Italy 1948)
Leben der Anderen, Das (*The Lives of Others,* Florian Henckel von Donnersmarck, FRG 2006)
Leben ist eine Baustelle, Das (*Life Is All You Get,* Wolfgang Becker, FRG 1997)
leere Mitte, Die (*The Empty Center,* Hito Steyerl, FRG 1998)
Legende vom Potsdamer Platz, Die (*The Legend of Potsdamer Platz,* Manfred Wilhelms, FRG 2001)
Legende von Paul und Paula, Die (*The Legend of Paul and Paula,* Heiner Carow, GDR 1973)
letzte Mann, Der (*The Last Laugh,* Friedrich Wilhelm Murnau, Germany 1924)
Lisbon Story (Wim Wenders, FRG/Portugal 1994)
Lissy (Konrad Wolf, GDR 1957)
Location Berlin-Brandenburg (Partner für Berlin, FRG 2003, marketing DVD)
Lola rennt (*Run Lola Run,* Tom Tykwer, FRG 1998)
Lord of the Rings III, The: The Return of the King, (Peter Jackson, United States/New Zealand, 2003)
Los Angeles Plays Itself (Thom Andersen, United States 2003)
M (Fritz Lang, Germany 1931)
Majestät brauchen Sonne (His Majesty needs some sun, Peter Schamoni, FRG/The Netherlands 1999)
Man Between, The (Carol Reed, United Kingdom 1953)
Manhatta (Charles Sheeler and Paul Strand, United States 1921)

Marty (Delbert Mann, United States 1955)
Mauer, Die (*The Wall,* Jürgen Böttcher, GDR 1990)
Mein Führer—Die wirklich wahrste Wahrheit über Adolf Hitler (*My Führer,* Dani Levy, FRG 2007)
Mein langsames Leben (*Passing Summer,* Angela Schanelec, FRG 2001)
Menschen am Sonntag (*People on Sunday,* Robert Siodmak, Rochus Gliese, Edgar G. Ulmer, Germany 1930)
Metropolis (Fritz Lang, Germany 1927)
Mörder sind unter uns, Die (*The Murderers Are among Us,* Wolfgang Staudte, SOZ 1946)
Morgen beginnt das Leben (*Life Begins Tomorrow,* Werner Hochbaum, Germany 1933)
Moskva (*Moscow,* Mikhail Kaufman and Ilya Kopalin, USSR 1927)
Mutter Krausens Fahrt ins Glück (*Mother Krause's Journey to Happiness,* Phil Jutzi, Germany 1929)
Nachts auf den Straßen (*The Mistress,* Rudolf Jugert, FRG 1952)
Nicht der Homosexuelle ist pervers, sondern die Situation in der er lebt (*It Is Not the Homosexual Who Is Perverse, but the Society in Which He Lives,* Rosa von Praunheim, FRG 1971)
Nichts bereuen (*No Regrets,* Benjamin Quabeck, FRG 2001)
Nirgendwo in Afrika (*Nowhere in Africa,* Caroline Link, FRG 2001)
Not as a Stranger (Stanley Kramer, United States 1955)
Octopussy (John Glenn, United Kingdom/United States 1983)
On the Waterfront (Elia Kazan, United States 1954)
One, Two, Three (Billy Wilder, United States 1961)
Opus I–IV (Walter Ruttmann, Germany 1921–25)
Paris qui dort (*The Crazy Ray,* René Clair, France 1923)
Paris, Texas (Wim Wenders, FRG/France/United Kingdom/United States 1984)
Pianist, The (Roman Polanski, France/FRG/United Kingdom/Poland 2002)
Possession (*The Night the Screaming Stops,* Andrzej Zulawski, FRG/France 1981)
Przypadek (*Blind Chance,* Krzysztof Kieslowski, Poland 1981/1987)
Pulp Fiction (Quentin Tarantino, United States 1994)
Raspberry Reich, The (Bruce LaBruce, FRG/Canada 2004)
Reader, The (Stephen Daldry, United States/FRG 2008)
Ready for Business (Partner für Berlin and Senate Department for Economics, Labor, and Women's Issues, FRG 2002)
Rebel without a Cause (Nicholas Ray, United States 1955)
REDUPERS—Die allseitig reduzierte Persönlichkeit (*The All-Around Reduced Personality,* Helke Sander, FRG 1978)
Regen (*Rain,* Joris Ivens, The Netherlands 1929)
Rien que les heures (*Nothing but Time,* Alberto Cavalcanti, France 1926)
Rock Around the Clock (Fred F. Sears, United States 1956)
Roman einer jungen Ehe (*The Story of a Young Couple,* Kurt Maetzig, GDR 1952)
Romeo + Juliet (Baz Luhrmann, United States 1996)
Rosenstrasse (Margarethe von Trotta, FRG/The Netherlands 2003)
Runscape (Laurent Guitierrez and Valérie Portefaix, Hong Kong 2010)

Salt of the Earth (Herbert J. Biberman, United States 1953)
Schmerz geht, der Film bleibt, Der (The pain goes away, the film remains, Jan Ole Gerster, FRG 2004)
Schule (*No More School,* Marco Petry, FRG 2000)
Sheriff Teddy (Heiner Carow, GDR 1957)
Sherlock Jr. (Buster Keaton, United States 1924)
Sie (She, Rolf Thiele, France/FRG 1954)
Sissi Trilogy (Ernst Marischka, Austria 1955–57)
Sliding Doors (Peter Howitt, United Kingdom/United States 1998)
Sonne der Stadt, Die (The sun of the city, Elektrowerke AG, Germany 1925)
Sonnenallee (*Sun Alley,* Leander Haußmann, FRG 1999)
Speed Racer (Andy and Lana Wachowski, United States/Australia/FRG 2008)
Spur führt nach Berlin, Die (*International Counterfeiters,* Franz Cáp, FRG 1952/1958)
Stadt der Millionen: Ein Lebensbild Berlins, Die (The city of millions: A living portrait of Berlin, Adolf Trotz, Germany 1925)
Stadt Stuttgart: 100 Cannstatter Volksfest (The city of Stuttgart: The 100th Cannstatt Folk Festival, Walter Ruttmann, Germany 1935)
Stage Fright (Alfred Hitchcock, United Kingdom 1950)
Stille nach dem Schuß, Die (*The Legend of Rita,* Volker Schlöndorff, FRG 2000)
Stille Nacht (*Silent Night,* Dani Levy, FRG 1996)
Straße, Die (*The Street,* Karl Grune, Germany 1923)
Stuttgart, die Grossstadt zwischen Wald und Reben (Stuttgart, the great city between woods and vines, Walter Ruttmann, Germany 1935)
Sunrise (Friedrich Wilhelm Murnau, United States 1927)
Symphonie einer Weltstadt/Berlin, wie es war (Symphony of a world-class city/Berlin the way it was, Leo de Laforgue, Germany 1943/FRG 1950)
Teufel spielte Balalaika, Der (*Until Hell Is Frozen,* Leopold Lahola, FRG 1961)
Third Man, The (Carol Reed, United Kingdom/United States 1949)
Time Code (Mike Figgis, United States 2000)
Tôkyô-ga (*Tokyo-Ga,* Wim Wenders, FRG/United States 1985)
Trainspotting (Danny Boyle, United Kingdom 1996)
Triumph des Willens (*Triumph of the Will,* Leni Riefenstahl, Germany 1935)
Unberührbare, Die (*No Place to Go,* Oskar Roehler, FRG 2000)
Unknown (Jaume Collet-Serra, United Kingdom/France/FRG/Canada/Japan/United States 2011)
Unsere 50er Jahre (*Our 1950s,* Thomas Kufus and Jan Schütte, FRG 2005)
Unsere 60er Jahre (*Our 1960s,* Thomas Kufus and Michael Wulfes, FRG 2007)
Unter 18 (*Under 18,* Georg Tressler, Austria 1957)
Untergang, Der (*Downfall,* Oliver Hirschbiegel, FRG/Austria/Italy 2004)
Untertan, Der (*The Kaiser's Lackey,* Wolfgang Staudte, GDR 1951)
Valkyrie (Bryan Singer, United States/FRG 2008)
Verbotene Filme (*Forbidden Films,* Felix Moeller, FRG 2014)
Versprechen, Das (*The Promise,* Margarethe von Trotta, FRG 1995)
Vorspiel (*Ready for Life,* Peter Kahane, GDR 1987)

Weg ohne Umkehr (Path of no return, Victor Vicas, FRG 1953)
Weltbühne Berlin—Die Zwanziger Jahre (World stage: The 1920s, Irmgard von zur Mühlen, FRG 1986)
Weltstrasse See—Welthafen Hamburg (Street to the world: World-class harbor Hamburg, Walter Ruttmann, Germany 1938)
Wild One, The (Laslo Benedek, United States 1953)
Winterschläfer (*Winter Sleepers,* Tom Tykwer, FRG 1997)
Wochenmarkt auf dem Wittenbergplatz (Weekly market at Wittenbergplatz, Wilfried Basse, Germany 1929)
Wunder von Bern, Das (*The Miracle of Bern,* Sönke Wortmann, FRG 2003)
Yamamoto—Aufzeichnungen zu Kleidern und Städten (*Notebook on Cities and Clothes,* Wim Wenders, FRG/France 1990)
Young Berlin (Partner für Berlin and Berlin Tourismus Marketing GmbH, FRG 2000)
Zugverkehr unregelmäßig (Irregular train service, Erich Freund, GDR 1951)
Zwei in einer großen Stadt (*Two in a Big City,* Volker von Collande, Germany 1942)
Zwei unter Millionen (Two among millions, Victor Vicas, FRG 1961)

INDEX

BRIGITTA B. WAGNER is a film historian and filmmaker based in Berlin. She is the editor of *DEFA after East Germany* and a member of the Berlin cinema collective WOLF Kino.